STRONG WORDS

LAURO MARTINES

STRONG

WORDS

WRITING & SOCIAL STRAIN

in the ITALIAN RENAISSANCE

THE JOHNS HOPKINS UNIVERSITY PRESS

BALTIMORE & LONDON

The Johns Hopkins University Press
2715 North Charles Street
Baltimore, Maryland 21218-4363
www.press.jhu.edu

Library of Congress Cataloging-in-Publication Data
Martines, Lauro.
Strong words : writing and social strain in the Italian renaissance /
Lauro Martines.
p.   cm.
Includes bilbiographical references and index.
ISBN 0-8018-6574-3 (alk. paper)
1. Italian literature—To 1400—History and criticism.   2. Italian
literature—15th century—History and criticism.   3. Literature and
society—Italy—History—To 1500.   4. Italian literature—Social
aspects.   5. Local color in literature.   6. Social problems in
literature.   7. Italy—Intellectual life—1268–1559.   I. Title.
PQ4075. M345 2001
850.9'355—dc21
00-010276

A catalog record for this book is available
from the British Library.

for Julia O'Faolain, carissima

Recovering . . . [the past is] at all events on this scale much like entering the enemy's lines to get back one's dead for burial.

HENRY JAMES, *The Sense of the Past*

Contents

Acknowledgments

Historical writing is always morally a team enterprise. The whole collective, however, living and dead, cannot be named, or one ends by thanking half of humanity—a current fashion. But I must acknowledge Christiane Klapisch-Zuber and Yves Hersant in Paris, of the Ecole des Hautes Etudes en Sciences Sociales, where I offered seminar sequences in 1992 and 1994. They provided the first forums for the arguments of chapters 4 and 9, later published in France (*Annales HSS*, 1996, 1998).

The following chapters have been published in England: chapter 2 in *the italianist* (1994); chapter 7 in *Language and Images of Renaissance Italy*, ed. A. Brown (Oxford, 1995); chapter 10 in *Art, Memory, and Family in Renaissance Florence*, ed. G. Ciappelli and P. L. Rubin (Cambridge, 2000); and chapter 11 in *The World of Savonarola: Elites and Perceptions of Crisis*, ed. S. Fletcher and C. Shaw (London, 2000). All, however, were conceived as parts of the larger plan for this book, and all have been revised.

The earliest studies, chapters 2 and 6, go back to their delivery as talks in 1985–87 at the Getty Center for the Humanities (Los Angeles), the University of California (Berkeley), and Brown, Cornell, and New York Universities.

Lois R. Crum, my remarkable copy editor, reminds me to indicate that the translations are mine. The rare exceptions are carefully noted.

In London now, I am most grateful for the working space provided by the Warburg Institute and the Institute of Historical Research.

A Word to the Reader

In working the contested ground between two different fields, my aim in *Strong Words* is to negotiate an entry into history through literature. The Afterword reviews the enterprise as a whole; so it is there, rather than here, that I deal with the question of how the book's themes and ways diverge from current work on the Italian Renaissance.

"Strong words" is my shorthand for words of love, anger, and fear, of high compliment and low abuse; words of prayer, complaint, and supplication—spontaneous, ritualized, or metrical; rhetorical and posturing words, neighborhood words, and rhymed words for fixing things in memory. The sweep, in short, takes in literary forms as well as idioms for critical exchange in everyday life. All these will help to guide us into the society of Renaissance Italy.

The implied scatter of meaning is not, however, nearly so wide as one glance may suggest, for the unity of this book belongs to a method and a vision. I shall be slanting my questions and pursuing hidden forms until what is submerged or disguised comes forth and is identified, gradually treating us to an anatomy of conditioned sensibilities and to strategies for living in city-states where the stress and strain of hierarchized authority, gender, and well-defined urban spaces pervaded human relations.

Our historical universe comprises the cities of the Italian Renaissance—Florence, Venice, Ferrara, Rome, Siena, Milan, and the others. Here custom and social class, orality and entrenched hierarchies, power and gender all contributed to a flow of fundamental rituals in word and gesture. Summoning "strong" words and phrases, the critical transactions of daily life utilized a language tempered in the ethos of social structures that were more fixed and coercive than anything in our experience. Among such transactions were the finalizing of arranged marriages, the fending off of bankruptcies, dealing with superiors, joining a confraternity, wooing women, commencing a business ledger, keeping a family log book, jockeying for public office, drawing up last wills, shouting abuse at a neighbor, salvaging honor, and of course imploring divine help. Each of these required verbal formulas and strong locutions.

Literature offers us a unique highroad to the past, for the simple reason that its expressiveness may be as plain as blistering insult or so devious and artful as to suit the most subtle social situation. In its engagement with experience and resolution to imitate human subjects, it is more likely, however, to course between the two extremes. And try as it may, it can never truly conceal its origins in a time and place. This is because imaginative energy and authenticity issue, in the end, from lived experience. These comprehensive claims, plus the fact that poetry and fiction are more defiant and radiant than the conventional runs of historical documentation, underpin the reasons why literary texts are here claimed for the historical record.

Yet to take literature as a primary historical source is to discover that it offers no ready or predictable approaches to the study of material, such as we find, for instance, in biography, in the analysis of ideas, or in political and economic history, which at once lend themselves to established and well-trodden forms of inquiry. For historians, instead, the way into literary texts is almost certain to be varied, unexpected, deceptive, and occasionally daunting. But once inside, so to speak, where history and literature are joined, we soon confront solid or recurring themes and structures; and these also make for the unity of this book.

In the following pages, the sense of the tight urban community, as gleaned by citizens from the neighborhood or from relations between favor-seekers (clients) and patrons, is kept constantly in mind; this is so whether our terrain is tiny Siena or prepotent Venice. As in Renaissance cities, here also the protean face of authority has a certain ubiquity, not only because of law codes and the power of government but also because of the public weight (often disguised and at times illegal) of the groups and families that disposed of wealth and political heft. In this connection, therefore, fathers counted more than sons, men more than women, family more than the individual, and the fashionable religious confraternities—in ceremonial and public life—more than modest ones. As expressed in the all-pervading call to conform to its mores, the watchful community was yet another shaping force in the urban arena, and it is never forgotten in *Strong Words*.

The main themes of the book—diverse but interrelated—are language and social strain, the give-and-take between patrons and clients, men versus women, amatory stances and sexual relations, anguish and prayer, the incidence of cruelty, the emotions collected around the polarities of "insider" and "outsider" (where being outside the group could bring terrible distress), and, not least, the violence and bitter pill of politics and partisan government, which cast a shadow nearly everywhere.

I could only get at this formidable assortment of affairs in the history of Renaissance Italy, and draw them all together into an orbiting system, by taking "literary" writing as my gateway and archive.

Some historians will think there is too much literature in this book; and students of literature will perhaps more often feel that there is too much history. How to reply to such contradictory complaints? Whenever cross-disciplinary study really breaks out of the established boundaries of academic fields, it is fated to provoke a small number of specialists, who must, after all (and rightly so), dominate scholarship. I have no quarrel with the work of specialists. On the contrary, I rely on it, and I have happily done it myself. In *Strong Words,* however, I am seeking a more catholic reader; and if this makes me a vulgarizer, may I be a "high vulgarizer" at least.

ONE

NEIGHBORHOOD
VOICES IN POETRY

THE PAROCHIAL MATRIX

Every society has a range of stories and anecdotes that serve to inspire a sense of community. After their "miraculous" victory over feared Florence in 1260, at the Battle of Montaperti, the Sienese had an event to exult in for generations. Talking about it induced inspiration and enhanced their identity as a people.[1] Pavia, as the former capital of the old Italic kingdom, long saw itself as more glorious than powerful Milan. Venice, Pisa, and Genoa had their patriotic yarns about the sea and distant conquests. Venetians could happily dwell on their heroic victory, in 1380, over a Genoese fleet at Chioggia, well inside the southern loop of the great Venetian lagoon.

Moments of this sort were the stuff of storytellers and chroniclers. In our day, off the eastern shores of the Adriatic and in parts of Africa, we see much the same kind of narrative activity, if not always in the best light, when people there, in the name of justice, rehearse the details of an old battle or massacre, reaching out thereby for a moment of tribal passion and cohesion.

All Italian cities—Florence, Perugia, Bologna, and the rest—had their narratives of bonding: miraculous events, founding myths, stories of patron saints, floods or famines, local victories, near defeats, infamous treacheries, and so forth. But their parishes and wider neighborhoods (*parrocchia, contrada, gonfalone, rione, sesto, quartiere*) had more localized repertoires of galvanizing incidents and tales: narratives that also pulled parishioners and adjoining folk

I

together in a commonality of feeling. These word-of-mouth accounts might be about a neighboring church, a guild, a leading family, a notorious miser or simpleton, a local political boss, remembered marriages, strange murders, or other odd occurrences. The stream of parochial anecdote was endless. Moreover, from the late thirteenth century, in a fluctuating rhythm that lasted for more than three hundred years, a pullulation of religious confraternities in the different cities brought groups of residents together in "narratives" of prayer, hymns (*laude*), and ritualized flagellation. In time these brotherhoods also developed collective memories.

Our urban dwellers, then, looked for cohesiveness; and any peaceful activity that served this end, while also serving the ends of the urban commune, was sure to win approval. But the first drawing together of people by the pull of narrative and incident—and the point merits emphasis—belonged to the local scene, to the neighborhood, because this was the place of every individual's first and daily communion with others. The effects of this influence could not fail to be profound.

In this chapter I identify some of the emotional and psychological traces of the neighborhood presence, not by noting the resonance of local events and tales, which abound in the pages of chroniclers,[2] but rather by seeking the deeper marks of this influence in ghost and substance.

In the love sonnets of the well-born Sienese poet Cecco Angiolieri (c. 1260–c. 1312), the beloved is a local lower-class girl, Becchina, daughter of the leather tanner (*pela le coia*) Benci, both of whom are named in the verse, she repeatedly so.[3] When we consider that the high amatory style of Italian Renaissance poetry (see chaps. 2 and 4) either suppressed names or wholly transcended them by avoiding all local reference, doing so in a policy to ennoble and generalize the experience of love, we begin to understand that Cecco's realism ties his love verse to the neighborhood, whether or not his Becchina (who later married) was partly imagined. Hence the sonnets also offer us the nicknames or first names of locals, including, often, his own: Cecco, Moco, Migo, Ciampolin, Tano, Mino di Pepo, Mita, Turella, Poggese, and others. The love poems even refer to his *babbo* (dad), in a startling sign of informality.[4] But since the familiar local scene constituted the first order of social and family reality, its entry, via the familiar name, into the poetry of idealism could only deflate and destroy the idealism, in a gross violation of genre. The high lyric verse of Lorenzo de' Medici's *canzoniere* (1470s) never slips into the neighborhood mode, although his raw political power snaked through all of Florence's neighborhoods. We might almost say that the idealizing love poetry of the Renaissance, reaching back to the period of Dante and Cavalcanti, the 1290s, defined itself by negating the neighborhood in its stance against realism. Not surprisingly, therefore, Cecco Angiolieri, who began by writing sonnets in the courtly and idealist manner of the *stilnovo,* then turned against it to become one of its first enemies and parodists.[5]

PARISH AND PATRONS

In our broad search for the meeting points between history and literature, let us move away for a moment from the dominion of the local scene, but only to return to it directly, by turning to a later realist.

Francesco Berni's seventy-six-line *Capitolo a suo compare,*[6] composed in Rome in the summer of 1518, is addressed to his young patron, Antonio Dovizi, nephew of the well-known literary cardinal, Bernardo Dovizi da Bibbiena. In this *capitolo,* Berni chides messer Antonio for chasing after Roman prostitutes night and day. He makes his case not by means of moral argument but by talking money and good health; whores, he asserts, will take your money, clothing, jewels, and time. All their parts reek and they may infect you with syphilis. You and other great lords and patrons (*gran maestri*), why not use your boy servants (*paggi, ragazzi*) to satisfy your needs? They are far less dangerous, and so is masturbation.

Although it would have outraged certain religious folk and no doubt lots of women, the entire poem is jokey, forthright, misogynous, and eager to amuse a patron. All the same, a number of questions arise at once. Did Berni mean to publish this *capitolo,* or was it intended only for his patron and a restricted circle of readers? Is the plea for sodomy ironic or in good faith? Interestingly, the poem itself can yield no answer to these queries, even though the question about irony would seem to be purely literary. We must therefore go outside the poem, to the historical setting, for some answers.

Berni's lines seem to be toying with dreadful dangers, because the laws of every city in Italy carried brutal penalties against male homosexuality, from castration and death by fire to public flogging, branding, prison, and heavy fines.[7] Yet Renaissance preachers and many other observers railed against the reign of sodomy; they believed that it was rampant;[8] and a recent quantitative study of Quattrocento Florence, Berni's native ground, concludes that by the age of forty, two-thirds of all Florentine men had been charged with the "abominable vice."[9] In other words, even if this figure is grossly exaggerated, the crime seems to have been common, not least of all in literary circles; hence we must favor the assumption that Berni's summons to sodomy in clerical Rome was not ironic. He meant it, and it appears that he himself was so inclined.

Although serial and other study now rather underlines the matter, at all events for Florence and Venice too, the fact is that we already knew about the high incidence of homosexuality in the Italian Renaissance, but lacked the courage to rely on our literary evidence, as is regularly done in the study of classical antiquity. For Italian verse and prose of the fifteenth and sixteenth centuries abounds in the male homosexual theme pro and contra;[10] and if we make the hermeneutic effort to examine this literature in the light of the love poetry of the age, we encounter the whole question of male and female, of misogyny, and of highly idealized gender relations. The dominant fictions in the amatory verse, where women are turned into strange goddesses, betray a troubled consciousness: they rest, queerly, on a fierce element of misogyny.[11] To make sense of the obsessive fictions (of the beloved as both goddess and beast), we are led out beyond manners, mores, and high culture to a cluster of economic and social structures and to one of the stickiest of all areas: the institution of the arranged marriage of convenience, the celebrated question of the female dowry, the powerful ideal of the chaste wife and daughter, and the acquisitive energies of the male lineage in matters of property.[12] These structural features of urban life—material, restrictive, and socially defining— cast a gigantic shadow over the literature of the age, and it is time we used this testimony to help us chart the consequent mental world.

Although I have taken shortcuts here in order to cover more ground, I underline two claims: (1) poetry is a part of the historical record and ought to be used by historians, even to the extent of basing provisional generalization on it, and (2) if historians use history to throw light on poetry, they must accept that poetry may in turn throw light on history; the relationship is reflexive. To illustrate these claims, I again turn to Francesco Berni, because much of his verse has local voices and patrons as points of departure; and these points, as it happens, when related to the idea of the urban neighborhood, are in the foreground of much current historical work on the Renaissance.[13]

Berni's poems are riddled with references to his crowd or little in-group (*la brigata*); he continually uses real or invented first names to convey the sense of

the well-defined group; his insistent and sometimes hectoring tone is familiar, racy, demotic, as if he is talking across a breakfast table or to a friend across
the street; and his language is laced with *gergo* (slang) or the words and turns of
a coterie. Thus he has *signor marchese* for menstrual blood, *la pace di Marcone* for
a royal screwing, *chiasso* for brothel, *sparviere* for penis, and *cavalcar*, a popular
verb, to describe the male side of sexual intercourse.[14] In using proper names
to convey a feel or sense of the familiar group—for the tactic is defining—he
may have recourse to outrageous invention, as in his comical poem on the
entry of Emperor Charles V into Bologna in November 1529,[15] which drew a
huge concourse of Romans to that city. Here he pretends to name all the noblemen and citizens who went to meet his imperial majesty. In fact, the poem
is little more than a jeering catalog of 137 ludicrous names, most of them
invented, all cunningly arranged to pour scorn on the occasion. Who was
present? Well, "Cornelio Cornazzano, Lodovico Beccadello [cuckolds] . . .
Battista Cazzetto, Antonio della Coscia [buggery] . . . Luigi Asinari, Ambrogio Muletto [beasts of burden]."[16]

In Florence, where Berni grew up, the neighborhood was the basic religious, fiscal, political, and social unit; it had been so since time out of mind.
But this was true, as we have seen, of all cities in Italy. It is not chance, therefore, that much of the poetry of the long period from the thirteenth to the
sixteenth centuries is inflected by the push and pull of the close-knit group:
friends, neighbors, relatives, patrons, and others in the receding vicinage.

Let us pause for a moment and look at my procedure. The family unit to
one side, I have noted that the neighborhood was the main building block of
the Renaissance city and one of its structures of dominance. Looking for
traces of this phenomenon in the poetry of the period, I detect them in the
language, turns, and tone of Francesco Berni and indeed in the poetry of
many others: Cammelli, Bellincioni, Pulci, often in Poliziano, and in a whole
school of lesser poets in Quattrocento Bologna.[17] A few distinctions, however, have to be borne in mind, for the language expected by patrons and the
one imposed by neighborhoods may seem to be identical though they issue
from different calls on the imagination.

The Renaissance neighborhood imposed informality, conformism, and
the need for easy communication, though always strictly respecting social
barriers;[18] a poem to a patron might require these too, but it would also offer a
current of tonalities against neighborhood speech, as in the need to flatter, to

charm, and on occasion to be nonconformist (see chap. 2). In the case of a powerful *personaggio,* flanked by a clientele of servitors, we have someone whose ability to offer favors and protection gave rise to a human network that was likely to include the psychology of a neighborhood, of an array of people drawn together by common ties. In addressing a sonnet to this group, say to a circle of Tuscans in Rome, the poet might seem to be addressing a neighborhood, and in one respect, of course, he was doing just that. But we have now passed to a place or space without a physical presence, to a neighborhood of the mind. Here, men living near or far apart may be held together by a core of shared interests, like the fifteenth-century humanists of Rome, Florence, Milan, Ferrara, and Venice, who constituted an intellectual neighborhood.[19] In this modality, Berni's poetry could speak to specific men in Rome and Florence, but all his other readers would be outsiders, nonneighborhood men, and they might have trouble fully understanding certain words, expressions, and attitudes. For Berni, who was well versed in the classics, had no trouble floating a learned cargo of quibbles, puns, and studied absurdities, usually of a sexual nature, onto the easy flow of his vernacular. In other words, the coterie part of the language of patronage is a sort of exclusive neighborhood speech.

We begin to see why patronage and neighborhoods were, so to speak, natural allies. The two operated in a linguistic zone that imposed speech parallels or similarities: the members of a neighborhood, like the members of a patronage web, favored certain nouns, phrases, accents, anecdotes, or neologisms. Here, finally, it is clear that the direction of my analysis has turned right around: I am using poetry as historical documentation, using it to help bring out the ubiquity and resonance of the neighborhood in the Italian city. In its effects on language, whether directly or through the bonds of patronage, the neighborhood was finding its way into the high culture of the Renaissance.

In the late fifteenth century, the poet Antonio Cammelli (il Pistoia), composed nine tailed sonnets personifying, petting, metaphorizing, deploring, and undressing the house he lived in: a ruined and filthy pile.[20] His purpose was to seduce his boss in Ferrara, Duke Ercole, into offering him the materials or the money to revamp the house. The sonnets are a conspiracy of contrived familiarity: they are jocular, self-mocking, witty, scatological, and decked with popular turns of phrase. Occupied chiefly by mice, ants, spiders, dogs, birds, urine, and feces, Cammelli's nonhouse becomes a fixation at the point where patronage, as experienced by the protégé or the servitor, turns into concrete fantasy and motor force. The poet objectifies and gives flesh to an abstract social relation by reversing or inverting the very thing he wants from his patron: he transforms it into a series of *un*desirable animals and objects.

> La entrata de la casa [mia] ha mille porte . . .
> Gli can la tengon forte,
> che mille volte l'ora a pisciar vengono
> e pontandovi un piè me la sostengono.[21]

> (The entry to my house is by a thousand doors . . .
> Dogs keep it solid:
> A thousand times an hour they enter it to piss,
> And pointing out one leg, they hold it up for me.)

Another sonnet claims that his house "par dal lupo un capra sbudellata, / un postribol di gatte o di carogna" (looks like a she-goat disemboweled by a wolf, / an official whorehouse of female cats and carrion).[22] A third and fourth sonnet transmute the house, one into a chicken, the other into a suckling infant: "[La casa mia] Grilla come un fanciul ch'a la sua madre / vede le poppe fuor per dargli il latte" (My house wails like an infant who sees / its mother's breasts out to give it milk).[23] And again,

> La casa mia somiglia una gallina
> quando schiamazza che l'ha fatto l'ova,
> e va gridando: Io mi farò pur nova;
> fuor fonghi, tele, stronzi; fuor salina.[24]

> (My house is like a hen
> when it clucks that it has laid an egg,
> and goes on cackling, "I'll yet remake myself:
> Away foul toadstools, spiderwebs, turds; away brine!")

The zaniness of this poet is moved by the desire or need to provide coarse, immediate amusement for a patron whom he knows to be forever busy. But Francesco Berni, a superior poet, takes a kindred program and at once elevates it in his wonderful "song" for a nonexistent cloak, *Canzon d'un saio*,[25] penned for his patron, Antonio Dovizi:

Messer Antonio, io son inamorato
del saio, che voi non m'avete dato.
Io sono inamorato, e vo'gli bene
proprio come se fussi la signora;
guàrdogli il petto e guàrdogli le rene;
quanto lo guardo piú, piú m'inamora;
piacemi drento e piacemi di fuora,
da rovescio e da ritto . . .
Quand'io mel veggio indosso la mattina,
mi par dirittamente che 'l sia mio. (lines 1–8, 11–12)

(Messer Antonio, I am in love
with the cloak you didn't give me.
I've fallen in love and love it dearly,
As if it were my lady;
I look at the breast and I look at the backside,
and the more I look, the more I love it;
I like it on the inside and I like it on the outside,
upside down and up aright . .
When mornings I see it on myself,
I really think it's mine.)

Having envisaged the cloak lecherously—although as the dearly beloved in the conventions of amatory verse—Berni changes gender in the second part of the poem and sees the nonexistent cloak as the god of war. Messer Anton, he asks, "Vedete questo saio, se non pare/ch'io sia con esso indosso un mezzo Marte?" (Look at this cloak, doesn't it seem/I'm half a Mars when I have it on?).

Similar in manner and intent is one of Poliziano's elegant Latin epigrams for his mighty patron Lorenzo de' Medici. Although he dedicates his poems to Lorenzo, he says, the "little people" laugh at him, the poet, because he goes around in worn-out clothing, mended hose, split shoes, and a cheap under-garment. Yet the young Medici lord greatly admires his works. So,

Hoc tibi si credi cupis et cohibere popellum,
Laurenti, vestes iam mihi mitte tuas.[26]

(If you want this believed and wish to silence the little people,
then send me your clothes, O Lorenzo.)

We are seeing that the seductive, ludic, insinuating, and familiar language of a poem to a patron might gather obsessively around an image which, in Berni's case, pulls us up suddenly and makes us appreciate the hallucinatory weight of expectation that men might attach to their ties with patrons. In an urban economy in which opportunity was starkly restricted, in which office, favor, contract, lawsuit, or a lighter tax burden could pivot on the actions of a patron, this man became the sun, the light, one's father, a force of nature, a semidivine figure, the great healer, a fountain of grace, and so forth. What is more, like "my lady" in Renaissance love poetry, he also reaped a litany of proffered love, servitude, and near worship, as we shall see in the next chapter. Here, all at once, the language of patronage broke out of the confines of neighborhood and took on a universal hue. By adoring patrons and by making them larger than life, protégés were assuming the stance of the poet-lover in amatory verse. But they were also taking back what courtly love, in the twelfth century, had originally pilfered from the idealized diction for relations between feudal lord and vassal. By being made to echo the world of rural feudalism, the language of urban patronage turned the meeting point between patrons and clients into a moment of ideal perfection. And in that murky zone where words and feeling, or words and experience, have some congress, we are able to see the shape of the emotional world of patronage networks. To call a patron the light or the sun was hyperbole, to be sure, but it was not a brazen lie, for the epithet might well carry the power of an emotional truth; and it was certainly a formal utterance elicited from the poet by a social structure.

Let us clinch the meaning of these transactions. Patronage could be a matter of life and death. In the driven quest to exercise its power or to receive its benefits, men were capable of murderous physical assault. In Florence in 1433, was the humanist Filelfo not stabbed in the face for getting on the wrong side of patronage arrangements in university and political circles?[27] Did not Luigi Pulci and Matteo Franco shamefully maul one another in verse, with a view to retaining Lorenzo de' Medici's favor?[28] In Rome, Pietro Aretino was knifed in the face and hands by an irate servitor to a bishop in papal employment and then derided for his injuries in a savage poem by none other than Francesco Berni, a second servitor to the same bishop.[29] Berni himself died suddenly and mysteriously at the age of thirty-eight, almost certainly poisoned, a victim of the treachery of patronage.[30] It is no wonder that all the words for love and devotion were so easily bandied about in the compass of patronage; for as symbolic action, such a tribute of strong words was also a mode of insurance against the risks of disappointment and treachery.

The omnipotence of patrons ghosted through the whole of society. Yet literary and artistic patronage was the least of all that came under the control of princes, oligarchs, merchant bankers, and powerful clerics. What were the political life-and-death struggles all about in Bologna, Perugia, Siena, Florence, Rome, and Venice, if not about the spoils of powerful office? The long reach of the *gran maestri* at the peak of the patronage pyramid extended through all parishes and neighborhoods, down to the most humble shops and dwellings, in a system that circumscribed a citywide moral and emotional economy. Queller devoted a whole book to the spoils of office in Venice, where a rich and eminent nobility, in the determined pursuit of endogamous policies, ran a sort of "welfare state" for the multitude of poor, down-at-heel noblemen and their families.[31]

The poem of malediction and the popular verse letter, two different genres, may be inserted directly into this context.

I have already alluded to the snarling exchange between Pulci and Franco of sonnets, deeply and shamefully wounding, behind which there loomed the specter of Lorenzo the Magnificent's power to give and to take away. The devious links between patronage and a poetry of vituperation were also present in Francesco Berni's fleering attack on Aretino. Up in the Milan-Ferrara regions, the brutal verse exchanges between Bellincioni and Cammelli were matched by many others between lesser poets: quarrels all directly connected with the favor and influence of patrons.[32] But this is all known ground. The new point here is that the passions of loyalty, vendetta, love, hatred, and despair, as articulated in the verse of Renaissance patronage, help us to find the moral and sentimental guidelines of an urban setting riven by competing patrons and their clients, not to say "gangs." In a word, patronage *was* neighborhood. For the spitting verse attack on an individual, the purpose of which was to inflict as much moral and psychological pain as possible by releasing a formal shower of insults, only made sense if the abuse circulated among people who knew the victim or knew about him. With their many friends and acquaintances in upper Italy, poets like Pulci, Cammelli, Berni, and Aretino could cut a swath across the face of literary circles, which amounted to neighborhoods of the mind.

The injury was most painful and lasting, however, when suffered in the true neighborhood, somewhere in the city, as in the case of Pulci's sonnet war with the disreputable priest Matteo Franco. All of upper-class Florence must have howled with laughter at the scurrilities heaped upon him by the priest. For the immediate community was the cockpit of public shame and ridicule. The eyes, ears, and wagging tongues of neighbors and local acquaintances were, after all, what kept poetic abuse and injury alive. A vituperative poem was for the here and now, not for future literary scholars. At its most primitive, the abuse might be a foul rhyme passed on by word of mouth and having absolutely nothing to do with patrons. A local unpleasant encounter sufficed to elicit *verba iniuriosa,* the legal term for such abuse when it was prosecuted as a misdemeanor.[33] Indeed, insults were occasionally posted outside houses, or they might circulate throughout the city—Ferrara, Parma, and Venice, for example—in the form of five- or six-line jingles, as in the case of important men, such as rich tax farmers or a naval commander.[34] But in its artistic form, the vituperative attack might be a sonnet passed around among people in the locality, and they—not just the author—inflicted the moral pain by their conniving interest and laughter. The Florentine poet Giovan Matteo di Meglio (fl. 1440s) produced four virulent sonnets against two unnamed priests and two local women, also unidentified,[35] though neighborhood readers would certainly have known who they were. Poetry in Quattrocento Florence blazes with personal abuse. It is the fire of an intense neighborhood life, where favor and advantage belonged to clusters of dependents and patrons.[36]

If the verse letter can be enlisted to help complete these considerations, it is because the genre reproduced the emotional "system" of the neighborhood, where human relations were rooted in familiarity, intimacy, anger, playfulness, affection, and wounded pride. What is more, the genre expressed these in the spoken language of the day, as evidenced, for example, in the common practice of apocope after vocalics (e.g., *vo* for *voglio*) or the suppressing of the intervocalic *v* (*beono* for *bevono*), precisely as in testimony gathered by legal clerks for use in court.[37] This vigorous, everyday language is to be found in the verse letters of Franco Sacchetti, Francesco degli Alberti, Burchiello, Lorenzo de' Medici, Berni, and dozens of other writers.

Wherever the evidence has survived, such as at Bologna, Florence, Ferrara, and Rome, it is clear that poets favored the verse letter as a form of direct communication. The Florentine poet Feo Belcari (1410–84) attracted all sorts of religious and theological questions in rhyme, and his replies went out in verse letters.[38] Usually, however, such letters broached just about any ordinary topic, such as love, taxes, office-holding, marketing, scraps of gossip, domestic matters, travel, moral advice, and outright nonsense. Written, generally speaking, to a friend, acquaintance, or patron, the verse letter was the most constructed type of missive and nearly always intended for someone in the real world. But the world men knew best in Renaissance Italy was the one bounded by their neighborhoods; and some of the larger cities, as Dante detected in Bologna, even had distinct neighborhood accents. It was also the case, however, that as people ascended the social ladder, the local world gradually opened up for them, to take in an ever larger circle of contacts and familiar faces, until, indeed, the entire city became their working neighborhood. This was certainly so for leading politicians and merchant-bankers in Florence, Venice, and Genoa; it was no less so for the influential men at court in Mantua, Milan, and Ferrara.

The high sense of honor and powerful shame, a sense of *public* being, that sweeps through Italian Renaissance literature arose first and long endured in the embrace of the neighborhood. Here is where *cittadini* most enjoyed or suffered the elemental passions of pride and shame. This must be why the moral and emotional climate of the neighborhood always remained a prime mover in the great body of verse letters and poetry for patrons. And if we ignore this literature, we are turning our backs on a vast archive, in which the testimony is at once direct, subtle, and devious. Humanity?

TWO

THE VERBAL WEB

OF PATRONAGE

LOVE

In a letter of 14 May 1477 to the Magnificent Lorenzo de' Medici, Luigi Pulci confesses to being "your debtor for many things," acknowledges a loan of one hundred gold florins, a minor fortune for which he was being dunned at the time by the Medici bank, and rehearses a client's allegiance to his patron:

> Though I seldom come to you now, know that I am always with you, that I am yours more than ever, and that the little I know and can do, along with my possessions and my life, I would put at your disposal . . . be sure at least of this, that I have not forgotten the numerous favors done me both by your father and yourself, and I for one know that you have not helped an ingrate, inasmuch as I have it all carved in my heart. So may your [business] partners not think that I am dodging you in order not to pay up, for I love, venerate, and fear you. I have long valued your grace [unmerited favor toward me] and friendship more than anything else in the world, and so will I value them always.[1]

Pulci's letters to Lorenzo, often very seductive (far more so, in fact, than appears here), are an education in courtliness of the sort for dealing with powerful men and patrons. I begin with the preceding quotation because it introduces an illustrative phraseology and set of feelings: notably, I am yours; I give you my life; I have the memory of it sculpted in my heart; I love, revere, and am afraid of you; I esteem your grace (i.e., the grace with which you have done things for me) above all other things in the world. All these subjects and predicates, or the designated feelings, turn up time and time again in the love poetry of the Italian Renaissance.[2]

In this chapter, therefore, I seek to establish two claims: (1) that the language of patronage and the language of love poetry in Renaissance Italy were so alike as to verge on being identical, and (2) that the nervousness and instability of patronage networks could also evoke a vocabulary of anxiety, anger, and invective, which in its turn casts light on the wider compass of politics and social organization.

Revealingly, as it happens, the links between patronage and love verse were more "natural" and necessary than might appear at first sight. For patron-client and lord-servitor relations in the Renaissance urban world were so pervasive, or the conductors of such heft, as to affect other human relations and their attendant vocabularies. At the points where social differences were most manifest, as in encounters between lords and underlings or patrons and clients, social structure was served by a language that both ransacked terms for heavenly bodies and invaded perceptions of love. Even in communication between obvious equals, it was often necessary to treat and negotiate by means of words for unequals, each side paying verbal tribute to the other in sensitivity to the envies generated by social and political gradation.[3] Although language might be as rich as or richer than all its referents in nature and society, some zones of social experience were so resonant, and feeling there so deep, that their field of diction influenced the language of adjacent or analogous fields. The particulars of this process may be observed in the give-and-take of patronage.[4]

Wherever we come upon letters between clients and authoritative patrons,[5] we find that each side has entered into an exchange, the action of giving and receiving; and we need no high-blown anthropological theory to make sense of this. The client gives love, praise, devotion, and sometimes completed action (say a poem, a picture, or a musical performance); the patron offers favor, payment, place, or at least encouragement, and some dash of affection or loyalty.[6] In its courtly or elevated form, the language of love poetry mimes the exchange of love and favor in patronage. In the love lyric of the fifteenth century, the poet-lover offers love, praise, and himself to his lady; in return he may ask for tolerance alone, for the right to see her, or even for love and favor. If he receives little or none of these, he grieves.[7] To express his love and admiration, and to profess his absolute fidelity, he enlists and highlights terms garnered from feudal ties (*lord* and *servitor* or *vassal*), the hierarchy of heavenly bodies (*stars* and *sun* chiefly), government (*ruler* and *ruled*), and domestic or economic relations (*master* and *servant*). The lady becomes his moral, social, political, or cosmic superior: his lord, light, guide, star, sun, or sovereign.[8] From the thirteenth to the seventeenth centuries, the diction for vertical social relations, for status high and low, all but dominates the love lyric in the job of describing the fundamental stance there: that is, it describes a transaction between loved one and lover, cast almost obsessively as a harmonious or discordant relationship between lord (loved one) and servitor (lover), master and servant, ruler and subject, proud and humble, powerful and weak, or rich and poor.[9] But far beneath them in the world of this verse are the *vulgo* (the common herd) and all those who are *vile,* base both socially and morally.[10]

Patronage gave rise to a similar stance. In dealings between clients and patrons, the lexicon of binding words is dominated—as in the imagery of the appropriate body language—by a vocabulary of love, flattery, service, fidelity, or the diction marking a failure of these, such as in complaint or even invective. Indeed, in a homologous sense, much of the religious poetry and painting of the Renaissance may be viewed as conforming to the paradigmatic stance of patronage: the worshiper bows or kneels, offers praise, makes avowals of love and faith, and implores favor, as he or she (suiter-sinner) prays to one of the saints or to Mary to intervene with the Lord of lords. Certain historians, drawing on anthropological models, would at this point urge the existential priority of the religious posture over the act of obeisance in worldly patronage.[11]

So long as sharp gradations of rank and station loomed importantly in consciousness, that is, as long as power was the exclusive business of princes and oligarchies in the closed spaces of Renaissance cities, so that they seemed an elite fixed by nature and right of birth, so long did an aura of lofty authority cling to them; whereupon love poetry, in its stretch and search for effective trope, metaphorized the difference between lover and loved one as a difference in power, or rather as a distance in rank and status between them. The pain and despair of the yearning lover were turned by metaphor into the condition of the underling disdained by his master, lord, or governor. In the semiotics of this polarity, light (including heavenly light) could belong only to the side of the social and political superior. Hence the sun and stars figured or symbolized kings, princes, patrons, or the beloved lady of lyric verse.

It would appear, therefore, that love poems were most likely to observe the foregoing metaphorical conventions if produced for readers or an audience at court, as at Ferrara, Mantua, Urbino, or Milan, where the princely establishments were the apex of power and the final arbiters of social degree. But this was not necessarily the case. Poets and sophisticated readers at "bourgeois" Florence and aristo-mercantile Venice were ready to read and imitate "courtly" love verse, because they saw it as more skilled, knowing, elevated, and somehow right about matters of the heart.[12] In addition, however, and more importantly, Florentine and Venetian social structures and gradations were enough like those in the princely cities, particularly as articulated in the reciprocities of patronage, to justify the linguistic conventions of "courtly" love poetry. In brief, the social organization of patronage in Florence, Venice, Bologna, and elsewhere gave structural and psychological support to the essential metaphors of noble love. And most poets of the period, from Malatesta Malatesti (c. 1370–1429) to the Florentine barber Burchiello (1404–49), were personally caught up in the web of patronage.[13]

So, then, the language and attitudes of Renaissance love poetry provide us with the words and turns of patronage and tell us, in ideal terms, what patron-client relations were all about. Since lords and dependents could be depicted as lovers, poems for patrons often hinged on the metaphorical conventions of love poetry. In its catalog of utter impossibilities, Cosimo de' Medici's friendship poem for his powerful military patron and ally, Francesco Sforza, keeps strictly to one of the standard amatory forms of the day:

Fia prima stato seminato il mare
e per montagne e per la piana terra
e pesci si vedranno a passi andare
[then a list of other impossibilities,
capped by the conclusion:]
che io non ami continovo e sempre
Francesco Sforza sopra ogni altra cosa.[14]

(Sooner shall the sea be ploughed and planted, and fish be seen taking a stroll over mountains and the flat earth . . . than that I should not ever and anew love Francesco Sforza above all other things.)

The reciprocity between amatory verse and patronage was made all the closer by poetry's filching of (and giving prominence to) the key words for vertical social relations, such as lord/subject (*signore/soggetto*) or noble/base (*gentile/vile*). Here too, implicitly or explicitly, depending upon the text and the passage, there was a diction for divisive social relations; for in love, as in patronage, the parties might draw apart and be in conflict. But of course we must beware of the alchemizing work of the imagination in the migration of words from social-structural concerns over to those of love in poetry. Love converted patronage, oddly, into a kind of matronage. The beloved lady became lord and master, as in this exercise octave (*rispetto*) by Poliziano:

> I' non ardisco gli occhi alti levare,
> donna, pe'rimirar vostra adornezza,
> ch'io non son degno di tal donna amare,
> nè d'esser servo a sì alta bellezza;
> ma se degnassi un po' basso mirare
> e fare ingiuria alla vostra grandezza,
> vedresti questo servo sì fedele
> che forse gli sareste men crudele.[15]

(I dare not raise my eyes up, lady, to gaze upon your high adorned self, for I am not worthy to love such a lady, nor even to be the servant to such lofty beauty; but if you would condescend to look down a bit and do injury to your greatness, you would see so loyal a servant here that you would perhaps be less harsh to him.)

Now the male was the lowly supplicant, suitor, or client. His true place in patriarchal and paternalistic society was turned right around in "literature," and the self-image that came back to him was that of the ardent but suffering, patient, pleading, powerless lover. His actual historical place put him apart from and above women, in a psychosocial distancing imposed by the power of men—in practice as in doctrine—over women.[16] All of a sudden, however, in highbrow love verse, the male could see himself as victim. Yet the objective historical reality—a distance, a submissive female, *or* a problematic difference—persisted stubbornly in relations between men and women. Indeed, it was now luminously confirmed by the metaphors of light and sanctity that divided the lovers in their patron–client relations:

Ma quando el lampegiar del dolce riso,
Amor, tu me mostrasti, caddi infermo:
riso che par che s'apra el paradiso.[17]

(But when you showed me, Love, the flashing of her sweet laugh, I fell
down, weak: paradise appeared to open in that laugh.)

With the luminous lady above the lover, the world was turned upside
down, but it was still, emphatically, a divided world.

In the love, praise, and obedience due from subjects and servants, and in
the support or affectionate concern due from their lords, were contained the
basic ingredients of a doctrine evolved to soften and validate the lineaments of
an entire social system, with its up-and-down transactions between superior
and underling, patron and client, husband and wife, father and son, lady and
lover. In this alignment only the last of these may strike us as curious, because
hyperbole and metaphor enabled the love poet to turn the patriarchal world
over on its head, to make women the mighty ones. But this inversion, in its
ironic and stagey contrast, served, I reckon, to underline the force of patronage and patriarchy in the world around. Poliziano's invitation, "Would
you but deign to do injury to your *grandezza*," already betrays a tincture of
mockery, although any derision always threatened to negate or parody the
genre.

Patron and lady both benefited from the alchemy of metaphor. Just as the
beloved lady of the Renaissance lyric is the stars, the sun, and the light of day,
so is she also routinely associated with sanctity.[18] The lover may seek moral
enhancement in her aloof virtue, or he may merely perceive his distance from
her by her blessedness. At the courts of princes, in courtly language, and in
the vicinity of the powerful, differences in social and political rank were easily
reconstituted, I have suggested, as moral and supernal differences. In gratitude, fear, or self-serving flattery, the servitors of princes and prepotent oligarchs ascribed Olympian or heavenly virtues to them; such ascription came
naturally. Piero della Francesca, Botticelli, Domenico Ghirlandaio, Raphael,
Titian, and most of the great painters of the Renaissance inserted their patrons, whether by easy request or natural choice, into the pictorial world of
saints and sanctity. The poetry of patronage did much the same sort of thing.

In April 1435 Giovanni di Maffeo directed a thirty-seven-line poem to
Cosimo de' Medici, urging him to intervene in a case that would certainly go

against the poet unless Cosimo stepped in.[19] The first line, "Pietà per dio del mie grieve dolore" (Pity my grievous pain, in the name of God), could easily be the opening line of a love sonnet, being fully in keeping with the amatory code. Cosimo is told that Giovanni is "senza amici, / povero, vecchio, infermo e peccatore" (without friends, poor, old, ailing, and a sinner), that he is being treated unjustly, that his case is neither heard nor understood, and that the officials concerned look upon him as an enemy. Then, with a quibble on Cosimo's family name and Christ's deeds, the verses declare that only he can help "il quale santificò nel medicare" (who in medicating also sanctified). And Giovanni adds:

> Nor do I see another way to my rescue
> than in the worthy ointments of this just man,
> fit to cure every incurable disease.

> (Nè altra via ci veggio al mie scampare
> se non di quest'uom giusto i degni unguenti,
> ch'ogn' incurabil mal fanno saldare.)[20]

He attributes to Cosimo the thaumaturgic touching powers of an anointed king: "And so I beg that [on my malady] he lay his holy hands" (Supplico adunque le suo sante mani / porga) (lines 25–26).

Power is the realm of light, virtue, and blessedness, the same properties ascribed to the image of the lady in amatory verse. Client and lover can approach their superiors, patron and lady, only by strewing the way with metaphors in salutation of their loftiness. In the whole of fifteenth-century Florentine poetry, no family excelled the Medici in the power to attract the nouns and adjectives that marked and celebrated authority—not the Albizzi, not the Alberti, nor even the Strozzi, the only Florentine families fit to have rivaled the Medici early in the century. At Bologna only the Bentivoglio family took in a similar harvest of adulation,[21] though in this regard they were easily surpassed, to be sure, by the Este of Ferrara, the Gonzaga of Mantua, and the Sforza in Milan.

The light that radiated from "my lady" in love poetry came forth, in the poetry of patronage, from the patron. Here are some verses apostrophizing Piero di Cosimo de' Medici in 1466, a year of grave political danger for him. Florence speaks:

Tu se'el mio Petro e sopra questa petra
ho rinovato il tempio a libertate
. . . .
O splendor rilucente, o santo raggio,
che'l cor m'infiammi di sì lieta gioia
ch'ogni molestia e noia
è da me tolta, el mio novello stato
è oggi più che mai per te beato![22]

(You are my Peter and on this rock I have restored the temple to liberty . . .
O shining brightness, o holy ray which so inflames my heart with joy that
all my troubles are shorn away: my new state is made happier than ever on
this day because of you!)

A sonnet written about 1420 by the younger Buonaccorso da Montemagno
for his patron, Palla di Nofri Strozzi, then the richest man in Florence, is
centered on the imagery of Palla's light:

Spirto gentil, che nostra cieca etate
di tua chiara virtù lustri et adorni,
. . . .
Sì potrò poi maravigliosamente
viver nel miser mondo ancor sereno,
e, stanco, a l'ombra tua chiara bearmi.[23]

(Noble spirit, whose bright virtue shines on and adorns our blind-dark
age . . . still serene, I shall be able, astonishingly, to live in this wretched
world and, though tired, find happiness in your bright shadow.)

Verse in Lombardy also turned patrons and princes into sources of light, as in
certain of Bernardo Bellincioni's sonnets for his Milanese masters, the Sforza,
who are identified with stars, the light of heaven, and the sun.[24] And Pietro
Bembo, about 1500, had much the same to say about the duke of Ferrara,
Ercole I, "the light of this our dark age."[25]

Looking back to the Renaissance poetry of patronage, historians may be
repelled by its facile hyperbole and assume that "good" poets avoided rhetorical exaggeration. But this was not so; and in any case, how shall we measure
exaggeration, by *our* good taste? Luigi Pulci and Angelo Poliziano abound in
high flattery. In the *Giostra* (1469–74), a poem of 160 octaves, Pulci regrets

the prospect that the Florentine people ("o mio popol, contento!") will never again be so happy as they were in Lorenzo de' Medici's day, a time of renewal more splendid than even that of the mythic Golden Age. For here among us was "the sun surrounded by other stars" (talented others and members of the Florentine oligarchy)—that sun which one of Pulci's letters to Lorenzo (in verses put into the mouth of Lucrezia Donati) calls "my only hope on earth and my Parnassus/my supreme good, my God, my paradise."[26] Written for the same patron, Poliziano's poem, *Stanze per la giostra* (1475–78), also apotheosizes il Magnifico's life and surroundings; as we see in the poet's invocation to him, Laurentius is slyly transformed, via the common ploy of playing on his name, into the tree of triumph, glory, and immortality:

> E tu, ben nato Laur, sotto il cui velo
> Fiorenza lieta in pace si riposa,
> nè teme i venti o 'l minacciar del celo
> o Giove irato in vista più crucciosa,
> accogli all'ombra del tuo santo stelo
> la voce umil, tremante e paurosa;
> o causa, o fin di tuttle le mie voglie,
> che sol vivon d'odor delle tuo foglie.[27]

(And you, well-born Laurel, under whose foliage gay Florence in peace reposes, fearing neither the winds nor the threats of heaven, nor angry Jove looking still more irate: receive under the shade of your sacred trunk my humble voice, trembling and timorous, O end and reason of all my desires, which draw life from the odor of your leaves alone.)

One truth at least was perfectly evident in the sustained metaphor here: Poliziano's ambitions and desires had certainly been stirred up and well satisfied by the city's (and Poliziano's) most powerful patron, Lorenzo. And whatever literary scholars may do, historians of the Italian Renaissance cannot afford to ignore praise or flattery. To do so would be to underestimate the impact, as then perceived, of political *padrini*[28] in patronage. They altered the moral air and the very speech around themselves. In its way, therefore, the amplified language of love and patronage was accurately profiling the magnitude of individual and group puissance at the local level, and it was suggesting something about its direful character when it was turned against enemies in the confined spaces of walled-in or water-bound cities.

In the eulogistic literature of the period, patrons were models: big-souled dispensers of employment, money, favors, clemency, and goodwill. They were foci in the political and social constitution of cities; and around them, in the different neighborhoods and main squares, orbited clusters of clients. Ultimately, these clusters knew and made for a larger social unity, in which again—back to poetry—patrons most embodied light and worldly virtue, owing to which they rightly deserved love, loyalty, and lauding.

Yet love was a slippery business.[29] Christianity had sought to make it all-pervasive. In issuing from charity and the love of God, no ideal could be higher than love. But in confronting the hard demands of everyday life—with its narrow occupational ways and constricting patriarchal structures—love always ran the danger of slipping into self-interest, as in this unlikely assertion: "I pledge love and faith to the Virgin Mary with a view to what she can do for me, and I love my patron and my lady with a similar view in mind." This surely was seldom if ever said. Instead, as if by instinct, the lover or suppliant played down all the signs of self-interest in his vows and ennobled the desired interchange by investing the object of his love with every appropriate virtue. But however we may see it, love was a reciprocity—an exchange, a contract, a transaction. And so, as an ideal emotion for sublimating human relations, love could be attached (or its words could) to all those persons and places freighted with the self-interest of the would-be lover. In this process, patronage and sentimental exchange between the sexes inevitably purloined ways of speech from one another and from religious expression. All the same, the stamp of power appeared in the resulting verbal forms and their expressive content, for the naked thrust of authority rather determined speech, gesture, and communicable content. To take the obvious example of a negotiation in the affairs of patronage: the classic recommendation requesting favor for an individual was bound to appear in a letter from one patron to another. Here, too, certain ritual terms were likely to be used in statements charged both with the diction of love and a strong sense of the client's *belonging* to the recommender, to someone who had, by implication, a whole company of such individuals under his protective patronage. In a letter of 10 June 1516 to another prelate, following a ritual salutation, Cardinal Ippolito d'Este begins thus:

> We greatly love Friar Anselmo de' Conti of Padua, both for his own qualities and because his father and [near] relatives are very much ours, and we desire to please him in every way. For this reason, we commend him to Your Reverend Fatherhood in the highest possible degree, in order that

you may show him favor in the name of our love and count him among those most dear to yourself. Confer as much benefit and honor on him as you can, for everything which for our love's sake you do for him, we shall take to be as pleasing as if you had done it directly for our own person.[30]

Throughout the Renaissance, the variable locution "per amor nostro," "per amor mio," or "per amor di [followed by a proper name]," was at once weighty and deliberately ambiguous, because it was shorthand for an inclusive notion of mutual love that moved to and from each of the parties involved. So in urging his addressee to favor Friar Anselmo "per amor nostro," Ippolito d'Este was saying, Do it out of the love that I bear you and that you [presumably] bear for me. The expression, moreover, carried echoes of the most resonant of all phrases, owing to the obvious parallels in charity and higher sentiment: "per amor di dio" (for the love of God), the most common and significant ritual turn of the age.[31] Again, to *belong* to someone, that is, to have a man who was "very much ours" in patronal or amatory terms, meant that the client or the lover, counting absolutely on the other's love, had entrusted himself utterly, and having been accepted in the same spirit, was indeed very dear to the other. All this is the sense of Anselmo's relatives being "very much ours" or "very much our men."

In this exclusive world of love among patrons and between patrons and clients, it is clear that men could come to love each other in ways that might seem—but were not—homosexual.

HATE

Patronage drew men together, but in doing so it also pulled them apart. It flourished on contradiction. Every commission, every office, every favor accorded to one man (or lover) was denied to others. Men competed for different prizes: some to dispense them, others to receive them. When competition became more intense, as happened in the fifteenth and sixteenth centuries, with the gradual hardening and constricting of ruling groups, discord entered increasingly into the wide webs of patronage. And in Florence, more especially after about 1420, the mounting rivalry involved public office, tax levies, tax clemencies, favor in the law courts, and the hunt for more advantageous marriages. But let us bring poetry in again, now as our guide on the divisiveness of patronage.

If in social designation and the hyperbolized trappings of power, the prince and the luminous lady of love poetry stood at one pole, the despised prostitute and the ugly old woman stood at the other. Here suddenly, as explained in chapter 1, we pass from a transcending or universalizing language of love, a code for forms of loftiness, to a "lower" and more particular "neighborhood" idiom. Writers directed some of their most violent invectives against whores and "filthy crones," metaphor often seeking to expel such women from the party of humanity by figuring them as feculent animals or mere carrion.[32] Even the delicate and subtle Poliziano, probably on the occasion of a feast for his Medici patrons, produced a well-known travesty, the *canzone a ballo,* beginning:

> An old woman ogles me;
> dry and flabby down to the bone,
> she wears not flesh enough
> to feed a hungry maggot.

> (Una vecchia mi vagheggia,
> vizza e secca insino all'osso;
> non ha tanta carne adosso
> che sfamassi una marmeggia.)[33]

But how might patronage elicit derision of this order? The instigating amusement of patrons aside, it normally did so only in cases of bitter rivalry between patrons or among angry and insecure contenders for place—a common enough occurrence in university and humanist circles at Florence, Rome, Bologna, Milan, and other cities, where relations between cliques were at times riven by venomous jealousies.[34] Some poets, too, plunged readily into scandal. For instance, there is the case of Antonio di Cola Bonciani (fl. 1440–70), who had to leave his native Florence to go in search of place. He produced a ravening sonnet against his brilliant compatriot Antonio di Guido, the leading *canterino* (public verse chanter) of the day and a poet in his own right. Directly addressing him, Bonciani spouts insult:

> O puzzolente e velenosa botta
> . . . imperio singulare
> di tutti i vizi . . .
> cagione d'aver guasta e corrotta
> Firenze . . .

Semiramis tu terresti a scuola,
soddomitando il tuo merdoso sacco
. . . porco, gagliofo, scelerato mulo,
ch'eserciti la bocca equal che'l culo.[35]

(O stinking and poisonous toad . . . unique empire of all vices . . . the ruin
and corrupter of Florence . . . You could even be a school for Semiramis,
sodomizing your shitty sack . . . porker, dummy, evil mule, you use your
mouth much as you do your ass.)

Up in Lombardy in 1502, the humanist Vincenzo Calmeta relayed an
anonymous invective against the Modenese poet Panfilo Sasso "to my particular benefactress, my lady the Marchioness of Mantua." It was a reply to
"quelli sonetti et epigramma che fece stampare in Bologna contra el Duca
Ludovico Sforza" (those sonnets and epigrams that he [Sasso] had published in
Bologna against Duke Ludovico Sforza).[36] The Lombard plain thus also rang
out with quarrels between and among favorites, would-be favorites, and men
on the payroll at the courts of Mantua, Ferrara, and Milan; and poets struggled
to show that in all affairs concerning the arts of writing, praising, and loving
service, they were second to none. In the 1490s the Ferrarese poet Antonio
Tebaldeo, who served several princes, issued a mordant epitaph against the
late Bernardo Bellincioni (d. 1492), comparing him to a dog because he had
spent his life "biting others." Says Bellincioni, speaking from hell:

E ben che sia la scorza in sepoltura
Non però il mio latrare ancora tace,
Ma per compagno a Cerbero rapace
Son posto . . .[37]

(And though my hide is in a grave, my barking hasn't stopped yet, for I've
been made companion to the rapacious Cerberus.)

At about the same time, Antonio Cammelli (il Pistoia), a dependent—later
sharply dismissed—of Duke Ercole I of Ferrara, issued a cascade of scathing
sonnets against the poets Bellincioni, Sasso, and Niccolò Lelio Cosmico,
as well as against the Ferrarese functionaries Gregorio Zampante, Niccolò
Ariosto (the poet's father), and others.[38] Bellincioni and Cosmico replied in
kind.[39] No insult, vulgarity, or gross metaphor was too vile for the lexicon of

poetic vituperation, which was dominated, at the extremes, by an imagery most in keeping with the activity of butchers, farm laborers, pimps, and lepers: pictures of carrion, refuse, fecal matter, prostituting, sodomy, ugly disease, barnyard animals, and the excretory organs. The results made for a mode of abuse so different from anything in modern literary culture—and this consequence of Renaissance patronage has never been considered—that it casts a special light on some of the sources and forms of feeling in Italian society. We see, in effect, a highlighting of the explosive tensions that could be generated by the strictures of the city-state world, with its webs of patronage, constraining patriarchal families, narrowing opportunities, daily face-to-face occasions, and chronic calls to please or to amuse the mighty—which returns us to the intimidating authority of local elites and particular individuals.

Much like what happened in Rome to a newly elected pope, the raw power and glamor that attended Lorenzo de' Medici in Florence galvanized suitors all about him, provoking sulfurous rivalries in the scramble to win his favor and attention, as may be seen in the verse exchanges between Luigi Pulci and Matteo Franco.[40] Already broached in chapter 1, their sonnet war, conducted over a period of three years (1473–76), was fought by epistolary exchange, public recitation, word of mouth, or copy carried by wag, relative, friend, and foe. On the whole, in the exchange, Pulci aimed for more subtlety than Franco, was more shaken by it, and tried sooner to put an end to it. For having been a merchant (though now failed), being married to an Albizzi (a preeminent lineage), and hailing from one of the city's oldest and most reputable families, he had more to lose in the fight than the jumped-up monk and private chaplain to Lorenzo's family, Matteo Franco. Yet being aimed at his brothers too, Franco's shafts had struck Pulci, who felt so savaged by the experience that in a letter to Lorenzo, "my hand trembling from a fever [caused by rage and shame]," he claims that "no dog has ever been more torn to pieces than I."[41] In such a state, he was able, not surprisingly, to produce these scabrous lines for the eyes of the scribbling monk:

Ben sai con sì vil porco ch'io cincischio,
nato d'uno troiaccia schiava Agnesa,
bastardo, mulo, incesto, bavalischio.[42]

(What a low swine I waste my time on you well know, born of a nasty sow and whore, slave Agnes, you bastard, mule, pervert, and rabid snake.)

Generally speaking, however, the two rivals were more controlled and relied mainly on in-group (coterie) punning or cryptic allusion. They were not, after all, buffoons at one of the princely courts; and they were too closely associated with their great patron to make strident vulgarity—the most facile feature of the vituperative genre—the norm in the sonnets that were allowed to go out of their hands. This restraint was the more binding in that Florentines, and particularly in the circle around Lorenzo, saw themselves as the font of poetry in Italy.[43] Vituperative verse was charged with less squalor, on the whole, than we have seen above. At Florence in 1440, drawings on the walls of the main criminal court, the Palazzo del Podestà, depicted leaders of the exiled Albizzi faction hanging upside down, their lower parts thus cast above their heads or higher part, the seat of reason. The official poet-herald of the Florentine republic, Antonio di Meglio, was then commissioned to write a series of biting verses to go with the defamatory frescoes.[44] He composed a quatrain of sneering derision, done in the first person singular, for each of the ten figures. The first was for Rinaldo degli Albizzi:

Crudel Rinaldo, cavalier superbo,
privato di mie schiatta e d'ogni onore,
ingrato alla mie patria e traditore,
fra costor pendo il più iniquo e acerbo.[45]

(Pitiless Rinaldo, haughty knight, stripped of my lineage and every honor, ingrate to my country and a traitor, among these I hang, the most wicked and sour.)

Another read:

E più di mie stirpa han questa pecca,
d'essere o ladri o barratieri o pazzi o traditori,
e io de' Gianfigliazzi
son Baldassarri, detto Carnessecca.[46]

(Most men of my lineage have this sin, that they are thieves or swindlers, lunatics or traitors, and I'm the one called Bacon, Balzar of the Gianfigliazzi.)

As abuse goes, this is paltry stuff. But having been written under the patronage of the official commune, rather than for the unofficial (and more scurrilous) ruling group, which assembled in the mansions of the oligarchs, it could not give too much unseemly scandal. The quatrains expose the double-sided nature of Renaissance patronage: honey for one side was poison for the other. Quarrels over public office, war, taxes, or even particular crimes[47] revealed the divisions between contending blocs, each with its patrons and clienteles. The love and flattery intended for one bloc was convertible into hate and abuse for the other, so that social bonding and harmony, the ideal ends of the patron-client nexus, gave way to divisive action, to the language of hatred and scurrility.

In the autumn of 1434, when from his exile in Venice the chief Florentine patron, *padrino,* and eventually *pater patriae,* Cosimo de' Medici, returned triumphantly to Florence, the losers—the Peruzzi, the Strozzi, the Albizzi, the Gianfigliazzi, the Castellani, and others—became fair game for abuse in rhyme; not, however, immediately, because Florentine prudence held that it was best to wait and see. Earlier, the leading popular poet, Burchiello, had not waited. He had produced at least two swinging compositions against the exiled Cosimo. One begins with the thumping "O umil popolo mio, tu non t'avvedi/di questo iniquo e perfido tiranno" (O my humble people, you don't see this evil and treacherous tyrant).[48] The other, at its most cutting edge, refers to Cosimo's partisans as "a foul and ugly populace," "base and only fit for manual trades, but scarcely fit to fend off its own lice."[49] As it turned out, Burchiello had to flee from Florence for his life. Another poet, the well-placed attorney (*notaio*) Niccolò Tinucci, who vacillated between the Albizzi and the Medici, had been briefly imprisoned and threatened with torture in 1433. He was to end up, as we shall see, with a despairing vision of life under the Florentine commune. And Luca Pitti, feted in a poem for his service to the ruling group in the 1450s, afterward became the object of poetic derision, when he passed briefly over to the anti-Mediceans of the mid-1460s and then successfully deserted them to save his own skin.[50]

The short verse attack, very often in sonnet form, cannot of itself account for the popularity of this genre in the fifteenth and sixteenth centuries. Without a vitalizing audience of readers or listeners, any genre is bound to remain a lifeless form. We must look elsewhere, to patronage and the familiar urban space; for as the handing out of large favors fell more and more fully under the control and shadow of politics, or rather, as patronage gradually got a choke-hold on public life, so the roughing up of people in verse could be more often commissioned or even be seen as a corrective, owing to the vigor and seeming spontaneity of the genre. A great deal of censure in verse, however, either was anonymously produced or targeted unnamed individuals.[51] Neighborhood and "city-hall" experience taught that it was dangerous to speak ill of the powerful, and on occasion it was too risky even to name and vituperate the humble, whose contacts, after all, might come up trumps. In capital matters such as lawsuits, household taxes, eligibility for public office, the granting of safe conducts, marriage, and the right to bear arms, there could be no perfect guarantees of success or achievement because of the common practice of secret negotiation. To have the desired reality in hand was the only true guarantee.

Since major patronage in Florence, as in other cities, could not be severed from politics, all the less so after the Medici return from exile, Florentines (even among those caught up in its trammels) must on occasion have sensed, if not seen, its iniquities. As long as a man benefited from his place in the patronage network, he was doubtless ready to tender praise rather than complaint. Moreover, at the most influential points in the network, favor and good fortune were the expected returns. But when benefaction failed to materialize at the humble points of influence and string-pulling, then clients and little patrons were more likely to be made aware of the "evils" of the system,[52] though the culture could not itself provide the insight to mount a critique, precisely because patronage was all-pervasive and "instinctively" taken for granted. To refer to an earlier example: in praying for the intervention of Cosimo de' Medici's "sanctifying ointments" and "holy hands," Giovanni was saying that he expected no justice in his case because he was poor and old and without friends. In effect, the deciding influence and power (patronage) were on the other side. Now, therefore, only Cosimo's prepotency could set things right. The injustice of patronage, in Giovanni's eyes, could be corrected only by more patronage. The contradiction was egregious, but poor Giovanni could certainly not see it.

At Milan, Ferrara, Mantua, Urbino, or (say) Rome, the power of the prince was such that if he chose, he could take up almost any case or entreaty, whatever the justice of things, and affect the outcome. This was the force of absolute patronage, and all subjects in the city recognized it. Whether perceived as good or bad, *fortuna* there pertained in some fashion to the domain of the prince, so he was deservedly accorded public gratitude or secret censure. But in Florence and the other city republics, the visage of power was more diffuse or disguised and the way of patronage more serpentine. Here, therefore, the favors, jobs, and justice most coveted by men appeared to belong to a more inscrutable and chancy world, where justice, like injustice, was itself devious. In Florentine Tuscany, accordingly, we find a body of verse obsessed with the themes of trickery, deceit, injustice, false friends, and wicked fortune.[53] The essential message of this comfortless poetry is that cunning, deception, wealth, and silence (secrecy) have poisoned the world. Typical are the angry accents and pessimism of a tailed sonnet by Niccolò Tinucci (c. 1390–1446):

> Chi ben fa oggi, el mal gli è dato in dota,
> chi è leale, è condannato a morte
>
> .   .   .   .
>
> el ben se tace, el mal se dice e nota,
> Giustizia tien serrate le sue porte:
> Colui ha ragion che di pecunia è forte,
>
> .   .   .   .
>
> I ricchi, i lusingher godono il mondo,
> traditori, ruffiani e barattieri,
> quanto è maestro tanto è più giocondo.[54]

(Whoever does what is good nowadays is given evil as his dowry, whoever is true is condemned to die . . . the good is kept in silence, evil is spoken and listened to. Justice keeps her doors locked; legal right belongs to the man who is made strong by money . . . The rich, the flatterers enjoy the world, so too the deceitful, panders, and swindlers; the more a man is an expert of this sort, the more joyous he.)

The asseverating style is the style of direct accusation. Tinucci is describing the current situation; he is not moralizing in a traditional fashion, that is, in the vein of late-medieval Christian asceticism. In these very years (the late 1430s?), none other than Filippo Brunelleschi himself voiced similar sentiments:

> Io veggo il mondo tutto inritrosito,
> che chi de' dar dimanda a chi de' avere,
> e chi promette non vuole attenere,
> colui che offende accusa po' il ferito.
> Prosciolto è 'l ladro, il giusto è punito;
> e 'l tradimento tiensi più sapere;

così inganna l'un l'altro al più potere,
e chi fa peggio n'ha miglior partito.[55]

(I see the world all askew: the debtor duns the creditor, the man who promises wants not to keep faith, and the attacker accuses the wounded man. The thief is freed, the just man is punished; treachery is held to be superior knowledge. So one man tricks another into trying for more and more, and he who does the worst deed gets the advantage.)

Verging on allegory, Brunelleschi does not of course mean that the debtor, the poor man with no connections, is able to hound his creditors. What a revolution that would have been! No, he is referring rather to moral debtors or moral bankrupts, to the shrewd men who control life around them by means of deception and trickery, and thus to the masters of the new wisdom. The failed Florentine banker and poet Francesco d'Altobianco degli Alberti, writing during the same years, shared Brunelleschi's bleak vision:

Se mai il quinto elemento ebbe potenza,
oggi triunfa e guridico apruova.[56]

(If ever the fifth element [i.e, lies] had power, today it triumphs and the legal experts confirm it.)

A man plagued by partisan taxation, his patrimony eroded, the loser in a sequence of lawsuits, and denied all effective patronage, Alberti went on to draw a grim picture of Florence, as we shall see in chapter 6. His bitter testimony was not unique; a good deal of supporting evidence came from other contemporaries.

There was yet another but related strain in our forlorn verse, sharply sounded about 1450 by Giovan Matteo di Meglio: "Qual cerch'avere amici sotto'l sole/prieghi'Iddio 'l facci riccho e ppo' 'l mantegna" (Whoever seeks to have friends under the sun, pray God he be made rich and be kept so). And again, "Non è amicho ognun ch' è detto amicho" (Not everyone's a friend who is so called).[57] Like the charge of injustice, here was an old theme—friendship or the lack of it; but fifteenth-century urban society revivified it, for patronage was also a kind of friendship. To be without friends was to be without patrons.

No contemporary could assail "patronage" as such (*patronato* or *patrocinio*), because this is our term, coined to help us see and summarize a system of power-broking, a whole array of interpersonal relations and dependencies, held together not only by self-interest but also by the ideals of love and amity. The indictments by Tinucci and the others move from the general charge of injustice to a more specific stress on trickery, treachery, and money. They are touching the dimly perceived ramifications of patronage: corruption in the law courts, the slippery workings of money, the force of blandishments in interpersonal ties, and the betrayal of amity or trust. Active during the middle decades of the century, even Florence's great *canterino*, Antonio di Guido, descried and lamented the dirty work that went on behind the scenes:

E son gl'inganni e tradimenti e torti
tenuti più sapere; e la rapina
si tien cosa divina.
L'occulta offension dett' è più ingegno;
chi peggo fa son dett'i più accorti;
micidi, furti, strazi e gran ruina
è quella medicina
che passa di sapere ogn' altro segno.[58]

(Trickery, treacheries and wrongs are deemed to be wiser, and [crafty] robbery is held to be a thing divine. The injury secretly inflicted is said to show more talent. The people who do the most evil are said to be the most sagacious. Murders, thefts, manglings, and ruin are the medicine which surpasses every other mark of learning.)

In Antonio and others, the nouns or verbs denoting the idea of betrayal, *ingannare* and especially *tradire,* are particularly strong, owing in part to their Judas subtext, and particularly significant because they truly adumbrate a community rich in sentimental bonds and the sense of trust—the bonds that held friends or patrons and clients together, and the trust at the roots of commerce and urban trade. Appropriately, therefore, Meglio, Alberti, Filippo Scarlatti, and others were keenly concerned about false friendship and ingratitude.[59] And it is all but startling that the organizers of the most famous poetry contest of the age, Florence's Certame Coronario of 1441, chose friendship as the theme for the occasion.[60] Where patronage featured so importantly in social relations, and the suspicion or fear of deceit was common,[61] the question of "true" friendship touched a raw nerve; so that the Certame, we may say, both acknowledged this and was a transparent exercise in the compensatory mode. As Scarlatti put it in about 1470—in a city where one hundred taxpayers held "one-fifth of all the wealth of Tuscany"[62]—when you are happy, false friends surround and praise you, but find yourself without possessions and everyone turns into your enemy; so be at the mercy of no man; hold on to your property and make sure that it is always yours ("el tuo conserva e fa' sempre tuo sia").[63]

Writers in Quattrocento Bologna, another center of patron-client web-bing, also produced a poetry of despair. But the attorney and jurist Nicolò Malpigli (c. 1375–1430s) took the feeling one step further and parried his disenchantment into outright cynicism:

> Guardesi homai ciascun dal ben li sta,
> Nè se fidi d'altrui più che de sé,
> Cum vitio se nutrichi e bona fe',
> Spechiando i tempi che fortuna dà
>
> . . . .
>
> Ma perché 'l mondo ha perso ogni virtù
> Giochi cum dui mantelli ogn' hom che po,
> Volpegiando cum questo e com colu'.[64]

(Let each man beware of what [seemingly] befits him, nor trust in others more than in himself; nourishment should he seek in vice as well as in good faith, thus mirroring the times given us by *fortuna* . . . But since the world has lost all virtue, let every man who can go into the game with two coats, playing the fox with this man and then again with that one.)

As if miming the duplicity alleged to rule the world, this recipe for deceit starts with a crisply ambivalent first line—"Let each man beware of what befits him"—and goes on to offer advice which may or may not be tongue-in-cheek. Only the brazen cynicism of the sonnet hints at its possible irony; but in view of the strains in fifteenth-century urban life and the continu-ing closure of oligarchies,[65] it is more likely that Malpigli's prescription was mainly in earnest. In an angry and melancholy frame of mind, his Bolognese contemporary Bornio da Sala (c. 1400–1469), a leading jurisconsult, gloom-ily opined in a *canzone* on current mores that riches are looked upon as

denoting good sense and goodness; evildoing is called knowledge; justice is
for sale to the rich, while being false and wicked ranks as virtue and superior
judgment ("Devenir falso e rio/È tenuta virtute e gran prudentia").[66] Even
after discounting the exaggeration here, we may accept that the charges
contain some element of substance in coming from one of Bologna's outstanding jurists. It would appear, therefore, either that patronage was not
working adequately, because there was too much deception about, or that it
was working too well at the main points of leverage, with the result that men
who lived outside the web of reliable patronage could only groan or gnash
their teeth. In any case, some kind of legal thievery in civil-litigation cases
seems to have been more and more common. Judges were being suborned,
and many people felt that tricks, treachery, and injustice were rife.

In view of the sustained outcry against the reign of deceit (the quintessential denial of love) in Renaissance urban life,[67] I have returned full circle to my
opening claim, connecting love and patronage and therefore, by necessary
implication, also linking hatred and the injustice (or failure) of patronage. Just
as love, hope, and goodwill in patronage, broadly understood, could generate
their opposites in the passions of anger, hatred, and despair, so the amorous
relation in verse could end in palinodes and the negation of love. As noted in
chapter 3, the sharp about-face against love often had a religious motivation,
and in this mood poets inevitably distinguished a "base" or "carnal" love from
a quite different order of love, capped by the love of God.[68] However, the
upper-class Florentine Antonio Alamanni, writing about 1500, needed no
religious grounds to take the measure of earthly love. The hypocrisy and
materialism of urban life, at least as he saw it, had disabused him. He demystified love by simply seeing it as sex and grounding it in the world of
money and influence:

> Amor vuol pur ch'io l'ami, ed io non posso,
> perch'io non porto mai denari a lato
>
> .   .   .   .
>
> S'ei saettasse altrui con qualche grosso,
> sarebbe da più gente seguitato
>
> .   .   .   .
>
> Voi dovereste, amanti, esser pur chiari,
> che oggi li denar son fatti amore,
> e amore non è altro che denari.

L'un dice:—Donna, io son tuo servitore—;
quell'altro . . .
. . . dicele che muore.
E lei risponde:—Se vuol morir, muoia,
che chi hon ha denar, non abbia foia—.[69]

(Love [Cupid] even wants me to love him, and I cannot, because I never have money in my purse . . . If he would shoot some weighty coins [instead of silly darts] at others, he'd have a bigger crowd of partisans . . . About one thing, lovers, you should be utterly clear, which is that in our day money is made into love and love is nothing other than money. One man says, Lady, I am your servant. Another . . . tells her that he dies [of love for her]. And she replies, If he wants to die, let him die, for any man without money has no business feeling the hot itch of love.)

In a word, what good is love, since it can't buy money? Alamanni's verses deflate and deride love's grand pretensions, while also sniping at the society that is giving them sustenance. His moral ground lies beyond laughter, too, in the implied need for a redefinition of love. But could the lesson of his verses be carried over into the perception of social structures, to enable contemporaries to see through the snarls of patronage? That is, could poets and other observers single out and deride the streak of hypocrisy in the claims made for amity in patronage? Not easily, for the semiotic transfer of love for "my lady" to love for a patron collided with unforgettable self-interests, basic family and social arrangements, and everyday material necessities. The high Renaissance concentrated power and wealth in fewer hands; blood nobility became the new, all-important social ideal; and the strings of patronage were more tightly drawn by fewer men. How could clients afford not to "love" their patrons?

The loosening of traditional ties did not begin until the eighteenth century, with the coming of new structures of dominance. Meanwhile, in a process underpinned by Renaissance social organization, amatory verse and patronage long shared a vocabulary, thus sustaining one another. Poetry enlisted— and exulted in—the contraries (superior/inferior) of vertical social relations; patronage used the sentiment of love to valorize and justify interpersonal relations between overlords and subordinates. But common too were the anxieties, frustrations, and hatreds generated by the give-and-take between clients and patrons. These exposed not only the painful limitations of pa-

tronage but also the constraints imposed by the demands of loyalties to family
and to other corporate structures. The shining patron, the bright lady of
amatory verse, and the abused "other"—sodomite, traitor, or porcine personality—were powerful fictions: a currency of the imagination, continually
called upon to negotiate personal requirements, to facilitate up-and-down
social intercourse, and to civilize or to vent passions.

THREE

PRAYER IN THE
URBAN SETTING

Even in prayer, citizens did not get away from a sense of the neighborhood and the pull of the web of patronage. First there was the parish, the social reach of the local church. Then there were the religious confraternities, which took in people from the vicinage or, in time, from beyond the near locality, but only so as to enlist like-minded members. Religious observance, therefore, was much more likely to be local than metropolitan. There was next the pantheon of patron saints, and above these the Virgin Mary, to all of whom citizens might turn as to protectors and advocates. They were the patrons whose raison d'être was to help open the way to divine favor. Thus, in worship too, remarkably, the requests and entreaties of citizens turned into a mimesis of interpersonal exchange.

In this chapter, while keeping the parochial space in mind, I consider religious sensibilities in the light of prayer. We shall see how local and personal religious needs were satisfied by means of a ritualized language whose power lay in its adaptability.

MISE-EN-SCÈNE

Borne to the brink of civil war in the mid 1490s, Florence somehow managed to back away. Around the main protagonist, a Dominican friar, there swirled a storm of passion. The death of Lorenzo de' Medici (1492) and the demands of a blackmailing French army (1494–95) set off raging controversy in the city, stirring up a discontented patriciate and the anger of hounded taxpayers. Fusing religious fervor with republicanism, the friar Savonarola threw his weight behind political reform and split the upper classes, even dividing families. Swaggering opulence, brazen immorality, entrenched political privilege, and the views of a cynical elite all came under attack; but the intensity of feeling issued first of all from the friar's use of Christian ideals for political ends. These ideals were found all over the Italian peninsula, but other cities did not allow political emergencies to reel so far out of control that the values of religious asceticism could then be thrust into the middle of public affairs, to help shape the outcome of events. Just this is what happened in Florence when the exasperated political class cast the Medici out of government. Although later hanged and burned (1498), Savonarola, by his temporary victories, gave proof of the tenacity of ascetic ideals in the culture of everyday life. Let us look at the underpinnings of his appeal.[1]

By *Christian asceticism* I mean a measure of withdrawal from, or denial of, "the world." Italian Renaissance sermons and prayers and a flood of religious verse, including hymns or lauds (*laude*), speak obsessively of this blind, false, wicked, and ephemeral (*caduco*) world, where life is little more than smoke and shadows. Such metaphor and judgment pervade the extant body of prayer and devotional poetry, a good deal of which spurns riches, honor, position, and high estate, while also calling for a supreme commitment to the salvation of one's immortal soul by means of self-denial, love, prayer, and true contrition. The ascetic indictment of the world is encapsulated in the deep and uncompromising spirituality of this fourteenth-century octave:

> O blind world, full of flatteries,
> deadly poison in your every delight,
> fraudulent, full of cheats and mistrust.
> A fool is he who turns his bridle your way,
> when, for less than a fig, he loses that good
> which over every other love gleams and remains green.
> Let no man ever heed you
> who wants to taste sweet flowers' fruit.[2]

> (O cieco mondo, di lusinghe pieno,
> mortal veleno in ciascun tu diletto,
> fallace, pien d'inganni e con sospetto.
> Folle è colui ch'a te diriza 'l freno,

quando per men che nulla quel ben perde,
che sopra ogn'altro amor luce e sta verde.
Però già mai di te colui non curi,
che 'l frutto vuol gustar di dolci fiori.)

So concisely expressed, this view of life and the world may strike us as being the stuff of medieval commonplace and not to be taken seriously in the Renaissance urban setting. But it would be wrong to see it so. Needless to say, men piled up riches when they could, despising the poor, seeking earthly honor and prostitutes, coveting lordly place, and "staining" themselves with sodomy or the brutal killing of others. But action and belief are seldom united in history; and hypocrisy is a notion that moralists and politicians will find more useful than historians. Though often coupled with obvious pride, the evidence of piety in Renaissance art and architecture, as in the written record, is simply overwhelming, even when Christ and the saints are being "humanized," as in painting, or represented as near-burghers and citizens, as in religious plays (*sacre rappresentazioni*). The unstable power of religious feeling was always there, latently explosive. Suffice it to single out the dramatic moment in 1494 when two of the finest minds of the age, Pico della Mirandola and Angelo Poliziano, first one and then the other, having requested burial in Dominican garb, ended their lives dressed in white, in the Florentine convent of San Marco, all but in the arms of the consoling prior Savonarola.[3] The worldly Lorenzo de' Medici had himself been the instigator of the friar's return to Florence in 1490.

But having stressed the ubiquity of religious feeling, I should point out that in the midst of piety there was also blasphemy, religious frivolity, skepticism, and even fleeting evidence of disbelief, as is noted at the end of this chapter. Our theme here must be the one that dominates the historical record.

I propose to examine urban piety in the Italian Renaissance by considering rhymed prayers, lauds (sung verse in praise of God and the saints), religious poetry, and *sacre rappresentazioni*. For these take us into the religious sensibility of the age: to a spectrum of fears, hopes, and vivid images that will enable us to draw a bead on the history and anthropology of Italian piety in the period from the fourteenth to the sixteenth centuries. A Florentine wool merchant, for example, might levy fines on himself, to be paid to "the poor of God," for having sexual congress with his wife on Fridays.[4] When badly cut or wounded, hardheaded Venetian spice traders, who scoured the seas for profit, sometimes fingered religious charms to help stanch the flow of blood; or they clutched a strip of paper with magical religious abbreviations—for example, "Bx. c. t. g. d. q. r. p. s. a."—so as to ward off the evil of enemies. There was even a belief alleging that on the day you attended Mass, you could neither age nor die.[5]

Before the Reformation, Christian ideals and liturgy were much the same all over Western Europe. Antwerp, fifteenth-century London, Nuremberg, Barcelona: all held a great religious patrimony in common with, say, Venice, Bologna, and Florence. Since, however, every part of Europe had a different history, the experience of religion in the universe of Italian Renaissance cities was bound to have different accents and tonalities.

In assembling the parts to make a whole here, we may start with the fact that most of the cities of upper Italy began to spawn religious confraternities in the thirteenth century.[6] All parishes and neighborhoods, and in Venice all guilds, soon came to have their pious fraternal associations: flagellant (penitential), charitable, or hymn-singing (*laudesi*) companies, were organized in accordance with various social affinities and geared to satisfy the local need for devotional solidarities. These companies were usually (in Venice always) kept under some political surveillance, and the controls on them were generally tightened during the fifteenth and sixteenth centuries.[7] But at different times and places six or a dozen men might get together to form a new confraternity.[8] By the beginning of the fourteenth century, the clustered urban space already had parish and other churches almost everywhere, including convents, the larger churches of the different orders of regular clergy, and, in the bigger cities, the great metropolitan church whose bells resounded loudly throughout the walled-in space and could be heard in the deep countryside beyond. An intense "civic" religion sprang up, closely associated with the city's patron saint or saints. For example, Saint Ambrose was the patron saint of Milan, Saint Ercolano of Perugia, Saint Augustine of Pavia, Saint John the Baptist of Florence, Saint Mark of Venice, Saint Venantius of Camerino; Bologna had three patron saints (Peter, Ambrose, and Dominic), and the Virgin Mary was claimed by at least four cities, Siena, Parma, Piacenza, and Brescia.[9] On certain days, or in times of plague and famine, civic worship also collected around other saints, such as the Madonna del Impruneta in Florence, and writers might produce special lauds and prayers for the occasion. Topographically, the core of the ancient urban concentration, the space ordinarily delimited by the main government palazzo and the principal church, was likely to command more piety, a mixture of religious and secular sentiment; this was further endorsed by the fact that crimes committed there—theft, assault, rape—usually carried heavier penalties.[10]

Family, group, guild, neighborhood, faction, and even patronage webs often gave rise to a corporate sense, especially among the men of the middle and upper classes; and this sense was likely to involve the individual's pious sentiments, even when the association was not sealed by an oath. "I am a gentleman, a merchant, a jurist, an office-holding citizen, a butcher, a Strozzi or a Contarini, a resident of the parish of San Luca, or a member of the Flagellant Company of the Blessed Virgin." Such self-identities entailed loyalties to a kind of larger self; but they soon came up against the capital power of government, whether princely or republican. In its turn, this high temporal authority also fostered a choreography of reverential stances around itself, largely by means of a religious semiology, such as by highlighting swearing-in ceremonies, boasting official chapels, mandating religious processions, maintaining close visible ties with the clergy, and having chronic recourse to divine invocation. In many cities—Lucca, Siena, Ravenna[11]—taking part in devotional candlelight processions was de rigueur at least once a year, a duty imposed on all inhabitants: men, women, and children above a certain age. Moreover, in upper-class circles, where oligarchy had become an immemorial business by the mid–fifteenth century, family chapels or tombs, memorial Masses, or other church ties also heightened religious feeling (and very often pride as well).

Piety in the Italian Renaissance, then, as I shall track it in prayer, lauds, and religious verse, should be seen in the foregoing context of loyalties and converging influences. Here was a motor and shaping environment, without which we cannot rightly gauge the religious feelings of the age.

REMEMBERING DEATH

Into our rich setting, as delineated above, came the primordial fear of death, intensified by recurring plague and influenza epidemics and by crop failure, famine, and war. It was a fear relentlessly exploited by the late medieval Church, with its blunt emphasis on the brevity of life and the terrors of death. If after about 1500, war and syphilis filtered frequently into the imagery of death, after 1348 plague was to be the great nemesis always, with its characteristic removal, swift and "pitiless," of multitudes of people, especially in the cities. This, plausibly, is why so much of the poetry of the period echoes with the themes of death and the fragility of life—amatory verse for one, but also carnival poems and songs, moral rumination, occasional composition, and certainly religious poetry.

To top it all, there was a theater of death, promoted both by Church and state with a view to hammering home the lesson that crime does not pay. I refer to the spectacle of public execution, usually by hanging but also, occasionally, by fire, beheading, or the amputation of limbs. Famously, in Venice, the site of the gallows lay between the two great pillars in the *piazzetta,* which fronted the ducal palace.

Normally inflicted in public, capital punishment, with its staged exhibition of gore, gave rise in nearly all cities to a special confraternity, founded to bring solace to the felon, particularly on the day of his or her execution.[12] Some of the "brothers" would gather around the condemned homicide, thief, arsonist, or counterfeiter on the way to the gallows, calling for ardent prayer, pressing him or her to feel contrition, to pray to God, and to triumph over death by reaching out passionately for salvation. Such a prayer comes down to us, but it is in the form of chanted verse (a laud) and mutes the emotional violence. The author, Gregorio Roverbella (c. 1410–88), was a member of Bologna's Confraternity of Santa Maria della Morte and a well-known attorney (*notaio*) in that university city. Entitled "For those on their way to justice," his poem includes these verses:

Misericordia, o sommo eterno Iddio,

. . . .

Eccomi giunto a quello extremo passo,
    Caro Signor, che gusta ogni mortale
    Del mondo ladro, sospiroso e basso.

. . . .

E merto el fuoco eterno et infernale;

. . . .

Und'io pentito di mie' gravi errori
    Cum volto lacrimoso e con gran doglia
    Penso piangendo ai tuo' mortal dolori

. . . .

Hor fami del tuo amor si forte acceso
    Che per lo merto de tua passione

Io porti con forteza questo peso.

. . . .

Deh! trami, signor mio, di questi pianti
     E menami a veder quel dolce viso
     Ch'ai martiri tu mostri e agli altri santi;

. . . .

E l'anima venuta a le confine
     Gridando invoca il tuo divin soccorso
     Che tra l'altre beate le destine.
Ecco l'amaro fiele, ecco il dur morso
     Che Pietro col gran Paulo e gli altri toi
     Hanno per lo tuo amor sofferto e corso,
E tu il provasti ancora qui fra noi
     Cum degno esempio de tua croce sancta . . .[13]

(Mercy, O highest and eternal God

. . . .

Here I am at that final step,
dear Lord, that every man must take
in this thieving, base and sighing world.

. . . .

I deserve the perpetual fires of hell;

. . . .

I repent my criminal ways
with a tearful face, and sobbing
with great sorrow I think about your mortal woes [on the Cross]

. . . .

Now fill me with such a fire of love for you
that through the merits of your Passion
I may bear this weight with fortitude.

. . . .

O, Lord, take me from these tears
and lead me to see that sweet face
which you offer to the martyrs and to other saints;

. . . .

Arrived at the ends of the earth, my soul
cries out for your divine help
so that you may put it among the blessed.
Here is the bitter gall, here the hard bite

that Peter and great Paul and all those others of yours
have faced and suffered for your love,
and you yourself went through it here among us
in that high example of your holy cross.)

The prayer is riddled with commonplaces, as any such plea must be, so as to
draw the sinner back into the commonality through the voice of the liturgical
tradition. Moreover, the principal strategy likens the impending execution to
the martyrdom of Christ and certain saints. But we must try to envisage the
prayer as a sustained act of weeping and shouting, a prayer that went on in the
midst of hundreds or even thousands of spectators—mute or unquiet witnesses
to a willed religious frenzy. The terrors of death and its consequences were
here communicated as something awesome. Now and then the cart bearing
the condemned criminal to the gallows was already spangled with blood.

Yet dying was an experience for which the numerous confraternities prepared their members, not only by earmarking funds for the burial of brethren
and the celebration of commemorative Masses but also, in the force of prayer,
by continual reminders of the frailty and evanescence of life, the Day of
Judgment, and the horrors of hell. The theological claims of asceticism were
easily inserted into this picture, nowhere more effectively than in the poetic
dialogue with a confrere not long dead: an exercise always fresh though drawn
from Iacopone da Todi's late-thirteenth-century composition "Quando t'alegri, omo d'altura." No death poem was more widely copied, recited, and
chanted over the course of the fourteenth and fifteenth centuries.

Quando t'alegri, omo d'altura,
va' puni mente a la seppultura;

. . . .
e ppensate bene che tu di' tornare
en quella forma che tu vidi stare
l'omo che iace en la fossa scura . . .
"Or me respundi, tu, om seppellito,
che cusi ratto d'esto monno èi 'scito:
o' so li be' panni, de que eri vestito,
ca ornato te veio de multa bruttura?"[14]

(When you rejoice, O man of eminence, go think about your grave . . . and
consider that you must turn into the form of the man you see lying in a dark

ditch.—"Now answer me you, the one buried, who so soon departed from this world: where are the handsome garments you used to wear, for I see you decked out in lots of ugliness?")

This poem/laud goes on for another thirty-seven quatrains, to set forth in picturesque detail the frightening differences between the man once young, rich, beloved, and handsome and his current (ghastly) condition in death.

A later anonymous laud has verses in a similar vein:

> O voi gente che state nel mundo
> Aprite li ogi a me sagurato,
> Che senza fine starò nel profundo
> E dali demonii sempre sarò strasinato,
>
> . . . .
>
> E io misero quando era bello frescho e possente
> Tuto lucente più che li fiorini,
> Era amato da ogni gente . . .[15]

> (O all you who are in the world
> open your eyes to unfortunate me,
> down forever in the deep
> where I'll always be dragged around by demons
>
> . . . .
>
> And [yet] when I, wretch, was handsome, young, and lordly,
> all of me brighter than florins,
> I was loved by everyone.)

The lesson of such hymns and poems was clear: all you who read or sing these lines, give up your worldly and carnal ways; repent now; ready yourselves for the Day of Judgment. Death, in a word, became the choice topic for turning the fears and hopes of people to thoughts of the afterlife, for if this could not drive them into the arms of religion and the Church, what could?

The dominant imagery of the most popular death hymns, such as "Quando t'alegri" and "Chi vol lo mondo desprezzare," was gleaned from the world of rich and well-placed men, not only because this choice rendered the verse more forceful, as in perception of the dramatic divide between riches and the vile nakedness of death, but also because such lauds and poems were aimed, first of all, at the comfortable middle and upper classes. Thus the *lauda* "Chi vol lo mondo desprezzare" declares that death "breaks all walls," "despises wealth," and "strips men the way thieves do."

> No fortitude counts against it,
> nor knowledge or beauty;
> towers and palaces and grandeur,
> all these it empties out.

> (Contra liei non val fortezza,
> sapienza né bellezza;
> turr'e palazzi e grandezza
> tutte le fa abandonare.)[16]

In a word, death is the enemy of the rich above all; the poor have nothing to lose. So let fear go out first to those who most deserve to tremble when hearing—say, in the late fifteenth century—the death ballad intoned in a Bologna marketplace by the blind minstrel Simon, or in Venice by Antonio Farina, the best-known Venetian *canterino* of that day.[17] Here is how three of the most often heard of such ballads begin:

> 1. I am the great Captain of Death

> (Io son il gran Capitano della Morte.)[18]

> 2. My name is death,
> I wound those whose time has come

> (Io son per nome giamata morte
> Ferisco a chi tocha la sorte.)[19]

> 3. Death frightens me
> by its condition:
> with no man will it make a pact,
> what it says goes.

> (La morte me spaventa
> De sua conditione,
> Cum nullo vol far patto,
> Ziò che dice si è fatto.)[20]

The third of these ballads, reminding the "rich man" that he must leave everything and end in "the meanest of sacks" (*portaray / Vilissime sachone!*), closes with a prayer:

> Christ Jesus, give me strength,
> let me not end in that bitterness [hell],
> but come up to that loftiness
> where your mansion is.

> (Cristo Iesu dame forteza
> Che non vegna in quella aspreza
> Ma vegna in quella alteza
> Duè tua masone.)[21]

When plague was raging through Siena in 1400, neither rich nor poor needed reminders of the peril to their souls. And on an appointed day, all the people of the city, flanked by the heads of government, massed into the Siena cathedral to hear a prayer to the Virgin Mary, invoking her intercession for help and mercy: a prayer composed and recited by the poet Saviozzo, as he stood before a painting of the Virgin in his bare feet and wearing a halter around his neck.[22]

THE LANGUAGE OF PRAYER

Most prayer of the period comes down to us as verse and chant (*laude:* hymns, lauds), and it was often composed for religious confraternities or governing councils but occasionally for an individual.[23] Most of it, again, was addressed to God (or the crucified Christ) and the Virgin Mary, with the pantheon of patron and other saints receiving far less. The bulk of it is anonymous and frequently interchangeable. It aims not at originality of expression but at something closer to a conventional idiom, for its prime interest is the occasion and the stresses normally alleged to determine relations between the singer or suppliant and the imagined holy personage. Prayer, after all, was meant at least in part to be ritualized. That is to say, being directed to an authority beyond the here and now, it wanted a special voice, frequently— already by the 1320s or 1330s—an archaizing voice, because the frozen (idiomatic) turns of the tradition of prayer, working like a social weight, seemed to move the sinner closer to the holy. A prayer in sonnet form to the Virgin

Mary, written by the prince and *condottiere* Malatesta Malatesti (1368–1429), illustrates the practice:

> Come tu se' gentil, beata e bella,
> immaculata, dolce e glorïosa
> Vergine pura, a Dio dilecta sposa,
> chiara dïana, rilucente stella!
> Tu se' nostra advocata.
>
> .   .   .   .
>
> Così soccorri, Matre, ai duri pianti:
> el morbo invade nostra patria cara,
> devorando ciascuno, e crudel peste.[24]

> (How noble, blessed and beautiful you are,
> immaculate, sweet and glorious
> Virgin pure, beloved spouse of God,
> candid Diana, shining star!
> You are our patroness.
>
> .   .   .   .
>
> So come help us, Mother, in our tears:
> plague invades our dear land,
> a cruel pestilence, devouring everyone.)

By the late fourteenth century, the epithets of the first five lines above, making for a stereotypical stateliness, were already "archaic" in dating back to the 1200s; and behind the vernacular, in Latin, they were part of an ancient liturgical tradition. However, they drew much of their power from the felt correctness of their antiquity, and this, in part surely, is why Malatesta opens with them: they complete the poem as a prayer.

The emotive language of medieval and Renaissance prayer was ultimately grounded in the love that no other passion could surpass, namely, God's love for humanity as attested in the Incarnation and the Crucifixion. But that language also gained much of its power from three classes of metaphor, each of which rooted divinity and holiness in the energies of vital social relations.

First of all, there were all the words for family membership—*father, mother, son, daughter, children*—employed to name the suppliant's *desired* relations with God and the Madonna. Since the ideal and the reality of the family were fundamental for Renaissance society and were also the decisive constituent of

personal identity, this symbolic and phantom kinship with the supreme figures of Christianity was endlessly voiced so as to draw the votary closer to
them. Moreover, from the end of the thirteenth century, in the most moving
vernacular hymns and prayers, affectionate relations between Christ and the
Virgin Mary were so dramatically humanized and domesticated that when
praying or singing, worshipers may be said—*toute proportion gardée*—to have
stepped into a familiar household.

Second, in a patriarchal and deferential society, where the local power of
urban bosses was egregiously strong, and particularly in the tightening political and economic circumstances of the fifteenth and sixteenth centuries, the
reverential stance of the sinner in prayer mimed the caps-off approach to
powerful patrons, just as the deferential approach to bosses and patrons might
replicate the attitude of the cross-armed, praying suppliant, even to the point
of kneeling.[25] The strategies in the appeals made by submissive client and
praying votary were thus similar and sometimes identical, as when, in utterance, a client explicitly associated his patron with heavenly qualities (see
chap. 2). In short, although the supplicatory verbal stance was utterly conventional and well worn, it was always necessary, always fresh and natural in the
society of Renaissance cities. Inevitably, too, the urgent appeal to a patron
might be cast in terms of a plea to a father figure.

In vitalizing the force of prayer by rooting it in urban experience, the third
type of metaphor collected around the transactions of buying and selling.
Christ had redeemed us, that is, he had literally "bought us back" from
perdition with his blood; and verse prayer teems with this pawnbroker's
notion in the key verb *ricomprare*.[26] In a remarkable prayer, Lorenzo de' Medici offers us a variation on the metaphor by simply saying to Jesus, "Poi che
non fusti del tuo sangue avaro" (since about your blood you were no miser).[27]
He goes on in another laud to tell the sinner (that is, himself), in view
of God's sacrifice for you, "non essere si tristo pagatore" (don't be such a
wretched repayer [of the debt]).[28] The essential transaction of a commercial
society was thus spirited into the dynamics of salvation. Using a less felicitous
turn in a Christmas poem, Lorenzo's mother, Lucrezia Tornabuoni, simply
has Christ declare that he "bought" heaven for us "on the Cross."[29] In a dramatic amplifying of the commercial metaphor, a prayer might even speak of
God's goodness as "an infinite market,"[30] so that we are suddenly, as it were,
put before an endless display of fantastic goods, though they can only be
bought, of course, by our own goodness. And a fourteenth-century hymn,

"O virgo maria/di dio madre pia," from a well-known Pisan *laudario,* calls the Virgin Mary "a great female merchant"—meaning that in her quest for God, she had been like a long-distance entrepreneur or a great merchant adventurer:

> Picciolella
> navicella
> gran mercatantrice
> dio cercasti
> dio trovasti
> o navicatrice.[31]

> Little lady
> little boat
> great female merchant
> God you searched for
> God you found
> O [great] navigator.

In the light of Pisa's extraordinary naval and business history, these epithets went to the heart of Pisan experience; and the diminutives (*-ella*) work both to express a kind of cooing affection for Mary and to set off her greatness as a merchant and navigator.

In effect, then, while obviously tapping traditional and biblical founts, in both word and metaphor, the poetry of prayer also drew on the language and realities of social existence—on family relations, clientage, commercial trans-actions, and the ever present menace of death. This engagement with every-day experience gave a fresh force to prayer; but by using in addition an archaizing ritual language, the poetry of prayer also produced a lively tension between ancient and modern ingredients.

Giovanni Dominici (1357–1419), the son of a Florentine silk merchant, later archbishop of Ragusa and finally a cardinal, wrote a famous laud of the Virgin Mary, the allure of whose words is grounded in the capture of a mother's love:

> Di', Maria dolce, con quanto disio
> miravi'l tuo figliuol Cristo mio Dio?
> . . . .
> Oh quanto gaudio avevi, oh quanto bene

quando tu lo tenevi nelle braccia!
Dimmi, Maria, ché forse si conviene
che un poco per pietà mi soddisfaccia.
Baciavilo tu allora nella faccia?

. . . .

Io mi credo che tu penavi, quanto!,
quando Gesú la mattina vestivi
perché a toccarlo avevi piacer tanto,
che da te mal volentier lo spartivi;

. . . .

Ma un pensiero nel cor par che mi nasca
sopra un singolar tuo gran diletto;
io non so come per quel tanto affetto
il cor non ti scoppiò e non s'aprío.
Quando tu ti sentivi chiamar mamma
come non ti morivi di dolcezza?[32]

(Say, sweet Mary, with how much yearning
you used to look at your son, Christ, my God?

. . . .

O, how much joy you had, what great goodness,
when you held him in your arms!
Tell me, Mary, for maybe it would be well
to satisfy me a little just out of pity.
Were you in the habit of kissing his face?

. . . .

I think you were troubled, oh so much,
when mornings you used to dress Jesus,
because you had such pleasure in touching him
that you didn't want him out of your sight

. . . .

But one thought seems to well up in my heart,
about your one and great delight:
I don't see how from the weight of so much love
your heart didn't burst wide open.
When you heard yourself called Mamma
how is it that you didn't die of sweetness?)

In much the same fashion, Giovanni Pontano's twelfth Latin lullaby is also
an exercise that taps directly into felt or observed experience:

Pupe meus, pupille meus, complectere matrem
    inque tuos propera, pupule care, sinus;
pupe bone, en cape, care, tuas, mi pupule, mammas,
    pupule belle meus, bellule pupe meus;
Suge; canam tibi naeniolam. Nae . . . naenia nonne
    nota tibi, nate, est naenia naeniola?[33]

(My pet, my little pet, hug mamma
and quick, dear pet, get to her bosom which is yours;
good dear my little pet take those breasts that are yours,
my lovely little pet, my little lovely pet,
Suck, yes, and I'll sing you a little lullaby. Lul . . . Lullaby
D'you not know it, pet, your lullaby, your little lullaby?)

In contrast to the picture of serene relations between Mother and Child in much fifteenth- and sixteenth-century painting, the sentimental charge in Dominici's lines, expressing a near raw emotion, is explosive. Hence we note a puzzling disparity between the visual and the oral cultures: the one formal, idealized, and decorous, the other much more realistic and immediate. When focused on relations between Madonna and Child, prayer was rarely placid and detached. And however beautifully executed, most frescoes and panel paintings of this subject, whether in churches or in the home, required the rhetoric of prayer (i.e., the input of the votary) to instill them with an emotional charge, as in the following lines, where it is clear that the suppliant is looking at an image of Mary:

Verçene madre, i to' iusti ochi e belli
dàno alegreça quando tu riguardi
a chi nel cor te tien cum pura fede.[34]

(Virgin mother, your just and beautiful eyes
give joy when you gaze
upon those who hold you in their heart with pure faith.)

HOLY CRAZINESS

The resounding humanity of God and the saints in Italian painting is usually taken back to about 1300, to the art of Giotto. We may trace a similar line of development in the verse prayer of the Renaissance, though it is a crooked line, as shown by the ideal of *santa pazzia,* "holy madness" or "craziness."

If hideous death was meant to move sinners to fear and repentance, there was a special kind of death that promised salvation. I refer to the dying of the self in the rapturous love of God, a kind of insanity. The claims of *santa pazzia* in much fourteenth-century prayer, most notably in parts of Tuscany and Umbria, moved the penitent away from the practicalities of everyday life to so close an identity with holiness that the ensuing state of consciousness, viewed from a worldly standpoint, appeared to have all the signs of a mad mental seizure. In his "Laud on Mystic Love," Bianco da Siena (d. about 1412) is in this state, or praying for it:

Distruggesi 'l mie core
desiderando forte
di sostener la morte
per amor dell' Amore.

. . . .

già non aggio a sentire
cosa che a me piaccia
s' i' non so' nelle braccia
del mie dolce Signore.

. . . .

Per amor vo impazzando
con disideri acceso,
per amor vo gridando
si forte ne so' preso![35]

(My heart is being undone
by its wanting so much
to suffer death
for the love of Love.

. . . .

already I can feel
nothing which pleases me
if I'm not in the arms
of my sweet Lord.

. . . .

For love I am going crazy
with inflamed desire,

for love I go shouting,
so strongly am I seized!)

Here, God is not brought down to earth and vested in the trappings of a citizen, as we often find in religious plays of the Quattrocento. Instead, the suppliant is uplifted through the pure folly of love to a mystical state of wisdom and a voluntaristic unity with Christ. We may therefore associate the ecstatic colors and arbitrary (otherworldly) movement in some Sienese painting of the fourteenth century, especially as illustrated in the art of Duccio and Simone Martini, with the claims of *santa pazzia* and with an urban setting soon to be much moved by the emotional message of Saint Catherine of Siena, as well as by the horrors of recurring pestilence. Giannozzo Sacchetti, a Florentine follower of Catherine who was executed for treason in 1379, held that Jesus elected "to die drunken with love/for a foolish worm [man]," and he gets a whiff of that sacrifice in his poem "Maria dolze, che fai?"

Di questa dolce ebrezza
uno odor m' è venuto,
ch'i' non son quel ch'io soglio;
preso m'ha tal mattezza,
tal coltel m'ha feruto
ch'altro che lui non voglio.[36]

(From this sweet drunkenness
an odor came to me,
for I am not the man I'm used to being;
I was seized by such a madness,
such a knife wounded me
that I want nothing but Him.)

Sacchetti's poem turns up in a famous collection of fifteenth-century hymns, compiled in Venice by the nobleman and poet Leonardo Giustiniani.[37] And as it happens, Venice was not a bad venue, for Bianco da Siena died there in about 1412, the mystic lover whose soul had longed to be in bed with her spouse, Christ:

I am married to you, beloved,
but I haven't yet been taken [home],

and I haven't yet, Love,
got into bed with you,
and on your sweet breast
I do not yet repose.

(Sposata son a te, diletto,
ma non so' ancor menata,
e non mi son ancor nel letto
con teco, Amor, collocata,
e sopra del tuo dolce petto
ancor non so' riposata.)[38]

In the vernacular, the crazed love of God was first strongly enunciated by the minorite Franciscan tertiary Iacopone da Todi in the late thirteenth century:

Senno mi par e cortisia
empazzir per lo bel Messia.
Ello me par si gran sapere
a cchi per Deo vòle empazzire,

. . . .

Chi pro Cristo ne va pazzo,
a la gente sì par matto.[39]

(Good sense it seems to me and also courtesy
to go mad for the beauteous Messiah.
I think it such great knowledge
to want to lose one's mind for God

. . . .

Anyone who goes mad for Christ
must seem crazy to the world.)

Relying on prayer shot through with "carnal" metaphor and emotive language, the fourteenth-century interest in "holy madness" required a militant stance against the daily world of getting and spending. Yet how could a woman be a busy housewife, and a man be a merchant or an industrious artisan, not to say a wage laborer, and also be so swept away by love of God that he or she could think and feel almost nothing else? *Santa pazzia,* therefore, could never have engaged more than a handful of urban dwellers here and there; and men like the former wool comber Bianco da Siena, afterward a

Gesuate, or the "traitor" and bankrupt Giannozzo Sacchetti cannot be taken
to have been in the least representative. Nevertheless, something of the self-
denying element in the claims of holy folly passed into common prayer. In
one of the most common forms of the day, we get a tacit dialogue between
the suppliant and his soul, between body and soul, or between the soul and
God, or the soul and the Virgin Mary. In such a colloquy, the speaker may
look to his soul's Heavenly Spouse while the soul, instead, is locked into time
and the world, that is, into the delights of riches, honor, lust, gluttony, and
every other sinful attachment:

> Che scusa anima mia
> Ara' tu poi appresso al tuo Signore,
> El qual con tale amore
> Ti va cercando, e chiama tuttavia?[40]

> (What alibi my soul
> Will you have for your Lord,
> Who with such love
> goes in search of you and still calls?)

Here is another example:

> Infelice anima mia
> .   .   .   .   .   .
> La tua carne si fetente
>   T'ha privata di ragione;
>   Cieca e sorda della mente
>   Alla buona ispirazione.[41]

> (My unhappy soul
> .   .   .   .   .   .
> Your stinking flesh
> Has stripped you of reason,
> In intellect [you are] blind and deaf
> to all good inspiration).

The implied dualisms here assign all real triumph, naturally, to the ascetic side.
This intransigence, however, was easily subject to scornful attack, as we see
in certain religious plays (*sacre rappresentazioni*), which occasionally feature

nose-thumbers of the sort who quite openly derided pious people.[42] The pragmatic realities of the quotidian world all too sensibly, or too easily, over-whelmed religious ideals. And yet there was a way to defend the *pazzia* in question by simply turning the tables round. A ringing example of this is the much-copied anonymous laud in sixty quatrains "Or udite matta pazia / della stolta vita mia" (Now listen to the mad craziness / of my foolish life). It deals with the suicidal folly of the sinner who yearns for salvation but is yet dedi-cated to prating, flattery, profit, wealth, appearances, and ambitious energies (*lena*). There were at least six early printings of this *lauda,* and it turns up in more than twenty-three extant manuscripts in Florence, Rome, Bologna, Rieti, Padua, and Venice.

I' ho degli ani quaranta,
    spero menare vita santa

. . . .

Disio ho d'esere salvato
    e sto ne' vizi intrigato;

. . . .

Povertà, vergogna e pena
    è la via ch'al cielo ci mena,
    io ricchezze, onore e lena
    cerco, e salvarmi voria.

. . . .

Pe l'avere e pe l'onore
    sono di Cristo traditore;

. . . .

    veggio la morte venire
    e vivo in balocheria.

. . . .

Io sono el pazzo magiore,
    ché conosco el mio erore

. . . .

trino e uno in esinzia
sanami di tale pazia![43]

(I'm age forty,
    hoping to live a holy life

. . . .

I desire salvation

and am tangled in vice

. . . .

Poverty, shame, and sorrow
are the way that leads to heaven,
riches, honor, and [vain] energy
seek I, and yet I'd like to save my soul

. . . .

For possessions and mere honor
I'm a traitor to Christ

. . . .

Death I see approaching
and I live my life in play

. . . .

I am the first of madmen
because I see my wrongs

. . . .

O trinity and one in essence
heal me of my madness.)

In other words, if the message of Christianity, as then interpreted, was taken seriously, then the daily life of most people was a circus of insanity. Nor was it hard to argue this, because the program of Christian asceticism was ensconced in the culture and could be made now and then to flare forth, depending upon conditions such as famine, plague, and catastrophic war. Governments were therefore sometimes driven to keep a cold eye on fiery preachers or even to put a sudden halt to their sermons.

The theme of *santa pazzia* had a remarkable bearing on amatory verse, and we shall return to it in that connection.

LANGUAGE FOR THE VIRGIN AND THE SAINTS

Like religious painting in the Quattrocento, prayer moved away from frenzy, although various collections of sung verse reveal that the mad love of God persisted strongly as an ideal down to the sixteenth century. More generally, however, Christ, Mary, and the saints were brought closer to home. This change is particularly evident in the verse plays of the Renaissance, the *sacre rappresentazioni,* in which biblical figures, emperors, kings, and an array of saints appear much like contemporary bourgeois: they wear current dress, use the daily language within the meters of rhymed verse (octaves with irregular hendecasyllabic lines), and give sustained expression to many of the urban attitudes of the day.

As we rummage through Renaissance lauds and other verse prayers, we quickly find that addresses to the Virgin Mary far outnumber all others, with the exception of those addressed to God (or Jesus Christ). Thus, of the 110 verse compositions in the main part of a celebrated fifteenth-century *laudario* (a collection of lauds), 44 are addressed to God or Jesus, 37 are for Mary, and 29 are narrative, doctrinal, imperative, or addressed to a variety of saints.[44] In a number of fourteenth-century laud collections, Mary again runs Christ a close second, and in some cases "the *laude* to Mary equal or outnumber the Christ *laude*."[45] Not surprisingly, the great majority of religious confraternities were dedicated to Mary or had a particular devotion to her.

What, if anything in particular, does this predilection for the Virgin reveal? If we put all a priori notions to one side—such as assumptions about psychoanalytic mother fixations or anthropological earth mothers—it becomes clear, even tediously so, that in prayer to Mary the suppliant was often voicing direct experience of the compassionate or loving mother; and if nothing else, the stereotype was always to be observed in the life around. This is the emotional matrix. In the verse, accordingly, Mary is typically enmeshed in convoluted family relations. She is the spouse of God as Holy Spirit, the mother of God (Jesus), as well as daughter to God the Father; and much prayer glories in the flagrant illogicalities of this trinitarian dialectic, such as in the succinctness of the two lines "Madre, vergine, sposa, amica e figlia/Del vero e solo Dio, nostro Signore" (Mother, virgin, wife, friend and daughter/ of the true and only God, our Lord).[46] She was chaste and a virgin before, during, and after giving birth to Jesus—another paradox happily seized upon and bruited in many prayers, so as to score her perfect and unassailable chastity: "O sacre Virgo in parto poi e prima" (O sacred Virgin, virgin while giving birth, afterward, and beforehand).[47]

From here, in prayer to Mary, we move out via image and metaphor to a whole geography of beneficence, touching every facet of her goodness and salvational nature. If mathematics be defined as "the collection of all possible patterns," then in the prayers and poetry of the Italian Renaissance, Mary was the vessel (almost) of the good in all its possible forms. This claim is richly documented in a rather erudite laud, "In your arms, O Virgin Mary," by Enselmino da Treviso (fl. 1325–50):

Tu redimisti tuto l'universo,
tu transmutasti el corso di natura,
tu secoristi el mondo ch'era perso.

Tu renovasti l'umana creatura
essendo nato el suo Segnor in terra
de ti, Verçene dolce, in carne pura.[48]

(You redeemed the entire universe,
you changed the course of nature,
you came to the aid of the lost world.

You renewed humanity,
the Lord having been born in
your very earth, sweet Virgin, in pure flesh.)

But Enselmino then goes on in metaphor to picture Mary as a shield, a sword, a gateway, a school, a bright star, the perfect light, the road to paradise, a key, a bridge, medicine, a ship, a ladder, a vase, a temple, a mirror, the norm of justice and charity, the "title and example of every good," and the form itself of purity. Time and time again, moreover, in the great body of Marian verse and prayer, she is also our defense counsel, a port of refuge, and a sea of goodness—sea as in *mare* for *madre* (mother) in the dialects of Venice and elsewhere.

The secret of Mary's vast powers lay in the view, as expounded in dogma and hailed in poetry, that she had been morally large enough—shades of an earth mother!—to contain and bear God. Here was the notion of Theotokos, which emerged in liturgy in the course of the third and fourth centuries, collecting image and metaphor in the eighth and ninth centuries and finally bringing Mary into the fulness of her cult in the eleventh and twelfth centuries.[49] She was also, accordingly, the supernal "ladder": God had descended through her to be incarnated as man, and through her we could all scale the heights to become "divine" (eternal) in Renaissance terms. But these abstractions, endlessly repeated in poetry and hymn, were made "fleshy" or were focused in the image of the lactating mother. Mary had breast-fed the infant Jesus; and therefore afterward—thus the claim and such was the bond—He could deny her nothing. Whereupon she became the supreme intercessor and *avvocata*, both protectress and jurist pleading before the Almighty Judge. Turn to her in true contrition, and you could not but be saved. No wonder her popularity overwhelmed the name and fame of all other saints, if not quite that of the trinity.

But there was more, for verse prayer reveals that the image of the compassionate mother (not "the giantess" of the nursery),[50] as intercessor with an angry God, pilfered much of its resonance from the everyday world of Renaissance cities, where the power of the father, the *patria potestas* in law, was so considerable that mental ghosts and veiled symbols inevitably orbited around that image or memory. That is to say, in the individual's progression from childhood to mature adulthood, there ran a normative line of authority figures: father, uncles, tutor, parish priest, master in trade or workshop, local patron, political boss, prince or powerful oligarch, and God the Father at the end or summit. Some of these then came to have hidden interconnections via the elusive workings and semiotics of authority. So we can but speculate as to the temporary solace, the fleeting hopes and labyrinthine modes of relief that came to the praying sinner when he turned away from all this to the Madonna. Plague, moreover, extreme pain, death in the household, vendetta, and other dangers all brought fluctuations in prayer; and princes, no less than artisans and merchants, might suddenly have recourse to Mary. Here is Alessandro Sforza, Lord of Pesaro, intoning a plea:

> Vergene sancta, prega el tuo car figlio,
> > Per la pietà che mosse ad incarnarsi,
> > Gratia e mercede doni, che salvarsi
> > Possa la donna che per guida piglio.
>
> . . . .
>
> Vergene, ascolta el suo e il mio dolce prego
> > E tanta gratia sopra nui distilla
> > Che in terra insieme e in cielo ambe dui viva.[51]

> (Holy Virgin, beg your dear son,
> out of the pity which moved Him to take on our flesh,
> to grant grace and mercy, so that the lady
> whom I take as guide may be rescued.
>
> . . . .
>
> Virgin, listen to her and to my sweet prayer
> and trickle such grace on us
> that we may both live together on earth and in heaven.)

All the same, many worshipers must at times have felt that there was too great a concourse of pious traffic at Mary's door. Besides, particular matters might have particular intercessors; and so suppliants also turned for help to an array of saints.[52] Special powers against plague, for instance, were ascribed to Saints Sebastian, Roch (San Rocco), and Christopher, the last of whom was also singled out by travelers; Jerome and Augustine were saints for the learned; Lucy (*lux,* light) for those with eye ailments; Anthony for people who had lost something; Margaret, Agnes, and Agatha for women vowed to virginity or chastity:

> Divotamente sia sempre laudata
> Agata santa, martire a beata,
> Vergine pura, immacolata e netta.[53]

> (Be she ever praised with true faith
> Saint Agatha, blessed martyr,
> Virgin pure, immaculate and clean.)

And Mary Magdalen was for all Christians, of course, but she could be especially sought out by adulterous women and ex-whores:

> Sposa ti tolse Cristo in quel servito,
> Per dar speranza a ciascun che si penta,
> Vergin sarai nello eterno convito.
>
> . . . .
>
> Dolce speranza degli peccatori,
> Mia avvocata, di pietà ripiena,
> O peccatrice santa Maddalena.[54]

> (Christ took you as wife into that [his] service,
> to give hope to all those who repent,
> a virgin shall you be in that eternal feast.
>
> . . . .
>
> Sweet hope of sinners,
> my patroness all full of mercy,
> O sinner Saint Magdalen.)

Florence even called upon a particular image of the Virgin Mary, the Impruneta Madonna, in prayers against death and famine.

When written on commission, devotional verse also reveals that it was often composed for special occasions: against disease, debt, lust, war, urban discord, the travails of old age, and even against personal calumniators or the wicked influence of friends. There were also Christmas and Easter poems, as well as verse prayers of thanks and gratitude. Lorenzo de' Medici paid for Antonio Miscomini's well-known 1489 printing of a rich collection of prayers and lauds.[55]

The need for prayer against calumny merits particular notice, because it flags the demographic closeness and animus of the small urban community, a face-to-face society of familiar acquaintances and compact neighborhoods, where the eyes of local residents took in a man's every move, and even more a woman's. Here the gossip or lies of kinfolk, neighbors, and enemies might undermine name and honor, destroy trust, and hurt matchmaking in that great market for arranged marriages of economic and social convenience among the middle and upper classes. No one of any eminence was immune to scurrility; even priests, such as the Aretine doctor of laws Rosello Roselli, could be made to feel its pinch. He struck back in a fury:

Chi dice mal di me, Dio mal gli dea

. . . .

A quella falsa lingua maladetta
ch'a posto in mal parlare ogni sua voglia
seccar si possa el tronco e la radice,
O giustizia di Dio, fanne vendetta,
a chi mal dice, dagli tanta doglia,
si che non possa mai esser felice.
Gastiga, Signor mio, chi più mal dice
con giudicio crudele aspro e severo.[56]

(God strike at him who speaks ill of me

. . . .

Let that false cursed tongue
moved by the spirit of malicious talk
dry up from shaft to root,
O justice of God, wreak vengeance,
give the speaker of evil such woes
that he can never be happy.
Punish, O Lord, those who most speak ill
with a judgment cruel, bitter, and harsh.)

Prayer, in other words, could be uncharitable in being the pointed invocation of God's wrath against malicious neighbors and evildoers.

BASIC THEMES IN SACRED DRAMA

Hewing close to the spoken language in its diction and registers, sacred verse drama—for church, confraternity, convent, or piazza—sprang from the tensions between religious ideals and the commercial, profit-oriented attitudes of daily life. It lived off a conflict of values. In the most obvious case, plays for women's convents always exalted the virginal state above and against the mainstream of marriage, for nuns hailed from a world in which the arranged marriage for girls was the coveted, honorable state. Hence plays and prayers for would-be nuns rejected that condition in the name of a "higher," divine spouse, even to the point of expressly denigrating marriage as a sort of "carnal" bond. Thus the verses from an anonymous laud done in quatrains:

Tu sai, suor mia, che le mondane spose
    Portando e partorendo son penose,
    Per molti modi poi son dolorose
    E sciagurate.
D'esti mali son nette e liberate
    Quelle, che a Cristo amor son sposate.[57]

(You know, dear sister, that wives out in the world
are full of pain in childbearing and giving birth;
they then have many other sorrows
and are unlucky too.
Clear and free of all these ills are those
married to the beloved Christ.)

One of the sternest attacks on marriage, voiced in *La rappresentazione di Santa Domitilla,* was penned by a married woman, the Florentine Antonia Pulci (1452–1501), daughter of an obscure citizen and wife of the poet Bernardo Pulci, hence sister-in-law to two other poets, Luca and the brilliant Luigi. Much given, like her husband, to pious interests, Antonia became a third-order lay nun after his death in 1488, and in 1501, shortly before she died, she used her widow's dowry to found a house for Augustinian sisters.[58] Like most plays about female saints, *Saint Domitilla* exalts virginity and chastity (seen as all but one with the love of God) over every other value, with the result here that the ideal becomes the happy road to martyrdom and to a heap of charred virgins, female and male. The pagan emperor Domitian gives Domitilla, his niece, to the "baron" Aurelian in marriage; and since the latter is young, rich, regal, and "noble of mind," what could be better for a beautiful young woman? However, before the pledge can be carried out, Domitilla is suddenly converted to Christianity by two servants; and in a few verses of striking realism, they offer one of the strongest pleas against marriage in Quattrocento literature. Moving from the Christian idea of self-denial by claiming that "no one can be called happy" unless he or she turns fully to God and spurns the world, which is "fleeting as a flower" and "false," they argue that Domitilla cannot know how Aurelian will treat her in marriage. As his wife, moreover, she would have to change utterly and bend to his every will, however base. So let her not be deceived.

> Tutti gli sposi si mostran discreti
> quando la donna lor tengon giurata;
> voglion parer humili e mansueti
> prima che a casa lor l'habbin menata.
>
> . . . .
>
> Quel ch'io ti parlo spesse volte aviene:
> ecci chi tiene amiche e concubine,
> e le lor donne con tormenti e pene
> batton con molte dure discipline,
> per questo molti sdegni si sostiene;
> d'ogni cosa si vuol pensar al fine,
> alle pene del parto e grievi duoli
> quando si partoriscano i figliuoli.[59]

> (All men aim to appear reasonable
> when [formally] engaged to a lady;
> they want to seem meek and gentle
> before they take her home [in marriage].
>
> . . . .
>
> I tell you that this often happens:
> there are those who have lovers and concubines
> and who give their wives terrible beatings
> with very hard sourges,
> so that such women suffer much from angry contempt;

you need to think about everything,
including the troubles of childbirth,
with all the grievous pains attending it.)

We would have to turn to court and trial records to find testimony of the
beatings doled out to wives by some husbands. The testimony of moralists,
preachers, and the short fiction (*novelle*) of the period suggests that wife-
beating was not at all uncommon.

There was nothing in the least "revolutionary" about sacred theater: it
sought to change hearts, not to overturn social structures. Performances of
The Adoration of the Magi, for example, as put on in early Medicean Florence,
might involve a cavalcade of more than two hundred gorgeously caparisoned
horses; they were less ceremonies of humility shown to the infant Jesus than
spectacles of power, opportunities for Florentine grandees to show off their
splendor while also acting out a holy tale by parading through the main streets
of the city.[60] Most other *rappresentazioni,* stark by comparison, were therefore
intended for convents, local churches, confraternities, minor piazzas, and
occasionally perhaps, as in the sixteenth century, for a simple reading of them
in the new four-penny pamphlet. Such was the play by the Florentines Feo
Belcari (1410–84) and Tommaso Benci (1427–70), *San Giovanni nel deserto,*
where we see the youthful John the Baptist brusquely abandoning his parents
to go forth into the desert to prepare the way for Jesus. The desert, we are
told, is no place for "adulators" or "prating" (*parole vane*). And when John
tells Jesus, "I love you more than I love my father," the stony justification is
that "quanto più s'ama la terra / Tanto più contro a Dio si muove guerra" (the
more we love the world / all the more do we wage war against God).[61]

Yet more uncompromising in ascetic terms is *The Day of Judgment* (Dì del
Giudizio), also by Belcari but with additions by the Florentine poet-herald
Antonio di Meglio (1384–1448). A play from Bologna also on the Day of
Judgment, employing very similar strategies, is not nearly so effective; and the
disturbing scene with a homosexual youth seems to have been lost or suppressed.[62] Most of the drama in the Belcari-Meglio play pivots on the arguments between the damned sinners on the left hand of Christ and the company of the saved on His right, where we also have the saints and God's
"standard-bearer" (*gonfaloniere*), the archangel Michael. To the outcry of the
angry sinners, claiming that "we are all made of the same stuff (*massa*)," the
simple reply is that "you" (the damned) died without contrition and pen-

ance.[63] Again, devotional companies of flagellants on the left are denounced for having used the confraternity to garner "honor and place, and to sell goods" (*spacciar mercanzia*).[64] We learn thus that religious brotherhoods could be much used for the cynical practice of making business contacts and hawking merchandise. An adulterous woman on the left blames her good husband on the right for having failed to take all due precautions against "those subtle traitors," her seducers, "kin, friends, and neighbors" (parenti ed amici e vicini),[65] the very people who were meant—according to historians—to provide the individual with social and moral subvention.[66] The merchants on the left-hand side are of course usurers, or false and avaricious men. Much more striking, however, is the boy who alleges his untutored youth in self-defense and yet is condemned for having been a gambler and a glutton, but especially because he was tainted with "the ugly vice of sodomy." He wheels round and curses his father, who also stands among the damned, for having failed to beat him when he was going to the bad. Whereupon a father on the right turns to his good son, there by his side, and tells him, "Now you see the fruit of all the blows I gave you."[67]

Here, as in many another play, filial obedience and the *patria potestas* serve to underscore deference and the ideals of patriarchy. In *Dì del Giudizio* the poor are said to be saved only if they bore their sufferings patiently and in the name of God. In effect, place and hierarchy obtain in the lower ranks as well.

Drawn from a story that went back to India via the ancient world, *Barlaam and Josafat,* written by Bernardo Pulci (1438–88), could not have been intended for large audiences, because the play's accent on death and its hard contempt for the delights of the world offered too grim a tableau.[68] Brought up in the lap of luxury and kept away from all suffering, Prince Josafat suddenly and belatedly learns about illness, poverty, old age, grief, and death. Thanks to the hermit Barlaam, however, to his secret instruction and catechism, Josafat is instantly won over to Christianity, or his new knowledge of the human condition would have plunged him into an impossible despondency. He is then able to convert his entire kingdom to Christianity, including his fiercely opposed father. All realism is cast to the winds; only the language of the play and some of its attitudes place us in a fifteenth-century Italian city:

> Il nostro serenissimo signore
> fa comandare a tutti infermi e vecchi

che son qui circunstanti, uscire di fuore
ciascun qui del paese s'apparecchi;

. . . .

Che vuo' tu far di noi? che diavol sia?
Che t'hanno fatto questi poveretti?

. . . .

S'i' mi t'accosto con questo bastone
io ti darò merenda e desinare.[69]

(Our most serene lord
decrees that all the old and sick
in these parts get themselves ready,
each of them, to quit this land [so that Josafat will not see them];

. . . .

What do you want to do with us, what devil is here?
What have these poor little people done to you?

. . . .

[To a beggar:] If I get near you with this club,
I'll give you a real snack and lunch.)

In the case of the anonymous *Prodigal Son,* drawn from the New Testament, we have a play that had at least three different versions and a variety of fifteenth- and sixteenth-century productions.[70] The action touches an exposed nerve in the world of the urban household, where strains between fathers and sons must often have been intolerable. After all, as the *Dì del Giudizio* strongly implies, a son was almost meant on occasion to say, "Thank you, dear father, for the blows you gave me. They were all for my own good." In propertied families most particularly, sons were usually under the authority of the patriarchal father deep into their twenties, because they depended on his decisions for their early education, subsequent trades, and all matters concerning property.[71] Their economic independence was not even guaranteed by marriage. *The Prodigal Son* idealizes the father, represented as being perfectly loving and responsible, whereas his younger son, the prodigal, is a wastrel, a gambler, a fool, and a selfish weakling. Losing in a card game right at the start of the play, the prodigal decides to importune his father for his inheritance, so that he can leave home and "go off into the world to have a good time" (pel mondo a spasso andare).[72] The father wants to discuss the question kindly, but his son is obstinate and rude. "Don't answer me at such length," says the youth, "give me what is mine . . . Don't be a nuisance with all your begging"; and anyway, "as far as I'm concerned, your words are worth nothing" (El parlar tuo non istimo niente).[73] Worn down finally, the father has ten thousand Venetian ducats paid out to him in cash, and the prodigal departs, only to return after some time, of course, a ruined man and a beggar. The good father, naturally, takes him lovingly back into the household.

Keeping with the public and domestic ideologies of Renaissance society, *The Prodigal Son* puts all humanity and virtue on the side of the aging father, who also commands the love and allegiance of the prodigal's elder brother. We may conjecture that fathers tended to like the play, although the easy disbursement of ten thousand ducats would have struck them as "biblical," for no Venetian or Florentine in his right mind would have parted so foolishly with such a vast sum.

LOVE: SACRED AND PROFANE

One of the more fascinating aspects of Renaissance piety was in the interplay between love poetry and prayer. More specifically, it belonged to the image of the adored lady as a quasi-divine figure, an ambiguous personage who often served as a devotional icon. As is well known, the troubadours had already hit on the idea of the ennobling radiance of love,[74] and this view passed over into Italy, to be made much of in the *Dolce stil novo* of the late thirteenth century. Famously, in Dante's *Divine Comedy,* the lady Beatrice is a metaphorical ladder to virtue and blessedness and thus shares certain characteristics with the Virgin Mary. Later still, in Petrarch's *Rime,* Laura, the beloved, is brought down to earth while still retaining supernal or heavenly qualities, now more and now less so, as she courses through his *canzoniere.* With the years, Petrarch sought to release himself from the grip of carnality and worldly pleasures, with the result that Laura becomes increasingly iconic and unreal. And even so, in the end he renounces her for Mary.[75]

Subsequently, in amatory verse as it evolves from the fourteenth to the sixteenth centuries, the image of the lady moves up and down continually between degrees of earthiness and lofty virtue or even blessedness, depending upon the poet, the occasion, or even his time of life.[76] In Bernardo Pulci, for example, the lady is always exalted; in Alessandro Sforza, usually so; but in the love poetry of the vastly popular Venetian poet (himself a nobleman), Leonardo Giustiniani, she comes across to us as earthy, even through the idealizations—all too transparent—of adjective and metaphor. In the best courtly poets of the Lombard Plain, such as Gasparo Visconti and Niccolò da Correggio, need and circumstance dictate the uplifting power of the idealizing lens, although the lady tends to remain a mere worldly icon. Here, therefore, the manner of idealization is more strictly keyed to the social virtues of grace, beauty, courtliness, lordliness, nobility, fine conversation, good breeding, and worldly wisdom. Intriguingly, the select adjectives *graziosa, bella, cortese, signorile, gentile, costumata,* and *savia* had been frequently applied to the Virgin Mary, as in the anonymous fourteenth-century laud "Madre che festi colui che te fece" (Mother who made Him who made you), where she is accorded the first three;[77] and this practice continued down to the seventeenth century. In *her* lexicon, however, the select adjectives denoted a moral or even a theological loftiness first of all, despite having been filched (and getting much of their aura) from the social diction of "courtly" love verse. In the love poetry of Correggio, Visconti, Lorenzo de' Medici, Bembo, and many another, the same adjectives were and are, to be sure, more thoroughly social, worldly, and upper-class.

But our theme is prayer, not amatory address. The poet may look to his lady as a worldly paradigm, as a source of inspiration, or to help him advance in virtue. If emphasized, however, any such operation puts the poem into the framework of prayer, in a tradition running back to the "Sweet new style" of the late 1200s. Here are the opening lines of a *capitolo* to his lady by Biagio Buonaccorsi (fl. 1500):

> O donna in cui pietà sempre riluce,
>> Honestà con bellezza et leggiadria,
>> De' mie stanchi pensier ricepto et duce,
> In te sol posta è la salute mia,
>
> . . . .
>
> Però felice son sendo suggetto
>> A donna non mortal, ma sì divina,
>> De' mie dolci sospir fido recepto:
> Gratia che a pochi el Ciel largo destina.[78]

> (O lady in whom merciful love ever shines,
> along with honesty, beauty, and grace,
> vessel and guide of my weary thoughts,
> in you alone is my well-being,

. . . .
Yet I am happy being subject
to a lady not mortal but divine,
Faithful vessel of my sweet sighs:
Grace which a wide heaven assigns to few alone.)

In these verses, as in the ones following by Nappi, we must discount some part of the cargo of heavenly qualities: the poet is treating us to sustained hyperbole. Yet there is no denying the insertion here of some of the Virgin Mary's stately qualities; and we cannot pretend to know how, exactly, Buonaccorsi would have read or recited the lines. The fact remains that they mime prayer.

We find the Bologna attorney Cesare Nappi (c. 1440–1518) writing in a similar vein. Born into a dynasty of attorneys, he was a well-known public official both under and after the Bentivoglios. Idolatrous, like Buonaccorsi's, and drawing fire from the tradition of Marian prayer, these verses were for a certain Camilla:

Chi vuol vedere el vero paradiso,
Angelica beltà, la fresca aurora,
Miri e contempli il corpo e sancto viso
In cui natura pose ogni arte allora.
Lucente stella

. . . . .
Fa di toa gratia degno el mio disio,
Ch'io t'amo e reverisco più che Dio.[79]

(Who wishes to see true paradise,
angelic beauty, and the fresh dawn,
let him look upon and contemplate that body and holy face
in which nature put all her art.
Gleaming star

. . . . .
make my yearning worthy of your grace,
for I love and revere you more than God.)

Was there more than silliness and blasphemy going on here? Metaphor exaggerates, of course, thereby distorting; but it may also disclose, and in this case it reveals that, though belonging to the party of "the world," Nappi was also calling on a kind of paraliturgy. Why so, why did he have recourse to religious turns? Petrarch had verged on an explanation. Toward the end of his *canzoniere,* he declares that love for a woman "made me love God less/than I should have."[80] This is to say—for Petrarch's confession belongs to a whole moral and emotional landscape—that at the end of the Middle Ages and down to the high Renaissance in Italy, there was something real, something substantial in the sentimental ties between worldly and divine love, in the energies devoted to one and thereby denied to the other, or devoted to the one as though it were the other. Let us pursue this briefly.

In his little-known play about Saint Mary Magdalen, commissioned by a confraternity and recited or performed in the Florentine convent of San Marco in the 1520s, Antonio Alamanni (1464–1528) puts the themes of divine and earthly love cheek by jowl in a dramatic fashion.[81] The play opens with two whores, as one of them is telling the other that Mary Magdalen, like themselves, "has sinned with many." Indeed, four different lovers currently dote on her, and we meet them all. A letter from her sister, the pious Martha, soon arrives, seeking to convert the sybaritic Mary, opposing divine to "lascivious" love, and directly attacking Cupid.[82] Martha then turns up; the two sisters quarrel; and Mary Magdalen finally agrees to go to Bethlehem to meet Jesus, but only after she learns that he is handsome (*bello*), young, attired in long red robes, and attractively bearded.[83] As it turns out, she is tempestuously converted (offstage) and goes on with Martha to Jerusalem to be near Him. There, already a zealot, the future saint meets the Virgin Mary and at once declares:

> I want to cry out like a mad woman, Jesus! Jesus!
> I don't even know whether or not I am me,
> and if I am and am not me, you [Mary] must know it.
>
> (I' vo' pazza gridare: Gesù, Gesue!
> I'non so s' i'mi sono o s' i' non sono,
> e s' i' sono e non son, tu lo sai tue.)[84]

These turns of phrase are not mysterious. They pointedly echo the rich body of Renaissance love poetry just at the moment when the lover has lost himself *in* the lady he loves, so that his heart and soul and identity are where she is, not where he is, which may be far from her. Earlier in the play, this conceit is humorously deployed when Tirsi, one of Mary Magdalen's suitors, comes on stage with all the airs of a suffering lover, claiming that he is not where he is and always where he is not:

> Lasso, ché dove i'son, quivi non sono,
> e là dove i'non son, son sempre mai!
> I' vivo in altri e me stesso abbandono;
> posso in me poco ed altri in me può assai.[85]

> (Woe, for where I am, there am I not,
> and where I am not, there am I always!
> I live in someone else and myself abandon;
> in myself I can will little and another much can will in me.)

Now, in the final act of the play, Mary Magdalen utters the classic refrain as cited above; but here, at last, it is wise and proper, a *santa pazzia,* for she has lost herself in Jesus. The author, Alamanni, had become a second-generation Savonarolan and an ardent republican in 1527–28, under the last Florentine republic.

Additional proof of the moral and emotional ties between the two loves, earthly and divine, appears in numerous palinodes, where the lover turns to seek his salvation in God at the very moment of his recantation. Breaking with the "false pleasure" of love, here is Pietro Bembo in one of his seven palinodes:

> Signor del ciel, s'alcun prego ti move,
> volgi a me gli occhi, questo solo, e poi,
> s'io 'l vaglio, per pietà coi raggi tuoi
> porgi soccorso a l'alma e forze nove;
> tal ch'Amore questa volta indarno prove
> tornarmi ai già disciolti lacci suoi.
> Io chiamo te, ch'assecurar mi puoi:
> solo in te speme aver posta mi giove.
> Gran tempo fui sott'esso preso e morto.[86]

> (Lord of heaven, if any prayer move you,
> turn your eyes on me, just this, and then,
> if I am worthy, let pity and your light
> bring help and new powers to my soul,
> so that love this time toils in vain to get me back into its loosened bonds.

I call on you who can protect me:
faith in you alone can help me.
Long was I held under it [love] and dead.)

In the same cluster of sonnets, Bembo alludes in fear to "the long offense [sinning] of my fevered yearnings" (il lungo error de le mie voglie ardenti).[87]

All at once here, we can see why a number of moral perceptions concerning love readily followed from the orthodox assumptions of the age:

1. In amatory verse, the passionate devotion to one's lady rightly belonged to God, because it amounted to a kind of *santa pazzia* for a mere mortal and so was horribly misplaced.
2. Profane love was a perpetual torment, vicious and self-destructive, precisely because it was misplaced.
3. In claiming to be elevated and noble, ardent love for a woman was always a hypocritical lie, because the lover's true aim was a base seduction.
4. Consequently, the scale and intensity of earthly love could have no bearing on the practical harmonies of marriage, which belonged to a different order of reality. After all, how could a *transporting* love have anything to do with the domestic routines of married life?

Viewed in this light, *all* amatory verse amounted to a type of parody or grotesque prayer in which the yearning, pleading, and suffering had been robbed from a fund that belonged, in Christian terms, to Christ and the Virgin Mary. It was, literally, idolatry. In his four invectives against love,[88] Benedetto Accolti opposes Cupid to "that benign fire / of just love" and lashes out at "lascivious" love for making the soul "earthy" (*fa l'alma terrena!*), while also seeing "a dark place" and a "furious fire" in the perversion. His own lady, "pitiless Jewess" (*dispiatata giudea*), had caused him to care nothing for "honor, / virtue, joy" or "rest" of any sort. Therefore, "Be cursed [love] for making / false things appear true to our eyes" (Maladetto sia tu, che fai parere / Cose false per vere agli occhi nostri).[89]

No wonder, therefore, that when poets turned against love, the about-face was so often blistering and violent. In his bitter recantation, Alessandro Braccesi (1445–1503) denounces "the kingdom of love" by summing it up as treachery, wrath, scorn, evil emotions, lascivious fixations (*pensier fisso e lascivo*), hates, furies, "dark and empty gaiety," biting repentance, an unhealthy mind (*mente insana*), and the "stink" of its "great poison."[90]

Put into a different key, the reaction against love, as we shall see in chapter 4, often ended as misogyny.

OPEN QUESTIONS

In sketching the historical context for the devotional themes of this chapter, I have emphasized the importance of religious companies. Yet we must beware of appearances. Membership in such brotherhoods was not in itself a proof of piety. We have seen confraternities relegated to the left hand of Christ, damned for having turned themselves into marketing conventicles. So much for "literature" as historical testimony. And recent study has begun to note that men—"new men" especially—often used confraternities for social and business reasons, quite apart from any thoughts about their future death and burial. In the late fifteenth century, with a population of about one hundred thousand people, how could Venice truly have needed more than two hundred confraternities for *devotional* purposes?[91] Lots of Venetians, we now know, belonged to several such sodalities. Florence, Bologna, and other cities had similar patterns of membership.[92] Lorenzo de' Medici belonged to at least eight different companies,[93] purely, it appears, for political reasons. In Quattrocento Venice, all noblemen in the great companies (*scuole*)—flagellant confraternities all—were excused from whipping themselves; and earlier still, in the later fourteenth century, they had negotiated the right for all noblemen and rich merchants to "buy out" of the requirement to flog themselves by making individual cash payments of twenty-five gold ducats.[94] But more revealingly in Florence, we have the diary (*ricordanze*) of the Florentine *calderaio* (coppersmith and kettle maker) Bartolomeo Masi, who was enrolled in five companies and founded yet another for thirteen men, contracted syphilis (*male francese*), seemed to suffer no moral pangs about this, and demonstrably used his memberships chiefly for social and comradely ends.[95] In brief, for the truly devoted personality, why, in most instances, would there have been no sufficient spiritual satisfaction in the doings of one or two serious companies? Did cities not swarm with clerics and have churches everywhere?

For all their pious clustering, neither Venice nor Florence (which had about one hundred confraternities) ever teemed with saints, not the least little bit.

In the universal need for prayer and a kind of moral accounting, there was always the immediate push of history, whether in the form of religious flurries caused by famine, epidemics, and war, or even by profound political crisis, such as in Florence in the 1490s, Milan in the early sixteenth century, and Venice in 1509–10. But other influences, much harder to pin down, also affected religious feeling: for instance, the heightened corruption and career-ism of the clergy, which issued in a major call for reforms by the early sixteenth century.[96] The millennial movement of the "Whites" (*Bianchi*) in 1399–1400, coming in the midst of the papal schism and bitter hatred be-tween contending popes, drew in merchants and artisans as well as country folk and noblemen.[97] And long before this, there was the explosive religiosity of the early thirteenth century: a flare-up, I have argued, set off by the tremendous economic and demographic energies that shattered the old social and political structures of Italy's northern cities.[98] Heresy therefore was also rampant. City and countryside saw a swift proliferation of lay preachers; and in the early thirteenth century, the new mendicant orders, Dominicans and Franciscans, came forth to combat heresy and to reach more people with correct doctrine.

The history of religious feeling cannot be sealed off and taken in and by itself.[99] There are no impenetrable zones in history: the life around breaks in to shake up and pollute purities. Hence in movements of religious devotion, we must always look for larger social and cultural wholes. That is why we dare not ignore the testimony of religious poetry. For here and in lauds and prayers, as in letters and the memoirs of those who are passionately religious, we shall find the field of social associations—worldly love, family feeling, commerce, patron-client relations—that put piety into a place, a time, and a rhythm of change. To enhance fervor and courage in 1496–98, Savonarola's followers turned some prayers into marching songs and one into a hymn (*lauda*) that called for confraternal togetherness.[100]

The theme of divine love—of God's love for man and man's for God—is extraordinarily slippery in contextual terms, social and political. For if tilted in the direction of charity and brotherly love, as a basic part of the Christian's compact with God, then love of Jesus Christ can be turned out and directed into action in the world, so long as it is done in the name of God. But if the stress on love be in the rapture, in proximity to God, in a passion wholly internal and penitential, then it may bring a flight from the world, hence a flight from brotherly love, charity, and the needs of the poor. Prayer, religious verse, and hymns of *this* sort may thus be said to adumbrate a "conservative" political and social stance. In this connection, I would point out that much of the large body of extant prayers and hymns tends to be penitential, internal, and conservative. Oligarchy, princes, and a corrupt clergy had no trouble with this stance. The trouble with the related ideal of *santa pazzia,* in institutional terms, was that it wanted to carry rapture too far—far enough to disrupt households or the practical routines of everyday life. And the trouble with Savonarola, both for the papacy and for the Florentine oligarchy, was that his love of God was directed out to the world and to man, to the poor, to the business of entrenched privilege, the possibility of political and social change, and the reform of the clergy. Between *santa pazzia* and Savonarola there was a slippery divide. The seemingly small matter of where the emphasis ought to be—whether to love inwardly or to push out in a concern for others—could issue in dramatic historical differences. The outcome, the winning direction, would depend upon the weight and play of the impinging social interests.

As early as the outset of the fourteenth century, it was possible to deflect the Franciscan concern with poverty away from the truly poor and wretched by an emphasis on voluntary poverty, on poverty within the Church, or on poverty as a kind of moral state or standard and not as a pitiable condition that was already disfiguring urban communities.[101] Much later, between about 1490 and 1495, Savonarola was to turn a passionate eye on the scandal of the poor in Florence.

If the evidence of literature points to the power of religious feeling in everyday life, there are also scattered hints—though this side of things wants much study—suggesting that some men verged occasionally on what would have counted as "atheism" in orthodox terms. Questions concerning the immortality of the soul might be debated, to be sure, in theological circles; but when such querying passed over into the conversation and verse exchanges of the laity, we must surmise that more was going on there than has previously been suspected. In a sonnet to the count Guido Pepoli, the well-connected Bologna attorney Cesare Nappi reflects pessimistically on the brevity and treachery of human life. Reasoning along lines that the two had previously discussed, he concludes that if death ends in nothingness, then there is something to be said for it, since it eliminates our pains and woes. But if I am my soul—that is, if there be a soul—then there *is* immortality, and this is good.

Se morte è nulla, or quella non è male;
     Perchè del mal ne tol l'aspro sentire;
     Se l'anime poi sum, s'tu vol ciò dire,
     Ben adunque è, perchè te fa immortale.[102]

(If death be nothing, well, that's not bad,
because it removes our sharp suffering.
If then I am my soul,
if that's what you want to say,
then that's good, because it makes you immortal.)

A tenacious demand for logic and rationalism in pondering God's nature, or the claim that paradise was possible only in this life, particularly as witnessed in the life of rich people, would also have been seen as bordering on a godless heresy. In an oblique, riddling, angry, twenty-three-line sonnet by Alessandro Ciacchi, written in the late Quattrocento, we get a derisive attack on orderly notions of the cosmos, the idea of the soul's immortality, and "the blind fools who await the Dove" with their "fastings, absolutions, and Our Fathers." These only serve "to fatten the orchard for friars and cloisters!" Better to know that "From summer to winter the rich are / in paradise and the poor in hell" (E ricchi stanno dalla state al verno / in paradiso e'poveri in ninferno).[103]

Was it a joke for an anonymous love poet to claim that he had purged his sins in the fires of love? Probably, but he ends the octave (rispetto) by declaring that "the only hell is the evil life of the world."[104] In other words, to be safe when being serious about such matters, poets often passed into a humorous mode. Yet for joking about the immortality of the soul and deriding the miraculous in three famous poems, Luigi Pulci turned Ficino, Lorenzo de' Medici, and others in Florence against himself; and the social pressures on him became such that some years later he issued an orthodox "Confession" in verse, in part a prayer to the Virgin Mary.[105]

In a poetic duel (tenzone) with another writer, a pleasure-loving poet who haunted the princely courts of Padua, Verona, and Milan, Francesco di Vannozzo (d. about 1390), scoffs at the idea of order in the universe and holds that chaos is eternal, not heaven and hell. But then, in caution, he hurriedly drops the subject, turns, and agrees (or pretends to agree) with the orthodox views of his challenger.[106]

Ups and downs in the magnitude of manifest papal and clerical corruption turned certain men violently against the clergy, and the poetry of the age conducts a current of fierce anticlericalism. Reaction of this sort must have seemed, at times, to neighbor on fundamental disbelief. Yet evidence of atheism, even of the sort cited above, is so hard to find that we may be tempted to conclude that the phenomenon was nonexistent;[107] such an inference would be mistaken. For in those conformist societies—Renaissance Siena, Ferrara, Florence, Bologna, Venice—people did not easily voice unorthodox views; it was dangerous to do so. What is more, in the context of the times, as we know from fifteenth-century anthologies, collectors of poetry were likely to select (hence to transmit) amatory, devotional, encomiastic, and occasional verse, rather than dissenting expressions of late medieval and Renaissance atheism, if indeed poetry of this sort even came to their attention much. In his book of accounts cum family log or memoir,[108] Machiavelli's father, Bernardo, studiously avoids the name of God and all other religious turns at the points where contemporary diarists automatically had recourse to religious locutions: for instance, at the mention of family marriages, births, deaths, serious illness, and other moments of unusual stress. These remarkable absences in Bernardo's *ricordanze* come through as the evasive demeanor of a man made uncomfortable by knee-jerk piety; and it is possible, even likely, that the author of *The Prince* grew up in the shadow of a father who spat priests and friars out of his mouth.

The anticlerical strain in Italian life was in some cases directly connected with the experience of the sacred as a moment of primary physicality. Any easy belief in or emphasis on religious relics struck certain men both as simple-minded and as a type of credulity that only catered to the mercenary interests of the clergy.[109]

Experience of the sacred was often, at any rate, strikingly physical, certainly so as apprehended in prayers, lauds, and verse. Here the Virgin Mary may give off the odor of roses and the parturition of Jesus that of flowers; and he is milk, honey, unguents, or the best of smells.[110] The saints are always tasting honey. Heaven rings with the sound of games, feasting, song, and dance.[111] The love of Christ takes place in His arms, on His wounded breast, or even on His bed.[112] And one may languish and swoon for Christ, die for Christ, bathe in His "holy liquid,"[113] or be urged to lock into details of the Passion—the flogging, the face-spitting, the crown of thorns, the nails, the lance wound, and the spurting blood, as in many pictures of the period. Who does not know that all such invitation was meant to project the sinner beyond the senses into the realm of the spirit, into the purely *un*sensual? But it was also taken as literally true that Christ had died on the Cross for us and that the Virgin Mary smelled of roses—no difficult or curious assumption this in urban societies that were rife with stench. In prayer, therefore, and at the peak of piety, poets and sinners were right to make the experience of the holy a moment of true physicality. So in relics, in church ornamentation, in the visual cult of the saints, in fasting, and in the bloody practice (so far as it went on) of self-flagellation in the penitential companies, there was a bedrock physical quiddity that possibly repelled a minority of men and women, stirring up their anticlericalism.

On the question of the sacred and the sensory, it remains only to highlight the fact that the floods of hymns, prayers, and poems to the Virgin Mary often bring out in vivid metaphor the emotional, physical, and domestic side of Mary's relations to Jesus. She *is* the weeping, loving, caring, compassionate, anxious, agonized, utterly human mother.[114] And it is difficult to overestimate the force and lure of this appeal. Here perhaps, down to the Reformation, was the one zone of religious sensibility that lay beyond the anger or derision of Renaissance skeptics.

If we think in terms of a broad demographic context, taking in the multitudes of country folk and urban illiterates, the strong suspicion arises that some prayer, a good deal of religious verse, and the true sense of many hymns (*laude*), however seemingly demotic, were not easily understandable by the multitudes of people. Down to about the 1340s or so, it is true that certain confraternities required younger brethren to memorize two or three basic prayers, as well as "the ten commandments, the twelve articles of faith, the seven mortal sins . . . the seven works of mercy," and to know the different sacraments.[115] Hence any confrere with a religious bent could easily acquire the basic teachings. In the course of time, however, religious companies tended to go lax, and they came to disburse a lot more money for chapel and church ornamentation, or for other nonascetic purposes, such as banquets, than for works of charity outside the confraternity. Consequently, in a world of ecclesiastical pluralism and absenteeism, where half-literate priests often acted for well-off absentee clerics, especially in the hills, market towns, and villages, it makes sense to ask how many prayers most men and women truly knew. How many could they recite in full, and how well did they understand them?[116] The Pater Noster and the Ave Maria were, it seems, in universal use. The Apostles' Creed was already recited far less often. But then what? A reliable answer is at this point impossible. If my suspicions are right, however, and I had to generalize, I would conclude by noting that much of the material treated in this chapter touched the lives of a minority of people in the cities, although, to be sure, a large minority: the people of the middle and upper classes, including certainly the ranks of shopkeepers and craftsmen of all sorts, and perhaps a scatter of wage laborers.

FOUR

LOVE & HISTORY

Men against Women

※ ══════════════════════════════ ℃

In chapter 2 I look at the ways in which love poetry and the select idiom for patron–client relations gleaned their special diction and metaphors from the same pool of words and images. Here I take up the question of why "high-brow" (upper-class) amatory verse remained vital and persisted for so long, while yet always keeping to its formulas. We shall see that the reasons lay in the subsoil of society and politics, in the special relations between men and women, and in the institution of the arranged marriage of social and economic convenience.

POETRY AS CHRONICLE

Love poetry has been a feature in the life of all Western societies, which have been haunted by the powerful desire for a deliverance from practical cares and anxieties.[1] The persisting desire for some kind of worldly perfection courses through modern love songs. Thus love in poetry and song always makes a shadowy social critique: it rejects things as they are and wants to bring in a new day, a new order. This is the anthropological dimension of our subject. In the physical bliss or imagined perfection of love, lovers spurn the imperfect world. The production of love poetry must therefore fluctuate. Wherever historians find sharp rises in anxiety and dislocation, there too, I suspect, love in verse and song is likely to have flourished.

In the thirteenth century, the cities of upper Italy were alive with raging civil strife and swift social change.[2] Religious passion ran high. For the first time, the Church and local secular authority mounted fierce campaigns against urban heresy, often ending in mass executions.[3] The last third of the century (after 1260) saw the rise of a new love poetry, as attested above all by the *dolce stil novo* (sweet new style), best exemplified in the verse of Guiniz-zelli, Cavalcanti, Dante, and Cino da Pistoia. Henceforth, too, there was to be a new stream of religious, didactic, narrative, political, occasional, and familiar verse.[4]

Relying implicitly upon thousands of poems and more than a hundred poets,[5] I consider the love poetry of the Italian Renaissance (c. 1370–1530), with a view to seeing how love and history intersected: that is, how the envisaging and expressing of love responded to the stresses of time and place. For although most of the love poetry of that period observed a polished, elegant, and noble ideal (chiefly Petrarchan and *stilnovista*),[6] the pertinacity of this ideal, with its diverging accents, indicates that it was readily adapted to individual social situations. The universality or anthropology of the love theme was shifted to a specific historical ground, where local strain, ambition, patronage, the sense of class, misogyny, and the spur of princely courts all *used* love to make their plea. Next to the religious longing for salvation, love was the dominant literary theme. But being directly in contact with the stresses of existence, love poetry was also a witness for the historian; it was born as historical documentation precisely because it encoded responses to realities.[7]

Florence, Siena, and perhaps Perugia and other cities each employed an official poet-herald, whose job was to produce political and other verse on commission.[8] The cultural and propaganda needs of the leading fifteenth-century courts also attracted a clientele of poets; and in some provincial cities (e.g., Rimini, Urbino, and Bologna in the entourage of the Bentivoglio), lesser princes frequently hired poets as secretaries.[9] More significantly, the public recitation of poetry in a popular vein was a common, almost daily or weekly, affair. Itinerant and stay-at-home *canterini* intoned or improvised varieties of narrative, timely, didactic, carnival, and religious verse, usually at points reserved for this, such as in Florence's little piazza of San Martino, situated almost midway between the cathedral and the main government palace.[10] News found its way into cities by means of emissaries, merchants, letters, and travelers; but major events, such as the sudden overthrow of Bernabò Visconti of Milan (1385) or the near dismemberment of the Vene-tian mainland empire (1509), were quickly taken up in verse for the piazza, complete with detailed descriptions, laconic political lessons, and resounding moral judgments (see chap. 10).[11] So we may say that poetry and word-of-mouth reports figured among the major human-interest and news carriers of the day. Making their rounds on horseback, town criers, with a blare of the trumpet, got immediate local attention and then made their official announcements. But a rich chronicle, seasoned with anecdote and ideology, was also provided by the public "chanters" of verse (*canterini, cantambanco, cantastorie*) and by printed flyers after about 1500. In addition, there was an irregular circulation of rhymes, scurrilous sonnets, and rude songs.[12]

Poetry, then, was a daily mode of communication, and in some circles it was eagerly gathered into anthologies, glossed, altered, plagiarized, or shuffled around.[13] But the orality of Renaissance poetry is testimony to its essential movement in public space; hence it was an obvious vehicle for expressing matters to the larger community. In fact, given the nature of the medium, even when a private statement, such as a prayer or a vow of love, was shunted into verse form, it was thereupon converted into something public, into a gesture of public intention.

LOVE AND RELIGIOUS FEELING

Since love poetry served a rich variety of needs, they may be best discussed here under their different topic headings. It goes without saying that the obvious, continual, and alleged aim of love poetry was to woo the loved one.

We have seen that the force of worldly love, when considered from a religious standpoint, conduced to a perversion by giving to an earthly creature that which belonged to God. So it remains only to tie up some loose ends here.

The religious element in the appeal of love poetry is tricky to pin down, because religious diction and metaphor run through amatory expression. This was the case, moreover, in cities dense with churches, religious occasions, clerics, the signs of ecclesiastical property, and the meeting places of confraternities. In this urban world, the beloved lady of lyric verse—angelic, heavenly, saintly, having a face from paradise, blessed or unique among mortals, and so on—shared some of the properties of holy personages, notably Mary. Among the *stilnovisti* (c. 1300) the lady might be an inspiration to, or a way of, salvation. Petrarch (d. 1374) retained the language of blessedness but put his loved one more fully into the world. And right down to the late sixteenth century, most love verse employed an idiom that associated the be-

loved lady with the authority to make the lover excel both in moral sensibilities and in courtesy. But even where the religious connection was minimal,
the singularity of *madonna* (my lady) rested on supernal qualities, indicated by
adjective, noun, or metaphor.

Thus, Antonio Cornazzano's sonnet 24, which ends with an image of his
lady's breasts, "two apples from the garden of Atalanta" (duo pome del orto
d'Atlanta), begins with a heavenly vision: "I saw a holy angel in an earthly
paradise, a living idol sculpted in ivory" (In terren paradiso un angel sacro/Et
in scolpito avorio uno idol vivo/Vidi).[14] Some conditioning in the poet, even
as he craved the real lady, impelled him to "sanctify" her. Princes and oligarchs aside, since haloed figures—Christ and the saints—constituted the
governing imagery of his culture, the poet was driven, as if by a natural
process, to borrow the words and turns that exalted saints and angels and to
assign them to his lady. In this *translation,* however "base" (carnal) his intentions, his language labored to transcend the merely carnal. It is significant,
too, that poets continually linked love and death, particularly in love complaint, where dying or the threat of it is often assigned its theological values,[15]
thus again putting the experience of love into a religious calculus. At one
point at least, Bernardo Pulci and Pietro Bembo actually associate love with
the death of the soul and so pray for God's intervention against it.[16]

Love's religious dimension was to a large extent a game of metaphor, to be
sure; but when combined with the strong interest of readers, the energy and
adaptability of the love theme argue for the close links here between life and
letters. In the urban spaces of Renaissance Italy, ruled by religious sights
and sounds and holy occasions,[17] the conventions and expectations of love
called in the sacred; and there was no telling exactly how poets and their
audience might process this feature for themselves. Nevertheless, to understand the workings of love in Cavalcanti, we need Aristotelian psychology;
Saint Augustine helps in the case of Petrarch; and Lorenzo de' Medici's
Neoplatonic commentary on his own amatory verse (c. 1480) seeks to repel
the charge of frivolity and alleged sin by highlighting the lover's devotion to
beauty in a rather religious sense.[18]

We may say, accordingly, that the religion of love poetry had a particular
appeal for the learned, for "elitists," and for anyone who found it as meaningful to seek spirituality in a cherished earthly creature as in prayer or in other
pious exercises of a routine and "vulgar" sort. By crossing erotic love with
religious feeling, the verse in question added urgency to the experience. Yet

the combination could also lead to conflicts of the spirit over questions of right and wrong or of dignified and contemptible social conduct, as we learn from Gasparo Visconti's remarkable 1490s admission. In the dedicatory preface for a book of love poems, he tells the duchess of Milan that "whoever departs from [virtuous love] enters a labyrinth full of deadly infamy, of disdain, wrath, deceit, treachery, brawling, wounds, manglings, and especially into such a bitter passion of the soul that by comparison I would consider death and even worse . . . most happy."[19] He had gone into that labyrinth in times past, and he continues: "Whether from carelessness, insanity, tender age, or the disposition of the stars . . . even now I cannot say that I have emerged from it fully and freely," though he confesses that his "ruin" would have been far worse had it not been for "these poetic zeals [the poems]," which served to take "the ventings of a passionate heart."[20] All this was to say, as we can overhear in Visconti's words, that love (and love poetry) could either satisfy errant religious yearnings or violate them and plunge the lover into a sense of acute sin and anguish. In brief, a history of religious feeling was being routed through amatory verse.

MISOGYNY

How could the male fear or distrust of women, alleged to have pervaded medieval and Renaissance Europe, have anything to do with the love poetry of the age? More to the point, how could a flourishing urban society foster the readiness to fear, suspect, or despise "the weaker sex" and find certain classes of women nauseating?[21] A way to deal with these questions is given by love poetry itself.

A commonplace view holds that misogyny issued from the old tradition of the clerical bias against marriage, especially strong in the Middle Ages. Spreading beyond the clergy to all sectors of the society, the tradition was based upon a mix of biological, juridical, and theological assumptions that held women to be irrational, unreliable, carnal, and by nature inferior to men.[22] Folklore also contributed to this view.[23] Italian city-states imposed, in addition, their own exigencies, namely, the legitimacy of heirs, family honor (based in part on the strict chastity of women), the supremacy of the patrilineal family, patriarchal domestic controls, and the disbursement of substantial dowries. These called for unquestioned authority over children (particularly over females), a decline in the legal status of women, and arranged (utilitarian) marriage, which weighed more heavily on women than on men.[24]

In a well-known Florentine lawsuit of the 1450s, centering on a contested marriage, we learn that one of the troubling and damning things about the beautiful plaintiff, Lusanna, widow of a Florentine linen maker, was that she dared to look men in the face when walking in the streets of Florence.[25] And because she was a widow, her effrontery was all the worse in its violation of the universal rule that imposed passivity and modesty on women. Yet the same rule did not apply in amatory verse:

Chi è questa che vèn, ch'ogn'om la mira,
che fa tremar di chiaritate l'âre
e mena seco Amor, si che parlare
null' omo pote, ma ciascun sospira?
O Deo, che sembra quando li occhi gira.[26]

(Who is it comes there, making the air tremble with clarity, and bringing Love with her, so that every man stares and none can speak but only sighs? O God, what she seems when she turns her eyes.)

In this vision, the lady was not only gazed upon; she could also look back and, in so doing, fill the gazer with love, fear, and reverence. The love poet transformed his beloved into a species of prime mover and giver of light. She became the sun, the stars, lord, master, moral guide, ruler, and the paradigm of virtue, worthy to be loved, served, feared, obeyed, and held in awe.[27] As we found in chapter 2, love poetry turned the social world over on its head: the passive and legally inferior female became powerful, and the powerful male became the humble servitor—loving, worshipful, self-divided, and complaining. From Petrarch in the fourteenth century to Giovanni Muzzarelli in the sixteenth, Italian love poetry is charged with the tropes of this topsy-turvy imagery.

O possanza d'amore, o tirannia
Che obligi tanta fe' d'un pizzol suo
A tanto alto signor crudele e forte
Di cui la gloria, forza e signoria
Adoro, temo, honoro, seguo e servo.[28]

(O power of love, o tyranny compelling so much faith from one of its little ones for so lofty, cruel, and strong a lord [the lady], whose glory, force, and lordship I adore, fear, honor, follow, and serve.)

There was no manifest misogyny here; yet love's revolution could take place only in a world ruled by a misogynous morality, or how could there be a fixed social politics to turn over on its head? To be as it was, our idealizing love verse required misogyny not only outside itself but also within, in poets and lovers. For the psychosocial division between men and women, remarkable in all the structures of everyday life, was thoroughly observed in poetry, although the polarities were reversed. Indeed, poetry aggravated and reified the alienation by turning the female into a figure of perfection whom no male could even approach, let alone match. Angel, supreme beauty, goddess, paragon of all social graces, endowed with a heavenly voice and laugh, she was most unlike the women of everyday life and the radical opposite of the evil crone, the whore, the vain or crafty female, the foul old woman, and the sordid procuress. These were the central figures in the period's misogynous verse, which was often written by the very men who distilled subtle sonnets about noble love. Angelo Poliziano imagines a hideously disgusting hag who insists on ogling him; Filippo Scarlatti describes a "muttering old woman" (vecchia . . . burbuttando) who had suddenly unbuttoned herself and bared her breasts to him; Cesare Nappi assails a scolding wife, an ugly girl, a treacherous crone, a deceitful mistress; and Giovan Matteo di Meglio produces four bloody-minded poems against the fetid bodies of women, one of whom, a poisonous gossip, is in part depicted as her genitalia.[29]

The Virgin Mary was a possible foil for, or antidote against, the society's misogynous formulas.[30] Laying a heavy burden of restraint and degrees of distrust on its propertied women, Italian Renaissance society yearned for Mary and for the beloved of poetry, as if to correct in semiotics and fantasy the great gender disproportions of everyday life. In the end, however, this correction was self-defeating, because poetry's idealizations, its unreal polarities, intensified the gender splits. To imagine Mary as a woman who had been amazing enough to "contain" God, or to see one's lady as a near holy creature, was not in the least to challenge society's misogynous tenets; rather it reinforced them by sorting out and doting on the shining exceptions. One extreme (misogyny) elicited another (worship), but the two worked very well together in imaginative interplay, as in conditioned perception.

The voluntarism of the beloved lady, evident in her effects on the lover, is often in fact an illusion: a reflection of the lover's fervent business. Down to the early sixteenth century, the writing of amatory verse in Italy was almost exclusively a male enterprise.[31] Hence the lady's powers are likely to belong to the arms of Cupid, or she may be so passive as to seem an absence. But even when she appears in her blazing glory, she just *is*. The lover, on the contrary, moves things, praises, grieves, prays, meditates, rejoices, despairs, rants, raves, and even scolds. He is a changeable being; she is a moral quiddity. He is a personality, however much in type; she is not. This is the disguised truth of the period's love poetry. At the heart of it, quietly at work, is a misogynous vision, for the lady is gazed-upon and flattered essence, whereas the lover is all agent, the sole maker and prime mover.[32] Here love and history intersect: the subordination of women, as a datum of social attitudes and social structure, is overturned by the hankering imagination of the male, who longs for an end to his self-division, which is imposed by his very alienation from women. But the ghost of his subordinating work and estrangement returns to perplex and plague him in the unreal image and cold perfection of the loved one. In other words, denied any initial place in marriage, as we shall see later in this chapter, the erotic charge ("love") floated out into fantasy or into imagined and "noble" adultery.

Dante claimed that it was love that first led Italian poets to the sustained use of the vernacular tongue, for they were seeking to address women, an audience ignorant of Latin.[33] The claim is ingenious but dubious. Although it is true that around 1300 the lay women of Italy had no Latin, it is not at all clear that the *stilnovisti* were more interested in conveying their amatory erudition to women than to other males. At any rate, misogynous strains always echoed through love poetry's ritual language, not only in the sharp strictures of the complaining lover but also in the obsessive imagery of hunting, war, and lord-servitor relations. Beginning with Cupid's darts or arrows and moving on to all the metaphors of falconing, chasing, netting, liming, hooking, binding, assaulting, and besieging, love is a confrontation between active and passive, hunter and quarry. The most predatory and active of male occupations are enlisted to help represent the dramatics of love; but reality is again reversed. The lady often seems to be the assailant, when in fact, if we read with more care, we soon see that she is little more than a passive hunter or phantom presence:

Invisibili nimici mi fan guerra,
I lor cavalli son penser sfrenati,
Amor gli corre e la morte gli ferra.[34]

(Invisible enemies make war on me, their horses are [my own] unbridled thoughts, Love rides them and death catches at or shods them.)

E fo come augellin, che si fatica
per uscir de la rete, ov'egli è colto;
ma quanto più si scuote, e più s'intrica.[35]

(I act like a little bird which struggles to escape the net it's caught in [love],
but the more it shakes about, the more it entangles itself.)

The lover appears to turn the male world against himself; yet even in the
midst of his suffering, he orchestrates the entire affair. Much the same is
true of love's war imagery: the siege and assault machines are assigned to
the lady, although *her* fortress or city is impregnable when attacked. And so
in patriarchal city and court society, where women are under legal handi-
caps and the tutelage of their men, love poets promote "my lady" to the
status of (and call her) *signore, sire, duce, governatore* (lord, sire, leader, governor). The lover recruits the male world of public life—politics, patronage,
rank, courtesy titles—in policies and campaigns against himself, ever insist-
ing on the role reversal, thus again reproducing the gulf between male and
female.

In any given sequence (*canzoniere*) of love poems, the first stage was the
time of idealization. Thereafter, the writer customarily passed over into a
period of keen lamentation, a phase sometimes followed by disenchantment
and touches of overt misogyny. Any frankly erotic element in the love sonnet
or *canzone* violated the genre, which imposed linguistic, moral, and social
decorum. But whether explicit or concealed, eros went to the root of any
subsequent palinode. I refer to the claim or confession that love of the sort
sung by poets was by nature carnal and base. In one of his moods of repentance, the prince and poet Malatesta Malatesti confesses:

Chi segue amor carnal come ho fatto io,
li viene in odio la propria salute,
li viene in odio l'operar virtute,
li viene in odio ogni honesto disio;
gli viene in odio ogn'atto sancto e pio,
el ciel, le stelle grandi e le minute.[36]

(Whoever follows carnal love, as I have done, comes to hate his own well-
being/salvation, hates doing the virtuous thing, hates every honest desire,
hates every holy and pious action, heaven, and all the stars.)

The literature of the Italian Renaissance is rich in attacks on love, founded invariably upon love's damnable and vile carnality.[37] As noted in chapter 3, the claim was that such love was tantamount to a travesty of man's love of God. After all, it overpowered reason, the most divine part of man. It masqueraded as a noble sentiment but was at bottom lascivious. In an indictment of "Love, the father of Judas" (Amor, padre di Giuda), written about 1450, the Florentine poet Mariotto Davanzati invites Christ to consider:

> . . . i modi inniqui e disonesti
> d'esto crudo tiranno [Amore], el suo governo
> e' vizi che pel mondo ha sempre sparti;
> vedi suo' ngegni e arti
> d'omicidi, adulteri e tradimenti
> incendi e rubamenti
> fornicatore, strupo e sacrilegio,
> sepolcro d'ogni egregio.[38]

(the evil and dishonest ways of this cruel tyrant [Love], his way of government, and the vices that he has always spread throughout the world; see his talents and crafts in murder, adultery, treachery, fire and theft, as fornicator, in debauch and sacrilege, [this] sepulcher of every excellence.)

In this reasoning, the critique of love could easily be turned into an attack on woman—that unclean or unreasonable vessel. The whole legacy of asceticism was at work here. In effect, then, poetry's polemic against love issued directly from the thematics of love in lyric poetry itself and provided yet another reason for regarding women with suspicion. That is to say, owing to the social insistence upon family honor and female chastity, in addition to the claims of Christian abstinence in the impinging mental world, love poetry—by its secular and hence "pagan" stance—already carried the rudiments of an indictment against love and therefore against women. To bring it forth took little more than the beginnings of resentment or contrition in the lover. In the Renaissance urban world, the passionate lover always verged on misogyny.

Scholarship in a psychohistorical vein, affecting to enter more deeply into the problem of misogyny, has argued that the cold perfection of the angelic lady of lyric verse betrays a fundamental Oedipal ambivalence in the feelings of the lover, who applies for love to the powerful female figure in an unconscious mimesis of the child seeking his mother's love.[39] On the one hand, he craves his mother; on the other, he resents her sexuality and is strongly hostile. But feeling guilty about this, he punishes himself by according her an aloof and even disdainful perfection. The flow of feeling here is circular: the poet's distancing of the lady is both a self-imposed penalty and a continuing reason for resentment. Where, moreover, as in Renaissance Tuscany, infants of the middle and upper classes were routinely put out to wet nurses, moved "cruelly" around, and then, in the case of boys, often taken from the mother and sent abroad to learn the trade of merchant or to be bred to arms, there the mother—and so women generally—takes on a problematic and menacing semblance.[40] This is likely to issue in misogyny (hence the perception of fickle and irrational *fortuna* as a woman), although the persisting ambivalence in the "need" for the mother continues to fuel both the fear and the idealizing process that distances and magnifies the beloved. I shall return to this interpretation at the end of this chapter.

LOVE AND SOCIAL STANDING

From the moment of its appearance in the late thirteenth century, the new love lyric took an ideological stance. Borrowing an argument from the troubadours and investing it with a prime importance, the poets of the "sweet new style" (the *stilnovisti*) of Bologna and Florence redefined nobility (*gentilezza*) and put it at the heart of their enterprise. Their immediate setting was an urban world whose streets and piazzas were riven by fierce conflict between the prosperous middle classes (the *popolo*) and the remnants, imitators, and servitors of the old communal baronage. Defining nobility as "virtue" and "gentility of heart," a vision of mansuetude and inner loftiness, the *stilnovo* seemed to advance a claim against the haughty families of ancient vintage and swaggering ways.[41] Not at all. The knife-wielding guild of butchers, often in the front ranks of the combative *popolo*, was no candidate for *gentilezza*. What is more, the new style flourished on an elegant manipulation of contradictions: (1) the revolutionary use of a lucid and rather simple vernacular, yet a shunning of the diction of everyday life and a commitment to complex or even fussy ideas of love, and (2), the promoting of a more egalitarian *moral* nobility over the grand and ancient patrilineages, yet with accents and preoccupations that removed the new elite far from the vital concerns of merchants and guildsmen. Consistently enough, the founders of the *stilnovo*—Guinizzelli, Cavalcanti, Dante, Gianni Alfani, Cino da Pistoia—were all educated noblemen or well-connected lawyers.

The coagulating of riches and power in the walled-in or waterbound cities of the Italian Renaissance resulted in spatial arrangements that brought out social disparities, such as in the spontaneous practice of naming streets, squares, and neighborhoods after the most prestigious local families. Chapels in local churches, the remains of battlemented towers, and fortresslike mansions also bore the great names and displayed carvings or depictions of their coats of arms. The effect of this system of signs was to infuse imagination and daily feeling with class distinctions, social ambition, snobberies, and envy about political standing. Appropriately, the refined dream of love, with its yearning for perfections, came to be pervaded by dichotomies that collected force and matter from the principal social schisms: rich and poor, haughty and humble, powerful and powerless, rulers and ruled, fine and uncouth, learned and illiterate. The "high" love lyric of the Quattrocento had its characteristic social stance in a repertory of binary oppositions, attained by means of pronouns (she, I), antithesis (*gentile, vile*), oxymoron (*dolce nemica*), and metaphor ("my lady," the sun illuminating a base world). Equaling light and lordly authority, the noble lady (*donna gentil*) is love poetry's primary pole. The opposite pole belongs to diverse images, ranging from the servant (the poet-lover) and the routine (lowly) world to anything or anyone ignorant, coarse, vile, ugly, vulgar, or unworthy. The key pronouns, *she* and *I,* are filtered through the class distinctions of the social world; and though, of course, the oppositions are chiefly moral, they are imagined in terms of a social and political ladder of high and low. The moral counterpoint, accordingly, as we saw in chapter 2, is rendered in the imagery of lord and servant, nobility and *vulgo,* grand and humble, courtesy and boorishness, or even sacred and profane. The point for the lover is to be worthy of the lady, a hope fully justified by his fidelity and amorous suffering. But even before this, lady and lover would seem to belong to the same party, because he is endowed with the ennobling gifts of love, service, and fidelity—properties that distinguish him from the vulgar crowd. He belongs to a moral elite that is also, by semiotic extension, an aristocracy.

By the late fourteenth century, the *stilnovo* and Petrarch's *Canzoniere* had helped to turn the taste for noble love into the dominant amatory idiom; but the taste was nourished by social need, because the idiom became as much a means of social identification as a way of expressing the heightened passion of love. The question now arises—and it is the nettle needing to be grasped at this point in the analysis—What did the lover think he was doing when he made a verse chronicle of his love? This question is historical, as we shall see, so I list the possible answers.

1. He was simply exercising his craft as a professional poet, and love was an obvious theme. Most poets, however, were not professionals; often there were real women involved; and a surprising amount of love verse, occasionally intended for particular people, was written on commission.[42] Furthermore, the poet had to observe the accepted amatory conventions and rituals, or his theme was not the love theme. This turned the poem into a conditioned social gesture, charging us with the need to identify the impinging cultural or community ideals.

2. He was making a declaration of love, at all events when he read or relayed the poem to his lady. Action of this sort, however, was not common, save perhaps exceptionally at some of the courts or in cases of commissioned love verse, when it was thus a matter of x (the poet) speaking for y (the patron, friend, or payer). And in comfortable bourgeois milieux, occasions allowing for the delivery or recitation of sonnets were undoubtedly rare, if, in cases of an oral delivery, not altogether unheard of. But in addition, many a commissioned poem was written as a litany for the delectation of the lover; hence it was perhaps never read or heard by the loved one.

3. He was drawing up a personal statement, in response to joys, strains, or other needs. Much love poetry of the period may be regarded in this light. The poet-lover is often addressing himself and merely affecting to talk to his beloved. I say affecting because, in the actual life of the times, the lady was likely to be hedged in by her social standing, marital status, virginity, or the necessity, in any case, to protect her name and honor. Certain conventions of the idiom itself—the mention of dress, jewels, or a lordly bearing—establish her social identity.

4. He was talking both to himself and to others, and perhaps indirectly too to the lady, in the hope that some rumor of his passion might get back to her. When combined with elements of 2 and 3 above, this is the most plausible and best-documented reply, and most Renaissance love verse may be read thus. Now the nettle-grasping question changes slightly, and we must ask, What did the poet-lover think he was doing when addressing himself and others? What was his talk about? Here at once the inquiry broaches considerable complexity and contradictory intentions.

Although the talk, to be sure, was "literary" talk about love, the guiding imagery was keyed to heavenly, social, and political hierarchies. I have already discussed the first of these as a paraliturgy in which the love poet, pursuing his quest for happiness or blessedness, calls on a ritual language rich in words for the heavens and heavenly doings, in order to satisfy both his own yearnings and the expectations of his audience. His vision therefore was colored by a sociopolitical hue: heaven was a kingdom with a court, gradations of light, and tiers of blessedness. The resulting verse was uplifting, but the lift was stubbornly envisaged in political and social terms.

Just as heaven excluded the underworld of hell, so the kingdom (*regno*) of love excluded the unworthy (*indegni*). By explicit statement or continual implication, poetry confined love to a charmed circle: to the beloved lady of angelic stripe, to the women worthy of holding conversation with her (the lover often directly addresses them), and to deserving lovers—those who shun everything base and common. This attitude was no mere *topos;* it came forth from vivid feeling in the *stilnovisti,* and it was taken over by their Renaissance legatees, who used it to hint at social positions, to promote careers, and to introduce discourse that enabled them to define themselves. Men at court, for example, Malatesta Malatesti, Giusto de' Conti, Niccolò da Correggio, and Bembo, assumed that the sentiment of elevated love was the business of courtiers, nobles, and leisured and learned men; that they alone had the time, experience, and breadth of soul to cultivate both theme and feeling. Thus, observing that Jove himself committed rape and incest, having been moved by the force of Love, Correggio (1450–1508) taunts:

Se Idio fece già questo, onde procede,
vulgo ignorante, che tu imputi errore
se uno om di carne, giovene e signore,
per qualche effecto transformar si vede?[43]

(If God once did this, how is it, O ignorant mob, that you level the charge of sin if a man of flesh, young, and a lord, sees himself changed by such an effect?)

Love poets in republican Florence also held decided social and class views. Indeed, owing to the more "bourgeois" or profit-turned nature of Florentine society, they sometimes gave a greater emphasis to the socially invidious face of love. In the early Quattrocento, in a poetic exchange with the Malatesta lord of Pesaro, a Florentine poet—uniting courtesy with civic humanism—urges him to follow the banner of love for the sake of virtue, poetry, arms, eloquence, fame, glory, and honor.[44] Nothing in this cluster of ideals had anything to do with the cloth industry, trade, or moneylending. Later, the poetry of two other Florentines, Francesco Accolti and Bernardo Pulci, will convey a kindred message in their passionate uniting of virtue, nobility, and love, a trinity that they oppose to the "vulgar" and "ignorant" approval of place and base wealth.[45]

Was there any substance to the view that noble love was the business of an upper class? There was, for it was imposed by literary convention itself, no less than by the love poet's ways of reasoning in poetic conversation with himself, with peers, with "my lady," and with other ladies. The central image required a beautiful young woman who was well-spoken, well-mannered, well-dressed, of lordly (*signorile*) bearing, and in excellent health. She stood out among women and was worthy to win the adoration of those devoted to the refined amatory idiom, which was also a school of manners. Nothing about her was in the least domestic or practical or common. And when she was seen to be holding anything at all—fan, flowers, ring, or letter—the focus shifted to the beauty of her hand, as in the title *Beautiful Hand* (La bella mano) of Giusto de' Conti's *canzoniere* of 1472.

Apart from the topoi of praise and lamentation in his interminable love talk, the lover's reasoning touched *fortuna,* the heavens, the times, shame, honor, mercy, and ignominy. He spoke of war, peace, harmonious speech, classical deities, historical parallels, flights, arrivals, and departures; of horses, falconing, and the ungrateful (princely) court; of poetry (*rime, carte*), style, and the need to pen verse; and he flaunted fanciful syllogisms:

Ogni animal che viva de rapina
Per suo cibo miglior s'elegge il core,
E similmente la virtù divina
Dal peccator non vòle altro che'l core.[46]

(Every animal which lives from prey picks the heart as its choice morsel; so too divinity seeks nothing in the sinner if not his heart.)

This complaining love octave ends in condemnation of the lady, because she disdains the best part, his heart.

All in all, then, he was a man of the world, ever rehearsing the keening complaints of love, yet articulate, well-read, traveled, ironic, leisured, and so deserving to be read or heard. Or at least he had to have enough self-confidence to believe that other well-read men and a few women of the upper class would want to listen to him. For the preferred love genres, sonnet and *canzone,* were not only verse forms but also ways of moralizing and ruminating, ways of seeing the world and of conducting self-analyses. Much of the love chatter, admittedly, was riddled with conventional metaphor and cliché; but if the lover was to make a good show of his praise and complaint, if he was to achieve some degree of freshness, he must demonstrate sufficient mastery of the idiom to manage it with novel touches from his own experience of the world. Accordingly, though most poets could occasionally produce poems in the high scripture of love, to issue a whole cycle, a *canzoniere,* required the accents of a male voice from the ruling class. In fact, nearly all the amatory cycles of the fifteenth and early sixteenth centuries were written by princes, courtiers, noblemen, and well-placed lawyers: Malatesta Malatesti, Alessandro Sforza, Angelo Galli, Giusto de' Conti, Rosello Roselli, Bernardo Pulci, Matteo Maria Boiardo, Lorenzo de' Medici, Antonio Cornazzano, Niccolò da Correggio, Gasparo Visconti, Pietro Bembo, and Giovanni Muzzarelli. The most modest of these thirteen men, Roselli and Cornazzano, sprang from prominent families of jurists and were themselves active as judges. Pulci and Conti hailed from the old municipal nobility of Florence and Rome, and Conti was also a jurist. Four others were princes or could claim princely blood—Malatesti, Sforza, Correggio, and Visconti. Lorenzo de' Medici was quasi-lord of Florence. The rest were noblemen and courtiers.[47]

THE MYSTERIES OF SOCIAL IDENTITY

The idiom of noble love—select, elevated, ritualized—was the amatory voice of Italy's urban elites. Everything in it, from diction and topoi to modes of reasoning, worked to keep it so. But though a point of arrival for us, this knowledge was the Renaissance poet's point of departure, precisely because his knowledge of self, as a condition refined and grasped by means of words, began with knowing how to use the love idiom as a language of class. The self-regarding stance of love, brought about by love's moral predicaments, by self-division and self-searching, motivated writers to use the idiom to identify, examine, and know themselves. Hence every man who sought to use the high idiom of love had to guard its conventions and rituals, ever renewing in this fashion the amatory voice of the society's privileged groups. In certain cases the process of manipulating the idiom also enabled him to know or to identify his desired place in the social world as he saw it. However, as a trained reader or listener—a different incarnation—he might look for the metaphorical accents (heavenly, social, or political) that confirmed his dream of love.

We begin to see why the elevated language of love, in Italy as in Renaissance Europe generally, was a vehicle for socially ambitious writers: it displayed familiarity with a privileged code while also offering its devotees the psycholinguistic resources to help form or reform themselves.[48] Yet every man used the code differently, even if the differences were in little more than nuanced matters; for semiotic systems, viewed as "equipment for living," can only be "read"—computers aside—by individual nervous systems.

Two outstanding poets, Francesco di Vannozzo (c. 1340–c. 1390) and Saviozzo of Siena (c. 1360–1420), spent their creative years in the service of princes and *condottieri*.[49] Producing verse on commission in a refined amatory vein, they could also turn the tribulations of the lover into oblique commentary on their own hard fate as servitors of the powerful, as in these lines by Vannozzo:

> Io veggio ben che i cieli ora mi sfida
> e sento contra me la luna e il sole,
> nè pero mai di me verun si dole
> poi che fortuna e povertà mi guida.
> Ai, tristo quel che mai d'Amor si fida.[50]

> (I see that heaven defies me, and I feel the moon and sun arrayed against me, and yet no one ever sorrows for me, because I am led by *fortuna* and poverty. Ah, wretched the man who ever trusts in love.)

In Saviozzo's case, more interestingly, we have a poet who occasionally used the amatory idiom to mask and ennoble homosexual interests. Disgraced in obscure circumstances and cast into prison, as we shall see in some detail in chapter 5, he committed suicide, having first laid a curse on the world and himself.

Poets, as we know, were often to be found at the princely courts. Here, in the shadow of the men who radiated power and consequence, hyperbolic compliment was a basic part of the currency of everyday speech, and learning to pay it belonged to the art of survival and success. Moreover, as established in chapter 2, the language of patronage—and princely courts were its great centers—was a language of love and praise. Therefore, in mastering the high amatory idiom, poets at court were also perfecting their use of one and the same courtly language for love, for daily life, and for patron–client relations. The great nobleman Niccolò da Correggio links love and life at court by linking their injustice to the servitude and unhappiness imposed by each:

> Da Amor sbandito in solitaria villa
> e del favor di corte in tutto privo,
> tra fere alpestre incognito mi vivo.

(Banished by Love to a lonely villa and stripped of all favor at court, I live as one unknown among alpine beasts.)

A later stage of love and courtly life brings melancholy and regret:

> In una cosa sol me stesso danno:
> de l'età persa vanamente in corte,
> e ch'io non venni qui al vigesimo anno.
> Qui non ha forza Amor, né ardire ha Morte.[51]

(For one thing only do I blame myself: for the years wasted at court vaingloriously, and for not coming here [to my villa] when I was twenty. Love has no power here, nor Death any impudence.)

Love, clearly, was not about love alone; it was also about a more complex social existence and a style of communication. It involved the profiling of a social identity. *Faith* and *fidelity in love* (*fede, fedeltà*) were words redolent with the whole quality of expected service at court.

The same idiom in "bourgeois" Florence would inevitably have different accents and applications, as we may readily discern in the career and voice of Francesco d'Altobianco degli Alberti, to whom we shall turn in chapter 6. Another Florentine, Bernardo Pulci, writing just after Alberti, utilized the grand idiom of love allegorically, thus displaying in this aspiring gesture his own "spiritual" bent in the very years when his ancient and distinguished family verged on financial collapse and public scandal. *His* loved one is often little more than a symbol of abstract virtue with a strong religious cast.[52] And though the great humanist Angelo Poliziano issued a more delicate, clever, and playful version of the idiom for his Medici patrons,[53] Lorenzo de' Medici made it do multiple service in his own verse. Consummate politician, "veiled" lord of Florence, patron, collector, and poet (though with nothing of the banking skills that had distinguished his patriline), he issued poetry of a high and sustained polish, revealing the artist and lover, suppressing the politician and power broker, while also promoting Florentine vernacular literature throughout Italy, all of which made him the literary arbiter of Florence in the 1470s and 1480s. The language of his *canzoniere* is self-consciously literary and selectively generalized, a production carefully pondered and wrought over a period of some twenty years.[54] His is an idiom that converts the ruthless politician into a wounded and grieving lover-artist, Neoplatonist, and student of Dante, Petrarch, the *stilnovisti,* and the classics. It is both high art and, as the voice of injured love, an astonishing masquerade.

At Bologna, meanwhile, a line of poets had adapted the idiom, again confirming it as the language of an elite.[55] Most of them came from the city's celebrated legal profession, a corps that proudly distinguished itself from the "illiterate" laity, who had little or no Latin. Their love poems circulated among friends, usually other lawyers; and they exchanged knowing literary comment, decried the vulgar herd, scoffed at the boorishness of provincial burgs, spoke to patrons in the exalted language of the amatory code, and used love to identify themselves as a cultivated coterie.[56] The more workaday or "bourgeois" quality of the Bologna group and the adaptability of the love code may be deduced from the attempt by one of them, Sebastiano Aldovrandi, to use it to mourn his dead wife.[57] At Milan or Ferrara this would have been seen as indecorous, inappropriate. Other poets might mourn a man's wife, particularly if the bereaved was a prince or a political magnate, but not the grieving husband. Paradoxically, the "natural" voice of our lawyers from Bologna, a voice more in keeping with their social condition, surfaced in their occasional attacks on love's hidden immorality.[58] For in that city, the urban crown of the papal states (not counting Rome), this was a stab at oblique criticism of the great nobility, whose ways, as practiced in the lord-servitor relations of the powerful Bentivoglio circle, called for all the stuff of flattery, dalliance, and ritual compliment.[59]

It can be no surprise to find that the code of noble love was most at home in the ceremonious life of the princely courts, where the amatory verse of princes and courtiers—Malatesta, Galli, Sforza, Boiardo, Correggio, Visconti, and Bembo—betrays an easy naturalness with "great ladies," grand compliment, faithful service, prepotent authority, and the immeasurable narcissism of the lover. There too we encounter the underlying sense that the world of the court *is* the world and that a cosmic importance may be more naturally ascribed to the joys and torments of the lover based at court. The sun, the stars, the seas, the seasons, the winds, the animal kingdom, heaven, the gods, fate, time, and *fortuna,* all conspire, as it were, to foil or figure his love passion. We have the syndrome in the great Milanese courtier Gasparo Visconti, caught up in "cloudy and turbulent times" (tempi nebulosi e turbulenti), his life "like a sea of sand and violent winds" (come un mar darena e venti/Impetuosi), while his "agitated mind like a riotous wave strikes the rocks of [her] disdain" (agitato penser come onda a turbo/Urta nei duri scagli del disdegno); for, he continues, "heaven's wrath is turned against me" (el cel me volto in ira). Or, more serenely and succinctly:

> Il cel nemico e la fortuna ria
> Et le stelle maligne insieme agionte
> Son contra a merti de mia longa fede.[60]

(Hostile heaven, wicked *fortuna,* and the spiteful stars, all joined together, are against all the worth of my unending fidelity [to my lady].)

More significantly for the ties between poetry and daily experience, the classic and persisting metaphors of the amatory code were all tied up with the practical life of courts and their business: diplomatic negotiation, intrigue, favoritism, war and peace, hunting cavalcades, the daily exigencies of service and patronage, and a continual coming and going between town and country. This whole life shines through the tropes and images of noble love; so also does the sense that *fortuna,* that pivotal force in love, involved princes, courtiers, and powerful men, not little folk, because it was all about the fall of the mighty and the climb up to great eminence.[61] Finally, being thoroughly accustomed to an unchallenged political and social (male) ascendancy, men at court (and the men of the ruling classes generally) entered easily into the persona of the obsessive, self-absorbed lover who fully expects to be of interest to others. Here at once the narcissism and misogyny of the lover were clearly in evidence; and Renaissance love poetry, with its genius for turning the world of gender relations upside down, is itself overturned here to become, in one of its manifestations, a heady exercise in self-love.

LOVE AND ARRANGED MARRIAGE

Among the propertied classes of Italian Renaissance cities, adultery on the part of women was not generally a realistic option, owing to a variety of daunting barriers (see chap. 9). Among these were the puissant ideal of female chastity, telltale servants and slaves, the spying eyes of neighbors, the threatened loss of honor, and the forfeiture of property. The thought of these conditions would have haunted any noblewoman or well-heeled bourgeoise caught up in a hankering for adultery. Almost as much as wives, young widows too had to guard name and reputation, because their sexuality was often looked upon as a menace to family honor.[62] Yet passion on occasion certainly had its way, and we hear of adulterous middle-class and patrician women as well as "unchaste" widows.[63] Some amatory verse reveals the first name of the beloved, usually, however, in puns, acrostics, or more rarely in a marginal note.[64] The incidence of illegitimate men in high place—not all the sons of servants and "low-born" women—points to adultery by women of rank and property, although such liaisons called for the maximum secrecy, discretion, or long-term concubinage that looked much like marriage.[65]

How, then, did the common practice of arranged marriage touch the ambitions and strains of noble love? Apotheosized in poetry and song,[66] this kind of love—a keen, elevated yearning for a woman of the upper classes—had nothing directly to do with marriage. It ran along parallel, so to speak, with marriage, and though obscurely related, the two never met. A candid contract of material convenience, marriage was intended to be a sensible economic and social arrangement, or occasionally a political tie between two families. Its aims were status, reproduction, and the transmission of property.[67] Noble love, *par contre,* was the negation of the real world of marriage: it removed the experience of yearning from the routine pragmatic world, so as to exalt and put it to the test of destiny, storms, and heavenly forces. Even as the material of dreams, noble love belonged to the *public* world of upper-class men, whereas marriage and marital sentiments belonged to a private and domestic space. In noble love, known by imagination and longing, women seemed to be in charge; in marriage, men were. Paradoxically, the lover dreamed and penned his verses in private, but he did so in a ritualized and therefore egregious public language. This was his entrée into a world of male dreaming, male talk, and male preoccupations: a world of courtly conduct, of idealization in a public idiom, of substitute imaginary realities, and of enunciated or even "performed" social identities. This aspect of noble love responded to the demands or desires of political magnates, literate noblemen, lawyers, and other men who had proved themselves in a public space.

Insofar as marriage was an abode of routine domesticity, it freed the male for a parallel commitment in the idealizing mode. Here, in the feeling of love for another woman real or fictive (at times a woman who had been merely seen),[68] the love poet gloried or overcame strain and frustration by means of action in the symbolic world of writing: that is, by ritual refrain (a kind of prayer), by the manipulation of a code, by a self-obsession, and by imaginative reconstruction. Now he could cry out with the whole of a lover's yearning while also dealing, in effect, with his current ambitions and troubles. Indeed, love was not love; or, more accurately, it was that and much else too.[69]

At the summit of authority, quite atypically, princes were expected to have mistresses; and their paramours might attract love poems from client-courtiers around the prince, this being a roundabout way of wooing the prince himself. The married beauty Cecilia Gallerani, mistress to Ludovico Sforza, lord of Milan, elicited the love verse of a clientele.[70] The wealth and favors showered on her, allied to the glamor and might of princely power, worked the miracle of a transubstantiation on her attainted honor, rendering it enviable.[71] But such flagrant adultery, even in the years of Lorenzo de' Medici's primacy (c. 1478–92), would have been unthinkable in middle-class and patrician Florence. Reportedly lustful ("libidinoso e tutto venereo"), Lorenzo kept discrete trysts in the Florentine countryside, where he conducted a long affair with a Florentine bourgeoise, the wife of Donato Benci, Bartolomea de' Nasi, who used to receive him at night in her villa. But his earlier love for Lucrezia Donati, another married woman of the Florentine ruling class, though celebrated in verse, was concealed by the camouflaging of her name and the claims of platonic love. In the literary record, Lucrezia's name usually appears in puns, such as on "light" (*lux, luce, Lucr*ezia), hence on "sun" too.[72] It is possible that they had sexual relations, but we cannot be certain about this. It follows that making love to a married woman from the republican patriciates of Florence and Venice or, say, Lucca and Siena, would have been even more difficult than it was for Lucrezia and Lorenzo. In the republics, therefore, the penchant for amatory idealization must now and again have been unusually strong; hence the reasons for turning to an idealizing idiom necessarily varied. In princely circles, the idealizing of love had much to do with the art of compliment and flattering the powerful.[73] But in patrician, legal, or rich mercantile circles, it had more to do with compensatory or symbolic action of the sort connected with ambition, status, and personal crisis. Here men achieved temporary victories or satisfactions by constructing statements about an uplifting or transcendent love.

A recent claim[74] holding that "love" begins to appear in Venetian marriage about 1400 is quite surprising. For the word had an enormous undertow of meaning. The age itself favored its usage at four points: in action for the love of God, in patron-client (or lord-servitor) relations, in relations between parents and children, and in relations between lovers.[75] Contemporaries sometimes touched on the element of "love" in friendship, but this sense of our polysemous term pales by comparison with the frequency of meaning at the four other points. It often happened, no doubt, that couples in arranged marriage developed bonds of affection and strong mutual regard, as in the model of modern Indian marriage. And "love" is surely an appropriate term for such reciprocal sentiment; but there was nothing new about it in Venice circa 1400; it was already there in 1300, in 1200, and so on. Other senses of the word are also applicable to arranged marriage in Italy: for one thing, love between spouses was meant to be joined to the love of God. There were homilies on this subject.[76] But marital affection was no gateway to great suffering and tremulous joy: a feeling to be doted on, exalted, and charged with learning, *fortuna,* or cosmic forces. Even when noble love was hell, it was hell *and* heaven (a commonplace oxymoron); it was the stuff of utopian velleity, and wives (however dear) could not inspire it. They were at home and available; "my lady" was not.

As for wives and what *they* dreamed about, who can tell? Did they dream of the beautiful young man across the way? Of the exemplary life of the Virgin Mary? Of some passing, braggart soldier of fortune (*condottiere*)? Or were their reveries a mute revenge against their men, a matter of unadorned lusting? The last of these possibilities, as we shall find in chapter 9, had ample support in the Renaissance short story; and if such imagined or fictional lusting was little more than the expression of male fears, did men, our prime movers, not have a hand in all this?

POPULAR LOVE

In the present climate of historical inquiry, it would be gratifying to be able to head this section "Love among the Populace." The state of current study, however, does not allow it, and documentary sources for such an inquiry are either spotty or beset by problems.[77]

Marriage in Renaissance Italy had its best legal guarantees in the girl's dowry, the importance of which called for witnesses who could one day attest, if need be, to the marriage.[78] And in Venice, as in Bologna and other cities, ruling-class marriages were sometimes great public events—happy, sumptuous, ritualized.[79] More modestly, the failure to dower a bride was a risky business, as it might expose the marriage to serious challenge.[80] Owing to the cohesive force of property, therefore, we may surmise that marriage among the very poor was a more fluid institution than among their social betters. Here, too, far more than at the middle or the upper reaches of society, choice and burning desire ("love") were likely to draw people into liaisons or marriages.[81] But it is also among the poor that we hear of runaway wives or husbands or of "spouses" who deny that they had ever been married.[82] Passion cooled or could end in strife, whereas "sensible" (arranged and dowered) marriages endured.

In these circumstances, how may we imagine or conceive of "popular love"? As a way of feeling and thinking that had something in it of all social classes? Moralists and even authors of palinodes frequently argued that the high ideals of love in verse and song were nothing but disguised lechery.[83] Many contemporaries, including physicians, saw love as a malady, albeit as one to which young men of the upper class were chiefly prone.[84] From a Platonic viewpoint, reason lost control and there was a plunge into vulgar, base, bestial, or even plebeian love.[85]

Adduced by contemporary observers, these qualifying adjectives look very much like a mandarin's (upper-class) ascriptions. Did the "plebeians" espouse "base" love? Put thus, the question is obviously loaded with ideological presupposition. It is the case, however, that when the high amatory idiom was given a popular twist or turned into popular song, as in the verse of Leonardo Giustinian, Bernardo Giambullari, Olimpo da Sassoferrato, and much anonymous composition, language, imagery, and sentiment at once became more realistic and accessible.[86] Many of the standard metaphorical conventions were retained, as in the girl's lordly or heavenly authority and in her equaling the sun and the stars; but they were now turned into mere stereotypes and mingled with the key element that makes for popularity—a large dose of realism. Thus the poet is likely to refer to the girl's name, windows, balcony, street, or the fleshy parts of her body. And much use is made of the informal

diminutive: "Le picciole mammelle [de la brunettina mia]/paion due fresche
rose" (The little breasts [of my little brunette] seem two fresh roses).[87] Mixing
the popular and stately modes, Giambullari comes up with something that
verges on mock-stately:

> Andranne la mie ballata
> in sul monte fiesolano;
> porterai quest' ambasciata
> a chi ha'l mie core in mano,
> e con parlare umano
> la saluta riverente.
> Priega l'Antonia piacente
> ch' i' le sia raccomandato.[88]

(Go my ballad up to the Fiesolan hills; take this embassy to the one with my
heart in her hands, and greet her with a bow and courteous words. Beg the
pleasing Antonia that I be commended to her.)

Popular poets also put us in touch with the words and turns of everyday
speech: "S'i' fussi un cane e stessi con altrui,/i' are' pur le spese almen da lui"
(If I were a dog with someone else, I'd get at least expenses from him)[89] or "un
vermine ò nel cor che par che sia/un can che per istizza il cor mi pigli" (I've a
worm in my heart which is like an angry dog that snaps at it).[90] The lover may
persist in idealizing the girl, but now too there is a franker commitment to the
delights of the senses:

> Tenéa madonna discoperto el pecto
> fisa mirando le sua poma d'oro,
> el ricco et bel lavoro,
> et fra sé disse: O quanto seria lieto
> l'amante mio fidel saggio e discreto
> se toccar le potesse un poco un poco.[91]

(My lady had her chest uncovered, staring fixedly at her golden apples, a
work rich and beautiful, and to herself she said: O how joyful would my
faithful, wise, and prudent lover be, could he but touch them just a little.)

The adjectival phrase "fidel saggio e discreto" was a straight steal from the
highbrow idiom, but here it borders on parody.

Popular love, then, was more obviously sexual than its elevated counterpart; and it appealed to elements of *all* social classes.[92] Were contemporary critics right, therefore, to claim that when the posturing of the high amatory idiom was unmasked, nothing remained but the appetite for sex and sensual pleasure? There was doubtless something to this, but it would be simplistic to stop there. Far too much solicitude and intellectual energy went into the amatory cycles of the age, the *canzonieri,* for these to have been a mere labor of hypocrisy and lechery. As we have seen, the idiom had various uses, apart from that of wooing ladies, and so it cannot be fixed to a single purpose. Whatever the views of moralists or Cupid's turncoats, historians may reduce the theme of noble love to lubricity only at the expense of meaning and motivation.

On the question of relations between elite and popular consciousness, it seems clear, in the present case at all events, that the urban multitudes had little discernible effect on the high culture of Renaissance love, unless it was to make its votaries more snobbish. Instead, influence moved the other way: the conventional locutions of noble love leached "down" into popular song and verse, to be adapted to perceptions and feelings that were plainer or more immediate. The filtering down of elements of the highbrow code was connected, I suspect, with the setting of verse to popular music, which then both stereotyped many of the elevated turns of phrase and "debased" them by inserting them into alien verbal contexts. With their ardent interest in musical entertainment, the courts themselves had a taste for amatory realism in song; and if any part of this betokened a seeping "upward" of popular taste, the results were often mocking or satirical.[93]

But just as the courts might "descend" to earthiness, so the populace might "ascend" to idealization, for the strategies of symbolic action in imaginary escape were also at work in the popular love idiom, however demystified its borrowings from the highbrow code. From the standpoint of his humble position, the urban artisan or petty tradesman was dramatizing wishful thinking when he sang of a girl "loftier" than all others in the world or of a lady "che de splendor avanza ogni chiar stella" (who in splendor surpasses every other bright star). Insofar as he elevated her to "paradiso" by means of metaphor that hinged on rank and luxury, such as "poma d'oro" (golden fruit/apple), precious stones, and her "amena fronte . . . alta e serena, alta e spaciosa" (pleasing forehead . . . high, serene, and wide),[94] he was raising her and himself up to a social milieu in which all the amenities were superabundant. In his way, surely, the poor man had a greater oneiric need, a need to dream, than the man of wealth; but his hardships were of the sort to make him more inclined to dream of the Land of Plenty (*cuccagna,* Cockayne)[95] or to combine love, food, and riches in his dreams, as in the image of "my lady's . . . golden apples."

CONCLUSION

The way to use poetry as historical testimony is to commence by making historical questions primary. Study of the verse is then organized around these. The sustained task is to conduct the analysis continually back and forth between the external world of institutions and social structures on the one side and, on the other, the internal world of perception, verbal negotiation, and response.[96] Love obviously answers to individual need first of all, but it is instantly adjusted to (and brings in the voices of) the external, flanking realities. In his quest to give himself and to take another, the lover is at the same time hedged in on all sides by conventions, by social expectation, by received notions of the good life, and by hopes rooted in the resources of the surrounding world. All these provide the lover with his love talk, for without them his utterances can offer nothing but perfectly flat predicates, such as "I love you" or "I crave you." In other words, without the flooding into him of strains and contemporary predilections, the love theme is an empty form waiting to be filled in, a blank check that has yet to be written and endorsed. Precisely here is where love and history intersect. Every society fills in the empty form in its own way, though the individual may of course richly vary the details. Owing to Christianity, the cult of the Virgin Mary, Neoplatonism, and a marked stress on "love" in patron-client relations, our key word had gathered up so much meaning by 1500 that it was the bearer of a whole archeology, of some part of the history of Europe.

I have paid strict attention to language, because it is the "hard" evidence in the conversion of poetry to historical document. Renaissance love poetry was sodden with a residual religion—in metaphor, adjective, analogy, and simple asseveration. Some part of this has to be discounted, because of the semiotic play offered us by language. But we must remember, too, that Italian Renaissance cities coruscated with religious signs, images, and places, with an art that was overwhelmingly religious and a daily speech riddled with religious expressions. Encircled and invaded by this rich semiology, the grand idiom of love was also at the service of serious religious intention, so much so, indeed, that certain men turned it into a surrogate religion. This also tells us—poetry tells us—that there was some staleness or notable want in the official Church, at any rate for an elite of worshipers.

As a source in which linguistic concerns are critical for the study of history, poetry is not singular but exemplary. In traffic between internal and external worlds, language is the chief vehicle of discernible transactions. The words of poetry, however, have to be read with more than customary skill and care. This is well illustrated by our identification of Renaissance misogyny. Here was a strain, a cause and effect of subordination, a deep-rooted mental habit that is not necessarily best studied in explicit statement but rather in the undercurrents revealed by the strategies of language. Misogyny was distilled into amatory verse not just in lamentation against the cruel lady but also and above all in the ritualized use of hyperbolic compliment, in the religious diction spun around "my lady," in the quest for adjectives that put her outside the human race, and in the elegant but brazen overturning of the real world of gender relations. The result was a separation so striking between man and woman that the exaltation of the beloved, though seeming to heal the gender schism, confirmed or even enhanced it. This is why the reversal of feeling in the lover came so naturally: adoration turned into bitter complaint. The lady might now became a "wild beast" or a "rapacious animal" (*fera, fiera*), thus being put, yet once more, outside the party of humanity. In Giusto de' Conti (c. 1390–1449), the reversal could come about "in men d'un giorno" (in less than a day), with the result that the two moods appear side by side:

Gloriosa, benigna, humele e pia,
Vaga, legiadra, bella, acorta e desta,
Magnifica, gentil, apta e modesta,
Real, cortese sopra ogn'altra dia;

Sdegnosa, altera, superba et empia,
Fiera salvagia, crudelle e infesta,
Retrosa, alpestre, crudelle e molesta,
Perfida, iniqua, dura, acerba e ria.[97]

(Glorious, kind, modest, and compassionate, Graceful, gay, beautiful, wise, and alert, Magnificent, noble, capable, and simple, Royal, more courtly than any other goddess; Scornful, haughty, arrogant, and pitiless, Savage animal, cruel and baneful, Contrary, wild, vicious, and vexed, Treacherous, wicked, harsh, tart, and evil.)

These extremes, her high glory and evil animality, mark the invincible self-indulgence, the narcissism, of the male love game. For by turning the lady into beast or deity, the lover denied her all parity (hence all give-and-take) with himself, and he could now deliver himself to an orgy of self-defining compliment or complaint.

A word next on the "problematic" mother of Freudian theory. If the analysis of language and metaphor helps to expose misogyny, psychoanalytic emphasis on the lover's infancy, that is, on putative relations with his mother,[98] obscures it by the a priori promoting of contentious theory over the claims of social and material forces. Patriarchy and its subservient misogyny were manifest in women's legal incapacities, in male rights over property, in the dominance of patrilines, in male-centered public and political worlds, and in the whole accretion of supporting doctrine and ideology. Yet if mother, or the so-called Oedipal triangle, was the key influence in turning the grown man (the lover) into a brooding and resentful critic of women,[99] how can we look for misogyny in institutions and property relations? These are all suddenly swept away. If, however, we take our bearings from external realities, we may assume that however untroubled the male infant's relations with his mother,[100] and however unstressful his education, his teenage contact with the world would soon fill him with the society's basic stereotypes. He would need these in order to make his way in life, whether in "bourgeois" Florence or patrician Venice, Milan, or Bologna, not to mention clerical Rome. In my researches I have come upon one instance only of a love poet, Comedio Venuti (b. 1424), whose language alludes to the mother figure in such a way as to raise the suspicion of a stressed childhood.[101]

Having identified the misogynist ghost in the amatory machine, I would point out again that this was only one of various interests at work in the enterprise of noble love. Depending upon the poet or the occasion, all of the following might also make their entrée: the need for prayer, wooing patrons, constructing self-images, displaying social credentials, and substituting or overcoming affliction. Each of these was satisfied by means of "language as gesture," whether as direct action (flattery) or as symbolic action (carefully crafted surrogates). It goes without saying that wooing ladies was always the avowed purpose of the idiom.

Although social historians have only just started to study the points and ways of contact between love and history, the nature of my argument implies that the basic structures of command and obedience in society would require some shaking up before love song and poetry would see any significant changes in their ways of imagining love. In this regard it is instructive to note that before about 1530, poetry by women was all but entirely religious.[102] The rare exceptions in the amatory vein tended to come from princely circles, and in some cases we know about them only because of contemporary reports.[103] Manuscripts indicate that fifteenth-century poets very occasionally penned amatory verse for—that is, as if written by—women, with ladies thus addressing the loved one; but it is impossible to say whether or not such verse circulated or was ever even seen by the addressee.[104] The subject has never been discussed. However, from the moment when the voices of women in love are first heard in the sixteenth century, as in the poetry of Gaspara Stampa and Veronica Franco, the phenomenon is closely associated with a new term: *cortigiana* ("classy" tart, or courtesan).[105] And although they write in the established male idiom, they are able to manipulate it for their own purposes.[106]

It should come as no surprise, however, to learn that at the beginnings of women's love poetry in modern Europe, the first voices to be made public were those of courtesans. They, after all, were "public" women. For in the gravely unsettled conditions of sixteenth-century Italy, at Venice, Rome, Florence, and elsewhere, the inveterate patriarchal structures were reinforced by prolonged war, narrowing economic horizons, and greater political inflexibilities. In this climate, women who dared to speak publicly of their amatory experience came perforce from the new demimonde of fashionable courtesans.[107] Any reputable woman, such as the aristocratic Vittoria Colonna (1490–1547), who wrote verse about love and allowed it to circulate was necessarily writing about love for her dead husband or love of God.[108]

Current work on the condition of women in late medieval and Renaissance Italy may be said to verge on sharp debate. The lines are drawn between historians who underline the subordinate status of women and those who look, rather, to a more felicitous condition.[109] Apart from the fact that most of the evidence on both sides involves women of the propertied classes, the chief problem has to do with the direction of generalization. Which set of findings shall we generalize: the fact that there were notable cases of wives and daughters who, in addition to their dowries, were favored by bequests of cash, property, and interest-bearing government bonds? For this is the evidence in support of women's happier status, though we should bear in mind the question of how many swallows make a summer. Or shall we favor, instead, the generalizations offered us by a great body of law, the nature of public life, the significance of the dowry, and the dominance of patrilineages? Is it not obvious that the affective world of poetry should be interjected into this debate, in our effort to chart the feelings, mental habits, dreams, and unthinking reactions of people in everyday life? My analysis of the male love verse of the age reveals that the subordination of women was so deeply embedded in consciousness as to make for an abiding self-division in the male. This is to say that he was oppressed by the contradiction in his socially created image of woman: mother, wife, daughter, sister, and real or fictive beloved. He demanded chastity or virginity from the one but insisted that the other pity his lover's condition and give way to his entreaties.

FIVE

THE SUICIDE

OF A POET

In the preceding chapters, I approach individuals through a play of gener-alities, by focusing on neighborhoods, love, patron-client relations, and the strategies of prayer. Here, reversing the procedure, I turn to the particulars of a man who walked a tightrope between the demands of "commune" and patronage on the one side and, on the other, the furies of a volatile self.

BACKGROUND

We must imagine a poet who summons the powers of hell to come and claim him, crying out in hate against his own birth and hence against his parents, cursing his mother's genitalia ("vulva adulterata"), and wanting to tear his father to pieces with his teeth. This was Saviozzo (Simone Serdini) of Siena, poet and servant to princes and soldiers, sometime before he stabbed himself to death in 1419 or 1420. No man could have been more alienated, and yet there was a world of help not far away, in the swarms of priests and friars and in the many churches. To add gall to his words of self-loathing, he even cast his curses into rhymed maledictions and malign parodies of prayer.[1]

I propose to trawl through Saviozzo's life and art, with a view to tracking the circumstances that led to his gruesome end. That he was subject to occasional fits of depression, even of clinical depression in our terms, is likely to have been the case. If so, the episodes worked themselves out in ways and with accents that belong to history by being stamped with the many signs of a particular time and place. Saviozzo himself often made a point of connecting art and life by attaching captions to his poems, explaining the immediate background to their composition. Time and again, moreover, when he failed to do so, or when the caption was lost, the poems speak with the same high hyperbole and self-accusing or introspective voice that came to characterize his verse.

In a century that first saw the art of Dante and Petrarch, Saviozzo comes in, needless to say, on a lesser scale, along with, say, Antonio (Beccari) da Ferrara and Francesco di Vannozzo but above two poets then dear to the Florentines, Antonio Pucci and Franco Sacchetti. In his thematic range, commitment, control, and manipulation of the language, he was admittedly "a minor master."[2] Yet for more than a century after his suicide, he was much anthologized, keenly read by cognoscenti, and often copied or imitated. Some of his compositions were long assigned to others.[3] In short, when we look down from the great *trecentisti* and run a survey up to the late fifteenth century, we see our Sienese master almost at once. To be sure, this is a judgment for literary taste, not for social analysis; but I make it only so as to identify a poet whose value transcends the stricter historical interests of this book.

Saviozzo is often compared with Beccari (1315–c. 1373) and Vannozzo (c. 1340–c. 1390) because, like them, he sprang from modest social stock and took up an itinerant literary life. He migrated in employment from one petty court to another, or moved around in the field, heading the chancelleries of princely soldiers of fortune, mostly in the region stretching from Umbria and Tuscany east to the Romagna. His pen, like Beccari's and Vannozzo's, was also out for hire: he composed poetry on commission—love verse, eulogy, propaganda, occasional pieces, and devotional poems. At one point a preceptor to young princes, he was above all a secretarial factotum, a letter writer, and an occasional emissary. Had he lived a century later, patrons would have pressed him into taking holy orders, thereby aiming to assure him of a stable income, as was the case with so many writers then.[4] The changing economic and political face of the Italian peninsula also changed the material conditions and outlook for men of letters.[5] I want to suggest that as the holder of one or more church benefices, Saviozzo would have had a more secure situation and the benefits, in crisis, of a more confraternal community. The brilliant macaronic poet Folengo comes to mind in this regard. In brief, it was almost unheard of for Italian clerics to commit suicide.[6] Thieves, merchants, swindlers, and fornicators they might be, but not suicides.

Saviozzo was born in Siena shortly before 1360, but we have scant information about the first three decades of his life, apart from the fact that he was a married father by 1383.[7] We must assume that he was born into a propertied family, for he held major public office in Siena in 1401 and could claim some Latin, as well as an excellent vernacular education.

In 1388, in a bloody brawl, he clubbed Giovanni Ghezzi of Siena, hitting him on the head, and was condemned to pay a substantial criminal fine of 200 lire (about 53 gold florins). In December of the next year, he gave a member of the upstart Spannochi family, Nanni di Ambrogio di Ser Mino, three knife thrusts but drew blood only once, and this time was condemned to the more crushing fine of 1,400 lire (about 383 florins).[8] As in the case of the previous crime, if he failed to pay the fine within ten days, the penalty was to be hiked up by one-third. Having paid neither fine, Saviozzo was forced to steal away from Siena in exile at the end of 1389.

That a man of letters of that time should engage in bloody assault is not in the least surprising. In Elizabethan London two centuries later, Christopher Marlowe, Ben Jonson, and Edward (Lord) Herbert were all involved in brutal incidents. And back in Renaissance Italy, there were murderous attacks— endorsed happily by literary men—on Francesco Filelfo, Pietro Aretino, and others. Nor, after leaving Siena, was Saviozzo's changing milieu to be more civil. On the contrary, his years of residence in the Romagna and his employment in the ranks of the servants of *condottieri* drew him into close contact with cutthroats and ruthless professional soldiers, whose loyalties to princes and city-states lasted as long as their contracts or moneys. The great mercenary companies were, to a large extent, organized bands of armed and trained thugs.[9] Moreover, as it happens, wherever noblemen were free to bear arms in the streets of cities—Perugia, Bologna, Rome, the Romagna towns, and at times even Mantua and Ferarra—vicious assault and murder were not at all uncommon.[10]

THIS PEN FOR HIRE

Saviozzo is next found in Florence in 1390, although the city was then at war with Siena. He spent a year or two there and got to know the humanist chancellor Coluccio Salutati,[11] as well as three other writers and poets: Franco Sacchetti, Giovanni Gherardi, and the rich oligarch and love poet Antonio degli Alberti, who died in exile in 1415. The Sienese fugitive probably turned up at some of the famous colloquies held in Antonio's villa, the Paradiso degli Alberti.[12]

But Florence was only a stop along the way for the wandering Saviozzo. He moved on to the little Romagnol city of Imola, where he remained for two or three years (1392–95), a servitor to Ludovico Alidosi, lord of the city.[13] By 1396 he was already in the service of Roberto, the Battifolle count of the great fortress of Poppi, not far east of Florence. Here, however, we find him in an eighty-six-line *canzone* imploring the count to release him from prison and the threat of execution.[14] The plea is pinned to the example of Christ's clemency, and each stanza begins with the first verse of Psalm 38, "Domine, ne in furore tuo arguas me" (O Lord, rebuke me not in thy wrath). The count had jailed him because of "a certain lapse" (*un certo errore*); we know no more, although the wrongdoing was clearly serious. In any event, Saviozzo's artistic pleading worked, and he was soon released. His connections and skills were apparently good, for he passed on next into the train of one of the leading *condottieri* of the day, the great Roman nobleman Giovanni Colonna, at that moment a captain of Florentine troops.[15] Our poet, therefore, was to be in and out of Florence a number of times between 1397 and 1399. There he renewed his ties with Sacchetti and made amicable contact with two of the city's young patricians, Giovanni (Nanni) di Niccolò Soderini and Palla di Mainardo Strozzi. Now, interestingly, and almost certainly for payment or favor of some kind, he produced two love poems in the names of Nanni and Palla, one for each.

The *canzone* for Palla, "The brow, face, Diana really, and the sun,"[16] laments the departure of a beautiful Florentine girl, Palla's love, gone to a marriage in Padua, and scolds both her guardians and "blind" Florence for letting her go. Introducing Cupid, classical allusions, and the standard hyperbole of weapons in love, the poem is an amalgam of *stilnovo* and Petrarchan turns, ending conventionally in the dispatch of the *canzone* to "my lady." We may suppose that Palla's request for the verses, or Saviozzo's offering of them, was intended to satisfy the young Florentine's craving for a poem that exhibited his virility and identity—or indeed the vanity of a preening Strozzi cadet—in a statement of noble sentiments, all the more so in coming from the pen of a great lord's poet.[17] Nanni's *canzone* is more personal,[18] threaded with puns on the lady's name (*Cosa/cosa*), but still a hymn to her high social virtues and the "holy wounds" that she had inflicted on him. The poem ends by begging her, "by God," to be piteous, for to be merciful is what "nobility" (*gentilezza*) is all about.

In keeping with one of the widespread patronage practices of the day, Saviozzo went on to pen a series of such love poems for others, for princes as well as private citizens. Both the courts and the ranks of the urban ruling classes, as noted in chapter 4, had men who were eager to see their amatory games and passions raised aloft in verse and song for others to read, ponder, and admire. From the fourteenth to the sixteenth centuries, to provide this labor of love, to write for others as if they were the other, was one of the main tasks of court poets. And we find Saviozzo doing just this for his warrior prince "Gian" Colonna, first in Fiesole in 1398–99 and again at Pisa in 1403.[19] He himself identified this activity in his manuscripts, often providing names and explanations in the captions (*didascalie*) for particular poems.

In 1400, moved by chronic worry over depopulation, the Sienese government issued an amnesty for a broad class of exiles and "fugitives" with outstanding fines. Although Saviozzo made a late bid for repatriation, his supporters in Siena managed to guide a private petition through the requisite council, the two victims of his bloody assaults having, meanwhile, removed their opposition to his pardon; and after paying the *gabella* (tax) alone on his ancient fines, about fourteen florins (no risible sum), he was able to return to his native city in late August.[20]

Something of a celebrity by now, he must have known what awaited him— Siena was in the grip of deadly plague—and so he collected himself. For we encounter the man in the cathedral next, barefoot and with a leather halter around his neck, loudly intoning one of his own verse compositions, a prayer to the Virgin Mary, in a plea for the city's rescue from the epidemic.[21] He was standing before an altarpiece of the Virgin, Siena's patron saint, in the presence of the Signoria (the heads of state) and all the people of the city, the halter and bare feet signifying humility and servitude. It was an extraordinary way to enhance his new standing with Siena's rulers. Saviozzo obviously had a strong public sense of himself and could also double as a performer.

At this point too, apparently, he had decided to resettle in the city, and the dramatic prayer in the cathedral surely assisted his cause, for in the following year he was elected to the city's principal public office, the Signoria, for the summer term (July–August 1401).[22] In political terms the moment could scarcely have been more uncertain. Although enjoying local autonomy, Siena had been under the broad rule of Giangaleazzo Visconti, the duke of Milan, ever since September 1399;[23] and at this point he seemed more determined than ever to bring Emilia, as well as the whole of Tuscany, under his domination. Exactly a year later (30 June 1402), Giangaleazzo grabbed Bologna with astonishing ease. Saviozzo now moved fast and soon produced one of his most famous poems, "Novella monarchia," favoring a new Italian monarchy and urging Giangaleazzo to seize the crown, "in the name of every true Italian."[24] Along the way, he also savages the Florentines, "that odious seed,/ enemy to peace and charity,/ who say liberty," when what they offer is ruin and "tyranny."

> Now the time has come, now the desire,
> now holy justice for its revenge:
> now I see awakening
> beautiful Italy, and you [duke] it calls for vengeance!
> Lord [of Milan], you see that everyone awaits
> your holy banner and your wide rule:
> so that Florentine blood may purge its venomous itch,
> and we be freed from so much frenzy.[25]

Suffice it to add, parenthetically, that Florentine poets also composed rabid verse of this sort (see chap. 10). In a setting poisoned by the anarchic power and destruction of the great companies of mercenaries, politics could not but be a murderous business.

Yet again, however, something went personally wrong for our poet: Siena was no home for him. Full of the breath of discontent, the restless Saviozzo was back in the field in 1402, probably even before Giangaleazzo's seizure of Bologna and the composition of "Novella monarchia." Now suddenly he was in the service of the Romagnol lords Pandolfo and Carlo Malatesta.[26] If we consider the broken trajectory of his life, his temperamental ways, and the recurrence of certain motifs in his verse, the evidence indicates that Saviozzo was a swift, subtle, explosive, impatient man and fiercely proud (or touchy). Back home in Siena, after twelve years of travel, adventure, writing, and attending warlord princes, he would have found the local elite too proper, narrow, and even illiterate in his terms.[27] I suspect, therefore, that either his spying for a foreign lord, or one rash scene with local oligarchs, put paid to his public career in that depopulated city, now a far cry from the regional center of trade and banking that it had been down to the 1330s.

But whatever happened, Saviozzo was able, if somewhat cautiously, to pass through Sienese territory by January 1406, when he sent off a letter requesting a Sienese visa (*salvacondotto*), "just to be on the safe side, although I don't think I need one." Writing from Perugia, he tells Siena's heads of government that he would be traveling as "my Captain's" emissary (he was by now with Tartaglia da Lavello), then snatches the opportunity to ask for a meeting with them. "My lords, I am after all from Siena, and I have the bones of my forebears there, including those of my mother and brothers." Adducing his love and goodwill for the city, he plunges in and claims to have some secret information to offer them, regarding matters of the highest importance for the security of Siena.[28] Conceivably, he was going to speak for Tartaglia, but the letter assigns all the credit to himself. The dwarf republic of Siena, having been in the clutches of Milanese soldiers until 1404, had fully regained its independence; and Saviozzo, either as an oblique voice for his current employer or thanks to his dealings with leading mercenaries, doubtless did have some information to impart. But from this time on we lose all trace of any future contacts on his part with his native land.

However unruly, the Sienese poet had compensating qualities, one of which must have been a talent for giving pleasure in conversation, as was the case with many Renaissance writers, or few princes would have suffered their company. In the early and high Renaissance, the following writers, to name only a few, all had a quick wit and a considerable talent for keeping their princely patrons entertained: Fazio degli Uberti, Beccari, Vannozzo, Sabadino degli Arienti, Bellincioni, Serafino Aquilano, Francesco Berni, and Matteo Bandello.

Saviozzo remained with his Malatesta lords for a year or two (1402–3) and in this time wrote eulogies and love poetry for their delectation, as well as a long lament for the lord of Milan, Giangaleazzo.[29] But having a knack for troublemaking too, as we have seen, he again made a mess of things, this time with Carlo Malatesta, and had to offer an apology, "Esser non può che nel terrestro sito," in sonnet form.[30] His caption for the poem reads, "To the lord Carlo de' Malatesti, begging his forgiveness for a certain crime (un certo delitto) committed by me, Simone [Serdini], now many days ago." A blending of entreaty and outright prayer, the sonnet turns on the commonplace that to sin is human, to repent an "angelic virtue," but to persist in evil is "demonic"; hence, moved by contrition, he implores Carlo's pity. What the crime had been we can only guess, but certainly assault was not beyond his ken, nor was "bad-mouthing" an overlord.

The second of these crimes, the more likely of the two, would have been grave, as is plain to see in his enigmatic, undated sirvente, "If ever I said it, may

God cleave me/from the very light and I go blind." The fifteenth-century caption, not Saviozzo's, reads, "Entreaties made by Simone of Siena, in prison at the time and under a death sentence, accused of having spoken against his lord; and because of these entreaties, he was released."[31] Though the entire poem is a denial of his having done any such thing, we learn nothing about the offended prince or *condottiere,* save that he was a man who could be reached by poetry. Cast in twenty-eight rhymed quatrains, with an enclosing final verse, the sirvente pivots on a series of ritualized repetitions. The first and third lines of each of quatrains 1 to 9 begin with the emphatic conditional, "If ever I said it" (S'io il dissi mai), meaning the unspeakable derogation, and is then followed by a curse against himself, as in this quatrain:

> If ever I said it, may I see earth open
> to swallow and to suck me in;
> if I ever said it, may the fruit
> of Mary be nowhere at my death!

> (S'io il dissi mai, ch'io veggia aprir la terra
> per inghiottirmi e per sorbirmi tutto;
> s'io il dissi mai, che 'l frutto
> di Maria non si trove al mio finire!) (lines 13–16)

Each of quatrains 10 to 21 begins with the denial "I never said it" (Nol dissi mai) and continues with charges of malice in others, of false allegations, further threats to himself, or declarations (to the addressee) of his love and servitude. In his plea for pity, Saviozzo finally passes to a description of the merciful Christ on the cross and ends by proposing that if his name is reentered "in the book of life," the poet's lord would be canceling his own sins and securing a place in heaven. Powered by the effects of prayer and ritualized words, the poem is oddly and cleverly humorous, fanciful, and compelling, with the whisper of a court jester's voice: one of Saviozzo's most genial productions. So it is not surprising, as the caption asserts, that its 113 lines saved him from the gallows. No more practical use of art can be imagined.

We pass to the years 1403–4 and yet another change of scene. Although back perhaps in their good graces, after his apology to Carlo, Saviozzo was let go by his Malatesta lords and returned to the service of his former prince, Gian Colonna, now captain of the Milanese (Viscontean) garrison in Pisa. There he made a copy in his own hand of Dante's *Divine Comedy,* also glossing it with a commentary, and presented it to the Roman soldier (it is now lost). In fact, the evidence of Dante's influence runs through Saviozzo's poetry. On request from Colonna, he also composed a brief life of the great poet in verse.[32] Yet another composition from these years, dated 1404, is a "moral poem" on "the origins and virtue of the magnificent house of Colonna."[33]

Quite inexplicably, then, in the following year, as noted already, he turns up in the service of another great soldier of fortune, Tartaglia (Angelo Broglio) da Lavello, afterward a leading captain in the marauding northern army of King Ladislaus of Naples. And but for a possible period of employment with the count of Urbino, Saviozzo seems to have remained with the soldier for the rest of his (the poet's) life, finally killing himself in the man's Toscanella prison. A fierce fighter, Tartaglia ("the Stammerer") was also a rather mysterious and sinister personage and for some time a true rival to the great Muzio Attendolo, founder of the Sforza dynasty.[34] Tartaglia soldiered for Ladislaus, Florence, Braccio da Montone, the papacy, Roman intriguers, and Attendolo himself; but like others of his ilk, he was ready to betray his employers, with the result that about two years after Saviozzo's suicide, he was ambushed outside Naples and beheaded for conniving with Braccio while still in the pay of Attendolo.

Down to the death of Ladislaus in 1414, Saviozzo's major contacts were with some of Ladislaus's foremost captains, as we see in his 1409 "song" of praise for the lord of Urbino, count Guidantonio da Montefeltro, and for the king, who had just appointed Guidantonio captain general of his forces in the north.[35]

Let us now look more closely at Saviozzo's writings, with an eye to sharpening our picture of the man.

Research thus far has found only a second letter from Saviozzo. Undated, it is addressed to King Ladislaus's first secretary and is curiously rambling, in the vernacular, but with the intent, I believe, of sniffing out the possibility of a place at the Neapolitan court. Written perhaps about 1410, it is redolent with commonplace flattery.[36] In the world of Renaissance courts, and most particularly in dealings with petty princes such as the Malatesta and Colonna lords, flattery was the standard way, the only way, rightly to approach them and their top functionaries.[37] Inevitably, therefore, Saviozzo's writings, like the stream of humanist Latin verse, are a thesaurus of flattering expression, not only the eulogies, to be sure, but also the prayers, love poems, apologies, and laments for the dead. Christ and Mary, the various beloveds, princely bosses, and the select deceased all come in for a rainfall of adulation. In his 1402 lament for the dead duke of Milan, composed for Pandolfo Malatesta,[38] the extraordinary praise for the Milanese lord, Giangaleazzo Visconti, was surely seen by Pandolfo as rightly due to the greatest of contemporary Italian princes.

In the lament, the duke is mourned by a great throng of women clad in black, some of them personifying the virtues and weeping for all Italy. Among these are the four sisters, Justice, Fortitude, Prudence, and Temperance, who declare that these virtues have perished with Giangaleazzo. Next we see Faith, Hope, and Charity; the last of these, speaking for all three, emphasizes how much the duke had loved each of them. Then Italy, the most rueful of the ladies, voices her sense of being on an ungoverned boat and of distress over the death of the man who should have been "my dear husband." She is interrupted by the arrival of Mercury, at the head of "two formations of divine shadows." The first, made up of ancient Roman writers, includes Livy, Cicero, and Virgil, all in conversation about the virtues of the dead prince. The second formation brings Mars and an array of generals—Caesar, Alexander, Hannibal, and others—speaking in praise of Giangaleazzo's martial abilities. All finally resolve to let his body lie on earth no longer. Now "The princes of eloquence and war, / Caesar and Alexander on one side, / Virgil and Cicero on the other," take the duke's coffin and bear it up to heaven, not "with lamentations, but with song and pleasure," whereupon, waking from his slumbers, Saviozzo is released from his troubled vision.[39]

In formal terms, there is nothing fresh or innovative about Saviozzo's lament, save that the over-the-top hyperbole looks back to his 1402 "Novella monarchia," with its bold call for a new monarchy and a single state in upper Italy. No other poem just then, in Latin or in the vernacular, speaks out on this theme with the force of "Novella monarchia," even though irony leaps from the eloquence of the plea in coming from a man born and reared in a republican setting, little Siena. His hatred of republican Florence was a natural reaction for an alert citizen of Siena in those years, when Florence, in the midst of its armed resistance to Giangaleazzo's brilliant expansionist policies, sought to implement its self-image as the great fortress of liberty in Tuscany. The truth was that Florentines already thought of Lucca and Siena as expendable republics, provided only that these fell to the rule of Florence and no other state. Since this lesson was not lost on other Tuscans, Saviozzo's hatred of Florence was an appropriate reaction to that republic's contempt for its lesser neighbors. The Florentine conquest of Pisa in 1406 only intensified the fears of Lucca and Siena, already anxious about Florence's purchase of Arezzo in 1384.

Saviozzo did not change his mind about the leading Tuscan republic. In 1409, when King Ladislaus made the count of Urbino his commander in the north, the poet produced a eulogy of the count and his Montefeltro forebears, ending with this message to the king:

> Say [*canzone*] that his new general,
> the count Guidanton da Montefeltro,
> will be his mirror and perhaps the speedy hound
> against the rabid wolves, his neighbors:
> death and destruction of the Florentines![40]

Was Saviozzo the bought lackey of princes and preeminent mercenaries? Not quite. We need a picture of complexity, for the man had too many lights and darks. Politics to one side, his feelings about Florence, given his vagrant mode of life, must in part have been connected with what he had seen in the ordered solidity and self-righteousness of Florentine burghers. They seemed to him to look at life through the entries in their account books. Consequently, he was only too happy to denounce them for their vile treatment, as he saw it, of his beloved Dante.[41] Forced at times, in all likelihood, to beg at the table of his grand captains, he could treasure the proverb "When it is certain, / one shilling is worth a hundred." Not surprisingly, therefore, he issued a stinging verse attack on *gente nuova* (upstarts), whose money alone, in Siena and elsewhere, could seem to lord it over him.[42]

So long as he was in the employment of princes, his published views had to jibe more or less with theirs. His bread and olive oil required this. But with his religious bent, he could also see them for what they were in the age's moral terms of judgment; and this, given his indiscretions, sometimes got him into trouble. He writes in a sonnet to Gian Colonna:

> Let virtue (O bitter feeling) flee the courts,
> fount of malice and of envy,
> inn of iniquity and wretchedness,
> of arrogance and spirits void of reason.[43]

But then he fudges, grants that there are good *signori,* and attributes the "every vice" of courts to the "base servants" of princes. First, however, he had made his declaration.

With his dream of a new monarchy and his choice of King Ladislaus over Florence, Saviozzo (we might expect) would have had doubts about Venice and its republicanism. Not at all. Much taken by it on a visit, he wrote a *canzone* in praise of the city, and many copies soon went into circulation.[44] The poem has his characteristic play of extravagant hyperbole. "O dear to God, O place alone and inn/of the pure gods," he begins. We see a "courteous city,/placed wonderfully in the midst of water." This is Venice, "blessed lady," who offers "an example to our whole way of life" in its civil institutions. "Star" of the Adriatic "and every other sea," "you know all merchandise" and "the whole world honors you." "Just madonna," "merciful," "mother of reason," "perfect holder of the scales of justice," where "virtue is rewarded" and "law and reason rule"—thus is Venice contrasted with the ways of Babylon (a schismatic papacy), barbarians, and tyrants. "Go, song," he concludes, and look for the like, "nobility and great power," in other cities; but as to "liberty" (*libertade*), "this one alone is raised aloft in the world today," so let "people and princes draw example from it."[45]

Saviozzo was no mere apologist for princely rule, then, or at least not this alone. For even if he was courting some kind of favor in Venice, the point is that he could also lend his pen to other ideals and in part subscribe to them. To confirm this, there is his puzzling sonnet for a free city[46]—puzzling because we know nothing about its instigating circumstances; and although it was probably intended for Siena, after the city's 1404 breakaway from Milanese domination, in simple political terms, the sonnet could as well have been for Lucca, or even for Florence but for the fact that it issued from Saviozzo's pen.

> Ah, don't regret the cost and struggles,
> dear citizens of this city,
> to hold on to your liberty:
> look at others who don't have it.[47]

This prosaic start, surprising for Saviozzo, is followed by an invitation to think about what a tyrant is.

He gets all his wishes, the tyrant does:
here he takes, there he kills,
or he gets this man's daughter and that man's wife.

Let it please him, and the thing is done
with no regrets about inflicting grief on others,
and there's no point in saying no when he says yes.

So with a bold face,
never be tired of resisting:
better to die than to be stripped of liberty.[48]

Saviozzo offers this defense of urban freedoms in a flat, humble style, because plain discourse cuts through the rhetoric of grandeur, so common in the pronouncements of tyrants.

Even when he wrote to favor the government of princes, he stressed a range of ethical principles, among them the prince's sense of truth, justice, temperance, charity, courtesy, humility, peace, concord, and love of his "subject people."[49] Although the moral arithmetic here, as in his sonnet for a free city, may strike us as conventional or even trite, it stemmed from classical sources, as well as from his religious preparation, especially the latter.

As to this, the imprint of religion, we shall find it even in his verse of appalling despair. His religious poems include compositions on the Annunciation, the Nativity, the Cross, the Trinity, three to the Virgin Mary, three to God and Christ, one on the seven deadly sins, one prayer for old age, and finally his verse renditions, done probably late in life, of the seven penitential Psalms.[50] In their expression of sorrow for sin and strong desire for pardon, his choice of these Psalms (6, 31, 37, 50, 101, 129, and 142, in the Latin numeration), usually recited during Lent, reveals the troubled Saviozzo himself.

There was a strain of asceticism in his view of man and the world, that optic angle that sees earth's pleasures as something of a bauble (see chap. 3); and this strain became stronger with age.[51] As his powers dimmed, he knew that he should begin assigning less value to the senses, hence to "the world," so as to prepare himself for something more serious. His sonnet "Questa misera vita aspra e serena"[52] is a statement about how we are tricked by pleasure, letting it triumph over reason and virtue, while forgetting our rush toward death over the course of our short years. With so distinct a religious leaning, it is not surprising that

Saviozzo was repelled by the papal schism. In a cutting sonnet likening the papacy both to a whore (with her "lascivious eyes") and to a flower torn from its greenery, he tells it contemptuously to go on "languishing, naked and barefoot among the thorns, / disdained by the world, and poor and haughty."[53]

The religious theme provides a wider entrance to Saviozzo's life and concerns, drawing us closer to his unhappy end. His verse is shot through with moral rumination, very often supported by classical, mythological, and biblical illustration. *Fortuna,* however, that late antique idea so prominent in Boethius and perceived as a major force in the direction of human life, returns repeatedly to haunt Saviozzo's thinking, either to be contested or, more often, to help explain his lot and the lot of others. It puts individual and social life under the sway of obscure, irrational forces. Thus, when he accuses himself and seeks pardon for sin, Saviozzo ignores *fortuna* and accepts his full individual responsibility; but by linking his destructive moods to the dark powers of Dame Fortune, he utilizes a conception that rhymed almost too perfectly with his explosive episodes. In his amatory verse, he occasionally pins unrequited love to the workings of *fortuna,* a commonplace ploy. The "ungrateful whore," however (Saviozzo's epithet), is best seen in a moral *canzone* for Gian Colonna, a bitter lament against King Ladislaus's ingratitude and tricksy refusal to pay the princely *condottiere* all his due or promised moneys.[54] Much of the poem's force gathers round the poet's working of his own resentments and discontent into Colonna's first-person discourse. The exordium cries out against "disdainful Fortuna," seen in the guise of "cruel and hard fates," "evil influences, eternal movements / abhorrent stars and wretched augurs." Glancing at Roman history and his early forebears, Colonna then turns to indict the avarice and ingratitude of the age, with its reign of robbery, cruelty, and deceit.[55] Inadvertently, Saviozzo glides from the blameless Colonna, the victim of unjust *fortuna,* to the culpable others and the culpability of the age, in a contradictory and self-serving use of the whole idea of *fortuna.* After all, why were other people and the age itself not also subject to that inscrutable power? We are seeing, if somewhat indirectly, that the poet's own life was a flux of contradictory feeling.

SUICIDE

Saviozzo issued four or five poems of forthright homoerotic love and two others of an ambiguous cast.[56] For a long time, in the course of this inquiry, I entertained the possibility that a homosexual affair had led to his final arrest and that this had plunged him into disgrace, driving him to suicide. The record, however, will not support this interpretation. For one thing, the bulk of his amatory verse is about heterosexual love. For another, homosexual practice at the princely courts was seldom prosecuted.[57] Moreover, the ranks of the great mercenaries, teeming with men from all walks of life, saw and tolerated every manner of taste. So if our poet took an occasional fancy to a good-looking youth at court or in the field, the matter would have caused little scandal, all the less so in a man who left Siena without a wife,[58] who was subject to moods of keen alienation and loneliness, and whose sexual liaisons were likely to have been mainly with prostitutes. Generally speaking, the wives and daughters of colleagues at court or in the chancellery, and the whole array of noblewomen, would have been inaccessible sexually.[59] This means, as we shall see, that some mystery attaches to his love poetry.

We are forced to conclude that Saviozzo's last arrest and criminal doings, if this they were, concerned something more serious, although he never says what in the pertinent poems. Was his a case, for example, of theft, secretarial forgery, or even a kind of *lesa maiestas,* as in calumny of his overlord or in betraying secrets? Men like Tartaglia da Lavello, Gian Colonna, Muzio Attendolo, and others of their sort were petty despots with microstates; and servitors like Saviozzo, though ranking as important officials, were often short of cash, with payment of their stipends sometimes chronically in arrears.[60] What is more, aside from the ultimate violence to himself—and it was also psychological, as his poetry reveals[61]—we should bear in mind that he was a main actor in at least a half dozen other dramatic episodes, in one of them as victim. There was the clubbing incident, the knifing, three other arrests (two of them for alleged capital crimes), and a robbery in the Florentine mountains sometime in the 1390s or the first years of the new century, in which he himself was the victim, having been set upon and robbed by a band of "scoundrels" in the service of the mercenary captain Andreino Ubertini.[62] Right after the robbery, he made straight for Florence, where he identified his assailants and spent several months pressing the Signoria to recover the booty. Meanwhile, to offer him consolation, he tells us, *Amore* stepped in and made him fall in love with a beautiful young woman whom he saw in the streets of Florence. Whether or not this was true, he now produced the poem "Among the handsome loggias and great palazzi/of the city of flowers."[63] We are not sure that his claim against Ubertini's men was successful; but if it failed, since the thieves had stripped him, his animus against Florentines would have held fast.

Fortuna and his religious faith always returned to help or to foil him. To the latter he could turn for solace, or turn it against himself in censure and self-loathing; the former, as we have seen, he could use either against himself or others, depending upon his need and mood. In four melancholy meditations on *fortuna,* each in sonnet form, we find him accepting its role in his life, regretting and resenting it, and then delivering himself over in spirit to its most noxious possibilities.[64] He could be a man of extreme and volatile reactions.

The drama of unrequited love may now be added to religion and *fortuna.*[65] These were the zones of experience and reflection that made for his blackest moments. I have suggested that his loves were mysterious not only because we know almost nothing about them individually, a characteristic of the love verse of the age, but also and especially because reputable women in his milieu were not normally available for amatory dalliance. At once ascetic and a pleasure-lover, a sociable man who could yet be desperately lonely, Saviozzo no doubt turned to prostitutes, homosexual love, widows, or swift adulteries of the sort in which the married women involved soon turned against him in fear of scandal, loss of dowry and property, physical injury, or death itself. But whatever the nature of his loves—hence the mystery—Saviozzo's way was for deep involvement, in contrast to other Renaissance poets, for whom love, as voiced in verse, was more often and more nearly the striking of a social stance and a self-definition (see chap. 4). His about-face against love, therefore, could be vehement enough to carry him toward the desolation of his suicide poems.

In his farewell to the world, love, and women, "Addio chi sta, ch'io me ne vo cantando,"[66] he chooses Christ and Mary over *fortuna* and earthly pleasure, leaving usury to merchants, simony to priests, pomp and arrogance to those who never think that they must die, and vain delights to lovers and idiots. To elegant and lovely women (*donne liggiadre*) he leaves a mode of "blind desire" (*un voler cieco*), inconstancy (hadn't he been abandoned?), pride, hypocrisy (of course), simple-minded religious credulity (*pinzocarie*), easy weeping, tormented lovers, little faith, greed, and malicious gossip. Saviozzo's bitterness fairly pours forth. It is even more fierce in the *Canzon quarta,*[67] where love—here called "carnal love"—is impugned as "the enemy of God, virtue, and grace." However, a third invective against love, commencing "Cerbero in-voco," must rank with the more moving palinodes of the age:

> Cerberus I invoke and his cruel barking:
> may he draw my base arts to himself
> and make my verses darkly howl.[68]

Here the poet wants to die rather than be without the face of his beloved, the one he takes to be "every law and good custom" for himself. In ruin and black sorrow, he is ready to live in caves like a wild animal; he warns young men against love, glosses over a gallery of star-crossed lovers in classical mythology, and while still hoping for peace from "my lord" (the beloved), he sees himself as "an enemy to fate, fortune, and destiny," and rails against "this false Love," which "kills the body and soul," sending the lover "to hell."

The darkness and anguish of love also appear, even more movingly, in his narrative of "a girl betrayed and deceived by her lover."[69] Here he seems able to project his own rue and despondency into the figure of the wretched girl, thus intensifying the poem's impact.

Before turning to his most anguished poems, I want to cast a glance at a few other matters, the better to close in on his final days. In his office as secretary and sometime emissary to a sequence of leading mercenaries, men frequently on the move, Saviozzo traveled through much of Italy—to the Apulian coast, Perugia, Rome, Florence, Imola, Rimini, Venice, Bologna, Pisa, Cremona, and parts of the Florentine mountains. His poems or captions refer to all of these; but he certainly visited many other towns and cities as well. These travels, his facility with words and quickness of perception, a long familiarity with petty princes, the parvenu and actor in himself, and an acquired haughtiness all led him to regard the common people (*il vulgo*) with an air of superiority. Part of the socio-mental baggage of most humanists and men of letters of the time, this attitude also surfaces in Saviozzo's love poetry, where "the common herd" functions as a foil for the lover, love, and nobility.[70] In the poem on "my ignorance and ingratitude and the brutish *vulgo*,"[71] he skewers "the great vile populace" (*il gran vulgaccio*), who stand around like goats, eyes turning and ears raised, stupefied by the heat of summer; or, marveling and with open mouths, as though releasing sparrows, they listen to the prating, sermons, and superstitions of imbecile friars. Still in his youth, or nearly so (lines 42–44), he also turns to rebuke himself for his own laziness and ignorance, for charging "the fates" with his own failures, and for his vanity about being known to the *vulgo bestiale.* This autocritique is both prayer and resolution, as he urges himself to seek wisdom, to study philosophy and theology, to beware of God's wrath, and to live by the ideals of constancy, humility, chastity, abstinence, obedience, and solicitude: in short, the very virtues that he most lacked, in view of his pride, fickleness, lust, and unruly outbursts. The poem passes from dark humor to solemnity, and once more, as in so much of his poetry, we encounter a marked religious penchant and a streak of asceticism. Here was the wellspring of his guilt, of the nagging sense that he was living a basely sensual life, and of his need to accuse himself, to feel contrition, to have absolution, and to make things right with God.

But what about the worldly man? For he was this too, a love poet, a votary of earthly delights, of the pleasures of the flesh whether "straight" or "sodomitical." The invitation to be a worldling was in his circumstances, as an official in small courts, where his lords were leading soldiers in an age of prepotent mercenary armies. Ranging in numbers of up to four thousand or five thousand mounted men and foot soldiers, these armies often burned, looted, and raped at will in the vast rural expanses outside the large cities, and not seldom they lived best by holding whole towns and villages to ransom.[72] So we may assert that Saviozzo lived with (and from) some of the worst of men. On top of this, the friars and priests at the courts or in the military entourages of his employers offered no sufficient guidance, no ritual strategies compelling enough, to bring *him* peace. Instead, he rather despised their ignorance and vanity. The petty court might offer instant pleasures, but nothing long-lived, to an unquiet spirit like Saviozzo's. Nor did his itinerant contacts as poet and chancellor bring enduring friendships, for he seems to have died without a friend to raise a hand in his defense. And though his verse hints at occasional amities, it nowhere reveals the traces of real friendships.

The record outside his poetry is mute about his pitching into moments of grievous anxiety; but if he suffered episodes of severe depression, on a few occasions at least, before plummeting, he managed to write while still in perfect control of his medium, absolutely determined to make a searing statement of his condition. By using art, as it were, to achieve expiation and salvation, he broke out of the bonds of his immediate circumstances, thus pitting poetry and prayer against history. His relief had to be temporary, but yet somehow complete and transcendent in the act itself of writing.

Saviozzo's three poems of despair are driven by a nearly raging desire for death. They have moments that seem to tilt toward madness, but only one of the three is stripped of all hope. The least despairing of these poems has two captions in the key manuscripts, one claiming that the poet wrote it shortly before his death, the other adding that he was in prison at the time:

> Io non so che si sia, ombra o disgrazia,
> che mi s'avvolge intorno de la mente,
> tal che tutta è disforme a quel ch'll'era.
>
> (I know not whether shadow or disgrace
> wraps itself around my mind,
> now all out of line, not as it was.)[73]

This self-knowing start soon becomes a confession. We are told that he has been all but turned into "a wild beast"—shiftless, hating life, bereft of reason, and despising what he ought to love, that is, knowledge and the intellect. What his "insanity" is (*l'insania mia*) he does not know, as he runs towards the "sunset" (death), without "thought, order, and measure," "loaded with oblivion" and "a monster to the world." Mired in "muck," in vile passions and sloth, he craves death (*la morte chieggio*). For a moment he remembers his name and fame; but what's the good of being "known to the few and to the populace" (lines 58–60), when, for all God's proffered good,

> I never knew Him, nor [his] grace:
> always sensuality, always sin
> battered down duty, always was I deficient. (lines 77–79)

He closes with a direct prayer to God: you who, "made into flesh in the virginal cloister,/then opened heaven with your blood." And what he calls for in the final verse is "mercy, not justice" (lines 92–94, 102).

A second poem, also ending with a cry for help, cuts into a deeper despondency.[74] The caption reads, "Capitolo in which he curses all created things and finally, in guilt, offers himself to God." Cast in Dante's *terza rima* form, the poem has twenty-seven tercets with an extra verse at the end, closing the rhyme scheme—all carefully wrought. With a cold fury pushing through every line, up to the final triplets, the poem opens by damning the heavens, humanity, poetry, and learning.

Corpi celesti e tutte l'altre stelle,
sette pianeti, tutti i cieli e' segni
sian maladetti e le lor posse felle!
E ciascuno alimento sì si spegni
maladicendo la natura umana
e te, Fortuna, che sì falsa regni!
E maladetta sia quella fontana
di poësia e ciascuna scïenza
e ciò che più da loro omai s'intana! (lines 1–9)

(Heavenly bodies and all the other stars,/the seven planets, all the skies, their traces/and their evil powers be cursed!/And every element thus undo itself,/damning human nature/and you, Fortuna, who so fraudulently reigns!/And cursed also be that fount of poetry and every science/and all that most resides there!)

Saviozzo proceeds to lay a curse on the cardinal virtues, on trees, fruits, grass, "stones, words, and everything." For the first eight tercets, each malediction is brought forth as though meant for a factual list. He wants the heavens and paradise to plunge back into darkness forevermore, and Satan, "that fury," to rise up again to "the lofty seats and lord it over all," for—and now the poem lurches into the personal—"I am so purged of every good," sunken in such impossible sadness, "that many times a day I call for death" (lines 24, 28). A cascade of curses follows: on "the first heirs" (Adam and Eve), the first seed, marriage, Saviozzo's parents, all their wedding preparations and festivities, their sexual coupling, the seed ("that wicked little beast") that produced him, "the hole" (*tana*) that held it, the gore, the nine months of pregnancy, all his mother's labor, his swaddling bands, the milk he sucked, and his baptism, confirmation, and first friends.

> Anyone who ever said anything worthy to me
> be crucified in the eternal fires.

> (Chi mai mi disse un motto di valore
> sia crucïato nell'eterno foco). (lines 70–71)

All at once, again, Saviozzo does an about-face. With a warning to the reader to beware of his (the poet's) deadly game, he flags his dreadful distress and ends by invoking God:

Now, for all my pain or evil,
I call on Him for help,
surrendering in guilt for all my vices,
and mercy move him to my pardon. (lines 79–82)

The poem's rush of cruel malediction is calculated to offend by turning all established value upside down; but its real work is to keep Saviozzo focused, to hold him together in the midst of his furious reality, as he strives to transmute the horror. As for the concluding appeal to God, it is too summary and hurried to have more than a feeling of scant conviction. All the art has gone into the catalog of cursing, into controlling the malady.

His most famous poem, "Le 'nfastidite labbra," a *canzone* of overwhelming woe and anger, comes down to us in at least forty-five manuscripts, but hundreds of copies of it would have been made in the fifteenth and sixteenth centuries.[75] There are two conflicting captions for the poem, neither of which seems entirely correct. One states that Saviozzo wrote "the following malediction" after his "expulsion" from Siena for political reasons; the other, noting that he was chancellor to the count of Urbino, claims that he wrote it in prison and then "unhappily killed himself with a knife." Whether or not he was ever a paid servitor to the count of Urbino is a moot, though possible, claim; and if we date the poem around the time of his suicidal depression (1419), then it cannot be taken back to 1401–2, when, conceivably, he was expelled from Siena on political grounds.

Standing on the brink of hell—in his own mind at any rate—Saviozzo opens the poem, remarkably, with a bitter farewell to love:

> The loathsome lips that once I used to speak
> a thousand sweet and lovely things, and opened up
> and closed as Venus so desired,
> now with other powers, with other verses,
> mixed with anguished tears,
> here must sing their woes!

> (Le 'nfastidite labbra in ch'io già pose
> mille vaghe dolcezze, e quelle apersi
> sì come Citarea volse e serrai,
> con altri ingegni omai, con altri versi,
> mischiati con le lagrime angosciose,
> qui si convien che cantino i lor lai!) (lines 1–6)

Summoning "the eternal Furies" and selecting "Erito" (Erichtho), a Thessalian enchantress, he begs her to help him enter the underworld. Clearly he belongs there, as he cries out, "Be damned the seed" and the man who put it into "the demonic womb in which I lay" under God's malediction.

> O corrupted genitals horrid and vain,
> why did you not close up in pain,
> so that I'd have died with you?
> Or at least, once I was out,
> why was I not deformed or torn apart,
> and my heart then given to dogs to eat?
> Damned be the light and brightness
> that first ever reached my eyes.[76]

If only he could tear at his father with his own teeth, he wails, and then slides into a call for universal destruction. He wants the whole world at war, an end to the heavens, God's merciless and shrieking wrath, rivers rushing with blood, the dying of the grass, the cleaving of the earth by a great serpent and its poison, and derision of the papacy (lines 34–48).

A new stanza follows, and he rounds on himself with a list of evils:

> All my days be turned to a dark mist,
> running ever unnumbered into months and years,
> my nights be dark with grieving,
> and the hours counted in my woe. (lines 49–52)

Since his soul already belongs to the devil, and he can be subjected to nothing worse, a fierce logic moves him to implore death and again the Furies. In his cold frenzy, he pictures hell, where he shall be received into a crowd "of illustrious men," become food for wild beasts, suffer being endlessly torn apart and remade again, but be burned to cinders too: all this he longs for, "only let me be rid of this life!" (lines 65–80)

In the penultimate stanza, continuing his purposeful reversals, he sees death as a relief from the threat of death, such as in a sentence of execution; and he hankers for this release so as to have his eternal punishments, since his soul, in any case, is already the devil's "by supernal and divine law."

"Song," he ends, go look for Scylla and Charybdis, where hurricanes bellow, splitting the sea open, then on to the fires of Mongibello, and next out "among the evil stars."

> To the most desperate and wretched
> souls shall you speak: weep and sigh
> and say that soon will I join them,
> for God is against me and the world in wrath! (lines 103–6)

Saviozzo could not fail to know that in religious teaching then, deep and sincere contrition made salvation possible and even likely. In "Le 'nfastidite labbra," however, he rejects this knowledge; he craves not only death but also everlasting hell.

Was this infernal desire the mark of a breakdown in a religious Tuscan of the early Renaissance? The mark of a man disturbed in so finite a way that it could only belong to the said time and place? What were the sins exactly that had put his soul, as he saw it, utterly beyond rescue? He never says. His maledictions are specific, but his reported sins are general; hence we cannot securely anchor his shattering distress. Yet there is a hint in the poem's thematic structure. For the first line starts off at once with a despairing tribute to love, and the poet then returns to the theme in the final full stanza, just before the conventional dispatching of the "song," in the vivid image of the hellishly boiling Mongibello (Mount Etna): symbol, in Quattrocento verse, of the vain torments of love and the insane fires of passion.[77] In fact, this direction is not surprising, because he had often accused himself of sensuality, by which he did not mean an excess of zeal for food and song. The land of Eros, then, seems to have been the zone of his besetting sin. Once at least, in his younger days, he had credited the powers of love with all his talents and force of imagination.[78]

Nowhere in Saviozzo's verse is there a reference to a wife or children, however fleetingly so; to loves, yes, often and directly, but never by name. Although such reticence was customary in the poetic practice of the age, the Sienese poet often drew his life into his art, just as Antonio Beccari and Francesco di Vannozzo had done, Petrarch too, and as so many others were doing. Accordingly, in the poems of malediction, if a wife or a family had ever been close to him, he would have laid a curse on them. Nothing he loved, or that loved him, was spared. The absence of any such venom points, obliquely to be sure, to his isolation. This, then, of all conditions, leads us back to the life of the itinerant little courts of the great mercenaries. Here Saviozzo's modest origins, leavened by his literary skills and quick spirit, would have given him a slippery or even changing social status. Muzio Attendolo, it is true, sprang directly from peasant stock, but he had turned himself into a great lord by sheer military genius: he commanded armies of men. Saviozzo, instead, remained a talented clerk and servant; and in those coarse and cruel courts, he was seldom, if ever, to find any deep satisfaction or anything lasting. He could make his peace with those often lawless, proud, and brutal men; but could they make theirs with him? Too clever by half, too fast with words, and too indiscreet, he must have ended in their jails more times than we know. The isolation that gathered round him as he grew older—worldly young men sometimes laughed at him[79]—was deepened with each arrest: the alienation in his mind was matched by his physical imprisonment. No wonder, then, that his need of God was fierce; and no wonder, too, that in his terrible depressions, his orisons somersaulted into demonic litanies. He was desperate to pray, but the prayers turned into black hymns.

Across the centuries, many readers have found him curiously appealing.

SIX

ALIENATION

The Outsider as Poet

A MATERIAL LIFE

Born in the stormy twelfth-century commune, political exile held a place on the proscenium of politics down to the sixteenth century, when cardinals refused now and then to return to papal Rome, fearing for their lives, and Florentine republicans, seeking refuge abroad, lived in fear of assassination. These are well-known matters, to be sure. Power politics in Italy was a game in which the losers paid with their lives, goods, or exile, often a "voluntary" exile imposed by the dangers back home.

But what about the political loser and outcast who managed to survive and remain at home, not really in the scene and yet not out: suspect, stripped of the honors of public office, foiled in his efforts to arrange judicious marriages, the prey of partisan taxation, and vulnerable in law courts where justice was not seldom suborned? Here, indeed, was an internal or psychological exile—angry, bitter, resentful, in a word, alienated.

In Francesco d'Altobianco degli Alberti, cousin and close friend to the great Leon Battista, we have the exhibit of such a man.[1] Banker and landowner, poet, moralist, and exile, he was born in the first year of the fifteenth century to one of the most important of all Florentine families, political grandees and bankers with international firms and contacts.[2] Francesco's maternal grandfather, Rinaldo Gianfigliazzi, was possibly the most exciting speaker in the Florentine political councils of the day: "His true eloquence made him worthy of being called *il gallo.*"[3] So we may assert that in the years around 1400, no one in Florence—Albizzi, Medici, Strozzi, or any other—came from a household that was more political than his. Yet the world around this house was riven by faction, with the result, unsurprisingly, that in the very year of Francesco's birth (1401), his father, Altobianco, was banished from Florence, along with other members of the Alberti clan, all accused of having plotted against the ruling clique. When Altobianco died in exile in 1417, he was a banker in France; therefore Francesco, also in exile and bred to the business of banking, now inherited a large fortune. A decade later, using their lofty connections, the Alberti got Pope Martin V to intervene for them in Florence, and in 1428 all political charges against the family were at last dropped.

Already listed in the famous Florentine tax census of 1427, the *Catasto,* and one of Florence's richest citizens, with net assets of nearly 11,000 gold florins,[4] Francesco submitted a second tax return early in 1431, though at that point he was still a busy banker in Rome. And here again he declared assets of thousands of florins in houses and farmland, in addition to about 5,000 florins of negotiable shares in diverse public funds, the *Monte comune.*[5] Observing that he was a partner in a Roman bank, really to raise funds for his Florentine tax levies, he claimed that his profits from this enterprise did not suffice to pay for even half his taxes in a single year. In that year too (1431), returning to Florence to serve as one of the "Officials of the Bank," he was forced to lend this magistracy more than 3,700 florins; and in 1434 the office still owed him and his Roman company about 6,500 florins in borrowed moneys.[6] Astonishingly, then, eight years later his tax returns of 1442 are little more than the chart of a near-total catastrophe.[7] Over the previous five years, he had seen twenty-four family farms (*poderi*), twenty-seven land parcels (*pezzi di terra*), more than twenty houses, a large mill, and thousands of florins of Monte shares confiscated, distrained, or simply put up for sale, all brought about by the demands of debt and personal taxes.

What had happened? In brief, the big Alberti bank in Rome, together with its closely linked branches, had failed between 1434 and 1436; but largely ignoring this and calling ruthlessly on estimates of Alberti capital before their financial collapse, the early Medicean oligarchy continued to levy huge taxes, in the form of compulsory loans, on Francesco and other family members.

In his returns of 1442, Francesco confesses:

I am in debt for many thousands of florins to the commune, to others, and [because of] lawsuits (lodi e sentenzie) . . . I lost all my household effects to the officials [of the fisc]. They stripped me of my safe-conduct (rupponmi il bullettino), which was my final undoing, as all the people of Florence know . . . And I could show you more, down to the last silver coin (grosso): Monte moneys, jewels, silver, and all my other possessions, all gone in cash [to the commune] and to my creditors . . . Hoping for the best, I commend myself to your reverences [the tax officials], so that, given the truth of things, it may please you this once to release me from the chains [my house asylum] in which I've now been for eleven years or more (che chonsiderato il vero, vi piaccia una volta trarmi di chatena, dove sono stato già anni xi o più).[8]

In effect, as from about 1430, as we know from a stream of other sources, this is what it meant in Florence to be at once rich and without reliable, powerful friends.[9] On returning to their native city after years of exile, the Alberti clan got no warm welcome in high government circles; and although Francesco sat in the major emergency council (*balìa*) of 1434,[10] the "honor" seems to have done him little good. The Alberti were never again to shine in politics.

Regarded as enemies by the ruling group in Florence, they were consistently rated among the city's heaviest taxpayers throughout the period of their exile; and in 1415 Altobianco's branch of the house was forced to raise some fifteen thousand florins on the sale of farmland and other properties, solely "to pay taxes."[11] Yet 1428 and the retrieval of their political "clean hands" brought no respite.

Spanning the forty-two years from 1427 to 1469, Francesco's tax returns gradually reveal that in about 1430 he and other members of the lineage involved themselves in a banking *compagnia* directed by two older Alberti cousins, Benedetto di Bernardo and Lionardo di Nerozzo. Set up, in the usual fashion, to take deposits and make large loans, the partnership quickly became one of the biggest banking operations in Europe, with the main office in Rome and branches in Bruges, London, and Cologne.[12] At some point, then, house and branch heads made a number of large but risky loans; and when news was leaked that their big borrowers had defaulted, depositors closed in on the Alberti partners in 1435–36, driving them into bankruptcy and years of litigation in Florence's top court for commercial lawsuits, the

Tribunale di Mercanzia.[13] All the Alberti partners, including Francesco, were now suddenly liable as individuals for the moneys due to their depositors, and a process of seizing their personal assets was set in motion. In 1442 Antonio di Ricciardo degli Alberti, for one, claimed to owe thirty thousand florins in taxes and to creditors. "I find," he concluded, that "I have lost my livelihood and possessions and honor."[14]

Down to the mid-1430s, Francesco had lucrative rents from a diversity of houses in Florence and elsewhere in Florentine territory, including two large palazzi on "the street of the Alberti" (now via de' Benci), and from properties and farms not only just outside the city on the Ripoli Plain but also in and around Empoli, Poggibonsi, Legnaia, and Staggia. It was land that brought in wheat, wine, oil, barley, beans, millet, nuts, figs, poultry, eggs, pork, saffron, and firewood. His returns of 1433 already hint at the dangers of big banking partnerships and the legal frailty of some of the assets assigned to him by fiscal officials; for of the more than twenty thousand florins in titular Monte shares listed in his name, about two-thirds, he insisted, were the property of the Alberti bank in Rome, of Benedetto di Bernardo, and of Benedetto's daughter Masa [Tommasa]. Some of the shares, for instance, originally held by members of the Tornabuoni, Castellani, Torrigiani, and Allegri families, had been transferred to Francesco's name, although this was done in partial repayment of loans that had been made to them by the bank.[15] Here, apparently, Florentine tax inspectors chose to recognize an essential element both of collective ownership and of individual responsibility. Later on, the same assumption was made by big creditors of the Roman bank—men as far away as Bruges, important clerics in the papal court, and Florentine citizens from the Santa Croce quarter itself, the larger neighborhood base of the grand Alberti lineage. Consequently, right through the late 1430s and early 1440s, Francesco's properties, once an integral part of his personal patrimony, were alienated bit by bit to satisfy the claims of bank depositors and of the ravenous Florentine fisc. By 1442, with at least five mouths to feed, not to mention the continuing duress of creditors and taxes, he had seen his yearly income shrink to 143 florins, which in those years, let it be noted, amounted to about half the cost of a wedding dress for a girl of his social class![16] Such a sum for such a man could only have shadowed a frightening and melancholy prospect. Hence all too appropriate here is his little "ballad":

Spacciati, vaten via, Malinconia,
fa' ch'io non ti ci truovi; altrove allogia

. . . .

Vatti con Dio, che lui ti dia il malanno.[17]

(Be off, go away, Melancholy; let me not find you here; go lodge somewhere else . . . Go with God, and may He strike you with calamity.)

It would be fair to say that Francesco never untangled his financial affairs,
nor did he ever get them onto a sound footing. Lawsuits and tax inspectors
would not go away.

His inventory of properties and income for the tax census of 1451 shows,
surprisingly, a net yearly income of 385 florins! But this estimate was set by
the inspectors and turns out to be a cavalier glissade over some disturbing
liabilities.[18] For one thing, the two old family palazzi on the via degli Alberti
were in hock (*pegno*)—mortgaged, in our terms—for 1,700 florins; and Francesco could only raise this sum, he claimed, by putting "del più vivo capitale"
(his best properties) up for sale, which at that point, at least, he was loath to
do. Again, the rents on two large houses were blocked by debt to the lessees
proper. And finally, though it was a generous windfall, a large legacy from a
favorite cousin who was killed in a joust in Florence in 1447 had come to
him, inevitably, with a load of taxes to pay.[19] But the indisputable proof of the
continuing financial squeeze on Francesco, then and through the 1450s,
appears in his tax *portata* of 1458, with its inventory of properties alienated
since 1450:[20]

1. 1450: a small farm (sold for 150 florins)
2. 1451: three houses and a large farm (for 1250 florins)
3. 1455: a farm and a house (for 162 florins)
4. 1456: a farm, a large house, and two workshops (730 florins)
5. 1458: three farms and diverse land parcels (1,150 florins).

We pass to his final set of tax returns, submitted in 1469, which clinch the
evidence of inexorable loss. The mortgaged Alberti palaces on the via degli
Alberti were finally sold just after 1458, in a continual hemorrhage, as shown
above, confirmed first by the sale of two large farms in 1460 and, sometime
thereafter, a third farm, including nine other land parcels and bits of wood-

land. By 1469 the value of Francesco's net assets had dropped to their nadir: a mere 780 florins, not counting of course—in accord with Florentine tax practice—the house he resided in on the via degli Alberti.[21] And a big part of this, as it happens, was pure luck, for his largest remaining property, a good-sized farm with a "gentleman's house" (*casa da signore*), located in the Ripoli outskirts of the city (Alberti country) and having a gross value of 671 florins, had been willed to him not long since by a cousin, Simone Alberti.

The capsizing of the last Alberti bank, which had been organized along international lines, is a story still locked away in the rich records of the Tribunale di Mercanzia and awaits its business historian.[22] We know enough about our man himself, however, to draw several provisional conclusions: (1) He did everything possible to avoid being arrested and declared a personal *cessante* (bankrupt), because this would have landed him in debtor's prison, possibly for years, and peeled the very shirt off his back. (2) When in about 1437 his official freedom of movement was more starkly restricted and he faced the constant danger of a sudden arrest,[23] he drew on the right of asylum against debt by remaining at home, and for more than ten years, certain holidays excepted, he was largely a prisoner in his own house. (3) Until the 1450s he was plagued by lawsuits, some of the plaintiffs, but not all, running their claims back to the bank crash of the mid 1430s; hence the pursuit of creditors was unrelenting. (4) Throughout his adult life and down at least to 1469, his property and income taxes in Florence, levied mainly as forced loans and often verging on confiscatory practice, were at least in part the fruit of politics, or he would have had no need, time and time again, to sell houses and farmland to meet his fiscal obligations. Appropriately, Lorenzo de' Medici once confessed that unless rich men in Florence had the oligarchy on their side, life and affairs could go badly for them.[24]

When I turn to a discussion of Francesco's poetry, we shall see these cruel matters transmuted into anger, allegory, prayer, and a horizon of dark menace. What is more, there seemed to be no manner of institutional deliverance: he could not even escape the Church and its courts. For on 30 May 1454 he was excommunicated, following the verdict of a papal court in Rome, the Camera Apostolica, for having failed to pay 125 florins to Pietro Paolo Mercatello and 34 ducats, also in gold, to Filippo di Tommaso Argenti.[25] Calling on a well-known ritual of symbolic action, the ceremony took place in the Florence cathedral itself, immediately after a particular Mass. Read out to all those in attendance, the anathema was followed by the ringing of a bell, the lighting and sudden putting out of a candle thrust into the ground, and the raising of a cross, all in sign of the debtor's enforced separation from the Church. The sentence was also published in other Florentine churches. From that moment on, Francesco was denied all sacraments, could enter no church, and all people, at least in theory, were forbidden to hold any ordinary civil communication with him until he paid the delinquent sums and the anathema was removed. Since Mercatello was identified as an heir, his plaint harked back, I believe, to the demise of the Alberti bank; and it is likely that Francesco's 1455 sale of a house and farm was imposed both by the shaming social pressures of the excommunication and his religious fears.

Harassed for years by creditors as well as by a hectoring fiscal bureaucracy, and for more than a decade a prisoner in his own home, can Francesco—a family man, as it happens—have been an easy household companion? Let us consider an array of mostly new facts.

Married in 1432 to Nanina/Nanna (actually Giovanna) di Bernardo de' Bardi, when the girl was not yet fifteen years old, he eventually had at least five sons, but not a single one by Nanina. In fact, when the well-dowered girl, crossing over the river from the distinguished Bardi enclave, first entered her spouse's house, she found two of his illegitimate sons already there: Giovanni, born to a certain Monetta near Avignon in 1421, and Niccolò, born in Rome to a different mother late in 1430. Lanzalao (Lancelot), another son, had already seen the light of day, also in Rome, in 1429. His mother was a certain Tita, and he joined Francesco's household sometime after 1433. A fourth son and member of the family, Troilo (Troilus), was eight months old in August of 1442, and he too was born out of wedlock. In the record's frank words, the last "little bastard," Piero, not born until 1450, was Francesco's son by Marta, his slave, who is listed in his 1458 tax returns not among the family members (*bocche*), but rather under material possessions (*sustanze*), in a column that also includes a mule, a ram, and sixteen sheep. Here, suddenly, as so often in his verse, Francesco's ironic humor bounds forth: he notes that he sometimes mounts the mule, "playing the down-at-heel gentleman" (il fo gentiluomo di pocho pregio), and adds at once that his slave "called Marta, more than accustomed [to it], would happily serve me in the same fashion" (più ch'avezzata . . . ben volentieri mi serviss' ella).[26]

Indeed, his "carnal" life was not yet by any means over, for after Nanina's death in 1461, he took another wife, monna Andrea, as we discover in his returns of 1469.[27] We also find that Andrea was forty years younger than her husband and not averse to sharing the house with his son Giovanni, now age forty-seven (but said to be forty-four) and still called a "bastardo" by the ever watchful tax inspectors. The epithet meant that Francesco was denied the right to slash his net assets by two hundred florins, the happy deduction normally allowed for each of the family's legal "mouths."

These bare facts would breathe life into a novelist, but they belong, alas, to a different kind of story here.

White female slaves were not a rarity in Florence, nor was the welcome extended to a father's *bastardini,* who were not seldom brought up with the household's legitimate children. In 1427 the city had 130 slaves of childbearing age (thirteen to forty-two) who could produce, it has been calculated, up to one hundred children per year.[28] So far, therefore, Francesco's sexual conduct rather belonged to the ways of upper-class men in Florence. He was certainly not ashamed of his children; and if he had any illegitimate daughters by a slave or by servants, it is likely that he either dispatched them into the far countryside with a small dowry or had them put out to a foundling hospital, in keeping with the misogynous (and economic) practice of the day.[29] What is unusual is the number of his sons. In this respect he had gone over the top: he was not, after all, a Visconti or a Malatesta prince, although the Neapolitan humanist Panormita once observed that Francesco had lived splendidly in Rome—the life, it seems, of a stylish aristocrat.

So our man took his bastards in and gave them a home; and Nanina, once she saw herself unable to have children, made her peace with a force majeure. But never once in the corpus of his verse does Francesco allude to Nanina, his sons, monna Andrea, or his slave. These "familiars" did not enter into the transmogrified world of his literary imaginings. His masculinity did; so, too, did his "higher" fears and angers, as well as his keen interest in (other) women, God, and politics. Lots of questions regarding his illustrious social identity also course through his verse—questions of wealth, name, honor, shame, humiliation, possessiveness, self-knowledge, willpower, ideals, powerlessness, and sinister legal doings; but not domestic life, not Niccolò and "Troilus," who possibly died in childhood; and above all not Giovanni, who, like so many Alberti children and grandchildren of that generation, seems to have grown up without a trade or a proper start in business;[30] and not "Lancelot," who was executed in Florence in 1463 in a tangle of mystery.[31] How best to put it? In a classical set of Florentine *ricordanze,* entries in a family logbook, Francesco would have touched on most of these matters. But family and household concerns, however grievous, did not belong in his poetry, because this was a place, even when touched with humor, for coming to terms with his "higher" self and his moral knowledge of the world. In the society of Renaissance Italy, a man like him—a bourgeois aristocrat born and bred—could draw all his troubles into a preoccupation with what he was and the way he saw himself.

With his dense web of family connections and early wealth, once Francesco settled in Florence, he came to know "everybody," most notably, of course, the men from historical lineages such as the Ricasoli, Bardi, Baroncelli, Peruzzi, Castellani, Rucellai, and others.[32] Here was his natural social world; and he certainly knew the mainline Medici—Cosimo; Piero; Piero's wife, Lucrezia Tornabuoni; Piero's brother; and Lorenzo the Magnificent.[33] In fact, in 1459 Piero ("the Gouty") appears to have given him a hand in a lawsuit.[34] And when Francesco died in 1479, the news was conveyed in a personal letter to Lorenzo's mother,[35] herself a writer of religious verse. Outside this circle, our ex-banker counted the poets Burchiello, Antonio di Guido, and Scambrilla among his friends;[36] but he must also have known the Pulci brothers, Mariotto Davanzati, Feo Belcari, and Michele del Giogante.

In his own day, some of Francesco's poems already circulated among Florentine cognoscenti, and a few were at once included in collections drawn up by Giovanni Pigli, Giogante, Antonio di Meglio, and others.[37] When the great Alberti bank crashed in 1435–36 and the news raced through Florence's luxury shops, the Mercato Vecchio no doubt resounded with stories of the debacle, particularly around the tables and stalls of the big bankers and drapers. Then afterward, sooner or later, news of the family's gradual but systematic despoliation also reached all ears: this was the way of Italian Renaissance cities (see chaps. 7–9). In 1442, therefore, Francesco was merely stating a fact when he claimed that it was "known to all the people of Florence" that a special permit, safe-guarding his right to move freely through the city, had been "torn away" from him, with the result, as all Florence also knew, that creditors and tax officials could henceforth have warrants issued for his arrest. And what of his dreadful disgrace in 1454, when by bell, snuffed candle, and raised cross he had been publicly excommunicated in the cathedral? No wonder he charged his verse with dark doings.

Yet Francesco never lost his humor, though it turned caustic; and he inspired strong loyalties in friends and family. Two cousins made him heir to their ample patrimonies and the great Leon Battista dedicated book 3 of *Della famiglia* to him. As late as 1465, he and monna Andrea occasionally regaled friends with excellent fare and first-class company, as reported in a letter to Lorenzo de' Medici, written by the young humanist and budding oligarch Bernardo Rucellai. He relates that he was about to visit them out in the country, where he expected to have "a good time . . . because his wife, you know, gets up a good feast" (ché sai quella sua mogle fa buona festa). They also had an attractive local friend known as "la Morella," who must have added sparkle to the company.[38]

To round the man out before closing this section, I want to put Francesco's extraordinary worldliness into relief by letting a sonnet speak for him. And this one time only, departing from my practice everywhere else in this book, I offer an English version or reconstitution rather than a literal translation.

Io ho sì pieno il capo di non so;
non trassinar, pensi tu ch'io stia cheta?
Deh, fatti un po' più là, ché c'è chi 'l vieta.
Ve' tu ch'ognun ci guata a più non può.
Ma perch'io mi scontorca e dica no
e stia pensosa per non parer lieta,
non temer tu, ché convien che si mèta
secondo il tempo, e pero così fo.
Abbia pur pazïenza e non t'incresca,
ché sempre non ha luogo il ben parere,
mentre che 'l buon voler non cangia il verde.
Ma, come manifesto puoi vedere,
quel che ben si conduce par rïesca,
né tutto quel s'indugia non si perde.[39]

My head's so full I don't know what to think!
Don't scold, d'you suppose I'd keep quiet?
Oh, move over a bit. There are those who'd disapprove.
See, everyone's watching us as hard as can be.
Well, but even if I jerk away and say no
And frown to keep from looking happy,
Don't be afraid. We have to be on guard and act
Like all the others, and that's what I'm doing.
Be patient and don't let it bother you.
We won't always have to guard appearances,
And anyway just wanting a thing won't make it happen.

But, as everybody knows,
Something well managed is more likely to succeed:
We lose so little by waiting.

The following commentary draws on other parts of this book: I make observations that any Florentine reader of the fifteenth century would have taken for granted.

The sonnet is a monologue in which Francesco imagines an experienced woman (wife or young widow) in mixed company, possibly at a wedding party or a large family gathering that includes a few familiar outsiders. She finds herself, most unusually, beside her would-be lover and is talking to him in undertones. Since groups of watchful people stand or sit nearby, she is anxiously concerned about her honor but feels a certain tenderness for him. Her plain speech is a specimen of clipped compression, elliptically so; and her self-control works as a check on the impulsive male. Her pauses and jerkiness are responses to a real situation: she both wants him there and wants a discreet distance between them, in a counterpoint of feeling that opposes carnal desire to the urgent needs of decorum. I say carnal desire, though it is nowhere even hinted at, because, as chapters 4 and 9 reveal, in view of the mores of the age as well as the kind of intimacy and dangers suggested in the sonnet, there could not possibly be anything between the lady and the addressee except a strong desire for sexual relations. Our conclusion therefore must be that the perceptive Francesco had either witnessed such a scene, presumably by reading body language, or, more likely, had actually been the recipient of such treatment, that is, of a lady's combined invitation and warning. Sixteenth-century comedies aside—and they are late—I know of no other monologue like this in the literature of the Italian Renaissance.

It would be false to suggest, however, for all his own doings, that Francesco could ever have offered moral support to a woman's adultery. In this respect, as in so many others, he belonged wholly to his own time. Thus, if the above sonnet is considered in the context of his oeuvre, we come to see that he was quite likely using the monologue to dramatize a moment of flagrant hypocrisy. He appears to collude in the little drama, but all the evidence outside the poem points to a moral interest in the exposure of disguised or hidden turpitude. Shot through with details from classical mythology, his erudite 151-line poem "Aprasi Mongibello"[40] is a scathing philippic against an unnamed adulteress who had taken up with a priest. The angry Francesco cries out to have both of them, together with their paid go-between, borne down to Hades by mythic monsters.

This part could rightly be entitled "Poetry as Self-Inquiry, Solace, and High Vengeance," for these were the chief offices of Francesco's verse. He examines himself; he idealizes love and composes prayer, thereby rising above his troubles; and he engages in angry denunciation, acting out a moral superiority, his high vengeance. But the second and third uses of his poetry were predicated on the first, because he could achieve solace and oblique revenge only by means of anger, self-doubt, disenchantment, hope, and a surge of affirmation. The process zigzagged.

If we had nothing to go on but his general social background, we should be safe in supposing that he received the rudiments of a humanistic education. In fact, elements of this preparation filter through his verse, not only in the numerous references that betray his close familiarity with Greek myth and Roman history but also in his echoes of Latin poets and his occasional Latinate constructions, seen above all in his poem (*capitolo*) on friendship (see below). In a revealing touch, moreover, as we have seen, two of his illegitimate sons were given names from Arthurian romance and Greek myth, Lancelot and Troilus.

He seems to have written most of his verse between about 1430 and 1465; and although he dated certain poems and a few others can be approximately placed by internal evidence, most of them cannot even be assigned to a particular lustrum, and manuscript notes offer little help in this regard. All told, in the most complete collection to date, he is credited with about ninety-five pages of printed poetry, but a bit more remains to be published; and all of it, with the exception of a half-dozen poems, requires meticulous editing, because the manuscripts betray a great deal of variation.[41]

Francesco wrote sonnets, short ballads, prayers, verse letters, a rather acid *frottola,* and several longer poems of meditation, including one on old age and another on the nature of friendship for the Florentine poetry contest, the Certame Coronario of 1441. He uses diverse voices and registers: of the moralist, the lover, the joker, the pilgrim, and the malcontent, in a register that varies from the low style *alla burchia* up to Petrarch's elegant middle style of the sonnets. His themes are amatory, moral, political, religious, and occasional; and if love and politics often lead him to moral questions, his moral or didactic verse is likely to glance off the political face of urban realities and may be cryptic, riddling, aphoristic, humorous, allegorical, or vituperative. Some of the poems are fiercely satirical, such as the three sonnets about the pushy, crooked, *arriviste* attorney ser Goro Lenzi.[42]

The moral and psychological scars of Francesco's financial ruin trail through his poems; and everything about his poetry, much of it in the vernacular vein of "bourgeois" realism, smacks of Quattrocento Florence: its diction, to be sure, but also commonplaces, imagery, observed facts, a strong element of introspection, the doings of humbug preachers, misogyny, and a loathing for legal trickery and swindling attorneys. Declaring in one sonnet, "I have a woodworm sharp and vexing in my heart,"[43] he discloses a manner of dark brooding strongly reminiscent of the like in his contemporaries Buonaccorso Pitti, Giovanni Morelli, and Giovanni Cavalcanti, who also suffered some political disfavor. With good reason Francesco came to favor the sonnet form. By the early fifteenth century, it had been turned into a reflective and self-inquiring mode, well suited not only for the theme of love but also for other ends and passions, such as anger, despair, crisp didactic rumination, moments of hope, religious consolation, and even terse invective. Moreover, the shortness of the form gave Francesco, a restless and distracted man,[44] the opportunity to work in spurts and to abandon himself to rushes of feeling.

In striving to get a fix on our ex-banker, with a view to his most characteristic moments, I reproduce a key (tailed) sonnet, written probably between about 1437 and 1447:

1	Io so ch'io non so più ch'altri comprenda,
2	e non son più, ch'i' 'l so, quel che prima era;
3	e so che nulla sa chi troppo avvera
4	di saper tutto e ch'ogni cosa intenda.
5	E so che chi non vuol ch'altri il reprenda
6	è aprovata bestia soda e intera,
7	e so chi troppo in questo mondo spera
8	capita male alfin, se non si amenda.
9	E so che divario è dal detto al fatto,
10	e come in altri facil si consiglia
11	quel che in sé poi non se ne osserva tratto.
12	E so con quanta industria uon s'asottiglia
13	per far dell'altrui suo sanza contratto,

14   e come insomma il mondo si scompiglia.
15   So tener groppa e figlia,
16   uscir fra gli altri, e so far del restio,
17   ma non so tanto far che torni il mio.[45]

1   I know I do not know more than others comprehend,
2   and I'm no longer, which I know, the man I was;
3   and I know that he knows nothing who claims too often
4   to know all and to grasp everything.
5   And I know that he who'll not be blamed
6   is a beast confirmed, hard and whole,
7   and I know that those with too much faith in this world
8   come to a bad end, unless they check themselves.
9   And I know what a gap there is between word and deed,
10   and how we counsel others with such ease
11   to do the very things we fail to do ourselves.
12   And I know how assiduously man sharpens himself
13   to bypass legal right and grab the property of others,
14   and how in short the world works its own havoc.
15   I know the way to hold a bridle and a girl,
16   how to go out in company and hold my own,
17   but I know not all it takes to get back what is mine.

Dealing with his flawed knowledge of the world, these verses catch Francesco at a question and in a mood that were to haunt him for years. He is talking to himself and to unnamed listeners, not, as in the love sonnets, to his loved one or to the women who know about love. This is to say, leaving aside the dialogue with himself, that the *lei* and the familiar *tu* of the love sonnet have been turned into the unspecified pronoun in the second person plural, the implied *voi*. Francesco is addressing the world; but the world, as his didactic poetry attests, is the immediate urban community outside his windows: Florence. In grammatical terms, then, this sonnet is an exchange with his fellow citizens, and its focus is the event that convulsed his individual social identity, his financial undoing.

The first and final words of the sonnet are *io* and *mio* ("I" and "mine"), and therefore, although speaking to neighbors and citizens, Francesco also closes himself into a self-preoccupation. He wants to talk to his fellow Florentines, but in the bewilderment of his financial ruin, he ends by talking unguardedly to himself. In line after line, deliberately affecting the flattest of styles (as if to reflect or underscore his honesty) and obsessively highlighting the innocuous conjunction "and," he makes a series of claims to worldly knowledge, including his upper-class horsemanship, sexiness, and ease in society (lines 15–16), only to set them all aside in the pivotal final verse ("ma non so tanto far che torni il mio"), where he confronts the fact that for all his knowledge, he does not know how to repossess what is most his own in material terms. The sonnet is beset by an underlying query about his self-identity, not only because all the asseverated knowledge culminates in his not knowing how to retrieve what is truly his but also because the first two lines, with their play of vocalic sound similarities between the assertions *non so* (I know not) and *non son* (I am not) or between *so* (I know) and *sono* (I am), juxtapose being and not-being, knowing and not-knowing, existence and knowledge. Francesco is, as it were, touching bottom. And one manuscript completely confuses *so* and *son*.[46] In short, the vocalic bindings in the first two lines of the sonnet, the remarkable privileging of *io* and *mio,* and the litany of flat locutions all combine to reveal the urgency of his lesson, "ma no so tanto far che torni il mio." Even here, in fact, the wealth of meaning continues, for *torni* also suggests the balancing of an account ("il conto torna") and the wheel of fortune, as in the nonturning or returning of his good luck. Revealingly, the one moment of rescue or solidity in the sonnet is religious, in lines 7–8, with their glancing statement of faith in a world to come.

The essential diction in the opening lines, positing a self-inquiry that revolves around the puzzlement of relations between knowledge and being, also appears in at least six other poems and was taken over from the amatory frame, as we shall see. Here are three examples of the critical lines:

1. "Io non so s'io mi sogno o pur son desto" (I know not if I am dreaming or if I am still awake).[47] Again, *so* and *sono,* knowledge and existence. The movement of this sonnet is centered on fear of dangers to the person and to wealth (*dovizia*), owing to the "traps" and "snares" set by others, including workaday lawyers (*notai*).

2. "Io non so s'io son più quel ch'io mi soglio" (I do not know if I am still the one I'm used to being).[48] In this sonnet, expressing a divided self, as he speaks "to women" about love, he recognizes his amatory error and "fights" against his mistaken self but continues to court a lady who is harmful to his sensible self.

3. In a love ballad of hopeless self-division, "a gracious visage" has so robbed him of himself that he ends in wonder, declaring in the final verse

"ch'io non so s'io son più d'altri che mio" (that I do not know if I am more another's than my own).[49] The sense of possessiveness here, of *self-possession*, is as strong as in the last line of the key sonnet reproduced above.

Surprisingly—to us at all events—the loss of a great fortune and the woes of love could be closely related in the question of a man's identity. In a well-known commonplace of Renaissance love poetry, the lover suffers confusion and disarray because he has lost his identity in the loved one. In our key sonnet, Francesco seizes on this convention but applies it to the consequences of his economic devastation. Or better, tormented by self-doubt and disarray in the wake of his financial calamity, he is able to turn the lover's conventional crisis into the genuine article.

Sheared of its love theme, the sonnet form could be converted into a complaining, questioning, satiric, or didactic mode. In Francesco, the manner of this conversion is all tied up with property, politics, and social life, because he aims his complaints (the plaints taken over from the amatory stance) at flagrant injustices in the Florentine commune. Even in the key sonnet above, the poet casts a cold eye on Florence. Lines 12 and 13 say, in essence, and I know with what dedication men sharpen their wits, so as to take possession of the property of others without even the pretense of a legal document.

Concern with a public morality came to fret or dominate much of Francesco's verse and even affected—in mood, word, or allusion—some of the amatory poems. Love and rank had constituted the strong outlines of his identity; but when the one was all but overwhelmed by the chronic menace of bankruptcy and debtor's prison, the other could not remain intact. Wherever the lady seems to be real, the love sonnets tend to be argumentative or constrictingly logical; when, however, the lady is more surely emblematic, social ideals take over, and the questing "I" may border on a search for salvation:

> Gentil, leggiadra, grazïosa e bella,
> saggia, cortese, onesta e costumata,
> diva immortal, felice, alma beata,
> s'alcuna n'è quaggiù, certo se' quella.
>
> . . . .
>
> Credo ben io che in questa mortal vita
> el peggio fa chi non ne va per tempo:
> sallo colui che più s'accosta al vero.[50]

(Noble, elegant, gracious and beautiful, wise, courteous, decorous and well-mannered, goddess immortal, happy, blessed soul, if such a one there be down here, you certainly are she . . . Well do I think that in this mortal vale, not to go to her for a time is the worst of things: he knows this who gets nearest to the truth.)

The ascent here up to a certain kind of perfection is made through a worldly (and courtly) morality that rejects everything base. Into all that is lowly or vile, therefore, we may put the people and public vices reviled in Francesco's poems of vituperation, namely, fraud, deceit, secrecy, and malicious gossip.[51] Thus, in a sonnet that begins with a reference to divinity, he writes, "God deliver us from the man who most harms us," from injuries, officious judgments (*albitrio*), broken compacts, torments, strange assaults, suspicious walkways, and "from the sound of bells, grey beans, *polizze,* and added details" (da' suon di campanelle, / da fave bige e polizze e ragguagli), a riddling and typical passage.[52] In context, the sense of the quotation fully emerges when we realize that he is referring to the bells for the summoning of public councils or the commencement of business in the law courts; to the casting of votes in government assemblies by means of the standard white and black beans (hence the imagined, not-to-be-trusted, grey beans); and to officialdom, that is, to still more reports or details (*ragguagli*) and to name-tickets (*polizze*) of the sort that were kept in pouches for election to public office. From all this, then (that is, the bureaucratic commune, rich in opportunities for corruption), and from the bent attorney "Goro and his brothers" (line 12), "may God deliver us."

Time and again, when touching on the evils of law courts and politics in Florence, Francesco uses a hit-and-run technique or passes over into symbolism and allegory. Since some of his poems circulated, and Florentines were ever watchful, "publication" imposed political caution, and so he often favored symbol or ambiguity. His darkly humorous *frottola,* racy, cynical, incisive, even trifling in spots, has disabused references to public affairs. Sardonically, too, it urges cheating, devious ways, and being a turncoat as the best means of staying in harmony with Florentine customs.[53] In contrast, the oblique and angry sonnets offer us strange sights, bizarre meals, mysterious doings, free-floating suspicions and doubts, contracts repudiated, and bamboozled men. More specifically, we meet the imagery of bloated bladders (braggarts), mud splashes (disgrace), sweet and bitter fries, and strange poultices; a mix of every kind of herb and woodwormed attorneys; a kite and a falcon as impossible allies; a queer meal for owls, plus woodwormy reeds, greasy and stinking; a snake among the eels, an isolated smithy, a pregnant cow; and a time when four and three no longer add up to seven.[54] Francesco weaves these images into statements and meditations, frequently occultly so, with a view to dropping hints and warnings about the treachery, lies, dangers, and ruthless political power of the early Medicean oligarchy.

Was he himself a craven hypocrite? I ask because two letters and several poems for the ruling Medici offer conclusive evidence that he courted them, although, as one authority claims, not before 1458, when he first turned to Piero di Cosimo for help in a lawsuit.[55] The task here, however, is not to sit in judgment but to take hold of the man in his world. He was not, after all, a saint. To keep an eye on his affairs, he was forced to live in Florence, because all his properties were in Florentine territory. Born a rich and well-placed Alberti, once he returned to Florence, he naturally got to know the Medici. But when the fiscal muddles and strategies of the early Medicean regime went to help keep him on the brink of economic ruin, what was he to do, pretend that he had never met the family and so make matters worse for himself? Not living in an "open" or "pluralistic" society, he was forced—for all the good it did him—to seek a modus vivendi with them. Yet this civil necessity did not expunge his political views, nor did he always mask them in allegory or symbolism.

He issued at least four candid indictments of the Florentine ruling class in poems that, to begin with, only got into the hands of trusted friends. The tamest of the four, dated 1433, was written in a year of alarming strain between clashing political factions, in the midst of hatred that led to Cosimo de' Medici's arrest and exile.[56] Envisaging Florence as a heartlessly abused "little widow," Francesco laments both the divisions that "batter" her and the power of "new men" (*avventizi*) over her "ancient and dear sons," the old patriciate. A second sonnet, produced I believe in the later 1440s, opens and closes with mocking ironies:

> Ben ti puoi rallegrare, alma Fiorenza,
> s'ogni cosa a disegno ti succede
> a tempo meglio, e, misero a chi 'l crede,
> che chi può commandare voglia licenza.
>   Brighe a contanti, angoscia e violenza,

odî, cominazioni a chi possiede,

. . . .

    Chi mette il senno e chi mette i danari.
Qui si concluda, e così la 'ntendiamo,
ch'a ch s'aniega ognun gli serbi i panni.[57]

(Well can you be cheerful, noble Florence, if everything happens to you by
design at the best of times; and poor wretch he who thinks that those who
can command us want leave to do so. Plots and fights over hard cash,
anguish and violence, hates, threats to the propertied [this is what we
have] . . . Some put in their wits and others put in money. Be this the
conclusion, and thus do we understand it: let everyone save the clothes of
the man who drowns himself.)

As often in Francesco's verse, the concluding line wants to have a proverbial
flavor. I take it to be a statement of black irony: the mocking recommendation is that when fools drown themselves, we do the useless thing afterward.
Here, however, the drowning refers to the Florentines themselves.

    A third sonnet (tailed), like the first one, actually precedes the Medicean
reggimento and is datable to the summer of 1434.[58] It is a spitting attack on
Florentine tax policies, citizens, and ruling elite:

    Ispulezzate fuor topi isfamati,
ché 'l tempo a partorito nuova usanza:
morto è il catasto e la novina avanza;
ben v'arendesti presto, o isvemorati!
    Miseri mentecatti isciagurati,
non v'accorgesti di vostra ignoranza
a farvi servi e perder la civanza.
Quanti ce n'è che fien mal arivati! (lines 1–8)

(Clear out the well-fed mice, for time has given birth to a new custom:
dead is the *catasto* and the *novina* goes forward. You certainly gave in fast,
you halfwits! Miserable ill-starred idiots, you didn't see the stupidity both of
turning yourselves into servants and losing the profit. What a lot will end
up badly!)

The *catasto* and the *novina* were two different tax levies; but the *novina,* a levy
distributed and assigned by a different nine-man commission in each of

Florence's sixteen districts (*gonfaloni*), won out in 1434 over the *catasto,* a forced interest-bearing loan first introduced in 1427. Going on with mock applause for those who willingly seek their own economic strangulation, Francesco ends the sonnet with an ironic slur on the keeping of faith among Florentine citizens. It is a furious and acid composition.

His most outspoken and sustained blast against the Medicean oligarchy is a bitter mix of invective and meditation in 148 lines, his *canzone* "Firenze mia" (O my Florence), completed, "Praise God" (as the manuscript concludes), on 17 March 1450.[59] This angry poem was drafted in the wake of Francesco Sforza's siege, starvation, and takeover of Milan (26 February 1450), which made Cosimo de' Medici's political position in Florence all but impregnable, because of the banker's close personal ties with the great soldier of fortune. The Medicean party rejoiced, and "Firenze mia" was an answer, really, to a poet of the Medici circle, Michele del Giogante, who had produced a jubilant poem on Sforza's victory, ending it with a line in praise of Cosimo. On 8 March that poem was publicly "chanted by a boy with a noble delivery" in the little Piazza di San Martino, a minute's walk from the great government square.[60]

Opening with a pointed intertextual reference to Petrarch's "Italia mia," Francesco's "Firenze mia" targets the ruling group and its throng of jumped-up supporters and hangers-on, denouncing their trickery, secrecy, fraudulent ways, and "contempt for all but lascivious and raving appetites" (line 79). The central image, again, is a woman's, Florence personified as mother, but now a dissolute (*scapigliata*) widow, long guilty of inflicting "havoc, outrage, and injury" on her best "sons," the men from the old families, while yet nourishing the "occult" hatreds and treachery of "newcomers" and opportunists, who are, by implication, evil sons or intruders. Public affairs have been conducted "contrary to the old civic rites and ways," and the "lewd and corrupt" widow (scelerata e corrota) is without friends. Private greed reigns in government (lines 10, 15, 17–18). Strong echoes of Dante follow:

> Quante constituzioni, hordini e leggi
> Hai già rimosso e rinovato a posta
> Di chi, più sormontando, ogni or ti prieme!
> E gl'intimi e fedel' sempre più aspreggi,
> Rigida, istrana, ingrata e mal disposta.[61]

(How many long-standing codes, rules, and laws have already been re-moved and renewed at the instance of those who, mounting ever higher, constantly press on you! And those closest to you and loyal, you all the more mistreat, stern, strange, ungrateful, and unfriendly [mother].)

All important public matters, those concerning the many, are managed in secrecy for the benefit of the few (lines 34–37). Well,

> Già non è questo il consueto antico
> De' tuoi patrizii, onde pigliasti inizio,
> Ch'or sì sfacciata al vïolar consenti. (lines 39–41)

(This surely is not the old customary way of your patricians, from whom you had your origins, which now you consent so shamelessly to defile.)

In effect—in accord with other sexual innuendoes in the poem (*sormontando, prieme*)—this widow shamelessly consents to her own rape. Pressing on with his accusations and emphasizing the years of misrule, Francesco asks her, mar-veling, whether she thinks that there is no God above (line 77). Yet in the end he is able to conclude with the hope that "Our famously glorious mother" will change her ways, for he believes that a change is still possible. And he sends his "song" out with caution, warning it to beware "of the sound of rotten [deceitful] jaws, which in our day fill the world." Instead,

> Co' virtuosi e buon' sempre t'accosta,
> Agli altri ista' nascosta,
> Ch'oggi partorisce odio andar co'l vero.[62]

(Always approach the virtuous and the good; hide away from the others, for nowadays to go with the truth breeds hatred.)

The leading expert rightly argues that "Firenze mia" put Francesco back in the camp of the old Albizzi-Uzzano group of oligarchs, thus showing him as opposed to the Medici, who, in the late 1420s, assumed the leadership of a nervous coalition of "new men" and others from an array of older families.[63] Later, under the post-1434 Medicean oligarchy, as "bounders" like the Nic-colini, the Pucci, the Martelli, the Cocchi-Donati, the Cerretani, and others of this sort climbed to eminence, angry resentment naturally went through the ranks of families such as the Bardi, the Baroncelli, the Castellani, the Pazzi, the Peruzzi, and the Strozzi. And in private, these men must have recounted bitter tales of lost court cases, corrupt justice, partisan taxes, defeats in silent contests for public office, and the politics of "crude, cruel, and avaricious men." In most ways, Francesco certainly belonged to this constellation of disaffected men and families, so much so that his poetry may be said to speak for their fears and ire. But having been a political exile until he was nearly thirty, then a prisoner in his own home for more than ten years, and one who held public office only two or three times in the course of a long life, his discontent also transcended party and could turn against any ruling group. He penned, as we have seen, at least two stinging criticisms of the pre-Medicean oligarchy. And if in 1458–59 he was glad to have Piero de' Medici put in a good word for him in a litigious dispute, he would doubtless have accepted such assistance years before. This is not to say, however, that he would then have changed his private (and secret) views regarding the Medicean *reggimento.* To appear on the outside to support the Medici, while in reality fearing and hating them, was not in the least a rare business in Florence, as illustrated by the actions of the humanists Alamanno Rinuccini and Jacopo Bracciolini.[64] Secrecy and covert operation were the way of politics in Medicean Florence: the truth bred hatred. Or, as Francesco claims in a slantingly political sonnet:

> Se mai il quinto elemento ebbe potenza,
> oggi trïunfa e giuridico apruova.
> El ver fuggiasco in fondo si ritruova,
> ch'apena può fiatar sanza licenza.
>
> . . . .
>
> Che si de' far per chi poco ci puote,
> se chi può più la guida come vuole,
> sì che n'andiamo in precipizio e 'n preda?[65]

(If ever the fifth element [lies] had power, these days it is victorious and your jurist approves. Fugitive truth finds itself down at the bottom, where it can barely breathe without a permit . . . What to do when you can't do much, if those who can do much run things their own way, so that we rush headlong and are prey?)

All Renaissance states had sharp political restrictions; and if, under princes, they were outright constrictions, they could be sinister under republican oligarchy, where there was no such thing as an honored or legitimate political opposition, not even in Venice. Insofar as dissent existed, it was voiced in the shadows, secretly, and in oblique expression. This explains Francesco's diffidence and natural preference, in his political verse, for symbolism, puzzles, and enigmatic reference. The psychological duress, however, could also cause equivocation and contradiction, as revealed by his 166-line *capitolo* on friendship.[66]

Here, in the first part of the poem, friendship is "Sacrosanct, immortal, happy," a quality of the soul that always seeks honesty, truth, and virtue, while offering goodwill, grace, delight, good counsel, and forgiveness: "L'amico è un altro io proprio redutto" (line 25), that is, a friend is really another I. But then remembering his Florence and engaged in the poetry competition of 1441, he introduces the element of self-interest and quickly lapses into claims that fly against all the brooding suspicions and warnings of his didactic verse:

> In qualunque republica o senato
> > senza compagni fidi e diligenza
> > nulla può ben condursi in magistrato. (lines 79–81)

(In any republic or senate, without trusty friends and diligence, nothing in office can well be done.)

He repeats, "nulla sanza gli amici si può far" (nothing can be done without friends), but with them, one can rally forces and "purge shames and contempt" (lines 88, 97–98).

> Così né più né men saran graditi
> > nelle private cure, opre e consigli,
> > per cacciar via le ingiurie e spegner liti,
> sostener nimicizie e gran perigli,
> > conservarsi in istato e crescer gloria,
>
> . . . .
>
> A preservar la cosa familiare
> > dall'impeto e da fraude e da nequizia,
> > sol colli amici puoi salva guidare. (lines 100–104, 115–17)

(Thus will they [friends] be truly welcome in private cares, works and counsels, to [help] banish injuries and stop fights or lawsuits, to face enmities and great dangers, to keep us safe in decorous estate and to increase glory . . . To guard the family and household from assault, deceit, and iniquity, only with friends can you go safely along.)

For one whose verse often condemns the injustice and cunning violence of hidden networks, these lines betray a moment of notable disorientation. Whereas normally, looking on from the side of the powerless, Francesco sees straight to the dark core of things in political Florence, here he also sees straightly, but now from the other side, as if in sympathy with the ways in which the ruling group used its ties of patronage and friendship throughout the city. He fails to see, at all events in this poem, that he cannot have it both ways. Whatever its other features, friendship in political Florence was very much a matter of what was good for self-interest. And this guiding rule, as documented in chapter 2, made for keen partisanship and patronage, resulting in a near choke-hold on key office, on the assessing of personal taxes, and to some extent even on the judicial process.

In the late 1430s and 1440s, when Francesco looked from his high windows down to the street known by his family name, an exile in the middle of his native city because he could not step out of his doorway, save at the risk of being seized and arrested for debt and back taxes, he was driven to moralizing and dark rumination. But his verse also came out of the strains and gossip of a close urban setting, where the eyes and chatter of neighbors made up a good part of the surrounding, pressing world. This "neighborliness" pervades many of his poems. Note the opening lines of four different sonnets:

Do you hear? Don't say then, "Thus she goes."

Odi tu? Non dir poi: "Così va ella."

If ever I get out of Cerreto's snares,

S'io esco mai de' lacci di Cerreto,

Yet here we are, the matter is dubious and strange;

Noi siam pur qui, il caso e dubbio e strano;

If I stay, who goes? And if I go, who remains?

S'io sto, chi va? e s'io vo, chi rimane?[67]

In each case, the abrupt start seems sprung from an animated but confining civic environment, where life is, so to speak, an ongoing conversation, interrupted only to be taken up again in medias res. But in addition, in his angry or disapproving moments outside the love poems, Francesco's verse is always a reply to the impinging neighborhood or the ubiquitous oligarchy. One of his tailed sonnets is vividly cast around the Old Market (Mercato Vecchio) and a nearby piazza, where pedestrians enter into a fracas of "ugly snouts" (*gnaffi*), unfamiliar "stinks," "baskets and cages, little birds, thighs and torsos," "kicks and bites" and "comings and goings." His sarcastic advice to the pedestrian is:

Chi non intende il suon non entri in danza,
perché chi non va a tempo, o nol comparte,
manca l'onore e perde ogni sustanza.[68]

(Let him who does not hear the sound not enter in the dance, for anyone who doesn't keep the tempo, or doesn't share it, is without honor and loses all his property.)

Here at once we come on an oblique reference to his financial despoilment. Not to hear or take in (*intendere*) the sound, that is, the sound of Florentine life, is also not to understand it; and with six words, linking honor and wealth, he flags the society's materialistic ruthlessness. Passing from ugly snouts to the ugly mores that rule over the city, his view of the rude, smelly, and fleshy market fades into a glancing comment on evil government. And this presence, with its politics of injustice, often haunts his verse.

More concretely in this moral geography, his premier villain in three other sonnets is a real Florentine, the swindling attorney (*notaio*) ser Goro Lenzi, who always "has his eyes on your shopping basket and his ears at your door."[69] The choice and focus here are calculated, for Lenzi's profession necessarily associates him with public authority:

e sa sì far del publico privato
ch'egli è del popol tutto nuovo erede.
. . . .

Non li si chiude porta:
ognun fa largo al nostro ser Gorgoglio
come al senator proprio in Campidoglio.[70]

(and he knows so well how to turn public [rights and property] into private,
that he's the new heir to all the people . . . No door is shut to him: everyone
gives way to our ser Proudy-Goro, as to a [Roman] senator in the Capitol.)

A canny and practical contemporary like the widow Alessandra Strozzi
understood that the politics of Florentine oligarchy hinged on patronage, on
the business of wheeling and dealing among political bosses. She worked for
years from within the system to obtain the repeal of the exile of her sons.[71]
Francesco instead, unless he was being blisteringly satirical, as in his assault on
Goro Lenzi, tends to look beyond all particular patrons to the dim outlines of
secret proceedings, manipulation of the political system, and injustice. He is
trying to make sense of a constitutional order that flourishes on his social
abasement. But being a complex man, he traffics in complexities; he both
muffles and gives point to his pain. His preferred adjectives are *dubbio* and
strano ("doubtful" and "strange"); and snare, trap, noose, ambush, trickery,
contract, and anxiety (*laccio, trappola, tranello, agguato, inganno, compromesso,
affanno*) all figure among his favorite nouns. In moments of moral fervor,
these words, or others in their semantic range, enter into his verse to characterize his view of sinister public doings. He sometimes allegorizes the matter:

Io veggio tesi per diverse strade
occulti lacci, ispaventosi e strani,
per prender tal, che per li aperti piani
passa a periglio di taglienti spade.[72]

(I see stretching through diverse streets hidden trap-nooses, terrifying and
strange, to catch one who, going over the open plains, passes in danger of
slashing swords.)

There is mortal danger everywhere, both concealed and out in the open; but
Francesco's warnings belong entirely to his vision of life in the evil city. Some
of his sonnets, cultivating obscurity, step up allegory and are more problematic. In these, therefore, he seems secretive, while also laboring to echo the
dark intrigues in the inner chambers of politics. Thus,

Le strane voglie e imprese di parecchi
e lor fallaci vie, cupe e segrete,
col poco senno e l'insaziabil sete
ci faranno anche un dì sudar gli orecchi.[73]

(The strange desires and enterprises of lots of men and their false ways, being shadowy and secret, with little good sense and insatiable thirst, will one day even make our ears sweat.)

Another tailed sonnet starts off with a grotesque feast: "E' c'è pasto da gufi e barbagianni, / puzole di stagion vizze e stizzose" (There's a meal fit for owls and barn owls, skunks in season withered and vexed). We are then treated to a parade of rebarbative images, leading to:

gabbie da pazzi e trappole ritrose,
c'hanno nello scoccar sinestri inganni,
cumul d'errore e ripien di bugie.[74]

(cages for madmen and difficult traps which, in springing, have ominous tricks, a build-up of errors and fullness of lies.)

We pass on to "shames and disdain," "a hostel of jealousies and suspicions," "villanies and injuries," "ambitions and treachery," to end in the despairing anger of the last line: "e non a fondo la miseria loro" (and their wretchedness knows no end). Francesco's fellow citizens stand impugned. He takes the sonnet from an unlikely *pasto* for owls out to the abstract social vices (jealousy, villany, ambition, *perfidia*) that justify his quasi-religious conclusion: a self-inflicted misery that is endless.

His career in the world of high finance was over and done by the time he was thirty-five. The ten or eleven years of internal exile, as a man pent up in his own house, took their toll. And it seems clear that he became increasingly religious with age. Some of his sonnets are compelling prayers,[75] and various others allude pointedly to his faith in the possibility of salvation. Like most of his contemporaries (and like ourselves?), Francesco lived by commonplaces: seen, for instance, in his notions regarding the omniscience of God, the superiority of the intellect, the need for the central place of reason in human affairs, the necessity of prayer, the delusion of ambition, and the madness of any trust in "this blind world." In indignation, he could lash out derisively at individuals: at ser Goro Lenzi, for one, but also at the depraved, rich, greedy, anonymous old man whose rage is likened to the squeaking worst wheel of a cart;[76] or the unnamed preacher seen as a "lubricious Sardanopolis," weighed down by the unhealthy evils of his own flesh ("Carco di male carni").[77] Hyperbole makes the depravity of such men seem transcendent, so that it loops out symbolically to the surrounding social world.

Francesco was a man so distressed by his financial and social undoing, and so outraged by the city's political bosses, that he had to make his psychological peace with them or be overwhelmed by rage and despair. But how was he to make his peace, if not by a labor of mutation, by transforming his vision of political evil into a larger drama? By so doing he could, in his moralizing strictures, take in the lot: city, citizens, bosses, *tout court* the fall of man and the human condition. And this indeed was his way, the way of the moralist and didactic poet.

The need to survive in the unholy city, to rise above his troubles, also drove him to verse prayer. So now art and piety are joined together. His poetry is a way of conversing with himself: it is a secular prayer, a mode of self-examination and improvement, a diary irregularly kept. Therefore, he chooses a short and focused way, the sonnet form or even the twelve-line ballad. But since his ground is word-loving, gossipy Florence and he is driven by complaint, his poetry is also a conversation with others. A few of his poems go out to friends and do the rounds; others are answer poems; but most of them remain with him. Of all his poems, however, apart from the outright prayers, those that aspire to a higher happiness are the love poems in the Petrarchan and *stilnovo* modes.[78] Their yearning for an idealized lady discloses a troubled quest for blessedness, a flight from worldly cares; and so they take him farthest from the unholy city. In this light, accordingly, even his idealizing love poems turn into a critique and a rejection of Florence. In a sonnet of praise addressed to Petrarch, Francesco confesses to having "a style rough and wrong" (lo stil rozzo e scoretto), because his soul is not at peace.[79] Florence is too much with him.

If we ask what our man longed to be, one of the love sonnets provides an answer:

S'io posso mai riveder pur quel volto
che già mi tenne, or m'ha colto in piena,
piglierò forza, ardir, vigore e lena
avessi assai più pria mi fosse tolto.[80]

(If I can ever see that face again which held me once, now that it has fully caught me, I'll grasp strength, courage, energy, and drive [and] I'd have more than was taken from me before.)

Although apparently simple, the verses pivot on verbs to seize or take, and they ripple with complexity: for (1) they introduce conditionality, (2) *ardir-arder* means a mix of courage and passion, (3) the succeeding lines affirm that he cannot really break away from his present carnal condition, and the thought is tormenting, (4) yet his "soul" is ever with that face, (5) there are hints that he is now too old to go on striving, and (6) *lena* (strong will) here carries a pun on the name *Lena,* which turns up in other sonnets and most likely denotes a real woman.[81] But for a moment, at any rate, he wants to believe that if he could but see that beloved visage yet once more, he would again be Francesco in his prime, the young banker and budding patrician, for "forza, ardir, vigore e lena" would come flooding back, to lift him suddenly up from his wretched condition. Nowhere else in the whole body of his known verse does he make so trenchant a statement of what he had lost.

Subject for years to fits of anger, melancholy, and the nausea of self-doubt, he found his way to a devout religious commitment. Shame also possessed him, living, as he did, among those who had helped to dispossess him. Their power swelled and he looked on. His outer life was a show of silence and seeming collusion; but his inner life was a nagging protest, mollified only by prayer and poetry.

Francesco's poetry belongs to the history of Florentine exile literature from Dante to Luigi Alamanni, except of course that his was an internal exile, an alienation; and this condition has not been studied by historians. More specifically, in a political and social alignment, his poetry also belongs to the history of partisan taxation and faction in Florence. For in the fifteenth century, hundreds of upper-class Florentines, involving scores of lineages (including even a cadet Medici branch), mismanaged funds, fell in political estate, saw themselves victimized in the law courts, or suffered crippling tax levies, largely because they commanded no sufficient support in the decisive political forums. Sometimes, too, it was a matter of victims having enemies in high places. After 1450 the burdens of crushing taxation were much lightened for most families. But in 1447 alone, Florence had 155 serious tax defaulters among the members of the patriciate: of these, 1 was in jail, 45 had emigrated, 40 others were in hiding out in the city's rural hinterland, and another 40 were "fugitives" in contempt of the law.[82] Some of these, like Francesco, were no doubt prisoners in their own homes.

The glory of Quattrocento Florence had its shadows in the secret life of the citizens who nursed a corroding discontent: able men whose families had never belonged to the inner circle of the oligarchy; others who had been pushed out of it; and others still who were unhappy with its ways or with their place in it. Most of them, however, fell silent: they were afraid. Francesco's poetry gives them a voice at once direct, devious, complex, and fresh.

SEVEN

THE TALE AS HISTORICAL TESTIMONY

Thirty years ago, coming from a historian, the title of this chapter would have seemed odd or a challenge. Nowadays we live easily with the assumption that fiction and fictional modes have something to do with history.[1] On the one hand, historians tell "stories"; they use narrative techniques; on the other, they deal with the stories of others, whether in state papers or private accounts. But wherever we find sustained historical testimony, there the resources of language, or of semiotic systems such as ritual, are being used not only to convey meaning but also to present narrative structures. Can we get the early Italian tale into this wide net?

If he was to give pleasure to his readers and listeners, the Renaissance *novelliere,* from Boccaccio to Bandello, had to lace his accounts with all sorts of realistic touches.[2] Italian tales of the period from the later fourteenth to the mid–sixteenth century are persistently realistic in setting, details, tone, motivation, and language. This is where the historian may have an entry into fiction and may, by means of analysis and reconstition, turn any Renaissance tale into a fund of historical evidence.

In the *Decameron* tale (8.7) about the good-looking Florentine widow and the scholar trained in Paris, we have a drama ingeniously centered on the Petrarchan amatory metaphors of ice and fire: all very "literary." But other ingredients in the tale, such as the esteem for learned men, the courting of young widows, their slippery honor, the smooth traffic between town and country, the alleged credulity of women, the art of revenge, and the hint of possible savagery in human relations all belong to the quotidian landscape of cities such as Florence, Siena, Bologna, Lucca, and Perugia. Moreover, more than Boccaccio, fifteenth-century *novellieri* cast their fictions around many of the assumptions that guided and regulated daily life. In fact, revealingly, they did not even draw distinctions between invented anecdotes and stories taken from life: all were grist to their mill.

How many professional historians of the period know that if you were going to have guests to a meal in a Renaissance city, you were more likely to invite them to a heavy breakfast than to a dinner or supper? That such a meal was apt to be more formal than a dinner and that you were more likely to conduct business at the late-morning repast? Because of this pattern, when close friends had meals together, they tended to do so after sunset.[3]

But is this not scrappy knowledge for novelists rather than historians? Yes and no. Insofar as practices concerning food are looked upon as isolated tidbits, they are little more than patches of color for adding verisimilitude to a narrative. But insofar as they mark the organization of the day and bear upon the lineaments of class, business, gender, and other human relations, they must interest students of the history of social organization, ritual, and private life. One can spend thirty years doing research in archives and never acquire any sense of when and how and what people ate, as if this were trivial—and of course it was for the kind of historical writing long dominant in the profession. In the past generation, a contrary trend has strongly emerged in study of the so-called history of private life;[4] but I am suggesting that the historian's interest in food may go beyond the arbitrary (in part artificial) distinction between private and public life and pass fully over to matters of nutrition, social structure, and social attitudes, such as in the occasional urban contempt for root vegetables, which were often viewed as peasant fare.

Yet if we are working *as* historians, we cannot read Renaissance tales without having first steeped ourselves in the more conventional documentation of the period. We must not be taken in by the freedom of Boccaccio's mixed company of raconteurs. Among the upper classes in Florence, unmarried and unchaperoned young women and men did not breakfast or dine together. All congress of this sort was forbidden by the ideals of chastity and corporal honor that were imposed on such women. These high rationalizations, in turn, issued from the social requirements of property, patrilineages, family politics, the legitimacy of heirs, and womens' dowries, as more fully represented here in chapters 4 and 9.[5] Interestingly, this was also why upper-class families moved down socially in their choice of godmothers, for lateral godparenting, involving male and female equals, would have brought too many "honorable" women into closer contact, and hence dangerous social relations, with *uomini da bene,* respected men of substance.[6]

My caveat about Boccaccio suggests that the fledgling historian should not begin with the study of Renaissance tales, or at least not without strict guidance. Unaided, he or she would sink in a vast stretch of quicksand in the desperate effort to distinguish fictions from past realities, for the two do not come separately in Renaissance storytelling; they are perfectly fused. Which is only a special reminder—is it not?—that every historical document has to be "decoded" and imaginatively reconstituted before it can be inserted into a meaningful framework.

In this connection, let us take as an example the theme of the lubricious friar or sexy priest, who turns up continually in the tales of the period. Conventional historical scholarship and diocesan visitations confirm that members of the regular and secular clergy were not seldom guilty of sexual misconduct.[7] In the absence of pertinent quantitative historical studies, can we base any historical considerations on the image of the lecherous cleric in Renaissance fiction? A computer-based inquiry might miss the range and tangle of attitudes connected with the sexuality of the clergy. One of the attitudes present in tale after tale, for example, casually assumes and accepts a form of flagrant cynicism in its depiction of nuns and especially clerics as chronic seekers of sex, treating themselves to it grossly, systematically, and without any prickings of conscience.[8] Their holy vows and supposed religious beliefs seldom, if ever, trouble them. In a tale doing the rounds in the 1460s, penned by Marabottino Manetti for Lorenzo de' Medici, the nobly born curate of a country parish near Florence has propositioned every woman in the village.[9]

What are we to make of this cold cynicism? Was it purely in the mind of the storyteller and his communicant audience, rather than in those to whom it was by implication ascribed? And so, do the appropriate tales document a virulent strain of anticlericalism? Or are they devious expressions of toleration for the carnal needs of the clergy? More simply, are the storytellers, at least in this matter, serving as reporters and effectively chronicling an outlook and a reality? These questions draw us away from literary concerns to a preoccupation with an inner social consciousness—inner and social because the attitudes involved were both conflicted and community-grounded.

In many a tale the scandalous friar or priest gets his comeuppance: a beating, castration,[10] humiliation, expulsion from the community, the loss of his benefice, or even death. Sin is punished; hence there is intolerance. The fact that ecclesiastical authority often seemed to be indulgent with wayward clerics doubtless stirred up anticlericalism and intolerance. At the same time, however, owing to the literary frequency and banality of the sexual antics of men in holy orders, there is a degree of tolerance in the large body of short fiction. Coldly lascivious clerics are routinely taken for granted; the story-teller colludes with the angry or prurient desires of his lay audience; and it is this contradictory play of acceptance and censure that verges on turning the image of the lustful cleric into a true record. San Bernardino of Siena, the great preacher, was made uneasy by regular contact between widows and their confessors, trusting neither his confreres nor the troops of widows; and the Dominican Lombard Congregation ruled not only that confession was to be heard exclusively by elderly friars but also that these were "to be frequently changed."[11]

The cynicism of the contemporary layman who countenanced priestly lust, and of the man in holy orders who climbed easily into bed with his penitents or parishioners, summons forth the contrary theme of credulous belief: the creed of the man or woman who believes too simplistically in the word of clerics, in relics and miracles, and in the sacraments. Once the alleged hypocrisy of the priesthood had become a commonplace in the culture of the age, when people spoke of religious belief and of all the things avowed by the clergy, how were they to draw a line between credulity or gullibility on the one hand and a sensible, solid faith on the other? Renaissance tales teem with accounts of the cruel tricks played on credulous individuals. One of the classics in this repertory is Lorenzo de' Medici's *Giacoppo*,[12] the story of a Sienese upper-class simpleton who succumbs to the belief, under the influence of his confessor, a wicked Franciscan, that because he has seduced the wife of a young Florentine—in fact she is a clever prostitute in disguise—his own wife must now be fucked by the Florentine if he is to save his soul from eternal damnation. A game of tit for tat is mockingly made the vehicle of Giacoppo's salvation.

By means of this lively dialectic between cynicism and gullibility, or between anticlericalism and an uncritical stance, Renaissance fiction takes us into a divided consciousness, a conflict that often, I suspect, characterized the condition of particular individuals.[13] We may enter into this mental world by other, more traditional, historical means; but fiction brings the entire problematic out into the open. It raises questions for historians, provides diverging points of view, offers possible solutions, and gets a fix on things in ways that are ordinarily denied to prosaic documentation.

Credulous laymen cuckolded by local priests and priests moved by a sense of impunity were not mere figments of the literary imagination. They were "factions" (fact-fictions) at least. As recurring images or character types, they drew their vitality and resonance from the counterpoint of meanings in the consciousness of Renaissance readers and listeners, who lived in cities where privileged space was the immediate setting for a society of anointed men with their own courts and civil constitutions.

Accused of arrogance, friars and priests were proud men. They occasionally struck poor folk or workers with their own hands.[14] They often came from or hobnobbed with members of the upper classes. And modest laymen, out of respect, stood up for them.[15] Consequently, the ensuing social strains were perhaps converted into (and exaggerated in) sexual metaphor; but the strains, the resentments, and the erotic misconduct were real and were all represented along the line of contact between storyteller and audience. Fiction and reality were brought constantly together, mixed or put face-to-face along this line, as the storyteller invented some things and drew in others that could at once be verified by the pragmatic experience of his readers. In this mysterious but routine place of alliances between real and imagined structures, we have a region as yet largely unexplored by historians,[16] although the so-called new historicists have often claimed it for literary and semiological analysis.

Having glanced off lewd priests, food, and the fact-fiction conundrum, I turn to six other questions, with a view to identifying more of the many areas of contact between historical realities and Renaissance tales. The questions involve

1. the personal pronoun as social indicator,
2. dress and social structure,
3. social identity and urban space,
4. relations between city and countryside,
5. voices and metaphor, and
6. genre itself as a mode of historical testimony.

Unlike the practice in modern English or even modern Italian, Renaissance Italian usage called on the pronouns *voi* and *tu* (you and thou) to shadow forth a complex world of patriarchal and hierarchical (vertical) relations. It was always a matter of social negotiation between high and low, command and obedience, or tribute expected and tribute paid. The two pronouns, accordingly, were also highly subject to rhetorical manipulation. The more we understand the use of pronouns of address in, say, the fifteenth-century tale, the more accurately we come to see the ways in which people saw themselves, saw others, and saw the man-made world. For in their uttering of "you" or "thou," they were drawing lines and sketching in a network of lateral and vertical social relations: a practice that no historian of Renaissance Italy has ever bothered to examine in sustained inquiry.

Priests, we know, addressed their confessing penitents with the familiar pronoun.[17] Spiritual monitors and advisors, they held the commanding position. In everyday exchange, they gave the *tu,* in first encounters, to men and women of the lower classes. But at what point, in addressing people further up on the social scale, did such immediate familiarity and delineating break down in daily encounters? They also employed the *tu* sooner with the women than with the men of the respected classes.

Pronouns in private letters tell us a great deal about social proximities and distances. In the late fourteenth century, Margherita Datini's early letters to her husband show a steady use of the deferential *voi,* but even the later ones dither back and forth between *voi* and the familiar form.[18] Her husband, Francesco, always used the familiar pronoun with her, I suspect. More generally, men of the ruling class employed *tu* with members of the lower classes, such as workers and artisans; and in the country, they used it regularly with their own tenant farmers and sharecroppers. However, neither in town nor in the country did humble folk respond to their social superiors with any but the deferential form, *voi.* Although older men often used *tu* when addressing younger men of the same social class, I cannot say how general such usage was. We also come on startling exchanges and, being startled, realize that we have failed to understand the mysteries of late medieval and early modern social structure. In Antonio Manetti's *Novella del Grasso Legnaiuolo* (Story of the fat woodcarver),[19] we find that in exchange between the two intimate friends, Filippo Brunelleschi and Manetto the woodcarver, one trained as a sculptor and the other trained to work in wood, Filippo addresses Manetto as *tu* but receives *voi* in return. The woodcarver is somehow the social inferior. Since the story was penned about seventy-five years after the reported events

(1485 versus 1409), one of two things is true: either the author felt that the famous Brunelleschi deserved the pronoun of respect from a "lowly" craftsman, despite the fact that they were very close friends, that both had been apprenticed to work with their hands, and that the sculptor-architect was only six to eight years older than the woodcarver; or, even in the midst of friendship, Brunelleschi's superior family background and education rightly entitled him to the deference of the craftsman, indicating that the social divide in Florence cut right through the intimacies of republican friendship. Was the Florentine social world so measured, subtle, and opaque? I have no doubt it was.

Relationships between dress and social structure follow naturally at this juncture. In reading the *novellieri,* I have come to realize that clothing was much more an indicator of social station than most historians have been led to think by the ordinary runs of documentation.[20] We all know that urban codes required Jews and prostitutes to wear distinguishing insignia, that the rich often wrapped themselves in silk and fur, that in Venice noblemen and a special class of "citizens" wore a black gown, that high office always called for official dress, that men at the princely courts wore shorter and closely tailored garments, and that sumptuary laws aimed both to curb conspicuous consumption and to preserve visual (dress) distinctions among the various social classes. But my sense is that everyday dress in Italian Renaissance cities told a more complete story by representing social differences in finer detail, so that people were able at a glance to pick out married women, maidens, and widows, as well as merchants, attorneys (*notai*), shopkeepers such as apothecaries, and the varieties of craftsmen and workers, not to speak of peasants and rural noblemen. When in a verbal exchange with a stranger, how would you know which pronoun of address to use, if not by the way the other was dressed? You did not use the deferential forms *voi* and *signore* with everyone, for they were not merely polite forms, as they are with modern Italians, but rather terms of social identification and of tribute paid to status. There is a Genoa-based story that suggests, intriguingly, that the Genoese were among the first in Italy to sheer dress away from the judgments contained in verbal deference.[21]

Tales of the period show that personal identity, ambition, and fraud were often deliberately linked, in some fashion, with the social markers of dress. The visibility of social identities traced the lineaments of society in perception and consciousness; and all the transactions of everyday life, from greeting people to marketing, jibed with the signifiers of the dress worn. Tricksters and swindlers, therefore, sought to wear the appropriate raiment.

Pronouns, dress, and social identities—or words, visual matter, and what people felt themselves and others to be: we are seeing a world in which social signification was at the core of daily understanding; and it was certainly at the core of the Renaissance tale, which was always an urban production. For generally the setting is a city, or the characters are *cittadini* (urban denizens) on some business or pleasure jaunt in the country, or the tale is depicting *contadini* (rustics) strictly from the viewpoint of the domineering city. The representation of princes to one side, seldom do we find departures from these three situations.

Naturally enough, therefore, as if in response to the current interest in the social uses and gendering of space, Renaissance tales have much to say about this. It is clear, for example, that nighttime was male time outdoors; that the places where men often collected in the evenings to gossip and retail anecdotes, such as the Mercato Nuovo in Florence, were exclusive male enclaves; that government squares, with their companies of armed men, were also places preeminently for the male, and even the immediately adjoining churches there were more likely to be frequented by men than by women. Cathedrals, too, were nearly always male arenas, owing to their central locations, mammoth proportions, and suitability as metropolitan meeting places. *Par contre,* evidence from Venice indicates that local churches (not necessarily the parish church) were the outdoor places for women, particularly for "honorable" women.[22] But what if a church was in the care of a suspected lecher? And speaking of movement outdoors, did women from the propertied classes do their own occasional marketing? Therefore, were fruit and vegetable markets neutral territory? The *novellistica* suggests that although servants often shopped for well-off widows, in families of substance husbands did much or all of the important buying of food, cloth, and household objects. Hence it is most likely that upper-class women, say up to about the age of thirty-five or forty,[23] regarded open-air markets as male space. This subject matter, however, is still open to study.

Back at home, window space was feminine space. Although proverbs, preachers, and parental advice warned women against being at windows, fiction associates them with that very space, not only because here were points for the making of eye contact that led to love but also because, being more often indoors and under parental or marital surveillance, women rightly saw windows as their eyes to the world outside.

But we must beware of overemphasizing the blanket gendering of space. Individual women could throw down challenges. In Gene Brucker's *Giovanni and Lusanna* (1986), one of the claims made against Lusanna was that she dared to look men in the face when walking through the streets of Florence. Under her bold eyes, masculine space became problematic terrain.

In trying to get at the semiotics of place and locale, we must also consider the ways in which space was apportioned and understood among rich and poor, political citizens and the disfranchised, or among the well-connected and the people of no name, no family name. The way a man "read" the spatial units of Italian Renaissance cities had everything to do with who and what he was. The deeper study of urban space has to be predicated, therefore, on the study of social identities. In middle- and upper-class society, identity was derived from property, trade, kinship or neighborhood ties (*parenti, amici e vicini*), and emotional attachment to a locality—all often summed up by dress as a statement. Donatello would not wear a red cloak with a covering mantle given to him by Cosimo de' Medici, because it denoted too grand a social identity.[24] He was thinking of the figure he would cut in the streets of Florence: public space assigned or elicited true identity. In a comic tale by Giovanni Sercambi,[25] at the point of joining a large crowd of naked men in a public bath, the Lucchese furrier Ganfo, having peeled off his clothing (and hence the outer marks of his tradesman's identity), suddenly feels that his nakedness may bring the loss of all sense of himself; whereupon he sticks a bit of straw to his right shoulder, to serve as his identifying mark. When later on it floats away and sticks to another man, he is overwhelmed by fear and confusion. In effect, in public and in matters of identity, dress is everything for him: it has all the markings of class, group, and individual. Identity is also, in some sense, the visible continuum that belongs to one—clothing in this case, but in other cases it might be tools, a house, or a bed, thus making for a most physical view of the social world.[26]

In Piero Veneziano's story *Bianco Alfani,*[27] Bianco, descended from a grand but now ruined Florentine family, cannot accept his humble circumstances and has turned into a loudmouth. This grave social sin, prating, committed in public streets and squares, brings about his psychological mutilation and downfall at the hands of the men around him. In other words, he is destroyed by a society that is witness to the inconsistencies among his hail of words, his modest social standing, and his claimed prestigious identity. For at the very least, in the manners and mores of the story, descent from a distinguished lineage imposes discretion and know-how in the use of words, especially in public areas such as squares and marketplaces, where men of standing are most in evidence.

The most disturbing story of the age, Antonio Manetti's *Novella del Grasso Legnaiuolo,* hinges on the pitiless challenge to a man's identity, a plot to make him think that he is not who he thinks he is. The company of conspirators, close friends and acquaintances of the victim, see to it that he is denied all contact with the society that holds and is witness to his ordinary round of everyday activities. By hiving him off into the dark (night, jail, shadows, an alien neighborhood), they are able to substitute their small company for the large, true, validating society. In effect they counterfeit Florence as a social system so as to usurp its power to assign identities to people by the mere act of recognizing them. The counterfeiters then recognize Grasso as someone else, and for thirty-six hours—save for a period of drugged sleep—he is hounded by the terror of having become someone else.

The historical lessons of this story reside in the ways and in the extent to which personal identity in Italian Renaissance cities was a continuing function, and purely a function, of the society and transactions that circumscribed the individual, meaning chiefly his trade, family, and everyday street and shop routines. Take away the mirror of society, or let that mirror reflect another you, and in fact you become someone else,

There are other lessons here as well. City society in Renaissance Italy put its mark on you, so that you then "read" its streets and squares accordingly and with much less leeway or choice than is available to us. When carried back into the fifteenth century, our modern and ready distinction between public and private life breaks down, for the public dimension then was far more overarching and occupied more of the deeper consciousness of people than is the case today.

If the social pressures on men were as strong as we have seen them to be, we may begin to appreciate what they must have been on women, whose field of action was very much more restricted and who were more subject to moral constraints, stereotypes, and outright coercion. This is why Renaissance fiction bristles with tales of crafty, imaginative, and highly practical female characters. If women were in reality to get a better deal, the better to soothe the conscience of contemporaries (and conscience did, it is clear, needle them),[28] then tricks, ingenuity, and common sense had to provide the ways and means.

My elusive point about the relations between urban space and social identity may be seen more fixedly in literature that broaches relations between *cittadini* and *contadini*.[29] In prose fiction and poetry from the fourteenth to the sixteenth centuries, but most especially perhaps in Tuscany, city people have their opposite in country folk. The peasant is the other: dirty, dishonest, coarse, unlettered, and uncivil—unworthy of citizens and unworthy to live in the city. No Arcadia here. Insofar as sex is demeaning or base, it is summed up in metaphor that smacks of the country. When people are ugly or barbarous, they are countrified. And when stupidity is the sin, the disparaging metaphors again bring in the peasantry. It is as if the citizen in literature, *his* literature, is able to define himself only by conjuring up the peasant as a foil. The citizen is everything that the peasant is not, and vice versa. The one belongs in the walled-in city, with all its mansions and amenities; the other belongs in the country with his coarse food, root vegetables, barnyard animals, and lack of civil conversation; yet the traffic between city and country was absolutely essential. No major city could have survived without the food, immigrants, and labor that came in from the rural hinterland; and much urban wealth, not seldom the larger part, was the agricultural wealth of the absentee landlords domiciled in the city.[30]

In this commerce between urban landlords and peasants, so advantageous for the city, we have the historical setting for much that is going on in fiction: an aspect of the literary enterprise revealing some of the ways in which *cittadini* organized their mental world. The fact that citizens enjoyed remarkable material and political advantages over the neighboring peasantry did not incline them toward seeing country people in a better light. On the contrary, as if to square things with the needs of conscience—I don't know how else to say this—their literature demeaned the other. It made the economic and social inferiority of the peasant into a datum of nature, into something that was also moral and cultural; and we find this cultural policy of abasement not only in poetry and fiction but also in letters, family log books, and collections of advice.

I am broaching a variety of themes, with a view to pointing out some of the diverse connections between history and fiction. But let it not be imagined that themes alone here are the bridge. There is also the evidence of voices, metaphor, language, and genre.

By voices I mean the presence of a kind of chorus or social buzz in many tales, such as by Sermini and Sercambi, a buzz produced usually by different interlocutors and by characters cast as ideal or stock types. These are the voices of a lively oral culture: the serried urban community is here having its say. Proverbs and platitudes, but also neighbors, idealized ladies, merchant types, and go-betweens all introduce the axioms by which the society lives and flourishes. And the historian is wrong not to listen, just as the student of literature is mistaken to steal the social buzz away from its vital sources by regarding it as mere literary occurrence.

By metaphor, apart from technical definitions, I mean the way in which judgment and value sneak through trope into the language of description and supposed neutral statement, to reveal the imprint of class, group, gender, locality, or creed. And speaking of language, I would also note the ways in which turns of phrase, register, and everyday speech allow us to break into the circuit of undercover societal presences. By these means we come to see how practical, basic, and group-oriented the civilization of the Renaissance city was, and for all its religious impregnation, how earthy were its chronic cares in being fixed on the jejune physicality of sex; on the external trappings of personal identity; on the fear of neighborhood censure; and on money, food, looks, maladies, odors, and sights and sounds. If the language of the Renaissance tale ties country people to the earth, to smells, animals, and crass movements, it binds the citizens of the middle and upper classes to values that are less earthy but no less earthly, for even the lofty honor of families and girls is pinned to money, real estate, concrete political office, dowries, maidenheads, and visually attested behavior.

By genre I mean the different kinds of tales: amatory, misogynous, malicious, jokey, anticlerical, *fortuna*-governed, antipeasant, and so on. Keyed to contemporary experience and revealing remarkable spontaneity, these forms are testimony to the input of historical time and place. I shall take one genre, the tale built around the prank or practical joke (*beffa, natta*), and illustrate how form itself may be teased out into a mode of historical documentation.

One of the most popular of all genres was constructed around the machinery of the prank, and a large number of such tales all but dominate the *novellistica*.[31] Typically, character x is egged on by one or more people to perform a given action or definitely to expect the coming of certain events. Manipulated by friends, a spouse, acquaintances, a confessor, or confidence men, the victim is persuaded that the outcome will be good for him or her.

Character *x* is then cheated, swindled, cuckolded, or made the butt of scathing derision. The intention is comic; no pity is shown; the goal is to provoke laughter, and the more hilarious the better. Boccaccio's Calandrino fits this recipe of the dupe. The same may be said of Sercambi's good-looking widow Antonia de' Virgiliesi of Pistoia; of Sermini's upstart son of a peasant, Mattano; of Piero Veneziano's Bianco Alfani; of Giovanni degli Arienti's Friar Puzzo; and of Lorenzo de' Medici's Giacoppo.[32]

We may wish to stress the universality of the kind of story founded on the trick, joke, or deception. But universality does not do away with time and place. Although the love poem, for example, is universal, its multifarious forms, strategies, accents, and so forth, anchor it to place and need, and in Italy even to different cities, as we have seen in chapter 4.[33]

The practical joke as tale had a particular and enduring relevance for certain Italian cities of the late medieval and Renaissance periods. In Florence, for instance, as we learn from Ronald F. Weissman's analysis of the city's "agonistic" society, neighborly one-on-one relations were fraught with a contradictory mix of amity and hostility.[34] In response, "Judas the Florentine" looked for ways to transcend his aggressions and suspicions in the spiritual brotherhood of religious confraternities, and Florence had a hundred of these.[35] But the anxieties of parish and neighborhood were not thereby spirited away, for they arose from the stresses of political faction, from a webwork of patrons and clients,[36] nagging traditions of civil conflict, and the city's confining (walled-in) spaces. Thus the trick or *beffa* as tale, with its union of amity and animosity, of trust and perfidy, captures—and is the very form or paradigm of—the everyday hostilities and loyalties in, say, Florence, Bologna, Lucca, Siena, Perugia, and sixteenth-century Venice. The woodcarver Grasso[37] is liked by his friends and perhaps even loved by the most treacherous of them, Brunelleschi; and yet, Judas-like, they round on him; they cannot keep from teaching him a lesson so cruel that it drives him to a tempestuous act of ritual suicide. Grasso suddenly abandons Florence altogether, in self-banishment from a city where for two centuries exile had been one of the direst penalties directed against serious political dissent.

In this feature of the story—teaching by means of punishment—we have a second narrative element that links the trick as tale to the society of the Renaissance city. The victim is always guilty of a social sin or two: simplicity, vanity, eccentricity, or religious gullibility. That is to say, in our fiercely practical, alert, suspicious, and conformist city society, the individual has an intense street and neighborhood life. Therefore, she or he must beware of being overly trusting, odd, or foolishly vain, because this is to get neighbors and surroundings wrong. It is to misunderstand a society that punishes such obtuseness by means of tricks, humiliation, and laughter. Friends and neighbors are spurred on to teach the social sinner a harsh lesson; and what we, with our modern sensibilities, find strikingly cruel, they considered comical, necessary, and just.

Narrative as the account of a prank has yet a third feature that relates it to the urban milieu. It is the best kind of anecdote for word-of-mouth transmission. That is to say that it both renews and takes animation from the community's oral traditions. To the extent that the energy of storytelling resides in the social topography of a community, it lies outside any given tale. Or, to say the same thing differently, insofar as the ingenuity of a tale depends upon effective storytelling and therefore upon a primed and ready audience, neither tale nor ingenuity can be cut away from the community's oral culture.

Franco Sacchetti, in the late fourteenth century, tells a story about a rich Florentine citizen, Antonio, who hides thirty eggs in his underbritches (*brache*) just before entering Florence, in order to avoid paying customs at the city gate.[38] Secretly betrayed by his servant, he is offered a glass of wine by the customs officials and forcibly invited to sit down, whereupon the sound of cracking glass is heard; the eggs are shattered, and his stockings begin to ooze something orange. Heavily fined, Antonio then adds a generous gratuity and swears the officials to secrecy, moved by the fear that an account of the incident will get out into the city and do the rounds. And indeed this story is about the vivacity of the city's oral and gossipy life. For when Antonio reaches home and his wife sees his drawers, he has to tell her what happened. She is horrified. Knowing perfectly well that the *gabelle* officials will dine out on the incident and at once associating it with matter for popular songs and tales, she screams furiously at him, claiming that the story will race through the city, that he will forever be disgraced, and that she will never again be able to appear among women without shame.

Sacchetti refuses to give the surname of the contraband egg-breaker because, he claims, he wants to avoid further infamy to the family. In other words, he purports to be chronicling a real incident, and like so many other stories in his *Trecentonovelle,* it may indeed have taken place, but we are unlikely ever to know with any certainty. No matter, for the point here has to do with the liveliness and pedagogic malice of Florentine oral civilization and with the viability of its streets and squares as oral conductors. No rich man, no well-placed family, no distinctive figure or personality could escape having a place in the public consciousness. Moreover, the trick as tale, like gossip, flourished best at the expense of such people and in such a setting. In the name of literary understanding as the knowledge of mere form, the *beffa* may be divorced from its social milieu, but in their search for entries to an opaque mental world, historians must look for the marriage.

My plea is, again, that the Renaissance tale is both literature and historical document. The first of these may be the willed act of the writer; the second is an unavoidable condition. If, as history, the tale is to surrender its holdings to us, we will have to work on it, just as we work on any historical source. No document, however forthright or simple, ever speaks for itself. But whereas the conventional historical document comes to us with an a priori affidavit of reality, of its truth as the carrier of some quondam transaction in the real world, the literary product appears as something imagined, invented, or brain-spun. Which it more or less is. However, insofar as it is not, it has historical information to impart; but even where it is largely imagined, its departures from reality have much to tell us about the construction of alternate imaginary realities and therefore about social strain and stress in the real world. As demonstrated in chapter 4, the Renaissance love poem, almost never addressed to a spouse, is a response to (and an act of revenge against) the utilitarian, strictly arranged, upper-class marriage of convenience. Study the one, and you throw light on the other. Certainly, no less so than poetry, Renaissance storytelling engaged with life, took it on, and aimed to comment on contemporary experience, thereby mixing invention and reality at will. This means that the historical study of Renaissance fiction requires more strategies, knowledge, and professional experience—in short, more skills and work—than the prosaic document. But the prizes to be had are inestimable, for they come forth from underlying oral traditions and from the society's conflicted consciousness: that is, from those parts of a mental world that are likely to be flatly represented, or ignored altogether, in the ordinary runs of historical documentation.

EIGHT

CRUELTY IN THE COMMUNITY

A Bloody Tale

CRUELTY OR CONTEXT?

At the start of the sixth day of Marguerite de Navarre's *L'Heptaméron,* written in the 1540s, the assembled company of storytellers agree that Italians have a reputation for "the vice" of cruelty.[1] Given out in a Europe that was a public stage almost everywhere for bloody floggings, mutilations, brandings, and executions, this judgment must strike us as perplexing. Why should Italians be singled out thus? What did it mean, after all, to hang, draw, and quarter a man or, later on, as in Elizabethan England, to disembowel Jesuits? How fierce was fierce?

I propose to take up a slippery subject, cruelty: a protean, problematic, and relative sentiment that would seem to be more suitable for anthropological inquiry than for historical study. Yet precisely because the ontology of cruelty is so labile—and how well we know this in our own day—we have the grounds for holding that it belongs to the changing structures of place, time, and chance. It is, in short, historical; and nothing is more likely to produce it, we may suppose, than, say, catastrophic social dislocation, war, or troubled religious frontiers.

In this chapter, however, I want to pursue a more modest, if more difficult, aspect of the question, and seek to account for the supposed cruelty of prosperous and settled Italians by looking chiefly at Renaissance Florence.

From the twelfth to the seventeenth centuries, most Italians in northern

Europe—Italians of the sort likely to make an impression—came from cities in upper Italy: Genoa, Venice, Florence, Lucca, Milan, and some of the lesser towns. They were long-distance merchants, bankers, moneylenders, and in some cases "wily" clerics. Trading in currencies, goods, and commercial information, they moved about with an eye to the main chance; they were bred to this, brought up to seek "profit and honor."[2] This was why they went abroad. Here at once, accordingly, we can begin to see why these "foreigners"—often known as "Lombards"—would in due course come to be seen as clever, practical, and tough, in England as well as in France and elsewhere:

I am a Lombart and subtyl crafft I have
To decyve a gentylman a yemen or a knave
I werke by poplyse (*policy*) subtylyte and craught.[3]

Penned before 1542, these lines indicate that later on the Elizabethan and Jacobean image of "the crafty Machiavel" would fit comfortably into an old current of ready presupposition. "Am I politic? Am I subtle? Am I a Machiavel?" asks one of Shakespeare's characters.[4] These rhetorical questions suggest that Italians were also associated with sophisticated ways. From the Italian side of things, however, this had less to do with the very early Elizabethan translation (1559) of Castiglione's *Il Cortegiano* than with the world that had gradually given rise to its courtly social code: namely, an old urban society that went back to the twelfth and thirteenth centuries, when the institutions of the Italian city-states were first laid down.

But there was something about the city-bred Italians, perhaps especially the Tuscans, that also seemed to smack of cruelty, and it must on occasion have leached through their humorous ways and conversation. I refer to their love of the ingenious trick (*beffa, natta*), the aim of which was the public humiliation of a selected victim judged to be worthy of such punishment. And as we noted in chapter 7, this taste was strikingly evident in Italian storytelling. Over the course of two hundred years and more (c. 1350–1560), the Italian tale continually featured the drama of the devious but ruthless prank, which cast the loser to the jeers of the surrounding community.[5] In chapter 2, moreover, I called attention to a vivid line of vituperative verse akin in ferocity to the punishing prank. A poetry of malediction, feral, violent, brutal, and merciless, it circulated among the friends and acquaintances of the poet, thus making it a public business and certainly delighting many a reader. The hated person under attack may be reduced to carrion, feces, or a bodily orifice, or perhaps is simply made out to be a snake or a stinking swine. Alternatively, as in a solemn curse, he or she may be denied every good under the sun: light, water, food, air, song, and God's grace. Following are three examples.

A tailed sonnet by Giovan Matteo di Meglio (fl. 1440s), addressing a particular woman, possibly a neighbor, gives names to her that seek to pervert her essence:

> nesto di mula e d'asinel portante, socchorso d'ogni frate e ttregendiera,
> vulva arrabbiata, in chui la foia è 'ntera,
>
> . . . .
>
> O torcifeccio e di fetor ghonfiata.[6]

(hybrid of she-mule and shambling ass, demon and damned soul, succor to every friar, hot vulva where all is lust . . . O scum rag blown up with stink.)

Calling on similar devices in a wrathful sonnet, but adding the rhythmic punch of alliteration, the Pisan Lorenzo Damiani (1440s) excoriates a certain Piero di Pardino, who is identified in an acrostic formed by the first letter of each line:

> Porco putente pessimo poltrone,
> invido iniquo ingrato iscognoscente,
> e brutto e tristo e ville e da nïente,
> rustico rio rapace rubaldone,
> o serpe oculta odiosa, o condizione
> di mal dimon dannato, dira mente,
> inclino in male invidia, incontenente,
> perir presto pos'tu, perch'è ragione!
> Astuto a 'nganni, ardito allo sforzare,
> roba rubando ruddemente regni,
> degno di mala dannazion, di morte,
> iusto iudicio è 'n punire; indugiare
> nulla non voglio nel darti; né sdegni
> oscuro obrobio o forche o mala sorte.[7]

(Smelly swine, nasty coward, envious, unjust, mindless ingrate, ugly, wretched, base, and worth nothing, guilty peasant, rapacious rogue, o hateful hidden snake, o thing damned by an evil demon, bent on fury, bent on malice, unrestrained, may you hurry up and die! It's only right! Sharp at trickery, bold bully, you rule by your crude thieving and are worthy of damnation and death; it's just to hand out punishment, and I want no delays in sentencing you to infamy, dark scorn, the gallows, or bad luck.)

Benedetto Accolti (1415–64) curses one of his enemies in a seventy-six line *capitolo:*

Ogni grazia del ciel ti venga meno

. . . .

Dimandi il cibo, e non si truovi alcuno
Ch'abbi el cor per pietate alquanto piego.

. . . .

L'aiere chiaro a te diventi bruno,

. . . .

Non possan gli occhi tuoi mirar le stelle,

. . . .

. . . et ogni creatura
Per gioa tenga el grave tuo tormento.

. . . .

La tua sforzata vita morte fuggia,
Perché 'l morir a te saria diletto!

. . . .

E quel corpo maligno, infetto e vano
Di podagre, di gotte e parlasia
Correpto sia, e d'ogni morbo umano.[8]

(Heaven deny you every grace . . . Beg for your bread and find no man with mercy in his heart . . . May the bright air be black for you . . . Your eyes not ever see the stars . . . and may every creature have its joy in your grievous torment . . . Death flee from your hard life because dying would be a delight for you . . . And may that evil body of yours, poisoned and worthless, be stricken with gouts, paralysis, and every human malady.)

Although the foregoing examples, being snippets, cannot convey the full force of the emotive energies involved, their lesson comes through in the surpassing violence expressed. Every boundary has been shattered: there are no doubts or restraints, and no Christianity. We are witnessing a ritual of total exclusion and elimination, in which the person cursed, in the classic mode of killing without qualms of conscience, is denied every particle of humanity, the more easily to justify any degree of insult or injury. Indeed, *Schadenfreude* is the keynote: pleasure is taken in the pain and abasement of the intended victim. The writer wants his curses, his prayers in reverse,[9] to come true and be real. In Kenneth Burke's terms, this is poetry as symbolic action.[10] The deed was done, even if only in spirit; the key is in the intention and in the use of language as act or gesture.

The question thus arises, What exactly was there in Italian urban society, as attested most notably in Florence and other Tuscan cities, that fostered taking pleasure in the ills of others, the chosen others? Fostered it, that is, *as a communion of public laughter*? In asking this particular question, I circumvent the whole matter of the rise of torture and the practice of official violence against the person, which dates back to the decades around 1200. Italy was to have this procedure in common with the rest of the Continent, and its practices were no bloodier. The root forces behind Renaissance Europe's harsh penal codes have yet to be studied in sufficient detail; and although a start has been made, the task will require the cross-disciplinary labors of a team of historians.[11]

In upper Italy generally, the animus in primary vendetta could rely upon a good deal of traditional approval in the community,[12] and the practice made for countless instances of a kind of licensed cruelty. When rightly sought, revenge was often held to be morally justified, despite the fact that by the late fourteenth century it nearly always fell outside the law, above all in cases of so-called secondary vendetta: that is, when the injured or murdered party was an innocent relative of the original assailant. In Tuscany there were even some chilling, trenchant summaries in verse of the steps to be taken in the wreaking of vengeance.[13] And startling instances of cannibalism, triggered by the lust for revenge, were now and then reported by chroniclers, as in the Perugian countryside.[14]

Here, however, although my case has about it the distant whiff of a vendetta, I seek to chronicle a different kind of cruelty and to offer a "thicker" account of the pleasure taken in the ills of others, by fixing on a tale drawn from Anton Francesco Grazzini's *Le cene* (*The suppers*). A native Florentine, Grazzini produced his collection of tales in the 1540s. The one in question, the seventh tale of the second supper, is recounted by the festive Lidia, who believes that it will give her listeners "something to cheer you up and laugh about."[15] The plot is as follows.

Taddeo, a countryman turned teacher, lives as a tutor in the house of a Florentine gentleman. Having fallen in love with a beautiful neighboring girl, Fiammetta, born to a noble family, he tries to get a love letter to her by entrusting it to the girl's maid, who delivers it instead to the young man of the family, the girl's brother. Agolante, who appears to have the *patria potestas* over his sister, is outraged by this vile affront to the family honor and calls on the advice of a friend, Lamberto. By counterfeiting alleged epistolary replies from Fiammetta, Lamberto leads the "peasant" teacher on until an assignation is finally fixed, which is to take place in the house of the siblings on a night when Taddeo believes that Agolante will be away from Florence. The girl, meanwhile, knows absolutely nothing about the teacher or the developing plot.

Four other friends of Agolante are brought into the *beffa,* and once they have Taddeo in the house, the six men, dressed and hooded in the white garb of a religious confraternity (ironically, a company of self-flagellants, the Battuti), then teach "the pedagogue" a lesson, without ever so much as uttering a word to him. As two of them hold torches, the other four scourge him with leather straps until they are exhausted, although not before they have given him "some four thousand strokes," so that "his flesh is everywhere broken and bloodied" (di maniera che egli era tutto rotto e tutto sangue). Taddeo's cries for mercy have long since turned to groans. Next, taking his shoes and peeling off all his clothing, they lock him in a room and go into another part of the house, "in a tizzy of delight (gongolando) and with the jolliest laughter ever heard." There is to be no end to the fun, for two of them, sculptors and "master tricksters" (maggior maestri di far burle e natte), have made a life-size maquette of the teacher by using plaster, straw, and old rags. They now put his clothes and shoes on it, and shortly before dawn, still wearing their confraternal garb, the six companions take it and the naked, blindfolded Taddeo out to the Old Market and force him to look on as they attach the dummy to the pillory column and stick a sign to its neck, reading: "PER AVER FALSATO LA SODOMIA" (For having been false to Sodomy). They then drag the flayed teacher away to conceal him in a neighboring horse shed and go off to sleep.

Within two hours of sunrise, news of the strange sight has raced through Florence, Taddeo's image is quickly recognized, and more than two thousand people rush to the Mercato Vecchio to see the maquette. No one dares remove it, because all think that it may be there by order of a special police magistracy, the Eight. Agolante and his five friends soon turn up at the scene and move around among the crowd, cracking jokes at the expense of "pedagogues," presumably by emphasizing their reputed predilection for sodomy. Later still, having again donned their white robes, they go back to Taddeo, to find that he has rolled around in the shed, getting dung all over himself in the effort to keep warm, whereupon all urinate on him. Then one of them sets fire to his beard and hair, burning his "ugly mug" (il mostaccio) and raising blisters on his neck, cheeks, and head—an action that, but for the blindfold, would have blinded him. Now "even his mother would not have recognized him," for "he seemed the strangest beast that had ever been seen." Next, removing the blindfold and seeing him all "bruised, bloodied, and burned," they shove him out into the street, just as there is the burst of a sudden and violent rainstorm. Taddeo runs east, across the main government piazza, down the present-day Borgo degli Albizzi, ever east, past San Pier Maggiore to the Porta alla Croce, one of the main city gates, and out into the deep countryside, never to be seen again. Only the cascading rain saves his life, for on the way, looking like an escaped madman, naked, wild, and as if painted red, he would have been killed in the streets, we are told, by children and young hired hands, who would have rushed out in hot pursuit but who instead hurl heavy objects at him as he streaks past open shop fronts.

The narrator of the story, Lidia, leaves us with no loose ends. When the scandal of the dummy is brought to the attention of the Eight, they have it removed from the pillory and then angrily put out a call for the arrest of the event's perpetrators. Agolante and Lamberto, each of whom has a relative on the Eight, present themselves to this magistracy and make a full confession but also produce four love letters in Taddeo's hand in order to vindicate the justice of their case. Sharply reprimanded and then released, the two thereafter "went throughout Florence, gaily describing the whole prank, and bringing laughter to all who heard it."

To understand the tale of Taddeo, reluctantly and uncomfortably summarized here, we shall need an idea of the festive framework around it and around all the other tales in *The Suppers.*

Looking back to the mise-en-scène in Boccaccio's *Decameron,* the author, Grazzini, introduces a happy company of ten Florentine men and women during carnival; he depicts them first at windows and in a courtyard, engaged in a merry snowball fight.[16] Afterward, having settled down in the enclosing, spacious palazzo, all agree that they are each to tell a story during the course of each of three Thursday suppers, making thirty tales in all (although Grazzini completed only twenty-two). The company meet in the great house of a happy widow and include her brother, four other young men, the widow herself, and four young, good-looking, married women, whose husbands are away from home on business. Widow and brother serve as chaperones, for three of the young women are their close relatives and the fourth is a neighboring friend. All are rich, noble, or upper-class; and despite any ensuing titillation, the common tacit assumption is that honor and propriety will be observed. Grazzini would not have dreamed of violating moral expectations and custom by introducing an unmarried young woman into the group.

The carnival season, the mixed company, and the announced purpose of the storytelling make it clear that the goal of the three suppers is entertainment, the chief fare of which is to be the ongoing train of jolly, moving, or ingenious tales. But let there be no doubt of it: Lidia's *novella* about the teacher from the country, Taddeo, is meant to regale the company with laughter, and it does, as the narrative informs us at the start of the next story. We may ask, then what in the world would arouse the group's pity or charity? The rhythms of the supper itself provide an answer.

The fifth tale of the second supper, set in Roman times, is about the prince of Fiesole, the widower Currado, who marries a girl about the same age as his sixteen-year old son, though he himself is over fifty. In time, son and stepmother fall fatally in love; and soon discovering their adultery cum incest, Currado has them blinded, has their hands and feet cut off and their tongues torn out, and then leaves them together on their adulterous bed to bleed to death. The next morning the nobility and the people of Fiesole rise up and stone Currado to death for his "cruelty" and "inhumanity." With its emphasis on the beauty, grace, and tenderness of the young couple, this tale so moves the Florentine company to tears and pity that Fileno, the next narrator (supper 2, tale 6), is forced to offer a humorous tale so as to lift up and delight the spirits of his listeners. He is immediately followed by Lidia (supper 2, tale 7), who, also electing to keep the company in a jolly mood, tells her Taddeo tale, hoping that it will make them laugh "even more" than the previous one.

How are we to use Taddeo's story to illumine the question of cruelty in Florentine society? The way, paradoxically, is to use our knowledge of Florence to throw light on the tale, which in turn will give off its own light as we start to see its buried and oblique meanings emerging to take their place in social history.

If we try to see Taddeo from the standpoint of his tormentors, our horror of the tale can be diminished. In a society marked by sharp divisions of class, caste, wealth, and gender, and rather obsessed at the top with aristocratic ideals,[17] Taddeo's ambitions begin to make him seem a villain. In the eyes of Agolante and company, he is a lowly wage-earner, poor, a foreigner, a countryman, and decidedly ugly—his ugliness being the banner of all his moral and social inadequacies. Yet he is set on wooing, seducing, and dishonoring the well-born and beautiful Fiammetta, who is necessarily a virgin, no doubt richly dowered, and meant to be married by agnatic arrangements, in the ordinary practice of the age, to a man of her class and station, a man like Lamberto, the very orchestrator of the *beffa*. Taddeo boldly aspires far beyond the possibilities of his class, purse, and face, to a pretended love that can but render him an outright criminal. Since the girl would have been about fifteen or sixteen years old, hence without the customary authority in practice to dispose of herself in marriage,[18] he may be rightly seen, in law, as entering her house like a thief, prepared to take her virginity, to pilfer and destroy her good name and the name of her family, and to foil the rightful ambitions of that family in the politics of marriage. Furthermore, his lust—for how else can Agolante see the man's socially illicit passion?—could wreck testamentary arrangements (touching her dowry) and even, at the extremes, terminate a family lineage if Fiammetta's dishonor should preclude marriage and impose immurement in a nunnery.

Of course these matters are not articulated in the tale. They need not be; they are already lodged in the consciousness and expectations of Lidia's listeners and Grazzini's contemporary readers. Nothing else can even begin to explain the brutality of Fiammetta's would-be avengers, unless it is the author's possible psychosocial motivations, to be touched upon in due course.

For all the intended comedy of the tale, we are dealing with matters so serious that religious and civic rituals—in parodic form, to be sure—are made the backbone of the narrative, the more forcefully to underscore its lessons. The six young men appoint themselves Taddeo's religious disciplinarians, judges, and executioners. Attired in the white dress of pious self-flagellants, they hide their faces in hoods so that he cannot identify them, and remaining absolutely mute, as if in silent prayer, scourge him rather than themselves, in action that may be decoded as the castigation of sin. They then, as it were— the parody continues—turn the sinning criminal over to the secular arm of authority, the state, and have him pilloried in the Old Market. The object of wonder, Taddeo's effigy, is so lifelike and like him that there can be no doubt of his identity. To the gathering crowd of spectators in the Mercato Vecchio come Taddeo's own employer as well as numerous acquaintances, teachers, students, and learned men. In one respect this is the most dire of his punishments, for if the flogging rends his body, the dumb show at the pillory obliterates his social persona. He can never again live in Florence; he would not want to; he would be the eternal object of contempt and laughter, and no one would hire him. However mean and humble his honest standing had been, even this is now effaced by the lewd spectacle at the pillory: "For having been false to Sodomy." That is, Taddeo is there for having been untrue to the social habits of sodomy by lusting after a girl, when all the world knows that private tutors prefer boys! What is more, Agolante and his cronies would take the true story throughout Florence and dine out on their derision of his lofty, hence ridiculous,[19] love letters. Why, he had even written courtly love sonnets to the girl! No wonder he is never seen again, if indeed he lives on after his bloody exit from the city via the La Croce gate, which led out to the vicinity of the official place of execution. He has been ritually eliminated from the body social. The marks of his "true" identity and destiny in Florence are shadowed in his naked race through the streets and the rain. Flayed, blistered, and bloody, he seems the perfect picture of lunacy, as if caught in a mimicry of his earlier demented lot, when he was mad enough to believe that he could win the love of the beautiful Fiammetta, a name—meaning the flame of passion—from love tales, amatory verse, and noble families such as the Strozzi and the Adimari.[20]

As students of the history of Florence know, there was a cleavage in Florentine attitudes toward city and country dwellers. Owing to ancient stereotypes, but especially to the city's subjugation and ownership of much of rural and municipal Tuscany, Florentines often looked down on countrymen and particularly the peasantry. In proverbs, poetry, and tales, a line of Florentine caricature disdained and made fun of the Tuscan peasant. So Taddeo is cast as a country lout. Thanks to his clerical contacts (an uncle of his was a local priest), he had learned enough Latin to be able to teach it to children. But he was little more than a humble employee and servant, the owner of a single pair of cheap flat shoes (*pianelle*) and one set of outer garments—the very items that helped establish the identity of his likeness at the pillory. For 150 years or so the scholarly profession had always produced a few humanist stars; but rank-and-file teachers and small-time tutors eked out a living, unless they combined the instruction of Latin grammar with the matriculated skills of the type of notary who was also active in the drafting of legal instruments and court transactions. In Taddeo's case, a series of adjectives and epithets puts him in his place: "a pedagogue from a little castle in the region of our Upper Valdarno . . . a low rustic of no standing, poor, without any virtues, and ugly" (villano, dappoco, povero, senza vertù e brutto); also "a good-for-nothing rogue, a loser, and a dirty little teacher whose life isn't worth a handful of nuts" (gaglioffo, sciagurato pedante fracido, che non val la vita sua dua mani di nòccioli).[21]

The least of Taddeo's crimes is in his mad presumption that Fiammetta would stoop to have a man of his sort. Such a virgin, being readied for marriage in Renaissance Florence, would not have opened the door of her house to any man from outside the family, least of all to an ogling "peasant." Taddeo's immediate crime is in his brazen readiness to deflower the girl, and this point is cleverly highlighted. For when he enters her house, Fiammetta's maid shows him directly into a ground-floor bedroom, where she invites him to undress and get into bed, having first announced that a clean set of "white sheets" had been put on that day. When, therefore, the delighted Taddeo climbs into bed, the whole scene suggests that he is likely to be imagining the girl's blood on the sheets. Soon, only his own blood will spangle them.

To explain the cruelty, or what we see as that, in the tale of Taddeo is to refine our understanding of group consciousness in Renaissance Florence and to get a firmer hold on certain of its structures. Taddeo's savage beating and disgrace are punishment for his odious challenge to the upper class as epitomized in the honor, property (dowry), and beauty of the girl, where bodily beauty, in a common synecdoche of Renaissance literature, equals the innate, natural superiority of the dominant class. By resolving to make social and sexual contact with her, he resolves to violate a set of capital taboos.

Can any punishment be too cruel for this? Yes, certainly, but apparently not the one dished out to Taddeo, at least not in the eyes of his upper-class judges or of the laughing company gathered around the storytelling Lidia. The threat lodged in Taddeo's motivation is deadly serious because he is thumbing his nose at upper-class ideals, thereby arousing deep and fierce animosities. The final reaction against him, however, is not spontaneous; it is delayed and studied; and perhaps we shall want to fix the point of cruelty here, in the act of cerebration, in all the scheming that goes on at his expense. His judges decide that they must put him in his place by teaching him a devastating lesson. Church and state, in mimetic form, are thereupon brought in to ritualize and exalt their verdict. The white robes, the silent flogging, the pillory, all mime the participation of the spiritual and secular arms of authority. But the ensuing brutality was not at all unlike that sometimes seen in the streets of Florence in the public floggings, always aimed at drawing blood, meted out to petty thieves and vagrant prostitutes.

If the act of cerebration, the trick or *beffa,* carries the burden of cruelty, then we are back, full circle, to the notion of something too clever in the makeup of the Italians who traveled up to northern Europe with their account books, to engage in astute financial and commercial transactions. Except that back home, in the Tuscan cities at all events, that cleverness might also take the malicious form of the plot designed to teach a painful moral lesson. Apart from applying the laws, the most effective way of defending or inculcating taboos seemed to be in the tricky *beffa.* Here society itself—that is, neighbors, friends, witnesses, or even intended victims—took culprits in hand and did the punishing.

But the *beffa* required a certain kind of well-circumscribed urban society, one that accommodated a competitive, almost antagonistic everyday spirit[22] while also being familiar enough to foster local amity and to stamp the lives of its members with a singular public quality. Privacy, as we know it in the modern West, was unknown in the Italian Renaissance. With its strongly endogamous structures, small-town (Renaissance) society—Florence, Lucca, Siena, Bologna, Perugia, even Venice—was both a showcase and reflecting mirrors.[23] The moment men and women went into the streets, they were on show because they were known to all the world immediately around: known by their dress, trades, names, kinships, and local reputations, as much as by their faces; known also, in the case of citizens from the eminent families, by their grand dwellings, servants, coats of arms, and web of patron-client relations. In the mental world of symbolic or transferable values, men *were* their families, trades, dress, and what they stood for in the neighborhood. Take all this away, and what remained of them as individuals? Some fundamental quiddity had been removed. In the middle and upper classes, women *were* their chastity and the man they married, unless they were nuns or darkly clad widows linked to their natal or marital lineages. What people were was directly confirmed and ratified every day, on their stepping out into the showcase of their city streets. This is why exile had long been considered such a baneful penalty; it deprived you of much of your self (hence, one of Accolti's curses is "Be banished to strange streets"—that is, to a different city); and it is why Italian Renaissance society could produce a variety of tales, only one of them well known, conveying the lesson that personal identity was what friends, acquaintances, and neighbors recognized and had stamped on it.[24] The results made for a high, unusual degree of natural social conformism in group, trade, parish, and family. Understandably enough, therefore, Quattro-cento Florence, with a population of forty-five thousand people at best, had more than one hundred religious confraternities.[25] Although a competitive spirit, often verging on antagonism, was embedded in the economic and political traditions of the society—much verse of the period claimed that treachery and envy were rampant[26]—such transgressive rivalry also had its peace and transcendence in the unifying, symbolic action of confraternal or other local rituals, such as singing lauds, self-flagellation in groups, or giving small dowries to deserving, shame-faced girls.[27] Unfortunately for poor Tad-deo, the symbolism was organized against him: he was the lewd and trans-gressing outsider.

It appears, then, that the cruelty of the *beffa* came at once out of a strong social conformism and a countervailing sense of rivalry. The one imposed strict and acceptable group behavior, but the other fostered social climbing and interjected local strains. In that conformist setting, people who stepped out of line seemed to flout common sense, thereby rendering themselves, if caught, fully deserving of condign punishment. For those within the group, as many tales reveal, such punishment could be fierce. With so much suffering and death about in Renaissance Italy, brought on by appalling poverty and epidemic diseases, the rigors of daily life and a sense of rock-hard practicalities easily justified harsh punishment. And female infanticide, after all, seems to have been not altogether uncommon. It follows that transgressors from out-side the group would be shown no mercy. Grazzini's *Suppers* begin with an invocation to God and the pious hope that "all their storytelling will turn to His praise and the consolation" of the assembled company,[28] but not a scrap of Christian pity is spared for the ill-starred teacher.

That *Taddeo* contains a heavy dollop of class arrogance is undeniable. It was an attitude that came forth more emphatically, I believe, with the lurch toward aristocracy in late-fifteenth and sixteenth-century Florence, when the dominant class was putting an ever greater stress on endogamous marriage, exorbitant dowries, ancient links with high public office, and old blood lines.[29] This narrowing or tightening in the top social ranks exacerbated any preexisting sensitivity to questions of class, name, and honor, in addition to bringing a new disdain for aspiring men from the lower orders. And what was Taddeo, "the strangest beast that had ever been seen," if not a weird and impossible aspirant to Fiammetta's hand?

Yet class divisions did not eliminate the vertical solidarities in confraternities, patronage networks, or frequent shop and workshop encounters, above all when these involved artist-artisans. And it is noteworthy that two of Taddeo's six tormentors were sculptors, the ones who made up the maquette for the pillory. Evidently, Agolante and Lamberto commanded the allegiance of men who, as artists or highly talented artisans, continually carried out work for the men and families of the upper classes. Here were the people who opened the way to the important commissions for public works, churches, and private palazzi.

Having charted the social nature of the brutality in the tale of Taddeo, I have the sense that the analysis is incomplete; we need a word on the effects of latent sexualities.

Once Taddeo is stripped naked, just after the four thousand blows, he remains so for the rest of the tale, whereas his assailants are somehow always overdressed in his presence, being all but entirely covered up by their white (penitential and purging) robes. They scourge him all over, "here, there, above, and below." White sheets are provided for the expected deflowering of Fiammetta, who is ready for marriage. An ugly outsider has penetrated the walled-in city to pluck one of Florence's loveliest flowers: that is, to rob its golden boys of that which one of them is meant to have as a birthright. Consequently, the assault on Taddeo is tantamount to a sexual charivari, all the more appropriate because it is the carnival season. If, in a number of fifteenth- and sixteenth-century tales, lecherous priests are killed or castrated for preying on the chastity of women,[30] here the bloodletting caused by the vicious leather straps adds up to a ceremony of symbolic castration.[31] That something like this is being negotiated emerges more clearly later on in the tale when, at the pillory, the large lettering on the maquette suggests that Taddeo was not truly a man; he was a sodomite who had gone astray.

The tale ends with the phallic triumph, back at the horse shed, of Taddeo's six assailants. Enveloped again in their white garb, and finding that their victim has rolled around in the shed's fecal matter, the six expose their penises and urinate all over his face and body, as if to wash him down with the exuberance of their own high virtue. Then one of them quickly burns off his fashionable beard, a sign of Taddeo's aspiring status and remaining masculinity. In the economy of the tale, the sudden and violent rainstorm at the end—"the seas seemed to be up in the heavens"—may be read as a call for their own cleansing.

In France, Michel Plaisance, a well-known student of Italian Renaissance literature, has read *Taddeo* as "a sado-masochistic fantasy,"[32] the product of Grazzini's repressed homosexuality, "guilty conscience," and "castrating mother." Indeed, he claims that Taddeo is presented "with a great deal of sympathy," so much so that he is alleged to possess a tincture of something Christlike. In this reading, Grazzini is perceived as a man divided: on the one hand, he identifies with the martyred Taddeo; on the other, looking to punish himself because of his shameful homosexual cravings, he sides with the authority and justice of Taddeo's tormentors. Plaisance does not hold—although he could, in view of his Freudian grasp of the story—that the assault on Taddeo is an oblique and bloated homosexual gang bang. He would then have a more aggravated and complex split in the author of *Le cene*.

One thing is clear in any case: the six men who assault Taddeo are a kind of gang caught up in a delirium of action that may be said to have a nasty element of male bonding. I would emphasize, however, that in the Italian Renaissance tale, *beffe* are often the work of several companions or collaborators, as in Gentile Sermini's tale of Mattano da Siena.[33] But whether we term them gang, group, or collaborators, the *beffatori* (tricksters) of our cruel tradition are also the chorus: the voices or bearers of the community's ideals and values.

There *are* hints of homosexual leanings in Grazzini's poetry and in a letter, and Plaisance cites the apposite passages. But he produces no evidence whatsoever regarding the author's mother or upbringing, nor a scrap of evidence in the text of the tale (*Cene*, supper 2, tale 7) revealing the least bit of sympathy for Taddeo. Unable, I believe, to understand or accept the overwhelming brutality, the French scholar mysteriously converts part of the narrative expense into a Christlike martyrdom, thereby, as it were, rescuing Grazzini's art. Moreover, aside from taking the tale's violence right out of history and situating it entirely in the author's alleged psyche, his interpretation also rests on a proleptic or a priori application of psychoanalytic theory. These elements, it seems to me, serve to vitiate an analysis whose true value lies in having identified an odd and disturbing ingredient in the tale.

Lest I be charged with peddling fiction as fact, I want to emphasize that *Taddeo* is a fiction, and there is no suggestion here that anything like it took place. However, being rooted in historical realities, *l'imaginaire* seldom if ever wholly conceals or disguises them. As the text itself makes clear, Grazzini meant his readers to find the tale entertaining, funny, and even, possibly, just. Although not published until the eighteenth century, nothing in *Le cene* or in what we know about Florentine Renaissance society indicates that he was mistaken about his expectations. As a narrative exercise, his twenty-two tales rest on a lively tradition of some two hundred years of formal storytelling; and the anatomy of the cruel/funny *beffa* holds a privileged place there, obviously because it appealed to generations of keenly appreciative readers and listeners, not to say an audience that now and then encountered the *beffa* in its immediate experience.

What is more, Grazzini (1503–84) knew his Florence. Born there in the Santo Spirito quarter, on the far side of the Arno, he came from a family of attorneys (*notai*) and small merchants; but he himself seems not long to have practiced a trade.[34] Instead, he lived largely on inherited income and dearly valued his economic independence. Throughout his known life, as Plaisance rightly observes, he frequented men of the sort born above his own social station: aristocratic or well-connected Florentines, heirs to landed estates and to ancient public-office traditions. Deeply interested in the origins of the Tuscan tongue, he also wrote plays and poetry and was a founder, in 1540, of the first Florentine academy, the Accademia degli Umidi.

Bearing in mind the history of the Italian tale at the end of the Middle Ages and during the high Renaissance, I have located the reputed cruelty of the Italians in "an act of cerebration," the *beffa* or *natta*. Marguerite of Navarre's *Heptaméron,* however, finds the cruelty in senseless brutality and butchery. One of her storytellers, remembering his war experience in Italy, gives the example of an Italian captain who cooked and ate the heart of a dead enemy, killed the man's pregnant wife, dashed the fruit of her womb against a stone wall, "then stuffed the corpses of both husband and wife with oats and fed them to his horses."[35] I cite these details only to observe that cruelty may be of two kinds: one to be found in acts of sudden butchery, the other in planned activity that makes for sustained torment, either mental or physical. They may of course be combined. The example of the Italian captain already holds a brain-spun ingredient in the stuffing of the corpses with oats.

If we end with the trite observation that all peoples have a potentiality for both cruelty and kindness, the question for the historian has to be, What are the conditions and social structures that draw these forth and almost *make* them? Even in our day some societies are seen as being more cruel than others. When we turn to Renaissance Italy, and more particularly to Florence, we can easily detect a strain of cruelty in the literature of the period, as well in the poetry as in the prose fiction. Analysis, however, soon dilutes our facile perceptions, elicits our own presuppositions, and reduces the horror of the cruelties by putting them into a bed of social-structural motivation. Does this mean that we may thus excuse all cruelty, in seeming to explain it away? I do not see how this is possible, how we can disavow ourselves in the putting of a seal of *rational* acceptance on everything that history throws at us. As historians, even as we study the constitutive features or building blocks that make some societies less or more murderous than others, we tend to introduce a moral dimension into our analyses, into our diction and metaphors, but first of all into our ways of asking questions. We may as well accept the axiom that historians also moralize.

NINE

SEDUCTION &
FAMILY SPACE

"Love often leads lovers into mortal dangers"

DECAMERON, 9.1

One of the trickier seductions of the Italian Renaissance takes place in Machiavelli's comedy *La mandragola*. The protagonist, Callimaco, hires a go-between to help him gain access to the house of an old lawyer, where he proposes to have sex with the man's pretty young wife, Lucrezia. The trick is to persuade the lawyer that a compound of mandrake root will render her fertile and thus bring progeny and happiness to the childless pair. But since the first man to couple with Lucrezia after she takes the potion will absorb all the resulting poisons and die, he must be an ignorant stranger somehow pressed into the deed—none other than the young Callimaco in disguise. Once the old lawyer is made to believe in the powers of mandrake, he has no trouble, as Lucrezia's respected husband, procuring the cooperation of her mother and the connivance of friar Timoteo, Lucrezia's confessor and spiritual director.

Written about 1518, *La mandragola* enjoyed immediate success in Florence, Rome, Venice, and Faenza, a success due, no doubt, to the comedy's side-splitting ingenuity.[1] Yet much of the play is constructed of realistic elements, all of which are to be found, along with a wealth of others, in scores of tales written between the mid–fourteenth and the mid–sixteenth centuries. These elements, no less than their artful mingling in Machiavelli's concoction, helped to guarantee the success of the play; their cunning realism was the very thing that appealed to contemporaries.

In this chapter I examine the whole question of family space in the urban civilization of Renaissance Italy by concentrating on the theme of seduction in a multitude of tales. The mode of inquiry restricts my findings largely, but not exclusively, to the way of life of the propertied classes. This is, however, a customary limitation in most social study of the Italian Renaissance.[2] By *family space* I mean (1) the space occupied or much frequented by families, especially by the conjugal core, and (2) the space over which family elders or adult males claimed an unquestioned right, such as in all affairs concerning the vital interests of the family.[3] In illustration, suffice it to say that family space accompanied all women young enough to be sexual prey, wherever they might go, but it did not go with young men into brothels or market-places unless a fracas erupted there, involving definite questions of family honor.

The ploys of seduction were the stuff of the most popular kind of anecdote in Italian urban society. This is confirmed by hundreds of tales and by what these intimate about an underlying oral tradition. As material for storytelling, clever seductions were matched in popularity, if at all, only by malicious tricks or pranks (the *beffa* or *natta*), such as in stories in which vain or gullible men and women are duped and scathingly humiliated. Very often, too, trick and seduction were astutely coupled: a woman tricks her husband in order to be with a lover, or a man seduces a young wife by tricking her husband, as in *La mandragola*.

The ensuing observations are based on 251 tales and anecdotes, nearly all dating from the two centuries between about 1350 and 1560, including nar-ratives by such *novellieri* as Boccaccio, Sacchetti, Ser Giovanni, Sercambi, Ser-mini, Poggio, Piovano Arlotto, Arienti, Masuccio Salernitano, Firenzuola, Molza, Brevio, Grazzini, Bandello, Fortini, Straparola, and Parabosco, along with a scatter of writers of single stories, such as Lorenzo de' Medici, Mara-bottino Manetti, and E. S. Piccolomini. I list the authors in the appendix to this chapter and indicate the number of tales taken from each. Of the total number of tales, 150 are directly about seduction, and the other 101 are closely related thereto, either because the first sexual encounter has already occurred and we are in medias res, or because certain amatory ingredients link the plot to different aspects of the activity of seduction.

The fiction in question recommends itself to historians because it is steeped in practical, everyday particulars. And as we found in chapter 7, Renaissance readers longed for realistic settings and details. Hence foods, clothing, customs, work and prayer times, public office, crime and punishment, neighborhoods, specific places, street names, and so forth, all tend to be accurately presented or represented. Seldom is there a conflict with testimony from the conventional streams of historical documentation. Nor do writers ever idealize the act of sex. They depict it in an earthy fashion, naturalistically, or even humorously, and they may rely on the metaphors of horse riding, gardening, farming, wool-beating, tilting, or the action of putting money into a woman's purse. Knowing that their readers and listeners, largely a male audience, had a strong predilection for the lineaments of actual experience, writers sought to retail stories taken from real life or to spin yarns that commented on the injunctions of daily life. From Sacchetti to Bandello, they continually claim that their stories actually took place, and this indeed was sometimes the case.[4] But even when the anecdote was entirely invented or lifted from an exotic oral or written tradition, it is usually embedded in the observed realities of time, place, manners, and circumstances—indisputable ground for the historian.

In the course of my inquiry, I shall appear at times to blur the frontier between fiction (tales) and recorded event or detail (history). This procedure is deliberate, not so much because I seek to point out that some aspects of historical phenomena have this instability *ex natura* as because I aim to retrieve parts of the historical reality lodged in Renaissance tales.

SEDUCTION: THEME AND CHARACTERS

If in our time, in the Western world, the act of seduction is given no unique or privileged place in literature, this is because contemporary society raises no coercive barriers against it. Seduction has lost its drama. Institutions do not truly get in the way of adultery or fornication, nor have they in the West in any structural sense since perhaps the end of the nineteenth century, depending upon country, locale, and social class.[5] But in Renaissance Italy, every "honorable" family guarded carefully against the seducing of its women. Preachers and statutory law prescribed severe penalties for the seduction of virgins and other men's wives. Widows were sharply warned against sexual lapses, and young women, wives or widows, were meant to take as models martyred female saints of the sort who had preferred death to loss of chastity.[6] Kin, friends, and neighbors were always on the lookout for secret lovers, not only so as to join the chorus of voices raised against illicit relations but also, if they were neighbors, to get news of scandalous stories. Gossip seasoned the life, illustrated the moral codes, and fired the imagination of the close, paro- chial neighborhoods of Renaissance cities.

Seduction, then, was all about a fundamental taboo. Where poverty or economic hardship scattered family members, putting women out to work, female sexuality lost its dangerous features and the taboos fell largely away. Female servants could not depend upon the laws against rape for any true protection: their obvious poverty, in the eyes of police magistrates and courts, appeared to bespeak a readiness to sell their bodies.[7] But wherever property, dowry, status, good name, and honor held a plea, all these were endangered by the seducing of a woman; for her defloration or unchastity signified disor- der, disobedience, and a breakdown of authority in the household. And every man who set out to seduce a woman of the propertied classes knew the dangers, knew that he proposed to violate trusts, names, and honors, and knew that he himself would fiercely resist any such threat to a woman of his family. Consequently, there could be no seduction without fear both in the woman involved and in the would-be seducer, who was aware that he ran the risk of marriage, dreadful scandal, financial penalties, violent physical assault, or even death.

Owing, therefore, to the determining effects of property and status, seduc- tion in upper-class circles was only contingently about the carnality of sex and really much more about theft, disdain, and violation: the theft of intangible patrimonies (honor, name, and standing), disdain for the authority figures in the violated household, and violation of the sacrosanct because the action polluted present marriage, as in adultery, or ruined the prospect of future marriage, as in the dishonoring of young widows or the deflowering of virgins. Marriage among honorable people was seen as a linking of two families, a union based on religious vows or "words of present consent" (the *verba de praesenti*), a contractual underpinning of properties, and a fundamen- tal strategy for social and biological survival. Preachers might emphasize the free consent of the betrothed, but in the case of girls and young women, this was easily enough obtained or imposed, and the consenting words were sometimes even spoken for them by another.[8] For the whole business of marriage had to do with reproduction, the transmission of property, the maintenance of status and honor, and the perpetuating of a Christian life. In this sense marriage was what life was all about.

In the late fifteenth century, the Este and Sforza princes were delighted to be the chief brokers or fixers of important marriages in their respective cities, Ferrara and Milan. Lorenzo the Magnificent performed a similar office in Florence. Princes were wife-givers. They conveyed enhanced social being: virginity, properties, *fama,* and honor.[9] In this light they were makers of men, particularly because they disposed of considerable resources; and since they were always seeking to content legions of clients, they looked upon marriage brokering as an important form of patronage and gift-giving. Here again was evidence of the primacy of marriage.

This primacy is fully taken for granted in Renaissance tales of seduction, and we may gauge its importance by the dangers that threaten the act of seduction in fiction's treatment of the social space that goes with marriage, as well as in its stock of characters.

There are eight recurrent *personaggi:* the young wife or virgin, the old husband, the seducer, the clever go-between, the young widow, the lusty priest or friar, the trickster, and the gull or victim. Any given story is unlikely to utilize more than three or four of these, and some may do double or triple work. Thus Machiavelli's *Mandragola* employs only four of the figures: a young wife, an old husband, a young seducer, and a clever go-between. But the old husband is also the victim; the seducer and the go-between share the role of the trickster; and friar Timoteo, though not moved by lust, is the immoral figure in clerical garb. Nevertheless, it is well to distinguish the eight different roles, because each involves an aspect of the social vision that shapes the tales, thus helping us to convert these into nonfiction and historical testimony.

One type of union in the demography of marriage often made for much psychological strain. I refer to first marriage for the woman, in which the age difference between spouses did not reflect one of the regional averages, say from seven to thirteen years (the male always the elder)[10] but rather was in the range of twenty to thirty years or even more, as when a virgin of seventeen was married to a man in his late thirties or forties. Here was the young-wife cum old-husband syndrome. Speaking for an oral tradition of feeling or expectation about the consequent wretchedness, ballads about the *malmaritata,* the unhappily married girl, were common from the fourteenth to the sixteenth centuries.[11] Certain stories, moreover, such as those in which the old man is punished for having been vain and foolish enough to marry a verdant creature, are acid polemics both against him and the father or guardians who had arranged the unhappy union.[12]

But there were countervailing ideals, too, also articulated in fiction, sanctioning marriage between young and old; and these ideals went to the doctrinal roots of traditional, androcentric, patrilocal society.[13] Here property clings mostly to the male line, the old stand over the young, men stand over women, custom rules over novelty, and all authority is meant to go unquestioned. The young are conditioned to satisfy family and group needs first, not their own individual (antisocial) "appetites." In this purview, if a wife was to be absolutely obedient and to learn the ways of her husband, she must be young enough to be as yet unformed (ideally the early or middle teenage years) and he old enough to have had experience of the world, so that he would know how to mold and shape her. The girl's family provided the pure near-child, but her husband would make and fashion her. As the great courtier Castiglione had his wife declare in a verse epistle to himself, she missed him keenly when he was away, because having been "given to him" as a girl by her parents, she felt that "only you have been my husband, you only my parents" (solus tu mihi vir, solus uterque parens).[14] If too inexperienced himself, a young husband could not properly school the girl; indeed, owing to the power of feminine wiles, his inexperience might drag him under the sway of her willful and irrational desires.[15]

The older husband, therefore, was both a source of social strain and one of the key figures, like his young wife, in many tales of seduction. He was also, however—let us always bear this in mind—the fine old flower of traditional urban society, its custodian and principal incarnation.

Another of our stock characters, the young seducer, rather speaks for himself. But part of his significance is also coded in the symbolic resources of the narrative. In some tales he is the avenger of the woman whose husband is unable to satisfy her sexually.[16] In others, ironically, he is simply the occasion for misogyny: he brings out the treachery of women.[17] And in others still, he stands for the antisocial individual will, as it hurls itself against that socially useful union, the arranged marriage of convenience.[18] In the last of these, the dramatic outcome is often murder, suicide, mutilation, or a mysterious death. Social structures, as epitomized in arranged marriage, are thus seen to triumph. In other tales again, the seducer is none other than the closest friend of the woman's careless (taboo-breaking) husband, who violates the privacy or intimacy of his own conjugal space by introducing his friend into it, into the primal area of a sexually active young woman. The result is that the friend too will share in the fruits of that space.[19] The lesson here is not about the limitations of friendship—these are taken for granted—rather, it is about not letting any male enter into the reproductive space (the household) of the married couple unless he is one of the young woman's close kinsmen.

When the young wife is herself the seducer,[20] the causes of her aberrant behavior are always immediate and specific: (1) the sexual incapacity of the older husband, (2) the husband's demented jealousy, which drives the young woman to rage and desperation, (3) his manifest homosexuality and love of boys, or even (4) her superior social background and resentment at having been married down, whence her willful desire for a young man of her social condition.

The roles of the trickster and the go-between may be combined. They offer insight into the guarded or monitored space around women. The surveillance of propertied young wives and widows was likely to be such that any thought of seducing them demanded extraordinary forethought, cunning, and secrecy. There was no other way to get near such a woman. Her fear and the barriers around her were too great. Hence the remarkable variety of tricks used to approach her: for instance, snaring her through her piety, becoming godfather to one of her children or a servant to her husband, catching her eye in church, tracking her seasonal movements between town and country, employing clever go-betweens (the favorite means), or even, in a more inventive vein, cross-dressing and pretending to be a woman. The last of these devices is used in a tale about a beardless and slight young man who passes himself off as a girl so as to become a servant in the household of a young wife, where in due course he becomes her personal maid.[21] This ruse may be a pure fiction, but it is also roundabout historical evidence of the extent to which virgins, wives, and young widows were hedged in by marital, family, and neighborhood controls. In Verona maidens were veiled when they went through the city streets; and in Venice, down at least to the early sixteenth century, virgins of good class covered their heads so fully when in public that foreign visitors wondered if they had trouble seeing as they walked in the streets.[22]

We now see why the intermediary or go-between was often such a crucial figure. If well placed, he or she was the one plausible means of making contact with a woman whose movements were under surveillance, who was rarely if

ever seen alone in the streets, and whose entire upbringing would instantly
have caused her to spurn any advance from an unknown male. Indeed, even if
she was already ardently attracted, as in Piccolomini's *Historia de duobus amantibus,* she must indignantly reject the initial approach of the would-be seducer
or appear dishonorable and unworthy. The culture of the middle- and upper-
class young woman gave her no other choice, although there are exceptions,
of course, in the *novellistica.*

The role of the victim frequently belongs to the husband of the adulterous
woman, to the woman herself (wife or widow), or to her guardians. If nothing else, her neighbors and the wider urban society are seen to be cheated by
any successful seduction, for their laws have been flouted and they have failed,
despite all their nosiness, to detect the affair. Since the boundaries that circumscribed the protected young woman could only be crossed, as we have
seen, by means of some kind of treachery or trickery, seducing her, whether
in reality or in fiction, meant that there had to be a victim. In an intriguing
real case of seduction (Florence, mid-1450s), dug up and studied by Gene
Brucker in his *Giovanni and Lusanna: Love and Marriage in Renaissance Florence*
(1986), the widow Lusanna and her protective brother turn out to be the
victims of a sly and barefaced upper-class seducer.[23]

Of the eight roles in our amatory tales, the one involving the young widow
is the most recurrent and charged with meaning. Much more than the young
wife or virgin, she is the chief prey, the one first singled out by lechers and
would-be lovers. Anthropologists find a certain ambiguity in the widow, in
her unsteady position between two kinship groupings, her own natal line and
the patrilineage into which she has married. Her children belong to their
father's line, but in having to care for them (unless she remarries), she also
seems to drift closer to their line. The best studied of all Italian widows of the
fifteenth century, the Florentine Alessandra Macinghi, who married into the
distinguished Strozzi lineage, was herself all Strozzi in looking after her sons
with such devotion that she would have sacrificed everything for them,
including the material well-being of her two daughters.[24]

The ambiguity of the young widow certainly comes through in fiction,
but it has more to do with her sexuality than with family identities. Will she
surrender to her carnal passions or somehow control them? This was the
inevitable question. Men obviously saw her as the most accessible of all
desirable women, because her most jealous guardian, her husband, was no
more. In 1444 a sharp-eyed contemporary, afterward Pope Pius II, flatly

observed that the practice of keeping a close watch on women "is a common vice among Italians, each of whom locks his wife up as though she were gold" (Vitum hoc apud Italos late patet, feminam suam quasi thesaurum quisque recludit).[25] In the popular assumptions of the day, men saw the typical young widow as keenly desirous of the pleasures of the flesh, because she had been sexually aroused by marriage. If she remarried, some sexual satisfaction would evidently follow. But if not, she lived, it was thought, in a state of anxious sexual desire, which could be satisfied only illicitly.[26] If she lived with her in-laws because of her children, she came under a new scrutiny. If, instead, she returned to live with her parents or brothers, her movements were again narrowly circumscribed. Consequently, the prize widow was the one rich enough and free enough from family ties to live on her own, with or without children, out of the direct line of sight of both lineages.[27] In this rare situation, she came to occupy a place between two kinship lines. Now at last, if she had complete control over her servants, assignations might be possible, despite the intruding eyes of kin, friends, and neighbors. For these were folk who thought they knew all about the supposed needs of widows; they had an eye out for all unusual activity around their houses, and on occasion they no doubt imagined wooing where there was none.

Given the foregoing framework, we can at once see why contemporary opinion urged widows to cultivate religious fervor.[28] Customarily dressed in black, or less often in a shade of maroon, they were in the world but not meant to be of it, if they expected to guard name and honor. Tales occasionally show them sharing houses with other pious widows, attending church often and regularly, and being under the strong influence of one of the different orders of friars. Many widows were tertiaries or *fratesche,* devoted followers of a regular religious order, such as the Franciscans or the Dominicans, and they might also go about in a grey mantle, to be known as *ammantellate.* Others, *conversi,* actually went as lay boarders into certain nunneries.[29] Storytellers allege that many widows used piety as a cover for their sexual misconduct;[30] and there is no reason to dismiss this allegation as fictional license. The overwhelming need to conform could issue in useful hypocrisy. In the bruising struggle to appear honorable, why might a widow, if driven by sexual desire, not use the camouflage of religion as well to protect her honor as to give rein to her sexuality? Large parts of the clergy, after all, had scandalous reputations for gluttony and lechery; so if a widow had intercourse with a man in holy orders, her sin would surely have struck her as minor compared to his. He was the dominant, learned male, not she; he had taken holy vows of chastity, not she; and his misconduct therefore somehow diminished hers.

These observations lead us directly to the lecherous cleric, the last of our principal characters. Nearly all *novellieri* produced tales about lusty priests and friars,[31] young and old, handsome and ugly, learned and ignorant, fine noblemen in holy orders and coarse upstarts. As confessors and spiritual directors, clerics were the only men from outside any given family, the only strangers, who might be in direct or nearly regular contact with the women of that family. Where the evidence is available, we find that mothers and daughters tended to have the same spiritual director;[32] and if a woman of the upper classes went to confession even as infrequently as two or three times a year, she got closer perhaps to her confessor than she was ever likely to be with any other male, apart from, say, her brothers, sons, and husband. The two could actually hold conversations in private. Moreover, owing to their changed status, newly married or widowed women could abandon the spiritual directors of their mothers, select a different confessor, and so take a more independent moral route. Unsurprisingly, therefore, clerics themselves—for example, San Bernardino of Siena, Antoninus of Florence, Beltrame da Ferrara, and the rules of certain friaries—were sometimes suspicious of regular contact between confessors and female penitents.[33] They distrusted their confreres even more, apparently, than they distrusted young wives and widows. The contact between men in holy orders and women was certainly no secret to husbands and male relatives. And so, appropriately, our stories indicate that women of the comfortable classes, up to about their midthirties, were usually either accompanied when they went to church or their attendance was approximately timed.[34]

In the long period between about 1350 and 1550, the image of the goatish cleric appears in nearly every writer who issued a series of tales. In addition, since there is ample archival evidence of the sexual misconduct of the Renaissance clergy,[35] we must suppose that fiction's exposé of the priapic exploits of churchmen had historical foundations and that those who looked to their wives like misers to their gold worried themselves sick at times about the odd dangers that might attend the piety and churchgoing of younger women.

Another matter also worried laymen. Aside from the elite of humanists, most people seem to have assumed that clerics were knowledgeable men, owing to their Latinity.[36] All the more, accordingly, might parishioners fear their capacity for tricks and cunning. In rural and mountainous regions, according to the corpus of Renaissance tales, the urban-born part of the clergy were often haughty in their dealings with a peasantry that they regarded as ignorant and uncivil.[37] They could also be bullies, at least with humble and working-class folk.[38]

In amatory tales, the amphibious cleric may be the evil seducer and the trickster, the knave who is himself tricked, or even the sordid go-between who, curiously, can turn out to be innocent. But his ambiguous place near women is basic—he might even be a woman's *compare,* spiritual coparent to one of her children. The result was that literature could easily treat him as a slippery creature in the streets and culture of the age.

SPACE, TIME, AND SEDUCTION

Like the towns of Oxford and Cambridge for so long, Italian Renaissance cities were places chiefly for men. Women and girls were naturally to be seen almost everywhere, but it was the men mostly who frequented and dominated the large churches, the main streets and squares, the markets, and the areas around waterfronts, fortresses, city gates, and court and government buildings.[39] If they chose to go forth, men also claimed the night and the twilight hours of the evening. Working women and women of the lower classes, having to enter male enclaves such as markets, whether to sell or to buy goods, could not match the swagger of male preeminence. Who, after all, walked up and down streets in front of chosen houses, striving to catch the sight of some pretty face?

At dawn, in season, peasant women came in from the countryside to sell small quantities of food: fruit, eggs, or poultry. Among the urban propertied classes, *par contre,* the men and the servants did all or most of the marketing, such as for meat and fish, the basic fare for the large, late breakfasts of the day.[40] Well covered and looking respectable, older wives and widows (those without servants) ventured out alone to do their shopping. But this was not the office of virgins or of young wives or widows of good class; and when these women went out into the streets, if well brought up, they walked with their eyes turned to the ground. At Siena in the 1390s, Raimondo da Capua noticed that "it is not easy to see a nubile girl go out [into the streets]."[41] In all cities at given times of the day, certain churches, squares, bridges, and other places turned into out-and-out meeting points for men. Mornings in Florence, for example, the cathedral attracted gossiping men of the sort who could take time off from business or work. In Bologna in the late morning, the Piazza Maggiore belonged mainly to noblemen, knights, and doctors of law. At Pisa in the late fourteenth century, the men of the ruling class favored the loggia of the Ponte Vecchio.[42] And in Venice the bustling Rialto area and the square of San Marco always belonged to men.

I draw the foregoing outlines in order to hint at the restricted radii for family and especially female activity. If when in the streets, respectable women had to walk with their eyes averted, how could those spaces be regarded as anything but male? The brazen eyes of ambulant prostitutes could not alter this, even when, as in fifteenth-century Lucca, they were free to walk anywhere.[43] The required accessories of their trade, bells, a bright sash, gloves, high heels, or a special veil, were marks of shame and identification.[44] It followed that the doors and windows of houses were sharp boundaries; and in some cities the home was a safe asylum against debtors' prison. All "decent women were supposed to lock the main entrance the moment their husbands left home," and "windows were equipped with full shutters, bars, and frequently iron grates."[45] The sheds or single (rented) rooms of poor folk, a good 20 to 30 percent of urban populations, usually had no such fixtures; but it was also true that their women were less cloistered, less guarded, under fewer family controls.[46] Poverty held fewer dangers for name and honor, since there was little enough of these.

The large body of tales from Tuscany—from Florence, Siena, and Lucca— strongly suggests that the propertied women of Genoa and Venice had more freedom of movement, and so were more likely to be licentious, than their equals to the south, say from Bologna to Perugia. The Romagna, again, had an infamous reputation, but more for male villainy than for female infamy. Forgetting their own reputation for sodomy, Tuscans associated the alleged laxity of Genoese and Venetian mores with the mixed, international ways of great seaports but above all with the perception that Venetian and Genoese men were often away from home engaged in overseas enterprise, despite the fact that by the mid–fifteenth century, among the patriciate at all events, they were a more sedentary sort. In the eyes of Tuscans, the absence of fathers, husbands, and brothers meant looser (ungoverned) young women.

Alas, there are remarkably few extant tales from fourteenth- and fifteenth-century Venice and Genoa, so we cannot say how people there regarded themselves in realistic fiction. *Novelle* of the sixteenth century, with more closely observed Venetian settings—by Bandello, Parabosco, and Straparola—come from a period of changed mores. The cult of the courtesan or the classy tart, for instance, by that time much in fashion, had some effect on the outlook of the Venetian upper-class male.[47] Certain gentlemen in Venice even came to believe that neighbors should be more tolerant of the "carnal" needs of young widows, always provided, of course, that such women kept to one lover and prudently guarded appearances, for name and honor remained all-important.[48] In short, we cannot readily use sixteenth-century stories set in Venice to help us throw light on the customs of Venetian upper-class women during the previous century. There are findings enough, however, in the well-known study by Guido Ruggiero, *The Boundaries of Eros: Sex Crime and Sexuality in Renaissance Venice* (1985), to suggest that in the period up to about 1500, married women of the Venetian nobility had a little more scope for action than their like in Florence, Lucca, Siena, or Perugia.

Having roughly sketched the circumscribed urban space for female activity, I should add the spatial coordinates of local churches, of chaperoned or accompanied movement to and from these, of visits to relatives, and, in the summer and early autumn, of two- to three-month sojourns in the countryside, where the families of substance customarily owned farmland, orchards, or vineyards, as well as villas or smaller houses.

If we return briefly to Machiavelli's *Mandragola,* we can now clearly see why the young wife, Lucrezia, lay beyond the reach of any possible seducer unless the strange connivance of her own husband made her accessible. The aspiring lover, Callimaco, could not hope to approach her in the streets, in church, or anywhere else outside the house, because such women did not move about alone. Let us suppose that he had plotted to attend a wedding fete where the old lawyer and his young wife were also to be present. If for a moment then he got a fleeting chance to address her alone, all the girl's fear and conditioning, in realistic terms, would have risen in revolt against him, especially as she is made to seem a rather timid and very moral young woman.

My sanction for thus mixing fiction and reality, that is, for my glissade from *La mandragola* out to the question of real possibilities in the Florentine world of Machiavelli's day, is both in the comedy itself and in the rich short-story corpus. Relying heavily on different aspects of social reality, Renaissance tales and plays already have their foundations in history; and this entitles the historian, in the tasks of analysis, to negotiate his way back and forth between the real and the imaginary. In this connection, let us consider for a moment a calculated meeting at a wedding party.

In the 1470s Sabadino degli Arienti, Bologna's leading storyteller, produced a tale about a young man who had fallen in love with Sulpicia dei Tebaldi, a married woman.[49] Both lady and would-be lover sprang from distinguished Bolognese families. However, while giving all the names involved, Arienti's chosen narrator, a noblewoman from Tuscany, refuses to name the young man in order not to give offense. Still alive apparently, he was a boon companion to her father, Simone dei Bardi, in their youth.

Never having had the opportunity to talk to Madonna Sulpicia, the young man suddenly accosts her one day at a wedding party of the Fantucci-Ucellani families, where he is serving as an honorary attendant. Seeing her detach herself and go off with a female companion to a lavatory facility outside the house, he rushes up to her, although the other lady tries to bar his way. It is his one chance to speak to Sulpicia; time is of the essence; and so he makes an instant declaration of love in the elevated, upper-class fashion of the day ("Lady Sulpicia, queen of my soul," etc.).[50] Seeing at once through his refined posturing, Sulpicia laughingly responds by saying that she values his words but that the ground around them is dirty and that she would soil her beautiful silks. The youth replies that he will go and find something to put under her, whereupon she agrees to wait. Returning with a "sack"—*sacco,* a type of mantle[51]—he sees that Sulpicia has gone, and cursing his bad luck, he goes back to the festivities. There, finding her between dances, he approaches her respectfully and says, "Madam, come, I have found a sack." "Good," she replies, "now go shit in it before somebody else does," and turns away from him to speak to the woman sitting beside her. Crushed, the young man retreats in shame and humiliation.

Whether wholly invented or based on some related incident, this tale reveals both Sulpicia's strong conditioning and the difficulty of even approaching an attractive woman of the upper class. The key moments of invention are in the punning on "sack" and the pointed contrast between the lover's ritualized language and the reported filth around the cesspool area. Sulpicia's insult was not only perfectly appropriate in a culture where conversation could instantly swing from courtly love to basic bodily functions;[52] it was also a fair response to what the young man actually had in mind, namely, the dishonoring of an honorable married woman.

Since weddings offered one of the rare occasions that might bring unrelated young people together into the same private rooms, tales occasionally rely on them. But even then, up to about the early 1500s, a conversation between an upper-class woman and a would-be lover, out of the earshot of others, would have been difficult. Apart from the fact that there was much dancing between women on such occasions, a dancing man and woman conversed under some restraint, the eyes of relatives and others being fixed on them.[53] Moreover, if a woman turned her gaze away—and this too was obvious—she at once cut off, in Boccaccio's expression, "the language of the eyes."[54] So on the question of fixing possible venues for assignations, these considerations return us to the spaces and areas greatly favored by the Renaissance tale: the home, the front door and window areas, the darkened rooms within, the country villa, the church or priory, and the spaces that could be violated by peripatetic go-betweens.

The last of these suggests that no space was inviolable. There was also, however, as has just been noted, another possible transgressor: the language of the eyes. Here was a mode of speech that could violate all spaces, all frontiers; and Renaissance literature sparkles with such communication. Petrarch centers many of his lyric poems on the imagery of Laura's eyes,[55] and the love poetry of the age is shot through with the theme of the speaking eye. Why this was so is now all too obvious: the social restrictions of the urban upper classes imposed the language of the eyes wherever there was any desire to establish illicit or disapproved-of bonds of affection. Aspiring lovers could find some unique content in merely speaking with their eyes.[56] This too is why window and door areas, particularly the former, are so often singled out in Renaissance fiction: eye contact was made there and ocular signals were frequently transmitted at windows.[57] In real life, women and girls were often warned to stay away from windows, and the penalty for infractions was at times a beating.[58] Nevertheless, women and windows are obsessively linked in the corpus of tales, for window space was, paradoxically, female space. Kept mostly indoors, girls and women of the comfortable classes, as noted in chapter 7, must have regarded windows as their eyes to the outside world.

All men and women knew that eyes could be used transgressively. Writing about 1430, Gentile Sermini produced a story about two apprentice silk merchants, the Florentines Papino and Giovan Bello, who are bound by a close friendship.[59] After Papino marries, he insists that his friend come often to the house, even against the wishes of his new wife, "little Laura" (Lauretta),

who fears the malicious gossip of neighbors. Invited, in effect, to violate
Papino's marital space, Giovan Bello (John the handsome) will in due course
enjoy Lauretta too. Yet early in the story, when the friend's conduct is still
above reproach, Lauretta tells her husband that when the three are together,
even when Papino falls asleep at table, Giovan Bello is always careful to avoid
eye contact with her, thus attesting to his virtue.

In one of Boccaccio's tales,[60] the expressive nature of the eyes is foolishly
ignored by a husband who transgressively authorizes a scheming suitor, Zima,
to get close enough to his wife to talk to her. Offered a beautiful palfrey by the
young Zima, Francesco Vergellesi, a nobleman from Pistoia, agrees to the
stipulated conditions: he may have the horse to keep if Zima is allowed to talk
to Francesco's beautiful wife in Francesco's presence but beyond his earshot.
Unknown to Zima, Francesco imposes silence on his wife; she is not to say a
word; and so she is completely mute at the interview. The surprised but
inspired Zima then makes a moving love plea to the young woman, climaxing
it with tears in his eyes; whereupon she responds with her eyes and half-
suppressed sighs. Now Zima, imitating her supposed voice and speaking
for her, provides detailed directions for their first secret rendezvous. When,
therefore, a few days later, Francesco leaves Pistoia for a six-month tour of
office in Milan, his wife transmits the prearranged signal and Zima sneaks into
their house at night to "ride" her, while Francesco is riding the palfrey.
Though envisaged in a fictitious situation, Zima's fervent plea and the young
woman's eyes were features practical or realistic enough to bring about the
cuckolding of a slow-witted husband in a world of arranged marriages of
convenience. For the first time ever, thanks to Francesco's playing fast and
loose with his own marital space, his wife is the direct recipient of a passionate
love declaration, and she is able, against all expectations, to rise above her
strict conditioning. Indeed, in context, her ready compliance seems explosive—thereby coming through as a measure of the crushing constraints on
her.

We have seen that no domestic space was beyond the reach of sinful eyes
and messengers or go-betweens. For all its perils, the home of the transgress-
ing woman, whether in town or country, remained the preferred sexual
venue. As often illustrated by the *novellistica,* country villas at night were the
ideal place for trysts, owing to the relative sparseness of neighbors and the
absence of husbands or other male guardians, who were sometimes compelled to make business trips back into the city. In the 1480s Lorenzo de'

Medici's mistress, Bartolomea de' Nasi, regularly used this dodge when receiving her lover.[61] Honor, name, and life or limb were under a lesser threat in
the country. Illicit house entries were far less likely to be noticed there. But
villegiatura (a stay in the country) lasted three months at most, and not many
wives or widows had discretely placed villas. The urban home of the sinning
woman thus remained primary. Much as she feared the inherent dangers
there, she was more at ease and more in control in a well-known space. That
great male world, the alien and uncontrollable outdoors, held unknown and
hence more frightening dangers.

A medley of simple rules governed the violation of domestic or marital
space:

1. Generally in households, the secret presence of a male lover put lives in
danger; hence supreme caution was the rule, for he was at least a house-
breaker and a thief and therefore, in a common turn of the period, fit to be
"cut to pieces" with impunity.
2. Since servants had the first of spying eyes, they had to be bribed or
somehow kept utterly ignorant of the affair.
3. Signals to lovers had to be clear but innocent-looking, so as to draw none
but the right party's attention.
4. Since the question of time was absolutely critical if the eyes of neighbors
were to be avoided, illicit entry into a house nearly always took place in the
dark, whether over roofs, through a window, through the main entrance, or
by way of a rear garden.
5. The lover always left before dawn, again to avoid detection.
6. Since master bedrooms and main entrances were provided with heavy
bolts or locks, lovers carefully utilized these against surprise arrivals.
7. Bedroom lamps or lanterns were generally to be found in the houses of
the well-off. Nevertheless, lovers tended to keep bedrooms dark, either
from shame or fear or because there might be a small child or two in the
same room, though on a little bed and well below the top of the large, raised
bed of the master bedrooms of the period.

Any rule regarding the use of servant go-betweens was bound to be more
flexible. Their dispatch is often seen in the first stages of a seduction. They
elicit the first reactions and are a face-saving device, especially for women. If
dispatched by a wife or a widow, messengers had to be absolutely trustworthy,
for they could destroy her. The particular value of a female servant for a
woman was in the fact that she knew the house (the sexual venue), its habits,

its voids and solid masses in the dark night, and might indeed have a certain sisterly feeling for her mistress. Renaissance tales teem with servants who are more loyal than rascally; and although demography shows that women in domestic service were remarkably mobile, some remained in the same household for years.[62] The value of the go-between for the male seducer was that he or she normally provided the only means of making a first contact with the desired woman or with someone in her house—someone who, on being outwitted, would then present no obstacle to the wished-for encounter.

Renaissance fiction respects the historical possibilities of household space in that period. The tales never give us the account of a love intrigue in a house with an extended family of two or three married couples, which, in Florence for example, made up some 18 percent of households.[63] Here clearly, apart from incest, sexual violation of the marital space was all but impossible. Fiction's respect for this aspect of historical reality says much about the importance and fixity of true household and marital space in contemporary consciousness, and it is precisely why seduction, in our large body of tales, so often depends upon craft and trickery. For unless the predators are priests or friars, who can draw the woman away from home to a place of worship, intercourse usually occurs in that other "sacred" place, the home, and illicit entry here nearly always depends upon imagination and skill. Consequently, in affairs of love, the trick or *beffa* of the Renaissance tale begins to look very much like a payment of tribute to historical reality; and a play like *La mandragola* now seems less far-fetched than it might have seemed at first sight. However rare or brain-spun any given trick, ingenuity was in fact a form of pragmatic realism.

Let us not forget, meanwhile, that in addition to husbands and brothers, there might be other men in the house, including certain ones who came from the outside but with more or less right of entry: stepsons, brothers-in-law, the occasional male servant, a homosexual lover of the husband, or even *compari* (male relatives acquired through the ritual of godparenting). Since the sexuality of men and women is given its due not only in tales but also in much other lay and religious writing of the period, fiction does not ignore the possible dangers posed by men already in the house, often in circumstances in which the question of passage of time is critical. Certain tales highlight the machinations of godfathers who seek intercourse, hence a kind of incest, with their *comari,* the mothers of the children whom they sponsored in baptism or confirmation.[64] There are tales in which a homosexual lover of the husband, having been previously introduced into the household, is then seduced by the wife in the absence of her husband.[65] Other tales show men seizing auspicious moments to seduce a female relative by marriage.[66] Here, tellingly, the gist of the lesson is that a male authority figure has been a fool in failing to be sufficiently watchful. Still other tales show young stepmothers coupling with stepsons, in scenes that strongly hint at hidden values and fantasies.[67] In this connection, I want to summarize a tale by Gentile Sermini (c. 1430) that reveals both a dash of symbolic incest and an illustrative use and abuse of the domestic area.

A thirty-year-old Florentine widow, Gioiosa ("Joyful"), beautiful, rich, and clever, falls in love with the innocent ("emerald green") and handsome Smeraldo, a sixteen-year-old orphan who is rather rich and lives nearby with his four-year-old sister, Lisa.[68] She artfully circulates the claim in the neighborhood that she and Smeraldo are related. Doing the rounds, this allegation preempts any local suspicions and is unlikely to be challenged, because brother and sister live alone and have no neighboring kin to deny the claim. One day, knowing that Smeraldo often passes her street door, Gioiosa sits there and talks to him as he goes by. Her *entrée en matière* is his little sister, whom she affects to be warmly concerned about, all the more so in that she herself has a daughter of nearly the same age. Smeraldo innocently accepts Gioiosa's courtesies; and from washing Lisa's hair on Saturdays, to looking after her in other ways, the widow proceeds in time to washing *his* hair on Saturdays and to having them in to meals. She finally gets them to spend the night of Mardi Gras with her, in order, she insists, to keep Smeraldo from falling in with evil company on that wild night. In view of the furnishings and sleeping arrangements of the age, she has little trouble getting him to share the high great bed with her, while the two little girls sleep in a *carriuola* nearby. Then, commencing with a humorous tale about forging kinships by means of coupling, Gioiosa gently introduces the youth to the pleasures of sex. The author not only presents us with a realistic use of the larger domestic space but also represents time convincingly by fitting it to the practical needs of seduction. Not mentioned at all, Gioiosa's servant or domestic help come in, apparently, from the outside.

Sermini could have ended the tale here, but he was seeking a blunter message. Having spied upon Smeraldo, two older friends of the youth discover the affair; and in his absence one day, they confront Gioiosa, rehearse the particulars of what they know, and blackmail her. Either she has sex with them or they will expose, disgrace, and destroy her. She has no choice but to yield and then swiftly comes to enjoy this new turn of affairs. Soon a nosey neighbor, an envious crone, denounces them all to the authorities: namely, to Madonna Gentile (Lady Nobility)—here we pass fully over into fable—and this generous lady imposes silence on the malicious old woman, threatening her with death by fire.

An astute negotiator of domestic and urban space, the widow Gioiosa knows intuitively how to guard name and honor. She is the protectress or mother; but she is also the carnal woman of much Renaissance poetry and fiction, worthy in fact, in fifteenth-century Tuscan terms, to be called a whore, because for a time she manages sexual relations with three men and quite delights in the arrangement. Being a product, in effect, of the male mind and imagination, the fount of literary fiction in Renissance Italy, Gioiosa has three distinct incarnations: that of mother figure, of sex-mad young widow (the free female), and of the worldly woman who knows her way around the restricted spaces and mores of the urban upper classes. As mother, she occupies the center of household space; as near-whore, she has no part in that space and is its prime transgressor; and as sophisticated worldly intelligence, knowing enough to operate almost anywhere, she is man's possible peer, hence worthy to be both feared and respected. The last of these, the most problematic of the three incarnations, leads away from our concern with family space; I have tried to deal with it elsewhere.[69]

In light of the controls exercised over the movement of young women, the question of time had to be critical in illicit loves, down even to the reckoning of minutes. How many hours or days was a husband or brother to be gone? At what points during the night was it best to go through the streets, in view of curfews, the patrolling night watch, or laws requiring pedestrians to bear torches? How close to the dawn dare a man emerge into the streets, bearing in mind that some artisans were already out before daybreak? At home, how long could a woman delay before opening a door? How rapid was the climb from the ground floor up to the bedroom? And how long might it take to fetch a compound from a local apothecary?

Scenes of seduction and illicit sex in our short fiction are fretted with questions of this sort. In a tale by Giovanni Sercambi,[70] written about 1400, the thirty-two-year-old Vessosa ("Pretty"), wife of Veri de' Medici, is tormented by sexual fantasies that are fixed on the local miller—wife and husband are in the country outside Florence. Her minutes counted, Vessosa goes out to the man's mill one day, boldly walks in on him and reaches out at once for his private parts. In the days that follow, Veri's suspicions are aroused, and pretending to have business in Florence, he doubles back to the mill in disguise, eludes the female servant posted as outlook, catches his wife and the miller in flagrante, and instantly kills both, pinning one to the other, with a single, violent thrust of a spear. He then steals away, and the double murder, given little investigation, goes unsolved.

In another Florence-based story, having heard from her own husband—hence in a semiotic violation of their marital space—that his young barber has the largest penis in the neighborhood (for he has seen Nanni in the local bath), monna Piacevole da Rabatta fakes a bad toothache. The barber-dentist is thereupon summoned, and when the husband goes downstairs for some vinegar, she unceremoniously grabs the young man's member. In seconds the decision is made to dispatch the husband to a particular apothecary some way off, and while he is gone, wife and barber have two orgasms.[71]

The concern with orgasms is paradigmatic and no mere frivolity. If we reflect on the play of time in tales of seduction, where neighbors, guardians, or a husband (sometimes all of them) must be outwitted, we come to see that the obsession with numbers of orgasms belongs to a larger necessity and pattern. Humorous to be sure, the purpose of such tallies was also to flash forth a statement about how much could be done by two impatient lovers with limited stolen time, especially if the female partner normally had little or no sex. In that hardnosed society, numbers of orgasms put a quantitative value on the right use of precious time.

In this light, too, we can also see why seduction was so often a matter of cold sensuality, as we have just noticed above. There was little enough time for the "act of darkness" itself; there was no time for sentimental prelimi-naries; and when perchance a gush of noble words was possible, the lovers passed from elevated speech to direct action with (for us) alarming speed. Time and illicit (instant) sex were closely coupled. In arranged marriage itself, lovemaking must often have started as a formal or clumsy action, preceded by little preparation. When it was possible at all, therefore, extramarital sex had perforce to be a carpe diem activity, usually characterized, I suspect, by an immediate lunge for the orgasm. For similar reasons, *novellieri* sometimes ascribe this readiness to women in convents. The lecherous nuns in Boccac-cio and Sercambi, not to mention Pietro Aretino, are not squeamish or given to euphemism; their carnality is foremost; they go directly to the points of pleasure.[72] Yet the limitations of time and space in illicit coupling touched wives and widows above all: they had the most to fear and lose. In the world of the Renaissance tale, acting under the fear of discovery, sinning lovers turned time into a continuum numbered by orgasms. The storyteller's preoccupation with sexual climaxing was simply a statement about the acute pressures of time, space, and secrecy in illicit relations.

FEAR, FANTASY, AND SYMBOLIC ACTION

In a tale by Sermini,[73] monna Rosa of Siena, the twenty-four-year-old wife of a castellan who is often absent from home, eyes and smoothly seduces the eighteen-year-old son of the peasant who works her land outside Siena. Receiving the young peasant's sexual "service" in the mocking guise of what a servant owes to a master, she "rides" him, frankly preferring this position, but admits that she does not ride her husband. Another Sermini tale features a slick and evil Sienese citizen who seduces a peasant girl out in the country.[74] Pretending to prepare her for marriage, he teaches her to mount and ride him so that she may afterward show her future husband that she is boss at home and mistress of her private parts.

Cavalcando: riding, mounting, or straddling. Down to the sixteenth century, this is one the favorite metaphors for the act of illicit sex.[75] Lovers break out of their confined spaces and ride away, and by such symbolic action, in cases of adultery, the woman's husband, wherever he may be, also necessarily travels; only he goes to Cuckold Land, to Corneto or Cornwall, to wear horns.

The metaphor of riding was also about being on top, as the dominant, active, or even fertilizing partner.[76] Place was symbolic. If a woman gave a beating to a man, whether with kicks or her fists, she was "riding" him. If she mounted him sexually, he was cast as her social inferior, and she might, in the jocular folklore of the time, be about to impregnate him.[77] The *novellistica* suggests, therefore, that wives did not "ride" husbands, for this would have been to reverse natural relations and to bring disarray into the orderly household. But in adultery and fornication, wives and widows often mounted and rode, thereby acting out their violation of the law—and they "rode" as much by invitation of their lovers as from their own volition. The lover took pleasure in the sinning woman's license; and if there was a husband around, all the more reason to egg her on in her impudence, in revenge for her spouse's suffocating jealousy or for all the dangers and obstacles that had to be overcome.

Writers, then, were much drawn to the image of the horsey woman, thus unwittingly touching the subject of freer movement over space but also broaching the nature of authority in the male-dominated family. A woman could "ride" in marriage only at the expense of her husband. In any proper marriage, she bore the rider, and this arrangement helped to keep women in their place. Since there was something triumphalist about the image of the horsewoman, at all events outside the princely courts, she elicited fears and derision in decent bourgeois or mercantile society. The laws of some cities barred women from riding through the streets on horseback,[78] except when leaving for a stay in the country or on the occasion of their marriage, when the bride's family were allowed to publicize the event and to show off her finery by dispatching her on horseback to her new husband's house.

The sexual image of the mounted woman was also the visual equivalent of the crafty woman who could trick her husband and even her lover. She knew how to violate domestic space, while yet holding on to her good name and honor. To "ride," a woman must first have the wit to outsmart her husband or guardians and nosey neighbors. Only then could she unleash her carnality. In these assumptions, cunning intelligence made for the most dangerous kind of woman, the sort who knew no bounds. Bandello's picture of Bianca Maria, the countess of Cellant, actually taken from life,[79] answers to this model of cunning and carnality. Rich, beautiful, scheming, and estranged from her second husband, she takes lovers almost at will but ends on the gallows, victim of her own vices and perverse intelligence.

Fiction could represent the clever female "rider" in two modes: either her sexuality was rendered with sympathy because she was married to a homosexual or a horrid old man, or it was castigated because she was driven by lust. In the first of these, the right marriage would have kept her within the bounds of decency; in the second, nothing could restrain her. Normally, a woman guilty of adultery forfeited her dowry to her husband. In Florence the penalties against adulterous women might be commuted to moderate or confiscatory fines. To tighten the constraints, most cities decreed that the testimony of a few neighbors sufficed to establish a woman's ill repute; some even ruled that extramarital intercourse with one man could make a woman a whore; and in other cities, female adultery was punishable by death, if the evidence proved decisive and the accused woman was charged by one of her close male kinsmen—husband, father, son, or brother.[80]

We shall never know to what extent fear of the sly, lusty woman sprang from traditional misogyny lodged in Roman law, in folklore, in everyday prejudice, and in views inherited from churchmen.[81] This strain, however, was always there, at work in all sorts of serpentine ways, and no less so among the humanists, as exemplified by the brazen misogyny of Poggio Bracciolini's jocular anecdotes, the *Facetiae,* with their wisecracking about the "wide-open cunts" of widows.[82] If misogyny streaked through the heart of the courtly love verse of the age, as revealed in chapter 4,[83] then we may imagine its effects in the oral tradition of popular storytelling, from which *novellieri* often drew material. Renaissance fiction swarms with advice against crafty, lecherous, and perfidious wives and widows. The more society corralled women, the trickier they appeared in literature, as if they needed ever more wit to survive in their restricted circumstances.

It follows that in the closed households of Renaissance cities, made so by enclosing or cloistering the sexuality of women, incest was bound to occur. Those who rightly occupied the sacred space on occasion polluted it. Interestingly, however, for the period up to the mid–sixteenth century, I have yet to find a single story about incestuous relations between father and daughter.[84] Household space did not confine men and so was unlikely, as symbolic or emblematic ground, to suggest their possible involvement in the most "unholy" of domestic relations. In the first tale of the fourth day of *The Decameron,* Boccaccio flirts with the father-daughter incest theme but keeps the matter symbolic. Married off by her father, Tancredi, the prince of Salerno, the beautiful Ghismonda is soon widowed. Time passes, and though she is still young, Tancredi does nothing about her remarriage, preferring instead to dote on her. Ghismonda falls in love with Guiscardo, one of her father's servitors. When Tancredi discovers this by actually being a secret if unwitting witness to their lovemaking, he has Guiscardo killed and sends the youth's heart to Ghismonda in a golden chalice. The incestuous note in Tancredi's fiercely possessive love is echoed by the symbolism of incestuous space: Tancredi has direct access to Ghismonda's bedchamber, whereas Guiscardo enters the room from behind, through a cavern and a forgotten door. Father and lover thus have her in a space between them; and this spatial equation can only betoken incestuous feeling on the one side, because the other side belongs to the lover who would be her husband, but Tancredi will not allow it.

Most of the incest in our rich array of tales is between young wives and their stepsons or other affines.[85] In the most famous historical case (1425), retailed by Bandello more than a century later,[86] the marquis of Ferrara, Niccolò d'Este, discovered that his second wife, Parisina Malatesta, was making love with his son, the handsome Ugo. He had the couple beheaded. She was twenty-one, her stepson twenty, and the marquis himself was forty-two years old. Bandello tells the story with much sympathy for Ugo, who repented, and a good deal less for Parisina, although she took all the blame and pleaded for Ugo to be spared.

Predictably enough, our incest tales have a common situation: youthful protagonists sharing the same household space. And we need look no farther for the grounds of this than the high incidence of arranged marriage between girls (*fanciule*) and older men, especially since Renaissance fiction emphasizes the "carnality" of youth, often singling out the young wife or young widow, with her yearning flesh, as the avatar of sexuality. Sacchetti's late-fourteenth-century tale about a coupling stepmother and stepson is absolutely unabashed.[87] Bullied and tormented at home by his father's young wife, the young man is urged by his friends to get into bed with her. He does so, and relations between the two are at once turned into a honeyed peace. When his father finds them in bed one day, there is a violent quarrel, and neighbors quickly step in to help get a reconciliation. They sympathize entirely with the son. Thereafter, although more prudently, stepmother and stepson continue to make love. The tale does not in the least moralize; it hinges on the frank recognition of the sexual and generational tensions that coursed through certain households.

But the enclosed family space of the period, with its built-in strains, was most dramatically outlined in the incest between genetic mother and son.[88] The sacred core, as it were, of domestic space was the bedroom shared by wife, husband, and child. Here too was the place for the family's religious pictures: Madonna, saints, or the Crucifixion. If, then, in the course of time and despite all the taboos against it, mother and grown son came to imagine—no more than to imagine—having sexual relations, was this not the outcome of the logic and affective pressures in the closed household? In fantasy, fear, or dream, the constraints of such space would in all likelihood issue, at some point, in the imagery of the coupling mother and son. Here was a formal kind of perfecting or completing of love, fully in accord with the symbolic resources of cloistered family space. Whether entirely invented or reconstructed from real cases, incest tales gave a narrative shape and dramatic meaning to the logic of the sacred core of family space. They grasped at the implicit dangers.

A tale by the Venetian priest Giovanni Brevio, written about 1542, takes this logic a step further, in a twist that turns family space into a strange and fabled cage.[89] Lisabetta, a nobly born Venetian widow not more than about thirty-two years old, is seized "by a carnal and lubricious love" for her fifteen-year-old son, Girolamo, a handsome and gracious youth. Stricken with shame and guilt, yet spurning would-be lovers, she is unable to vanquish her feral love and in the end surrenders to "what the stars desire." Girolamo, meanwhile, loves his mother's beautiful servant, Elena. Keenly watchful and alert, Lisabetta secretly overhears their plans for a first tryst and, in the complete darkness of the house, cleverly substitutes herself for the girl, who is kept firmly occupied elsewhere. Mother and son make love, carrying on thus for months but only in the dark night (it is an act of darkness), as she disguises her voice and exercises absolute control over Elena. Pregnant, Lisabetta then withdraws to the country, gives birth to a daughter (Giulia), puts her out to a secret wet nurse, and returns to Venice, where she finally arranges a marriage for Elena. Two years later, on the pretense of offering a charitable place to a female child servant, Lisabetta sends for Giulia and lovingly brings her up at home. The child grows up to be a great and gracious beauty, whereupon Girolamo falls so deeply in love with her that he resolves to take her in marriage. Stunned, his mother uses all possible arguments, save the true one, against such a match, but Girolamo steadfastly insists that he must have Giulia or die. Lisabetta is forced to give way, "preferring her son alive and healthy . . . rather than dead or sick." Already father and brother to her, Girolamo now also becomes Giulia's husband.

In effect, the most shameful and forbidden relations were facilitated by a conditioning that had led Lisabetta to keep her existential space sealed off from the outside world. Though very much the exception, no doubt, in breaking a powerful set of taboos, Lisabetta's crime is readily imaginable in the spatial context of the Italian Renaissance household.

The Church, law codes, and social doctrine strongly condemned, in San Bernardino's words, "the act of marriage outside of marriage,"[90] and this spatial metaphor fits perfectly here. For "marriage" with lovers in that sacred place, the marital bedchamber, was a wicked parody, which, by its unholy reversal, spoke a language of symbolism. Action of this sort, however, always called for tricks and treachery, that is, for feminine wiles. So enter misogyny, or an attitude akin to it. Here the virulence of Boccaccio's tale about Lydia and old Nicostratus, her husband, is exemplary.[91] Having first killed Nicostratus's prize falcon before his eyes, yanked out a tuft of his beard, and extracted his best remaining tooth—all acts of symbolic castration[92]—Lydia then performs the act of marriage with her lover under her husband's very nose and convinces the old man that he is hallucinating. In this spectacular feat, she extends the marital bedchamber right out into Nicostratus's garden, as he sits there in a supposedly charmed pear tree and in a dream of hallucination (he thinks), watching Lydia copulate with his most trusted and loved servant, the handsome Pyrrhus. Thus is her husband's lordship, the whole of his male authority, pulled sneeringly to pieces, and all because he had taken too young, clever, and willful a wife.

Lydia is the most ingenious and brazen of all Boccaccio's heroines, but she has a multitude of daredevil sisters in fiction, even if not so imaginative as she: for example, Parabosco's monna Betta, Bandello's Bindoccia, Molza's Flemish servant, Salvi's Angela, and many others.[93] Misogyny, female cunning, homosexual or impotent old husbands, and outright male stupidity explain much of the action in our tales of lust and seduction. But there was something else at work in the picture: the effects of enclosed family space. This was coming back to haunt the prepotent male. Patriarchal society had laid it down that decent, honorable women must keep to certain areas, spaces, and ways. Now, therefore, in the fears and fantasies of men as filtered into Renaissance fiction—and *all* the known storywriters were men—there unfolded the action (the symbolic action) of wives, widows, sisters, and mothers sinning in the very spaces reserved for them.

There could be no greater irony. The male imagination turned against the male, and a rude justice triumphed. Men saw themselves duped and scorned, getting their comeuppance, confronting a resourceful schemer (woman) or even failing to have enough regard for this worthy partner-opponent. Calling out in the middle of the night from an adjoining room, where she is feigning an illness, Bandello's Bindoccia speaks sardonically to her insanely jealous husband while making love to his dearest friend.[94] That night she has nine orgasms. Boccaccio's Beatrice has lover and husband virtually in the same bed, and as she clutches the hands of one in the dark, she sends the other, her husband, off into the garden on a wild-goose chase, so that she may at once enjoy her lover in the place still warm from her husband's body.[95] Grazzini's Mante, sharing a large bed with her conniving mother and dim-witted husband, sneaks a lover into it and every night, for months thereafter, with her mother sleeping between herself and her husband, she and the lover "ride."[96]

Arienti's madonna Pippa, married to a one-eyed merchant and taken by
surprise, has suddenly to open the bedroom door to him. She covers his good
eye with a loving left hand, at once flattering him with a charming lie, while
her right hand makes an obscene (copulating) gesture over his sightless eye as
she maneuvers her young lover around and behind him out of the room. In
other words, says the gesture, screw your blind eye and—by symbolic extension—mine too.[97] In a tale by Masuccio Salernitano,[98] when the physician
Rogero finds a strange pair of male knickers or drawers (*bracche*) in the marital
bedroom, just after his young wife's "miraculous" recovery from an illness,
she assures him that they are a religious relic, once worn by Saint Griffin and
forgotten by the friar Niccolò da Nargni, who had brought them along to
assist him in his prayers for her good health and recovery. Soon after, receiving
secret word from her about his forgotten *bracche,* fra Niccolò and his confreres
quickly organize a religious procession to Rogero's house, where all the friars
kiss the garment and process back to their convent with it in great solemnity.

The astonishing proximity of husband and lover in the scenes noted above
mark off the quintessential space and place of the wife, the area in and around
the bedroom. She was compelled to operate there, whereas her husband was
free to roam anywhere in the city. Only her guile or genius could turn that
space into the very arena of her freedom, in her perfecting of a stance against
the authoritarian male animal. This is not to say that perilous forms of upper-
class female adultery were common in Renaissance Italy; they presented too
great a danger to life, limb, honor, and property. It *is* to say that the imagining
of those forms was testimony to the corralling of women, especially young
women.

Fra Niccolò's saintly knickers remind us of that other possible place for
women, the church or the religious house. The scabrous image brings us to
one of the least studied subjects in Italian history, the matter of intimate relations between women and clerics, and I can only touch upon it here. Although
a great deal has been written about mystic and holy women in late medieval
Italy,[99] often in connection with Siena, the pages of the leading Sienese
storyteller of the fifteenth century, Gentile Sermini, contradict that holiness
with the words and actions of lascivious women and clerics. From Boccaccio
to Grazzini, fiction reveals a powerful undercurrent of anger against the clergy,
aroused by evidence of their hypocrisy, immorality, and relations with women.
The anger surfaces not only in forthright diatribes against wayward priests and
monks but also in anecdotes that often seem merely "literary." A case in point is

the third of a trio of stories by Sermini, chronicling the adventures of two sinister friars.[100] One of them, fra Puccio, seduces a rich Roman widow, gets her to found a "house of holy widowhood" for young widows, none older than thirty, and proceeds to turn it, in effect, into a comfortable brothel for a string of friars, their confessors. Six months later, with nearly all of the house's twenty-five widows pregnant, the place is mysteriously burnt down, along with all its inmates, but the two villainous friars easily survive and flourish. A kindred anger or fury may be detected in Sercambi's tale about Pasquino, the parish priest of Gello, near Lucca.[101] This cleric gets one of his pupils, a seven-year-old boy, to try to pluck out several of his mother's pubic hairs as she is sleeping at night and to pass them on to him, so that he may use sorcery on the precious strands and get the young wife to lust after him. Boy, mother, and father sleep in the same bed; and when the boy is caught by the mother at his funny business, he is made to confess. The parents now substitute the hairs of a sow, and the boy gets these to the unsuspecting Pasquino, who then performs his magic and is afterward all but killed by the aroused beast, as it goes after him in a sexual frenzy. The sow has to be slaughtered, and the priest is run out of the village.

The snarling anticlericalism of this tale is clearly evident in the yoking together of cleric, sorcery, the corrupting of the child, and porcine lust. Only a venomous resentment can fully account for this mix of ingredients. We shall never know anything really about the numbers of priests and friars who had clandestine relations with women, but we do know that the priesthood itself worried about the problem.[102] Chastity, the primary female virtue, rested upon both religious and moral constraints; hence women could not reasonably be kept away from men in holy orders. When going to church, women ventured out into public space, some fraction of which was thereupon turned fleetingly into family space, because "respectable" women were everywhere the vessels or carriers of family honor. The infamy of an adulteress radiated out through space. She dishonored her husband, his lineage, her mother, and her own patriline; all these were shamed, soiled, and angered by the discovery of her sin.[103] And honorable women avoided her like the plague. Accordingly, when literature coupled a shifty friar and a sexy married woman or an imaginative young widow and a handsome priest, it was doing little more than dramatizing fears and fantasies that already echoed through social consciousness. History and storytelling were in this fashion joined, and the writer whisked controversy into the image of the cleric.

Since the institution of the arranged marriage of economic and social convenience looms in the background to much of this chapter,[104] I conclude with a statement about a possible rival: that is, marriage for love.

Aside from a paltry dowry, public shame and dishonor constituted the one fault that could destroy the marital prospects of any woman of good class. If knowledge of the widow Gioiosa's doings had leaked into Florence's neighborhoods, she could never have remarried reputably, and, with her financial means, her most likely destiny would have been a convent. No less scandalous were known liaisons with priests. However, the arranged marriage of convenience also generated another enemy, its imaginary or possible opposite: the reverie, fear, or tale of a young man and woman in love, yearning desperately to be united in holy matrimony, contrary to all family plans and desires. Renaissance fiction offers us dozens of such narratives.[105] It is as though alongside the tradition of arranged marriage there ran the fear or wish, or both, that marriage for love could stand as an alternative option (without the tragedy of the Romeo and Juliet story), thereby challenging the family's authority over matrimony. The outcome in fiction is not always predictable, for the two lovers may end happily or, more often, tragically. If tragic, their end may come with implied criticism of their elders, who could have authorized the marriage, especially if the lovers were social equals. If, instead, the end is a happy one, the story is likely to eschew realism and turn into wishful thinking.

Patriarchal reasoning had given rise to the proverb "Chi si piglia d'amore, di rabbia si lascia" (marry for love, break up in hate and anger);[106] and received wisdom warned men not to dote on their wives, because this turned women into petty intriguers and tyrants.[107] From the princely courts to the varied milieux of the solid middle classes, the individual was expected to marry in accordance with the dictates of parents and elders. Since, as a rule, these had a stranglehold on family economic resources, how could young lovers ordinarily go against their family elders and the expectations of contemporaries? Indeed, to be young lovers already signified that something had gone wrong: family rights were threatened. Private "lust" had to give way to collective (family) needs. In 1484 the duchess of Ferrara denounced a widowed Este princess who refused a recommended second spouse and instead married for love. She called the princess a "female brute" or "animal" (*femina bestiale*) who put "her appetites above everything else."[108] In Italian Renaissance imaginations, therefore, when the will of an individual was cast against a revered institution such as arranged marriage, if wishful thinking was put aside, the outcome had to be devastating. This explains the love tales that end in mysterious deaths.[109] In *The Decameron*,[110] the beautiful Andreuola, daughter of a Brescian nobleman, makes love with and secretly marries Gabriotto, a neighbor richly endowed with noble qualities, though also her social inferior. Each has a dream presaging his death, tells the other about it, and as they embrace at night in her father's garden, he suddenly dies. Andreuola ends her days in a convent. Here, as the narrative makes clear, their dark theft of authority—not alone their social inequality—brings about the strange, punishing death.

The mysterious death, as the fruit of love, results from the intruding, phantom presence of the institution of arranged marriage. In turn, however, this pattern of occurrence in our tales throws light on the institution. It tells us that the impact of arranged marriage in people's minds could have such resonance as to generate and foster an imaginary counterworld: the dream of love. Only powerful institutions are likely to have effects of this sort. Renaissance Italians had a very clear picture of the vices and virtues associated with the negotiated marriage of convenience; but when they reflected on the alternative, namely on marriage for love, they could see no realistic way to it. Storytellers either killed the secret lovers who longed for a publicly recognized marriage, or they abandoned reality altogether and concocted a fable-like happy ending.

A Chronological List of the Authors

Following are the names of the thirty-three writers whose tales provide the source material for this chapter. Next to each is the approximate time (year or years) of the composition or publication of the work. The two columns on the right indicate the number of tales by each writer in the total sample. The column under *direct* lists the number of tales directly about seduction; the second column is a tally of the tales that touch the theme indirectly. Composition often preceded publication by years. Thus, in Bandello's case (1554), the writing of his *novelle* went back to the 1540s.

	SEDUCTION	
	direct	*indirect*
1. Boccaccio (c. 1350)	28	21
2. Ser Giovanni (1378)	2	4
3. Franco Sacchetti (1390s)	3	5
4. Giovanni Gherardi (c. 1400)	1	1
5. Giovanni Sercambi (c. 1402)	20	19
6. Gentile Sermini (c. 1430)	19	2
7. Leon Battista Alberti (1430s)	2	2
8. Enea Silvio Piccolomini (1444)	1	0
9. Poggio Bracciolini (1440s)	5	8
10. Masuccio Salernitano (1460s–70s)	6	0
11. Lorenzo de' Medici (c. 1468)	1	0
12. Marabottino Manetti (c. 1470)	1	0
13. Sabadino degli Arienti (late 1470s)	8	4

	SEDUCTION	
	direct	*indirect*
14. Piovano Arlotto (1470s–80s)	2	4
15. Niccolò Machiavelli (1518)	1	0
16. Girolamo Morlini (1520)	3	1
17. Giovanni Guidiccione (1530s)	1	0
18. Giovanni Brevio (c. 1540)	4	0
19. Agnolo Firenzuola (1540s)	4	2
20. Anton Francesco Grazzini (1540s)	6	2
21. Girolamo Parabosco (1540s)	4	4
22. Anton Francesco Doni (1542–53)	0	5
23. Giacomo Salvi (1547)	1	0
24. Francesco Maria Molza (1549)	3	2
25. Giovan Francesco Straparola (1550)	2	2
26. Giustiniano Nelli (1550)	2	0
27. Ortensio Lando (1552)	1	3
28. Matteo Bandello (1554)	9	7
29. Pietro Fortini (1555–62)	7	1
30. Giambattista Cintio (1565)	1	0
31. Sebastiano Erizzo (1567)	0	1
32. Niccolò Granucci (1569)	2	0
33. Lorenzo Selva (1582)	0	1
Totals	150	101

P O E T R Y   A S
P O L I T I C A L   M E M O R Y

In 1420, during his stay in Florence, the noble Colonna pope, Martin V, became furious when it was reported to him that children were going about the streets of the city loudly proclaiming and delighting in the jingle "Papa Martino non vale un quattrino" (Pope Martin isn't worth a farthin').[1] An ambassador had to be sent out to mollify the offended pope. That single line purported to sum up his character. Where, if not into a rhyme or a jingle, could memory be more neatly crammed?

In August 1503 a sonnet libeling the king of France was doing the rounds in Florence.[2] How were communal guardsmen to find the author, how prevent the poem from circulating, and how stop the making of new copies? These questions worried the authorities, for local spies might get the sonnet into the hands of the king, who was, after all, a Florentine ally. Fearful of the possible reactions, the embarrassed republican government was forced to discuss a course of action; but what the outcome was remains unclear. And anyway, how could anyone put a stop to secret scribblers? In June 1527, after the Medici had been cast out of Florence, several sonnets in their favor were surreptitiously posted up in Bibbiena, a town under Florentine rule. The action so upset the local priors that they got in touch at once with their bosses back home and dispatched one of the sonnets to them.[3]

Already in the late fourteenth century, and no doubt much earlier as well, Florentine political leaders had been forced on occasion to hit back at the clandestine posting of mutinous inscriptions. In December 1394, for example, the city priors had offered an enormous reward of five hundred gold florins for the successful denunciation of anyone found to have posted defamatory statements against the regime ("scritta d'infamatione dello stato").[4]

But Florentines certainly held no monopoly on graffiti and secretly concocted verse of a vituperative or subversive sort. In Bologna, if the abuse was personal and put up in a public place, it was known as a *libellus*.[5] Such abuse could also go by word of mouth, in which case, as in Florence, it was often rhymed; and as *verba injuriosa,* it might also be decreed unlawful, as was blasphemy or the *libellus*.[6]

Most other cities bore witness to the same kind of activity. Venetian chronicles claim that when in 1355 the doge of Venice, Marin Falier, plotted against the prepotent authority of the Venetian nobility, one of his major grievances concerned a disgraceful rhyme, got up against him and his young (second) wife by a group of young noblemen:[7]

Marin Falier—de la bela moier,
Altri la galde e lui la mantien.

(Marin Falier has a wife too fair,
Other men lay 'er but he is the payer.)

Rome in the early sixteenth century, around the statue of Pasquino in the old Piazza di Parione, had a site notorious for the publication—the making public—of rhymed abuse and invective against popes and leading prelates.[8] In Bologna in 1506–7, when a great deal of anonymous political verse was flying about the city, the notary Ercole Ugolotti was hanged for composing and secretly posting a twenty-five-line poem against the fiery Pope Julius II, who had just dramatically ended the forty-four-year reign of the Bentivoglio family by driving Giovanni II into exile. The poem urged the people of Bologna to go out and demonstrate for the return of the Bentivoglio and to rise up against the government of "pitiless priests."[9]

If put into the public arena, a political statement in verse was no mere utterance without consequences. Whether in couplets, quatrains, octaves, sonnets, or longer compositions, such as the *capitolo* or the lament, the statement could not just be about present events. It had to be also a curt rehearsal of things past, done with an eye to recommendations for the present; and therefore the poem was a kind of memory capsule; it took hold of a history, however selectively, and sought to cast it into memorable form, giving it a voice, an edge, and ploys for easier remembrance.

Any political attack was bound to be a statement in favor of something else. Hence eulogy was the reverse of insult and censure, and a great mass of political verse was chiefly praise, usually based upon a bare or gilded catalog of the past deeds and present virtues of the prince, republic, or capital city. Republican Florence, Venice, popes, the Visconti, and other princely families were those most likely to be showered with verse of this kind, not least because they could hire professional poets.[10]

In our neglect of poetry, we forget that before it became a modern exercise in the esoteric probing or articulation of private experience, it was a public form, frequently sung or recited to a group and nearly always, at any rate, expressed in language that was immediately comprehensible.[11] This commitment to society and to communication, whether of fact or of feeling, made poetry the ideal vehicle for the office of commemoration, of trying to fix persons and occasions in memory. Let us broach the larger background to this question, for it is about why poetry as politics and memory constituted a dangerous activity.

In all Italian cities, new laws, bans, and other public news were communicated by word of mouth. Town criers on horseback, or special messengers, went from point to point, that is, to all the usual places (*in locis consuetis*) and there, after a few blasts of their trumpets, made announcements. Men might be summoned to court this way; and local guildsmen were occasionally assembled by the *podestà,* or another top magistrate, to be reminded of the main regulations governing their trades. Accordingly, a tremendous amount of official information in Renaissance cities was relayed by repeated public announcement and face-to-face encounter—in Venice, for instance, usually after Mass on Sundays. The names of fugitives were publicly proclaimed, and when an indicted man was absent from the city, a court summons might be nailed to his door for everyone to see.[12] In the familiar meeting places of each neighborhood, such as a local corner, church, or square, where the substantial and settled families had all known each other for generations, one sharp insult, publicly uttered, could shatter the bonds of neighborhood amity for years to come; and therefore verbal abuse was often made subject to legal penalties.[13]

More than for us, in short, the word spoken in public was likely to have a certifying value: it entered into a zone that was decisive for the community-centered individual. Noblemen, merchants, tradesmen, and outstanding families had their identities confirmed daily in their nearby streets and marketplaces, or in government squares, where dress itself, a rich sign language, profiled the lineaments of the different social identities. More succinctly, social/public being *was* being *tout court,* with the result that the publicly spoken word carried a weightier and particular pledge.

The distinctive appeal and validation of public statement is demonstrated by the practice of defamatory painting (*pittura infamante*).[14] To condemn traitors to death was final enough; but to depict them on the walls of public buildings, hanged or hanging upside down, went even further. It advertised their enduring disgrace, making the infamy live on for years and sometimes centuries, as indicated by nineteenth-century remains. Moreover, vituperative verse or doggerel then completed the commemorating of the infamy, since the custom was to tag each effigy with a few insulting lines, identifying the alleged criminal by name and tersely summarizing his crimes, as in this Florentine example (1440) against enemies of the Medici:

Aspido della mente e del colore,
strambo, travolto, ontuoso e pien d'inganno,
son di messer Rinaldo il brutto Ormanno,
che pendo allato al padre traditore.[15]

(Serpent-like in mind and color,
Queer, bent, shamed, and false,
I am my lord Rinaldo's ugly Ormond,
Hanged next to my traitor father.)

Such captions and images were bitterly resented by the families of those concerned, for the memory was being kept shamefully alive. Some cruel and unjust punishment seemed to be everlasting here. In February 1392 in Siena, twenty-seven rebels were depicted in this manner, ten of them from the preeminent Malavolti family. The charge was that they had tried to betray Siena to the Florentines for filthy florins.[16]

Nasty political rhymes of the sort used in defamatory painting were often penned by the community's official poet, such as Florence's poet-herald. In the fourteenth and fifteenth centuries, Perugia, Siena, Florence, and other cities employed poets not only to write verse but also to read and perform it in streets, public squares, government palazzi, and the halls of princes.[17] In republican Florence, the *buffone* or herald of the *signoria* composed and intoned verse for the lord priors, both to delight them and to offer moral edification.[18] These functions were fully set out in his contract of employment. Everywhere, moreover, down at least to the middle of the sixteenth century, itinerant tale or poetry "chanters" *(canterini)* were a feature of the urban landscape.[19]

Poetry, then, was not meant in the first instance to be a private affair for secluded enjoyment. It was more often seen as a public event: a performance, a circulating oral jingle, a longer composition passed from hand to hand, a verse letter or a riposte, some rhymes tacked up in a reception room,[20] a sonnet easily memorized and freely altered at will (it was in the public domain), or a piece done on commission for a special event. In addition, poetry was always put into a highly conventional (hence communal) form: the sonnet, the *frottola,* the octave, the ballad, the *strambotto,* the *canzone,* the *capitolo,* the long narrative with its regular rhymes and stresses, and the religious laud with its panoply of standard devices, most of which were easily recognized by readers or listeners, thanks to the hundreds of lauds for the Virgin Mary. The different cities favored or designated certain places for the public recitation of verse: in Florence the Mercato Vecchio and the little episcopal Piazza di San Martino, in Siena the great government square, in Lucca the Piazza di San Michele, and in Perugia the marketplace Piazza di Santa Maria. In the mid-fourteenth century, Antonio Pucci resented the fact that verse recitals were given everywhere in Florence, even in "disreputable places."[21] Written abuse or political criticism, when posted up at night, was also likely to go on a highly visible surface: a government portal, a church door, or, in Siena, the loggia of the Uffiziali della Mercanzia.[22]

I want to say—but I cannot prove it, so let it be a hypothesis—that the public force of the word of poetry must have borrowed part of its thrust from the universal experience of prayer and the rhythms of public preaching. In gathering patriotic or political sentiment into a sonnet or a lament, the poet pilfered rhythm, accent, or metaphor from the routines of prayer and profaned them, thereby getting an extra hold on expectations. From very early on, in any case, the sonnet, the madrigal, and other forms of verse had been invaded by prayers and religious themes.

We begin to see the powers and dangers of poetry. As politics, it was for emphasis and commemoration; it employed an everyday vernacular language, unless, of course, it turned to Latin hexameters and an elite of readers;

it was for praise of the powerful or for the calumny and destruction of enemies; it celebrated victories or tried to be a salve in the face of defeat; it might
be spoken to a crowd; and it might go up on the walls of a government palace
or, as rhymed abuse, outside a modest house, like a pair of horns over the
doorway of a local cuckold. At Bologna, on festive occasions under the Bentivoglio, celebratory verse was actually handed out to spectators on printed
sheets.[23] The poem caught the attention of passersby; it affixed a message in
memory; and the reward for the person praised was one of pride, whereas the
victim of an insulting poem took home a harvest of disgrace. A good deal of
pompous eulogy was produced in learned circles, sometimes in the Latin of
the humanists; but this was not, generally speaking, the idiom for the popular
occasions, for large assemblies of people, or for political *vituperia*. The vernacular and the demotic were more universally suited for these purposes.

What were the different forms of political poetry, and what were its occasions? How and why was it produced?

Verse about political matters could vary from the two-line lampoon to the
long narrative which, in passing, sings the praises of a princely house, for
instance of the Este, as in Ariosto's *Orlando furioso.* Long compositions might
be done on commission or simply come forth as the fruit of patronage. But
the hard-hitting political poem of the sort most likely to be repeated and
memorized, with its curds of remembered material, was bound to be short
and comparatively spontaneous: for example a sonnet, a *canzone,* or a lament,
rarely running to more than 180 lines, unless it was taken up by a professional
canterino, a declaimer or tale singer highly skilled in verse recitation.[24] In this
fashion, the poem seized upon the freshness of the occasion, and its topicality
won an immediate audience, while its focused strategies nailed argument
down and stocked memory. The great occasions for verse of this type were
military or naval victories, sudden changes in government, the fall of cities or
princely houses, political assassinations, acts of treason and political violence,
and the death or marriage of princes and powerful oligarchs. Many lesser
occasions were also a spur for poetry: the holidays of the patron saints of cities,
the arrival and departure of dignitaries, the drawing up of treaties, the election of new magistrates, and even mistaken policies, the actions of corrupt
officials, and the imposition of new taxes.[25]

What was the purpose of political poetry? In our own day, what is the
purpose of slanted government information and propaganda? Is it not to rally
support for government and policies or to allay hostile criticism? And is it not,

in the case of a poetry of dissent and opposition, to turn people against government and rulers? These aims were not in the least foreign and alien to the agendas of the princes and oligarchies of Italian Renaissance cities. After all, they occupied the middle of the urban space; they lived in the midst of their people and were physically vulnerable—the Venetian patriciate, the Baglioni of Perugia, the Bentivoglio of Bologna, and of course the Medici in Florence. In fact, at Milan, Mantua, and Ferrara, to separate themselves from the *popolo* in the middle of the city, the ruling princes lived in a *cittadella*, a moated citadel: thus the enhanced importance for them of looking out upon a surrounding world of goodwill. Knowing this, and being ever on the look-out for patronage, writers were prepared to pay a heavy tribute in verse eulogy. The ruling houses, in turn, welcomed the praise, finding it only too natural, because they wielded a near-absolute power within the urban saucer. Still, they were seldom so perfectly secure as to be able to do without a rainfall of continuing praise. We may put this observation paradoxically: their grand authority in the city was such that for them *not* to receive accolades would have been tantamount to their not truly having the power claimed. Consequently, the production of verse flattery for them was simply the expected thing. It came with political power, as light came with the sun.

In Florence no family—not the Strozzi, not the Alberti or the Albizzi—ever attracted as much poetry and praise as the Medici, even from a relatively early period, the 1430s, when they were far from being, as yet, the city's undercover rulers. This tells us something about a way of perception that did not easily enter into the ordinary historical record. The Medici were doing things and bearing themselves in such a way as to encourage verse adulation; they were marking themselves out in some special regard. By contrast, one of the richest and most learned men in Florence in the early fifteenth century, from a family more distinguished than the Medici, Palla di Nofri Strozzi, was accorded only one verse composition in Florence that I know of, though I have no doubt that there were others. Luca Pitti, a brassy oligarch, received a poem in 1463 commemorating his knighthood, though he was to end in disgrace and derision.[26] These examples were, however, paltry by comparison with the verse written in praise of Cosimo de' Medici and members of his family, who received verse letters, eulogies, and marriage, funeral, and other gift poems.[27]

Poetry reminds us that memory is selective—selecting with an eye for present need. The past is remembered for the sake of the present; but present need is no respecter of the facts and small truths of the past. History becomes the victim of memory. Thus Florentines and their poetry were fond of re-membering that they had long been a free people who descended directly from the Romans in the time of Roman triumphs or freedom; that republi-can Florence had always defended liberty (i.e., autonomies) in Tuscany. Then what about the Florentine seizure of Arezzo, Pistoia, and Pisa? Answer: the strategic stronghold of Tuscan liberty, Florence, had to be defended, even at the cost of conquering neighbors for the sake of standing up to outside tyranny. And so Florentines believed that it was right for them in 1429–32 to seek to overthrow the little republic of Lucca by force of arms. Memory had no trouble with contradictions. In a savage lament nearly one hundred years earlier (1337), the poet Antonio Pucci raged against the fact that Florence had failed to get its hands on Lucca, owing to a broken treaty and the dirty work of treacherous allies.[28]

Political poetry was no good unless it came to the eyes and ears of others, and the more so the better. We have seen that Siena, Perugia, Florence, and other cities employed and honored men who composed verse for public recitation. On holidays and special occasions, the Florentine herald some-times presented his verse in the cathedral or Piazza della Signoria. Elsewhere, too, in streets and squares, *cantatori in banca* intoned not only parts of long narrative poems, pitting Saracen against Christian knight, but also verse at-tacks on the Visconti of Milan and on other notorious enemies. When Pisa was finally conquered by Florentine mercenaries in 1406, that renowned seaport at once fell subject to the scurrilous abuse of Florentine poetry:

Al mondo non fu mai tal meretrice
Di tanta faccia data a ogni rio,
Como son stata io [Pisa]
Per compiacer di gratia a' miei figliuoli.[29]

(The world has never seen such a whore,
So shamelessly given to every crime,
As I [Pisa] have been,
Only to please my sons with everything.)

In the 1370s, as though to thumb their noses at Bernabò Visconti, Florence's rulers dispatched an insulting *canzone* to him, written by the well-known Florentine poet Franco Sacchetti.[30] The poem, "Credi tu sempre, maladetta serpe," held the lord of Milan up to ridicule and did the rounds in Florence in written form, if indeed it was not also publicly recited. Down to the late fifteenth century, professional court poets sometimes presented their verse to an assembled crowd (*coram populo*). Such were Antonio Beccari da Ferrara and Francesco di Vannozzo in the fourteenth century and Niccolò Cieco a century later.[31] At the court of Milan in the 1490s, Bernardo Bellincioni often spoke his poems out to Ludovico Sforza, and many of his sonnets carried a stinging political commentary.[32] For him the usurping Sforza lord was nothing less than the political genius of Italy; this at least is the message of a number of his sonnets.

In 1441 Mariotto Davanzati, a Florentine poet, presented his sonnet "Sacra eccelsa colonna invitta e giusta" to cardinal Colonna.[33] Much like a painted portrait that offers an improved, idealized, and justifying image of a man, this flattering verse composition offered both validation and inducement: the man's place in the world is proclaimed, his forebears are praised, and his alleged virtues enumerated, all this in meter and images that aim to seduce memory. In the case of princes or political bosses, such verse provided the manifesto or the lineaments of a social and cultural identity. Thus, to pass to another poet, Filippo Lapaccini's praise for Giovanni II Bentivoglio, lord of Bologna:

> L'eccelsa fama tua pel mondo sparsa,
> milite glorioso
>
> . . . . . .
>
> Benedetto sia'l seme
> ch'al mondo pose così dolce frutto,
>
> . . . .
>
> O fior di nobiltade,
>
> . . . .
>
> gloria del mondo e de la patria padre![34]

> (Your lofty fame strewn through the world,
> glorious knight
>
> . . . . . .
>
> Blessed be the seed
> That put such sweet fruit into the world
>
> . . . .
>
> O flower of nobility,
>
> . . . .
>
> Glory of the world and father of his country.)

In yet another example, by commencing with a cascade of adjectives, Michele del Giogante purports to describe Lucrezia Tornabuoni, wife of his powerful patron, Piero de' Medici, and mother of Lorenzo the Magnificent:

> Magnanima, gentil, discreta e grata,
> vaga, benigna, saggia, onesta e lieta,
> con l'ascendente del tuo bel pianeta
> sublime all'altre, se' dal ciel dotata.
>   Di stirpe degna e degnamente nata.[35]

> (Generous, noble, modest, and pleasant,
> charming, kind, upright, gay, and wise,
> with your lovely planet on the rise
> over the others, you are by heaven endowed.
> Well-born to a deserving line.)

If such a poem passed into the public domain, either by circulating in manuscript or being heard in a public place, it now attained its proper estate, for eulogy was one of the most public of verse forms. Consequently, the form alone gave it a strong community imprint, even if it was read or heard by none other than the dedicatee. The word of poetry transcended any private language; it wanted to partake in public occasions.

Florence and Bologna had lively enclaves of poets, copyists, amateurs, and collectors of verse.[36] Working for themselves or on commission, these men copied not only the poetry of the masters (Dante, Petrarch, and the *stilnovisti*) but also that of scores of lesser lights; and it was poetry of every sort—amatory, occasional, moral, jocular, political, religious, vituperative, and narrative. A familiar, animated commerce went on in the discussing, lending, and memorizing of poems. Collections were bound and unbound; their contents were reshuffled. And poets themselves, when in the act of copying, could not refrain at times from altering words and lines, unless they were copying a major work. This is why so many verse manuscripts come down to us with different versions of poems and with anonymous, mistaken, and conflicting attributions[37]—in part also due, of course, to the flaws of memory, as in cases in which the detailed knowledge of a poem came solely from its having been heard somewhere. Much of the give and take in all this literary traffic took place in private houses, shops, and favorite points of encounter. Burchiello's barbershop in Florence was certainly such a point, and so too were the houses of a half-dozen notaries in Bologna.[38] There a single copy, or a man with a good memory, could make any poem public.

Publication, then, came about by three different routes: by recitation in street and piazza, by means of hand copies or even printing (after about 1480), and by discussion and memorization in private enclaves or in public places such as shops. In cases of political *vituperia,* publication also had a fourth route: the secret repetition or clandestine posting up of sonnets and other shorter verse forms. But whatever the route, poetry and memory were closely linked.

The tendency was to make religious and political poetry swiftly comprehensible, because it was more effective this way. Thus in political poetry, the most common metaphor by far for a city, and for proud or violated Italy, was in the image of a woman: queen, chaste wife, honored mother, widow, female beggar, slave, or prostitute. She could be revered, abused, used, or raped. Her sons could sell or sully her, tear off her clothing, and reduce her to vile shame. This was Florence, Genoa, Venice, Pisa, or poor Italy. She could appear in resplendent dress (rich Venice) or shamefaced and in tatters (degraded Pisa). A great prince, Giangaleazzo Visconti, might die suddenly, leaving her (say, Italy *or* Milan) a poor and wretched widow. She might be queen of the sea (Genoa) or, straining the metaphor, the whorehouse of the barbarians. The changes to be wrung on such personification, on woman as metaphor, carried an elemental force, because they tapped the well of family feeling. By means of some ready alchemy, the chastity or lechery of mothers, wives, and daughters was easily reified: turned into a proud or battered city, then made to bear the honor or shame of the household. Nothing disgraced women, and hence the household, more than their sexuality; and so poetry as politics obsessively metaphorized this datum—so much so that no city could be concretely imagined except as a woman. Here political ideology and gender relations joined hands.

Two other image types, also common, were directly related to the labile female and household metaphors: bastardy and the imagery of brotherly peace or fratricidal strife. In the patriotic fervor of Italian Renaissance cities, especially in times of war or internal conflict, what better fund of images was there for the instant summing up of affairs than that to be found in the drama of household space? There, conveniently, the family could be seen at peace or war, in love or hate; and the passions were either under the control of reason and authority or on the rampage. When brothers all pulled together in the same direction, the *ben comune* (the "common good") was observed. In this

rich brew of family feeling, where the sense of property was a critical ingredient, repellent bastardy was associated with the mother's unchastity, never
with the father's promiscuity, and hence could only seem a horror, something
to be rejected and punished.

If the loving ties of family gave the ideal material for the metaphors to help
depict peaceful relations in government and public life, the wild animal, the
filthy prostitute, and the bastard were mostly at the imagistic core of angry
political verse. In politics as a war of words and a field of condensation for
memory, those who had poets in their employ had the advantage: they told a
better story. Consequently, poets were on occasion faced with grave dangers,
for politics and prudent discretion were very poor allies in strong poetry. The
political poet had to speak out more or less bluntly. In 1426 Florence set a
reward of one hundred gold florins, a small fortune, for information leading
to the arrest of the author of an incisive political poem that had been surreptitiously posted on the main government palace.[39] When Cosimo de' Medici
and his brother returned to Florence in triumph in 1434, the poet-barber
Burchiello fled for his life—he had harshly attacked Cosimo in verse; and
Niccolò Tinucci, another poet, was soon arrested, although the politics in his
verse was muffled by being put into the guise of moral censure.[40] Thereafter
in Florence, poetry as politics was to speak chiefly for the Medici, although a
line of secret composition, bitterly critical of the Medicean *reggimento,* was
gradually to come forth, as underlined in chapter 6 in my portrait of Francesco degli Alberti.[41]

The Church hierarchy was often the target of fierce attacks in verse, a risky
exercise; but these were most likely to be handed around in learned circles,[42]
except in times of war with the papacy, when poets and *cantimbanca* were
protected by their cities or by the prince in conflict with the Church. In the
1370s, Florence's War of the Eight Saints with the papacy drew forth some
wrathful poems against Pope Gregory XI;[43] and in the early fifteenth century,
Bolognese poetry raged against the three-headed papal schism.[44]

The world of high patronage could be deeply divided. In 1473–76, as
noted in chapter 2, the scandalous sonnet *guerrilla* between Luigi Pulci and
Matteo Franco was all about the politics of Lorenzo de' Medici's patronage.[45]
The more shameless and foul-spoken of the two, the priest Franco, was a safer
bet in the light of orthodox religious belief, and so the charming and talented
Pulci was largely banished from Lorenzo's company. Late in the century, the
well-known poets Bellincioni, Cammelli, Panfilo Sasso, and Niccolò Lelio

Cosmico engaged in vulgar sonnet wars over political and patronage differences.[46] Cammelli, in 1497, lost his post and the favor of the duke of Ferrara,
Ercole d'Este, almost certainly because he had attacked the wrong people in
verse.[47]

I want to close this chapter with a commentary on the so-called historical
lament, a full-fledged political genre, much produced in the period from the
fourteenth to the sixteenth centuries.[48]

Composition of this sort did not command a given form. It could vary in
length from less than 20 to more than 1,800 lines; and it might be a tailed
sonnet, a moral "song" (canzone), a capitolo, or a long narrative. The political
collapse of independent cities, the defeat of great captains, and the overthrow
of princes or powerful oligarchs were of all occasions the ones most likely to
bring forth laments. As a verse type, moreover, the lament was a meditation
on the fall of the mighty, hence on sin, on justice or injustice, and especially
on dramatic turns of the wheel of fortune. In fact, it was nearly always a
political statement as well. If recited in street or piazza, it was also a summons
to resignation and moderation, for its lesson of doom strongly suggested that
any middling or lower place in the world's hierarchies of power and dignity
was better than a place at the top, which could only beckon the fickle goddess
fortuna.

Most laments have the poem issuing directly from the mouth of the fallen
prince, captain general, or personified city. The speaker may be Bernabò
Visconti, Giovanni II Bentivoglio, or the city of Pisa; each lament delivers a
tale of woe in such a way as to arouse either our glee or our sorrow and
sympathy over the fall and abasement of the speaker. But the aroused sentiment was always a matter of pure politics, in frankly seeking to intensify fierce
current animosities or traditional (and current) amities. No true lament for
Pisa could possibly arouse the pity or sorrow of the people of Florence,
because in expressing its miseries, the Pisan voice would at the same time
enunciate the sins and crimes of the treacherous Florentines; and any make-
believe lament was patently ironic, nothing more than an occasion for stirring
up Florentine scorn and derision.

The best laments tell a story and offer us a biography or history of the
subject. Studded with detail, they are repositories of memory, with names,
dates, numbers, and descriptions of major deeds, events, and characteristics.
Passages abound that are all but chronicle, and I suspect that some of these

offer detail not elsewhere to be found. Among the truly memorable laments are those for Florence's duke of Athens, Pisa, Bernabò Visconti, Constantinople, Galeazzo Maria Sforza, Ludovico Sforza, Giovanni II Bentivoglio, Caesar Borgia, the flash dismemberment of the Venetian empire in 1509, Genoa after the sack of 1522, and Rome both at the time of the Great Schism and after the sack of 1527.[49]

In his lament for Walter of Brienne, known as the duke of Athens (1343), the Florentine poet Antonio Pucci has the nobleman give us a mini-autobiography. Here the late lord of Florence calls himself wretched, a traitor, a liar, lecherous, and unjust. Turning Florence into a sexual object, Walter admits that he had taken her by the hair and now murmurs his regret:

Omè, Firenze bella da godere,
che fosti mia quanto fu tuo piacere![50]

(Alas, beautiful Florence made for enjoyment,
Mine, but only so long as you took pleasure in it!)

The Florentine conquest of Pisa inspired no fewer than three laments, at least one of which was widely diffused in the Quattrocento, copied over and over again, and reprinted three times in the early sixteenth century, in the wake of Pisa's brief escape from Florence's clutches at the start of the Italian Wars.[51] Once a queen, Pisa is now called "the mother of fraud," "a slave and a whore."[52] She herself tells the story of her glorious territorial expansion, chronicling her bold seizure of main points and islands, in an empire to stretch from Majorca and Corsica across the Mediterranean to the Holy Land. Moaning and weeping in her downcast state, she implores pity and help from Ghibelline Italy. Now the emperor Sigismund makes a reply, granting that though Pisa was once "the flower of cities," she now deserves to die, owing to her pride, overly refined pleasures, and other sins. She had lived like a tyrant, from theft, with no regard for God or the fates, and had even "sold the Holy Sepulcher." Therefore, "O Pisa, worthy of death, now die!"[53] Another lament noted that the fall of Pisa would afterward provide material for sermons and be a rich source of sayings and proverbs.[54]

In 1385 the lord of Milan, Bernabò Visconti, was suddenly seized, imprisoned, and poisoned by the man who was both his nephew and son-in-

law, Giangaleazzo. This spectacular coup occasioned at least three different
laments,[55] which were often recited in public, copied, passed around, and
soon Tuscanized for the sake of listeners in other Italian cities. There we learn
inter alia that the ambush set for Bernabò threw his servitors into disarray, that
he had lived in France in his youth, was well schooled in Latin, gave his
daughter Catherine in marriage to Giangaleazzo, was a constant military
threat to his neighbors, had two friars burned alive and a woman from Mantua torn apart in Milan, put his falcons and hunting dogs above the good of
his people, and loved jousts and chess. One of the laments, redolent with
praise for Giangaleazzo, was almost certainly composed by a poet in the
enemy camp.[56] But another, written and later publicly recited by the Milanese *canterino* Matteo da Milano, was made more decorous and acceptable to
the continuing authority of the Visconti house in Lombardy.[57] It is done with
sympathy for Bernabò, though not omitting his sins and not censuring Giangaleazzo, whose compassion and good intentions are nicely highlighted. If
presenting such a poem in public was not to provoke anger or stir up resentment against the Visconti in the cities under their rule, then Giangaleazzo's
ruthless ways and Bernabò's barbarous cruelty had to be smartly played down.
Here the recent past was altered to serve the interests of public order in the
present; and so, introducing the needed palliative, the lament ends religiously:

> Tucti preghiamo Cristo, il re di gloria,
> Che mandi pacie infra l'umana gente,
> Contra'l dimonio che [ci] dia victoria,
> Essi perdoni a quel baron possente.[58]

> (Let's all pray Christ, the King of Glory,
> For peace among the human race,
> May he grant us victory over the devil
> And pardon that powerful baron [Bernabò].)

As a type of poem, the lament casts a clear light on the terrible intensity of
feeling, of brute patriotism and virulent hatreds and jealousies, in the political
affairs of Renaissance Italy. Men at times declared themselves ready to skin
others and to look upon rivers of blood.[59] Or, to underline their devotion,
writers might claim to belong to a prince or patron "in flesh and bones,"
blood and sinews,[60] as if mere matter were the only underlying reality. When

received in Milan, two laments, one calling for a Sforza takeover of Genoa (1464) and the other criticizing the takeover (1473), were copied directly into the state papers of the Sforza chancellery, the ducal secretaries thus aiming to keep a permanent record of the passions frankly expressed there.[61] Like oligarchs in Florence, Milan's rulers saw political poetry as a repository of strong public feeling. And such feeling was everywhere to be found. Across the years Venice too, for example, like republican Florence, aroused a vast measure of bitter resentment against itself. So when parts of the Venetian mainland empire rebelled and fell temporarily away in 1509, a well-written lament, lampooning Venice and charged with fierce popular accents, was at once put into circulation; and there the many sins of the proud Venetians are eloquently rehearsed.[62] A series of other anti-Venice poems followed, one of them avowing, through the personified Venice,

A lady I was, now a mere serving wench,
all my clothes have I lost

.   .   .   .

I've been stripped down to the skin,
peeled of my riches and chastity,
utterly abominated . . .
for all my adultery and evil deeds.[63]

The long reign in Bologna of Giovanni II Bentivoglio laid up a great store of hostility for his house. And his fall in 1506 was a spur to old, resentful memory, which released a surge of passion against him, his lineage, and his government.[64]

In effect, then, no eruption of political feeling seems to have been complete, or deeply enough felt, unless the anger also spilled over into verse. But however short, the best political poetry was always the encapsulation of a public mood and an act or statement of memory—of memory because the poet sought to base his praise or indictments on a recollected past, whether recent or more remote. The poetic defense of a prince or a city, or an attack on the enemy, was grounded both in current feeling and in a kind of reasoning about the past. Poetry was therefore a major accessory in politics. It defended friends and assaulted enemies; it identified and sharpened moods; its words, tropes, and meter created a mode of ritual expression, most succinctly rendered in the refrains of the best laments.[65] It was a form of condensed memory and a salient moment of public opinion caught in words. No man making a public recitation of political verse would have dared to depart from the views of his listening audience. His office was to refine, gild, emphasize, and illustrate. As poet, he was the better (and best-informed) conscience of his listeners; but in the ruthless political world of Renaissance Italy, he could also stir up murderous passions.

ELEVEN

CRISIS IN THE GENERATION OF 1494

The focus of the foregoing chapters moves from the compass of the local neighborhood out to the citywide scene and then glides back and forth between these; but it also passes well beyond, out to the larger world of Italy. Thus, in exploring the ideals of love and prayer, with a view to how they met the local needs of contemporaries, we turned to a metrical language of metaphor that was currency in all leading Italian cities, including the princely courts. By adapting the same images and a similar language, the citizen of a Renaissance city could pray or declare his love in Siena, Milan, Venice, Florence, Ferrara, or, say, Perugia. In the ties between poetry and politics again, as we have just seen, themes and topics could be locally based or could be called in from far afield; and they might deal with internal conflict or wars and tensions between city-states.

In the present chapter, though always bearing in mind the local urban setting, we shall see that the engine of historical change could come from abroad, via superior military and diplomatic might, and burst into the city, overturning governments, frightening local elites, and generally casting a fearsome shadow. But whatever the causes, any trauma had to be a matter of local experience.

Italy was not cast into crisis in the autumn of 1494: it was there already.[1] The new turn in affairs, the catalyst, pivoted on the cozy progress of the invading French army. Descending into the peninsula, it laid bare casually, as if by

accident, the burden of oppressive elites and unpredictable taxes, corruption
and favoritism in the administration of states, and a church driven by simony
and cynical careerism. At many points, arguably, the strains in civil institutions had become intolerable, and the cleavage between rulers and an alert,
articulate people was simply too great. No other reasoning can account for
the fact that the invader was often greeted with outright—not to say clamorous—approval. In Florence a Savonarolan populace believed that the foreigner had come to help purge Italy of its sins.[2] A few years later, in Rome,
many people were to believe that war and invasion constituted fair punishment for flagrant sin.[3] Political discontent, in short, ran so deep that it mingled with feelings of spiritual loss and salvation. God and politics were yanked
together.

Not for a while would the keenest observers, many of them poets, begin to
see that foreign intervention in the affairs of Italy might go on for decades and
that the arrival of "barbarian" armies—the specter of ancient Rome was at
once conjured up—conduced to the collapse of states. Every corner chronicler was soon making this observation.[4]

Local oligarchies were bullied or pushed aside by foreign armies, while the
larger community was swiftly affected by rising food prices, taxes, a fluctuating justice in the law courts, and the supine position of the productive countryside in the face of ravenous armies. In valleys, hills, and the vicinage of
cities, whole farming communities were pillaged or destroyed.[5] But the shock
of foreign invasion was of course chiefly felt at the top of government, in day-
to-day diplomacy, in military arrangements, and in public finance. Mistaken
policies could issue in disaster, in the infamy of leaders and the disgrace of
their advisors. Thus Piero de' Medici, Ludovico Sforza, and the last Ara-
gonese kings of Naples; thus, in other respects, the scampering about of the
lords of Mantua, Ferrara, Urbino, and the Romagna, in the breakneck effort
to keep to the winning side; thus the dizzying twists and turns in papal politics; and thus, in Florence, the republican policy of temporizing, in the desperate belief that the longer you waited the wiser your consequent actions.[6]

Since the most obvious failures in this age of instability were political,
political thinkers and writers—Pontano, Sanuto, Machiavelli, Bernardo Rucellai, Bernardino Corio, and so forth—were among the first to appreciate
the magnitude of Italy's dangers. Lesser chroniclers, often more socially humble, men such as Fabrizio degli Atti, Bartolomeo Masi, Leone Smagliati, and
Giovanni Marco Burigozzo, were overcome by distracting details and could

not recognize the larger shape or direction of events.[7] Like journalists, they were captivated and trammeled by immediate appearance.

But this is not to belittle immediate appearance, as I call it, for we all tend to live by its dictates. There, at any rate, is where crisis first revealed itself; and there too, in immediate appearance, is where political poets had their primary ground.

The moment we turn away from encomia and the copious love poetry of the age, which was often used by men from the upper classes as an imaginary exit from the real world of cares, we find a poetry charged with a vivid political content.[8] It cries out against Italy's selfish divisions, the savagery of war, "barbarian" armies, the hypocrisy of popes and prelates, the vanity and villainy of princes and other *gran maestri,* the treachery of mercenary captains, the credulousness of the common folk, and the nullity or fragility of truces and treaties. All such protest was pervaded by the instinctive knowledge that in the end the ordinary people of Italy would bear the costs, physical and economic, of the foreign presence on Italian soil.

Antonio Cammelli, Panfilo Sasso, il Cariteo, Giorgio Sommarriva, Antonio Tebaldeo, Francesco Berni, and dozens of other poets, many of them anonymous, pointed to the dangers and raised their voices in a chorus of eloquence. Long before Machiavelli, in the famous last chapter of *The Prince* (1513), called for liberating Italy from the barbarians, poets had much championed this cause. They were very often professional writers, attached mainly to princely courts or to grandees and near the centers of power[9]—watchful men, informed, quick to react, and directly caught up as clients in the major webs of patronage. Let us sound them out for a sense of the crisis, a sense of its outer limits and its buried or oblique consequences.

Unlike the chanted narrative verse of the *cantastorie* or *cantambanchi* (bench singers), the political verse of the age was sharply outspoken. This was one of its most striking features; so in many cities it was anonymously posted or even thrown into the streets, to be circulated without an author's name. Venice, Florence, Parma, Bologna, Milan, and other centers were all venues for writing of this sort;[10] and of course Rome had a celebrated site for the affixing of anonymous verse, often of a violent sort. Here in the early sixteenth century, the custom was to attach short poems to the statue of Pasquino (just off the southern end of the Piazza Navona) but also to points on the bridge of Castel Sant' Angelo, in the Campo dei Fiori, and in other places—poems usually charged with criticism, derision, or calumny. Pietro Aretino, Antonio Lelio,

Nicolò Franco, Francesco Berni, and even Annibal Caro are supposed, on good grounds, to have figured among the authors.[11]

Variously collected, the large body of this verse comes down to us in anonymity. And we may assume that the writers were mainly the secretaries or servitors of leading churchmen and temporal magnates, because most of the poems—the work of "insiders"—are skilled, cleverly turned, and exceptionally well-informed. Their language is comic, extravagant, paradoxical, allusive, frequently learned, spangled with *furbesco* (a coded "in-group" idiom), and at times swingingly obscene. No man—pope, prince, or cardinal—is spared. A rash of sonnets, however, posted about 1510 in the pontificate of Julius II, voices a sharp and melancholy awareness of Italy's prostration in the face of foreign princes and armies. The sentiment "Italy for Italians" is exceedingly strong, as is a sense of the horrors of war, the "barbarian furor," and that "evil and criminal dog" (quel cane iniquo e rio) King Louis XII.[12] Once ruler of the world, Italy is now a servant to France and Spain. Pope Julius is summoned to help free the Italians from "questa barbarica, aspra gente" (these uncivilized, cruel people). But you shall see Italy beautiful and green again, he is told, and see it bind itself to you against your enemies.[13] Other sonnets repeat this theme, calling him the "imperial warlike Vicar of God" and summoning the Italian people to rise up against the "cursed horde of barbarians."[14]

From about 1512 and the election of the first Medici pope, Leo X, the flow of "pasquinades" turns increasingly personal. Vigorous pleas for the Italian people continue, and the feeling of *italianità* is always there, but the new pontifical reign brings a leap in invective against cardinals and curial officials. Obscenity and scandalous blasphemy reach a new pitch (e.g., "Potta di Cristo" or "cul di Dio");[15] and Pope Leo himself, although held to be well aware of "the bitter laments of poor Italy," is boldly denounced as a brazen simonist.[16] He has his supporters in verse, to be sure, and is defended in the anonymous skirmishes fought around the statue of Pasquino; but the expressed deadly rivalries also come to reflect Italy's grievous political fractures and the wild instability of shifting alliances, with France on one side, Spain and the Empire on the other, and tilting back and forth between these Milan, Venice, the papacy, and Florence. Here was a political seedbed of passionate contradiction: to be for one side (it was claimed) was to be for poor Italy; but of course the other side made the identical claim. In this treacherous setting, poets could offer no solutions; and why should they? Neither could the

Venetian republic. Like the supposed toughest of all political thinkers, Machiavelli, in his more fanciful recipes, poetry could offer only rhetorical and psychological remedies; yet the heartache and the unhappiness, so movingly set forth in Guicciardini's *Storia d'Italia,* remained.

The death of Leo X in 1521 released a cascade of sonnets against all the evils and vices rampant in the college of cardinals; and every one of these gentlemen, all thirty-nine, in poem after poem, comes under blistering indictment. That any one of them could even think himself worthy of the papal tiara is a notion met with the utmost contempt. Sodomites and amorous lechers some are called; others are stigmatized as thieves, traitors, liars, beasts, Jewish dogs, misers, swindlers, vile peasants, madmen, and bastards.[17] If Cardinal Farnese became pope, one sonnet declares, "every whore and every ingrate bastard/ in Rome would triumph."[18] The late Medici pope himself, "a pig in St. Peter's stables," pawned Florence and the Church; if he had lived, "he would have sold Rome, Christ, and then himself."[19]

Although the adduced poems rank as *vituperia ad personam,* the charges all too often had a core of truth. Cardinal Giulio de' Medici was born out of wedlock; Cardinal Armellini, who flaunted a mistress, was a devious and squalid financial operator; Cardinal Monte had a widespread reputation for sodomy; Pope Leo had been a simonist; and many cardinals were surrounded by grasping, parasitical relatives, sometimes droves of them.[20]

The international status of Rome and the papacy meant that the conflict between states and among Italians had a platform in the college of cardinals, among their servitors and clients, and in the learned wars of well-turned poetry. Much more than letters or chronicles, this body of verse excelled in exposing the lesions and hatreds of the age, especially when the poetry was anonymous, for it could then say what other sources dared not say. In being repeated and circulated, the verse in question also, as it were, fingered the crisis: it kept touching the assault on political authority first unleashed by King Charles VIII, who seemed able, in his march through the peninsula, to turn subjects against rulers almost at will, thus rudely uncovering the fragility of power in Italy. This process of exposure, however, was then teased out into a more general rebellion, a fact attested by poetry's brutal attacks, both in Rome and elsewhere, on every kind of authority, secular and spiritual, princely, aristocratic, and even literary. No office or title, no place or dignity, was above mockery or sneering insult. And even when the poet as aggressor had the encouragement of a great patron, his invectives generally invited extreme replies. As a result, in the volatile environment of the day, the public spurning—often brilliantly done—of any prince, pope, or cardinal carried an innate charge against the loftiness of authority itself. If nothing else, the surpassing virulence of the language of political poetry knocked down barriers and opened the way to every kind of challenge. In a somewhat analogous situation, Martin Luther's in-your-face diatribes against the Roman Church were certainly seen (or miscast) in this light by the revolutionary German peasantry of 1524–25.

In the propaganda wars—that is, in poetry—Venice, Florence, Ludovico Sforza, Charles VIII and Louis XII, the French and the Spanish, and popes Alexander, Julius, Leo, Adrian, and Clement all are held up to public ridicule and venomous scorn. When forced to flee from Milan in 1499 and again in 1500, Ludovico Sforza fell victim to a poetry of sneers and scorn, and I have been unable, for that time, to find a single sonnet in his defense. A famous anonymous composition in the Milanese dialect, rare as a literary form, "Dove vet, dove vet, O, Lodovigh?/No l' e questa la via danda a Mira," is bitterly mocking, moralistic, and dismissive.[21] He is seen to be getting what he deserves. And another poem, a sardonic lament in the first person, "Son quel duca di Milano/che con pianto sto in dolore," makes him out as wretched, pitiable, and rightly surrounded by nothing but traitors.[22]

When the Venetian mainland empire was invaded by the armies of the League of Cambrai and temporarily dismembered in 1509, enemy poets rushed in gleefully with some long, ironic laments and short, pungent attacks on the republic of Saint Mark.[23] Propelled by arrogance and greed, the laments claim, the Venetian republic had gorged itself on lawless acquisition and brought war to Italy. But now, at last, it has got its comeuppance and is held up by heaven as an example to all the world. Expressing a sham regret, the sonnets see the Venetian republic as on the verge of death; the powers of Europe all prepare to attend Saint Mark's [Venice's] funeral; and if he has any honor left, he will truly die now; but first let him make amends for all his ill-got gains, his "mali ablati."

Venice, however, unlike poor Ludovico Sforza, had her champions, and they replied at once. Their chief tactic was to represent the republic as the defender of all Italy, a title earned by its alleged stance against the foreign element in the League of Cambrai.[24]

The emotional and moral climate that accompanied the political earthquakes of the late fifteenth and early sixteenth centuries—the keening anger, hatreds, fears, and outbursts of religious fervor—reveal that the crisis was profoundly social and cultural, not merely political, and so was likely to affect patron-client relations as well as other matters such as art, literary theory, philosophy, and religious phenomena. Some contemporaries held that war and the massive presence of foreign troops ushered in crushing tax levies, horrible blasphemy, contempt for priests, swaggering sodomy, shameless women, and a corrupt officialdom.[25] Later on, as is well known, Guicciardini himself was to pin the cause of the alleged drastic changes in manners and morals to the year 1494 and Charles VIII's descent into Italy.[26] Yet for all the period's alleged worldliness, fiery preachers continued to stir people up, as at Milan in 1516, and had sometimes to be silenced, from fear that the crying, chanting populace would get out of hand.[27] Moreover, traditional religious processions—the great strategy for social binding, and managed everywhere with expert care—were now used to satisfy new needs, for they also served to siphon off heady emotion. Here, however, in seeking to take the measure of the crisis, I want to pursue the larger challenge to authority.

Francesco Berni, the early-sixteenth-century Florentine poet, is in many ways the product of political upheaval and wartime emergencies. He paraded his joy in hedonistic pleasures and occasionally ranted, this man in holy orders, that he was ready to renounce God if his desires were to go unsatisfied.[28] Steeped in classical Latin poetry yet famous for his burlesque and comic verse in the vernacular, he was iconoclastic, rambunctious, brazenly homosexual, a client to powerful men, petted by ladies at the early Medici court, and finally poisoned—it seems certain—in strange circumstances in 1535. He embodied, in a word, flagrant contradictions.

In its most characteristic manner, his verse glorifies the commonplace and shameful, while denigrating and despising that which was traditionally considered noble and stately. Thus, in a sequence of clever *capitoli,* a verse form conventionally intended for serious moral matter, he sings the praises of a nonexistent cloak, of cooked eels, artichokes, fish, peaches, the penis as falcon, meat gelatin, urine beakers, the card game *primiera,* plagues and plague time, and a dreamed-of beautiful boy servant (he means a catamite).[29] In contrast, two popes, a new archbishop of Florence, and the god of love ("Love, I shit on thee") are all subjected to his merciless derision. The same treatment, as we saw in the first chapter, is doled out to the August entry of Emperor Charles V into Bologna in 1529, an occasion described by Berni exclusively in terms of a long, ridiculous, punning, and partly obscene list of names—the names of all the grand people who purportedly attended the event. It is a tour de force.[30]

In effect, Berni takes the world's values as traditionally known and turns them upside down or dismisses them out of hand. His distinctive achievement is in the poetic brilliance of this moral reversal. Authority had rarely been so consistently or insultingly challenged—in literature at all events. Although in holy orders, he detested clerical garb and produced at least one fuming sonnet against priests, who have turned the church, he alleges, into a tavern and thieves' den for "satiating . . . their strange appetites."[31] Yet all his literary activity went on under the protection of a variety of ecclesiastical patrons—Cardinal Bibbiena, Angelo Dovizzi (the well-connected apostolic protonotary), Giovan Matteo Giberti (bishop and powerful curial official), next Cardinal Ippolito de' Medici, and finally the first duke of Florence, Alessandro de' Medici.

War, a flood of foreigners, and the overturning of states had turned important patronage (not always a solid bond) into a dicey affair. With its changing popes and mighty curial officials, Rome had never offered infrangible guarantees to talented protégés. But as the chronicle of Michelangelo's life reveals, circumstances now suddenly became very much more precarious. Coups d'état at Milan, Florence, Naples, Bologna, Urbino, Perugia, and the Romagna scattered throngs of servitors—secretaries, men at arms, writers, musicians, artists, entertainers, grooms, huntsmen, and many another. Ferrara, Mantua, and even Venice felt the sharp military squeeze on cash and ready taxes, penuries that made for destabilizing uncertainties in the careers of artists and writers. This is why, in the early sixteenth century, as Dionisotti noted,[32] such an army of men of letters found themselves in holy orders, where they sought a more secure material existence. No wonder, therefore, that the idea of a capricious *fortuna,* harking back to the ancient world and often blamed or singled out thereafter, was now borne up to a fresh importance.[33] In their tormented new world, more thinkers and writers were seduced by the claim that no worldly place can be secure or stable, high place and honor least of all. The fashionable tales of the priest Bandello later on in the century are often darkened by a mute *fortuna.*[34] The priest Giovanni Brevio produced stories in which tragedy verges on being destiny.[35] Man / woman is pitted against forces of the sort that overwhelm reason and authority. And in the work of Machiavelli, Pontano, Ariosto, Guicciardini, and a host of other writers, *fortuna* courses its way importantly through the lives of men and the shape of political events.[36] Looking back, we can now see that the engine of instability really gathered around the invading foreigner.

From the very first, as documented by the propaganda war, Italians were haunted by a spirit of *italianità,* which later was to echo through Ariosto's *Orlando furioso.*[37] According to a contemporary Milanese chronicler, Cagnola, at Fornovo in July 1495, just before the battle that first tested the alleged invincibility of the French, the marquis of Mantua, Giovan Francesco Gonzaga, captain-general of the Italian forces, already proclaimed to his troops, "Dear Italians (*Italiani miei*), we are fighting against the French for the honor and good of all Italy."[38]

The Italianate feeling was more intense early in the period, when the battle lines were more easily drawn and political analysis cut more cleanly. Later, after about 1512, too many interests came to have a place in the contested scene, thoroughly clouding it, and the materials of analysis became intractable. Antonio Cammelli, il Pistoia, is the political poet par excellence of the early period.[39] In more than one hundred sonnets, he chronicles the political rivalries, events, rumors, and shifts in mood of the years from 1494 to 1500.[40] Dependent on Este patronage in Reggio but often compelled to worry about income, he turns in his verse to the Milanese court, which was allied to the Este by marriage, and takes Ludovico Sforza's side in the power struggle, in sonnets that at first see the lord of Milan as the genius and prime mover of Italian politics. But soon Cammelli begins to worry about French power and to sound warnings to all Italians. Informal, racy, newsy, knowing, insolent, and rich in proverbs, he gives out his particulars and dreads the second coming of the French. Florence, Venice, Milan, Rome, the rulers of Naples, Ferrara, Mantua, and even Genoa, Bologna, Lucca, and Siena, all are repeatedly alerted, admonished, or criticized. As events turn against Ludovico, so too does Cammelli, who in the end denounces the Sforza lord as a "base tyrant,"[41] although his fall, the poet insists, means the fall of Italy ("tu sei caduto e la Italia è caduta / e chi questo non vede è in tutto cieco").[42] Battered and divided Italy, however, gets his most sustained cry of sympathy. He takes sides, of course; he sees the Venetian and Florentine republics as predatory bullies; he curses Pope Alexander, "false priest," whoremonger, and "simonist";[43] and he bewails the treachery rife among Italian rulers. But he also brings a sharp clarity to the perception that a divided Italy is a recipe for lasting disaster. No more than the Italian statesmen of his day is he able to overcome the contradictions in his own sentiments. The sense of being a single people, noised about and sung in the literary culture almost every day, was also undone every day by the hatreds and fears that animated peninsular politics.

Cammelli's political poetry enables us to see the schisms, as it were, in the Italian soul—or better, to see the many souls of the different parts of Italy hankering to be one in the face of danger. Although less extreme than the anonymous poetry of Pasquino in Rome, Cammelli's poems, by their anger, ironies, and bitterness, pluck at religious sensibilities and adumbrate the profundity of the crisis. The Renaissance frankly tied state and religion together. No great political dignitary ever died without the massive, ceremonial presence at his funeral procession of all the local clergy—friars, monks, priests, and cathedral canons. Despite the cool detachment of many Italian statesmen, the urban multitudes everywhere, egged on by preachers, were only too willing and ready to relate political and military catastrophe to sin or the need for spiritual renovation. And whenever there was a transfer of power, such as into the hands of French or Spanish authority, the local clergy could be counted on to preach and to hold processions in favor of the new rulers. For Machiavelli and Guicciardini, therefore, the Church itself—that is, the papacy and the upper clergy—had helped to destroy the intelligence of religion in Italy, not only by its immorality but also by its opportunist and divide-and-conquer policies.[44] Now and then, after all, the papacy had spies even in the highest councils of Venetian government, for all the care and secrecy of those canny patricians.[45]

Reaching back to the age of Dante, anticlerical poetry attained a new pitch in the late 1490s and kept it up for decades. Let us not, however, get our bearings purely from themes. In the period before us, the modes and language of poetry also shadowed a troubled spirit. Thus, right around 1500, as Mario Martelli has emphasized, poetic forms were in rapid flux; experimentation flourished; the old genres were being recast.[46] As never before, contemporary events became the occasion and prime matter for verse, particularly satire, polemic, invective, prophecy, and narrative description, such as in war poetry of the period.[47] And soon there was a Tuscan *rifacimento* of Boiardo's *Orlando innamorato* in Francesco Berni's revision and translation. Yet at the very same time, cutting against the current of experimentation but answering to the crisis and its conflicting voices, there was the celebrated and partly successful attempt, in Pietro Bembo's linguistic program and in his followers,[48] to lock Italian literature into the language of Petrarch and Boccaccio, an archaic Tuscan, as if with a view to fixing that part of experience in a kind of mini-utopia. Here at least there would be a perfect and unchanging form in a distressingly unstable world. We shall see a parallel enterprise in Castiglione's construction of the ideal courtier.

In a genial analysis of Guicciardini's *Ricordi* (maxims), Alberto Asor Rosa finds a new literary form, "reflecting a moment . . . of transition and radical crisis."[49] Composed between about 1512 and 1525, the maxims verge, occasionally, on offering a vision of experiential chaos; for their guiding claim is that experience and reality offer no rules and regularities; contradiction there abounds and is natural, the world being, after all, the realm of the particular, the changeable, and the unpredictable. In Asor Rosa's analysis, therefore, the *Ricordi* are respectfully likened to *ghiribizzi*, whimsical notions or fantasies.

Ambitious and worldly to a fault, but in a world in which the capsizing of governments and the angry rejection of authority had come to seem a commonplace, Guicciardini was not alone in trying to make heads or tails of his experience. Why, indeed, had Machiavelli taken up his pen? The great macaronic poet and runaway Benedictine Teofilo Folengo, spurning all reason and with a fresh twist, frankly took to *ghiribizzi* in language and parody. In the very years when leading writers opened a debate on the capital question of the right and proper literary language for Italians, Folengo rejected the search for a utopian vernacular, producing instead, in macaronic hexameters, his comic but troubled epic *Baldus* (1517, 1521).[50] Blending Latin with dialect from Mantua, Padua, Brescia, and even Venice, which he then treats clownishly to the endings and syntax of Latin, Folengo, like Berni, turns the world upside down. He unfolds the picaresque life of the bastard grandson of a king of France, Baldus, who grows up in an imaginary village near Mantua as a roistering peasant. Here the displaced French nobleman collects a little gang of wild ruffians, among them the giant Fracasso and the half-dog Falchetto. We enter into a world of lawlessness, near-madness, and chaos.[51] Corrupt friars, effete courtiers, and local magistrates are mercilessly derided or cut down. Scatological, absurdist, anarchic, anticlerical, weird, hilarious, and marvelous, the epic takes Baldus and his accomplices into hell and raging battles with devils, sorcerers, and monsters. The action ends in a gigantic scooped-out pumpkin, where the teeth of poets and astrologers are unendingly pulled out—each then springs back again—as payment for all their lies.

Folengo's writings are driven by a mockery of themes and literary forms, from his burlesque of Petrarchan love in the macaronic pastoral *Zanitonella*

(1521) to his *Caos del tri per uno* (Chaos of three for one) (1526–27).[52] This obscure religious allegory relies in sequence on Latin, Italian, and macaronic, on prose and poetry, dialogue and narrative, thus answering in all to his professed three selves—macaronic poet, vernacular poet, and aspiring theologian. The gaping contradiction in his life, that he was an anticlerical Benedictine monk, was a wound healed by his eventual return to the cloister.[53] The age itself fostered such self-division: Berni, Firenzuola, Bandello, Ortensio Lando, Anton Francesco Doni, and others were all anticlerical clerics.[54]

In reviewing a line of literary evidence, I have passed from subject matter and the changeability of themes to questions of language and form, where crisis, if it is real, is likely to be imprinted. To testimony of this sort we had already turned by underscoring the pointed violence—in tone, language, and anonymity—of political and anticlerical poetry. Although still more or less dominant, the forms and language of Petrarchism were under sustained assault.

Meanwhile, another event was taking shape in the background to the practice of poetry: the new debate concerning the question of the most suitable language for Italian literature, the famous *questione della lingua*.[55] There was a new world out there, pressing in on the high culture of the age. The tumult and "barbarism" of foreign invasion had led many Italians to look searchingly beyond their traditional mental perimeters, with a view to transcending the municipal provincialisms of the tenacious old city-state.[56] In view of the period's limited network of communications, however, even including the new printing press, this larger cosmopolitan need could engage only an elite of writers and men in public life. With their fix on the ancient world, the humanists had long since crossed the intellectual frontiers, so to speak, of parish and cathedral. But after 1494 the call for a renewed dignity, for a new and grander ideal of unification, became dramatic. Humanists and statesmen—Calmeta, Castiglione, Bembo, Equicola, and others—soon stepped in with a model: namely, modern Italian literature, beginning with the masters of the fourteenth century (Petrarch, Boccaccio, and in part Dante). Here was a magnificent cultural construction and a would-be unifying language. It was a utopian solution and it was compensatory, a winning in the mind, in *l'imaginaire,* of that superior state that could not be won in war and politics.

But even in utopia Italian disunity reared its head, for the discussion was dominated by the question of the koine to be cultivated and used by modern writers. Once Latin, for all its persisting champions, had been edged over to the more erudite margins, three choices, as is well known, remained: there was (1) the language of the great *trecentisti,* excluding the demotic aspects of Dante (viz., Bembo's line), (2) a courtly and eclectic language, most common in Rome and best known to ambassadors and courtiers, and finally (3) the living speech of Tuscany, Florentine above all. All three offered elitist solutions, even the Tuscan option, which was selectively narrowed and based on the speech of the educated men of the upper classes. It was agreed that the dignity of literature could accommodate no other Italian dialect. In other words, if there was to be a solution, the peninsula's linguistic realities had to be rejected.

This vision of Italy, of a divided Italy united under a transcendent linguistic banner, is hauntingly reproduced in the most seminal work of the age, Baldasar Castiglione's *Il cortegiano* (The courtier), first published in Venice in 1528 and itself a key text in the language debate.[57] Here, however, the high ideal is lodged in the image of the courtier, who is second only to the prince as the most important political and social figure of the day, even in aristocratic Venice, where the top statesmen, as ambassadors, had to know how to conduct themselves in the leading courts of Europe. And once again, here, division and crisis ghost through the discussion as Castiglione, passing entertainingly from topic to topic, seems unable to find an organizing center. It ought to be, as recognized by the dialogue itself, a political question: namely, the courtier's raison d'être. Why is he at court at all? What is his distinctive business there? Not until about five years later, in the course of revising the work, was Castiglione able to bring the answer fully into focus:[58] in the axiom that the courtier is at court in order to provide the prince with the most effective and enlightened political counsel. All his arts, grace, and *sprezzatura* (masterly ease) are meant to win a place for him at the right hand of the prince. Otherwise, his mooted qualities turn into mere frivolities and ornamentation. Now other contradictions and structural breaks in the work come forth. I list them.

1. *Il cortegiano* was first dedicated to the king of France, Francis I, thus avoiding any narrow nationalism; but this dedication was removed when Francis assisted Pope Leo X, in 1516, in ousting Duke Francesco Maria della Rovere from Urbino,[59] the very site of the courtly dialogue. At that point, moreover, Castiglione was still Francesco Maria's ambassador to the papal court.

2. Certain passages, such as in books 1 and 2 of the work,[60] touch the painful memory of Italy's current "servitude" and military ignominy, while

also hinting at a strong feeling of *italianità*. Political realities thus break into the dialogue, to make for moments of pessimism that clash with the optimistic enterprise of molding an ideal courtier for Italy.

3. The realistic business of the courtier's political ties with the prince, briefly adverted to in book 1, is at last taken up for discussion in an afterthought, book 3 of the second redaction of 1520–21. There (chaps. 5–47), at once moralizing and glossing the subject with classical ethics, the author treats us to a fleeting picture of the peninsula's predatory courts and princes[61] but then truncates this discussion by introducing—to judge by its placement—the *more* important theme of love. This is followed by Pietro Bembo's closing peroration on platonic love and beauty. And this part too was a later addition, though one that cannot rhyme with the preceding section on the momentous true mission of the courtier. The closing theme and speech, nevertheless, in a genial use of the art of rhetoric, serve to conclude the work in the light of an ideal vision.

4. The image in book 4 (3 in the second redaction) of the ailing prince, morally enfeebled by his corrupt adulators at court, each of whom serves only his own selfish ends, metaphorizes fratricidal Italy as it is treacherously torn apart by self-serving elites. Moreover, the figures of both prince and ideal courtier come through to us in tragic isolation: the one sealed off from the world by a courtly circle of evil toadies and yes men, while the other, the true, perfect, or ideal courtier, stands apart from the claque of base noblemen and favorites at court as he seeks to find a way to the prince, so as to nurse and deliver him from evil. For he is meant "to turn with all his thoughts and the very power of his soul to loving and almost adoring his prince above all other things."[62] Yet how he is to reach that ailing personage in the face of so much moral and political pestilence is a question, ultimately, that goes untreated. Instead, the theme of women and woman's nature is playfully allowed to keep intruding. Consequently, with ladies present and with the beckoning of light flirtation, the apolitical theme of platonic love surfaces to become more rewarding; and we end with the philosophy for giving intellectual substance to Petrarchan love verse, Neoplatonism—the main speaker at that point in the dialogue being none other than the first great editor of Petrarch's lyric poetry, the Venetian aristocrat Pietro Bembo.

Castiglione seems never to have challenged authority. Nor could he, for he issued from it, in the sense of having been born to a leading noble house and then married into another (the Torelli), in the region of Mantua, where his lot was to serve princes at the highest level: first the marquis of Mantua, then the duke of Urbino, and finally Pope Clement VII. Understandably, therefore, in view of his experience, *Il cortegiano* is beset by the strains of a dire and violent political world—the *real* world of the Italian courtier. There is, however, an escape route, a way for the author to salvage his perfect nobleman, namely, the way of high entertainment: games,[63] fantasy, idealization, a dose of political moralizing, a highbrow philosophy of love, and, in the accomplishments of the ideal courtier, the graceful wearing of a mask that strives to fuse artfulness at court with truth in politics.

In view of the broad range of themes and examples in this chapter, a lean summary may help to highlight the argument. The markers of crisis in the literature of "the generation of 1494" were

1. the willful turning upside down of the established moral and social values,
2. terrible contradiction,
3. unusual experimentation,
4. the Bembian attempt to freeze forms,
5. violent literary cross-currents,
6. shattering diatribe, and
7. bizarre excesses, such as Pietro Aretino's pornographic sonnets (1527) on the different sexual positions, intended to serve as commentary for the engravings of Giulio Romano's erotic drawings of 1524.[64]

Only during the great age of its beginnings, in the conflicted thirteenth and early fourteenth centuries, had Italian literature been the forum for such a spectacle of activity, trial, and error. Indeed now, in the high Renaissance, the peninsula's literary performance was richer, more varied, more worldly, and for a time at least, in its imaginative daring, more vital than anything offered by the real world of Italian politics and economic enterprise.[65]

THEMES &

STRATEGIES

Looking back at this point over the book's trajectory, the reader will note that we entered a historical world through an ether, so to speak, of "strong" words—the literary imagination. Examined in their "material" context, such words led us to the heart of Italian Renaissance cities, to the forms of consciousness that moved patrons and clients, insiders and outsiders, lovers, neighbors, suppliants, victims, aggressors, and troubled or anxious citizens.

Literature, as we also saw, is an elastic idea and activity. This may be demonstrated by simply recalling the radical expansion of the canon in English and American literary scholarship in the years after 1968, when all-but-unheard-of writers (women, blacks, and others) began to enter the stream of study at major American universities.

In Italy the first remarkable changes came in the late nineteenth and early twentieth centuries, with the unification of the peninsula and the rise of democracy. "Minor writers" (the *minori*) such as Iacopone da Todi, Saviozzo, Franco Sacchetti, Leonardo Giustinian, Antonio Cammelli, plus a host of "Petrarchists" and "bourgeois realists," were fetched up from early printed editions and manuscript libraries, to be put on their way to respectability. Later, sixteenth-century female poets too were resuscitated. But it was to be three to four generations before such writers were truly drawn into the world of Italian university study; and even now most of them, the men especially, remain without critical editions. So the process of "elevation" to the canon continues, although often in the face of contempt. No tradition of literary scholarship has been more "elitist" than the one in Italy, where—at least for the Renaissance—the overpowering emphasis has been on the "greats." The sustained study of the Cavalier poets in England ("minor" writers?) has had no parallel in Italian scholarship. And I have heard professors of Italian literature ask, Since every little hick town in Italy has had its local poets, how can the *minori* be taken seriously?

This scorching judgment may give pause to literary scholars, but why should historians take any notice of it? We have a different and less invidious job to do.

Here immediately, however, I want to scotch the idea that writers of the second and third rank have more to say to historians than the "masters," because of being less accomplished, less "artistic," and so standing closer to the realities that interest historical scholarship. There is *nothing* to this notion, but it is dying hard. In their very departures from "reality" by means imaginatively secured, writers such as Petrarch, Boccaccio, Lorenzo de' Medici, Bembo, and Ariosto treat us to all the devices of idealization, wishful thinking, and evasive ambiguity. If we elect to study the wealth of these resources, aiming to see how major writers use them to negotiate their way through or around the constraints of social life, we begin to confront the complexities of consciousness in its more slippery, subtle, devious, or layered operations. Just here is the special terrain for the charting of relations between "high culture" and social forms, including politics.

In the foregoing chapters, however, I had a variety of reasons for calling more often on the *minori*. First, traversing an interdisciplinary field that is still new, I chose to reach out for the wider perimeters and to set down some of the main lineaments, never losing sight of the fact that my first commitment is to history rather than to the transcendent features of literary texts. Second, the major figures would have required more detailed analysis, more specialization, and a book three times the length of this one. Third, the *minori* often echo or adapt the rhetorical and imaginative strategies of the masters, thus helping to illuminate them: in a word, they are apt to offer shortcuts. Finally, it was most important to introduce a valid assortment of writers, in order to maintain a view of literature more in keeping with its spacious office in Renaissance Italy. After all, Ariosto wrote for women at court and dismissive patrons; the demotic Bellincioni wrote for the lord of Milan; "bench chanters" recited to mixed crowds in the piazza; Giambullari issued poems for a public ready to sing or recite them in the streets; humanists such as Poliziano looked to an elite of learned men; Correggio and Gasparo Visconti wrote for other courtiers; Lorenzo de' Medici wrote both for a select circle and (in his carnival poems) for a more vulgar taste; others (as at Ferrara and Bologna) wrote more strictly for friends; and the Venetian patrician Giustiniani wrote for a broad taste in popular love songs.

Clearly, I have kept intended reading and listening audiences in mind throughout the book. Though always problematic, bonds between writers and readers provide one of the keys to the tracking of movement between literary and social structures.

Here and there I have not hesitated to cite ditties and doggerel as entries *en matière*. Does this mean that I think of the like as "literature"? Many people would, nowadays; and when we consider that the Renaissance was very much closer than ours to being an oral culture, one in which verse chanters, for example, were a common phenomenon, we should not be so quick to dismiss street rhymes and jingles as unworthy of our attention. The fact that I myself do not think of doggerel as literature is beside the point; for whenever I quote such matter in the text, I do so to open things up and to ease the reader into a course of argument. Just as in the writing of political history we may pass from garbled diary entries and simple rumor to the ploys of diplomatic correspondence, so in the social analysis of imaginative verbal expression, we may need to cross over the space from penny rhymes to more sophisticated composition. Obviously, as we pass from one to the other, our analytical strategies will radically change.

In my treatments of Saviozzo, Francesco degli Alberti, love poets, and the tale of Taddeo by Grazzini, diction, metaphor, tone, mood, and even occasionally sound are made central to an unfolding analysis, aimed at teasing social milieux out of words and configurations. But while the literary critic is more likely to stay in literature when at the tasks of analysis, I endeavor, in addition, to look out to the historical world around the text.

For all its inclusiveness, need I point out that my working definition of literature sets the emphasis on composition of an imaginative sort—poem, tale, or dialogue? This would include letters, such as the one by Pulci that opens chapter 2. It follows that I have sought to avoid, except in passing, all traditional historical sources such as chronicles and other forms of flat (prose) documentation: these require no concerted analysis in the literary-social mode. The purpose of this book is to get at the evasive, formalizing, playful, aggressive, and idealizing imagination, but only so as to widen the historical stage by bringing in richer forms of consciousness. That is, I am seeking a more complex reality: one somehow closer, surprisingly, to the ways in which people both daydreamed and carried out their ordinary activities under an aura of social ideals and stresses. In this sense, I accept that literature holds the voices of more complete men and women. As a guide to the minds and sensibilities of people, the flat document, the prosaic record, must always be—if I may in brevity exaggerate—oversimple and perfunctory.

What to say, therefore, about the formal side of imaginative literature in relation to social strain and constraints? Having published a book on the subject in 1985, *Society and History in English Renaissance Verse*, I want here to keep strictly to the barest of statements and to *Strong Words*.

The love sonnet, the verse letter, the eulogy, the hymn, the moral statement (*canzone* or *capitolo*), the short tale, the dialogue—all these genres had their stylistic and formal conventions. In part, therefore, they bear the sound of past voices. But this aperçu is theoretical, valid up to a point but of no use in the task of contextualizing, say, a love sonnet 100 or 150 years after the genre got started. To read Guido Cavalcanti in the troubled context of his late-thirteenth-century world is one thing. However, when we find traces of his vision and of Petrarch's in the love sonnets of Francesco degli Alberti or of Lorenzo de' Medici in the fifteenth century, we also find that the later poets are adapting and adjusting the earlier voices to their own requirements. Now, therefore, the fresh use of the genre must be recontextualized by a new labor of analysis. Genre may bear the echoes of past voices, but if the form long persists and remains vigorous, then they tend to be muted or even extinguished by present need. A usable past, genre may be endlessly recycled.

There is a deeper connection to be made. When a form—hymn, sonnet, octave—remains truly vital over time, we should recognize that something about it is paradoxically protean. For it is able to take on all the new accents and modulations needed to make it conform with the vicissitudes of time and place. Thus, the sonnet could be more or less courtly, more or less learned and allusive, more or less imitative, more or less charged with self-inquiry, more or less "base" (popular and "carnal"); and it could also abandon love for satire, prayer, or even a statement of hate. Though the formal shell remained (meter, rhymes, and the fourteen-to-seventeen lines), the subject, treatment, and attitudes might all change. Lust, politics, moralizing, scathing abuse, patronage, and local gossip: all could have their say.

Of all forms, the popular tale and the verse letter got closest, in their transparency, to the kinds of events and doings that historians are likely to see as first-order social and political realities. The dialogue, the satire, and the "straight" political poem also approached transparency. But we have absolutely no warrant for privileging these forms over those with a more slanting, idealizing, or elusive démarche. Eulogy, prayer, the poetry of elevated love, and literary form itself also touched existential strains and were all the more challenging in that they made their contact by more devious, rhetorical, or subtle means.

Transparency, then, cannot be the sole measure of historical reality: the real also belongs to a more oblique and opaque record. The unstable and tricky relations between profound political crisis and literary form, as examined in the last chapter, illustrate this. In the climate of revolt against authority, the course of change fanned out into a sustained assault on the authority of literary convention itself. Passing into consciousness, the unhappy cavalcade of events ("crisis") was also refigured outside the confines of rational discourse.

I come to the book's themes and its treatment of social strain.

Nowhere in historical scholarship is there a sufficient appreciation of the orality of daily life in Renaissance Italy. On the one hand exceptionally literate and tenacious about their record keeping, urban Italians were, on the other, continually assailed by the words of town criers, sermons, confraternal and parish prayers, by government bells sounded to impart daily information, by the oral spectacle of public punishment, by keen neighborhood gossip, and by the recitations of street and "bench chanters." Some cities required prostitutes to wear little bells. Even if privately read, therefore, the poem and the tale, normally composed in a conventional "communal" form, entered easily and naturally into this setting. My emphasis on the spoken tale and on the poem, whether the latter was secretly posted or openly recited, highlights the orality of life in streets and piazzas: a mode, so to speak, of hands-on communication. Nothing better exhibits this feature of urban life than the line of political poetry considered in chapter 10.

The machinery of Renaissance oral culture is also revealed by a certain kind of cruelty, another topic all but untouched by historical scholarship. As related in chapter 8, which is cast around Grazzini's tale of Taddeo, the most harmful form of action against a select victim was done by word of mouth, often ending in the wholesale destruction of his or her community standing. In the theater of the cruel, physical pain was short-lived, but the injury done by speech to name and fame went on: the victim lived in the din of contemptuous words, whether spoken to his face or behind his back. Such a setting also accounts for the fierce power of the hate poem, the *vituperium,* penned not for reading in privacy but for circulation, to be repeated and if possible memorized, so that it would inflict the greatest degree of harm.

When we turn to adulterous women, unchaste widows, or fatuous men such as Bianco Alfani and the Fat Woodcarver (see my *Italian Renaissance Sextet*), we again find that speech—local gossip, street rhyme, or public proclamation by trumpet and town crier—did the fatal damage. In recognition of this, Venetian custom made it possible for a falsely defamed girl to have her honor restored by official announcement in her parish church on a Sunday— though, once the girl was attainted by scandal, however innocent she had been, we may wonder about how far such a restoration could truly go.

In the chapter on prayer, I refrained from discussing the character of its orality, because this seemed to me self-evident. Confraternal orisons—and much prayer *was* this—meant that a good deal of address to God and the saints was an open and public act of speaking or chanting. Certain feast days, as well as every city's periodic processions, enhanced this feature; and of course religious drama, at times performed in public squares, also promoted the resonance of the spoken word. Believing, however, that the study of prayer belongs in the mainstream of social history, I concentrated mainly on how its language and metaphor locked into urban experience, in a linking of God, commerce, and patriarchy. Beyond all their transcendence, the most noble words, the highest flights of religious fervor, also had roots that were more or less time and place specific.

Yet how did it happen that in a climate of prayer and a dense scatter of churches and religious confraternities, suicide and alienation were possible? In two case studies, I let the poetry of Saviozzo and Francesco degli Alberti speak in reply. The life of an itinerant writer could be nagged by uncertainty, material strain, and isolation, ending (in Saviozzo's case) in such anguish that the religious call itself, although in reverse (prayer as adamantine cursing), was made the road to suicide. Here is another topic, suicide *and* community, that has had no attention from historians of the Renaissance.

Alberti's political alienation, as traced in his writings, made him an internal exile. He used his love poetry and prayers to condemn the vile political enemy and to lift a proud spirit above the disgrace of having to claw the margins of social life. Prejudice against the validity of poetry as witness has led historians to overlook this mode of exile—men at home in their native cities, nursing rage and resentment against ruling prince or oligarchy, and carrying the bitterness of exile in their hearts.

The countless churches and floods of prayer notwithstanding, there was an occasional touch of skepticism or even atheism in certain men, although it surfaced lightly, discreetly. Here is another open topic for historians, not only as set forth in Luigi Pulci's antireligious satires but also as seen in the doubts and queries of more cautious men.

Both as place and idea, the urban neighborhood entered serious historical study only recently. The method of inquiry has rightly tended to focus on local organization and on the social character of the place. However, in considering the impact of the neighborhood on poetry and conceiving of patron-client webs as "neighborhoods," I try to enter a mental world and to get at some of the adhesive elements of consciousness. For clearly enough, house and the near locality were determining and could not fail to condition or mold the individual in the glare of the community and its words. The circumscribing perimeters of life—kin, daily contacts, church, shops, streets—were first in the shaping of speech.

In this connection, it is imperative to note that the study of patronage has neglected its language and *forma mentis;* hence the business of chapter 2. Obvious as it may now seem, when I first went to work on the question some fifteen years ago, I was amazed to discover the striking similarities between the words and locutions of patronage and those in the poetry of elevated love. Relations between clients and patrons could never have boiled down to a mechanical process of soliciting and giving favor. This give-and-take was governed by a play of ideals that muted or helped to soften power, wealth, social structures, name, rank, and reputation. This is to say that the claims of love, loyalty, respect, convention, and other niceties greased and rationalized an elaborate system of inequalities—though in these matters, to be sure, some men had more artistry than others.

Hate and vituperation complete the picture of patronage. You cursed your rivals and the enemies of your patron; or you might secretly curse his treachery and he, publicly, yours. In the hard world of the Renaissance city, where material fortunes and patronage were often closely linked, defeat and frustration in the quest for favor could well elicit bitterness and venom; but these were turned against the man, not the system.

Neighborhood and patronage lead naturally to the themes of "insider/outsider" and hence, in the hounded outsider, to alienation, exile, or even suicide, as in *Taddeo,* Alberti, Saviozzo, *The Fat Woodcarver,* or the adulterous wife and the unchaste widow. To be from outside the group or the city, to stand (friendless) outside the web of patronage, or to be targeted as a victim by representative groups: here were the makings of distress, unless the outsider, such as the Jew or the prostitute, belonged to an accepted or needed group. To be inside the group was to be in close conformity with it, whether as a nobleman in Venice, an artisan in Florence, or quite simply a chaste wife in any city. The manifest signs of the outsider laid stress on the importance of conformity, for the outsider too must conform, in testimony again, through a visual code, to the power of the oral culture. Thus, the prostitute had to wear the badge of her trade (sash, gloves, etc.) proclaiming her identity; the criminal wore his disgrace at the pillory or on his branded face, amputated limb, or some other sign of mutilation; the known adulteress was known by *publica fama* (word of mouth); the disgraced priest was simply removed from the scene, transferred, so that the silence itself spoke up; and urban codes of law required Jews to wear an identifying accessory.

The powerful call to conform in the bounded spaces of the Renaissance city is far from having received its due in the vital historiography; but until we gauge it rightly, the making of social identities, as a matter for investigation, will elude our inquiries.

Chapter 9's analysis of the problems of seduction, in the course of which I began to appreciate the extent to which young wives, widows, and virgins were corralled, finds that the eyes and tongues of the neighborhood were the great danger and deterrent for sinning women. The eye detected, but the word destroyed. In the gendered spaces of the age, women were more enclosed, and their cross-town movements were chaperoned. The findings of that chapter contribute to the current debate regarding the place and space of women in Renaissance Italy. As projected in literary form, the evidence indicates that their condition was not at all "liberating." It may be that the period after 1540 offered them more space, but the signs of this are fragmentary and relate to Venice alone. Genoa, the great unknown, may hold some surprises for us.

The fact that transparency, in the "plain" document, the poem, or the tale, holds no exclusive access to historical reality is demonstrated by chapter 4, with its inquiry into the windings of love. As I worked on the vast body of amatory verse, I myself was surprised by the emergence of the role and tenacity of misogyny. This discovery, however, needed sustained analysis: a patient peeling away of the layers of mystification, to reveal at the heart of "courtly" love the misogynous distances between men and women and the "infinite" narcissism of the male lover. Yet this by no means depleted the resources of the amatory idiom, for the articulating of exalted love on the page of poetry could lead to a calculus for dealing with social strain: with ambition and frustration, with personal and group identities, with troubled self-inquiry, or with the wish to alter realities by drawing them into the symbolic universe of the imagination. There was still more: the same calculus could also be converted into a mode of prayer and litany, to help drive away, however briefly, the "base" world. In searching for the links between history and "highbrow" love poetry, we are just beginning to make out their intricate meshing.

Although the literature of Tuscany, and Florence in particular, often stands foremost in this book, owing chiefly to the history and geography itself of Italian literature, I have sought to keep Italy's regional differences in mind all along the way. This is best shown by the chapter on love, which draws attention to the differing manners and uses of love poetry at the courts, among itinerant writers, in Bologna's legal circles, in "bourgeois" Florence, and at Venice in the strain popularized by Giustiniani. Revealingly, this most imitated and practiced of themes and forms could issue in rich variations; and this is demonstrable because amatory verse from some of the different courts and cities is copious enough to permit comparative study. Hymns and prayers, on the other hand, betray less regional variation, although the mystical strain, seeking actual union with the body of Christ, turns up with unusual strength in Umbria and parts of Tuscany.

All social historians of a deterministic or strongly materialist die must be defeated, it seems to me, by the fact that unlike, say, the Veneto and the Genoese littoral, Tuscany produced so resonant a literature so early and for so long. Yet even in Tuscany, what happened to the meager fortunes of the love poem in fifteenth-century Lucca and Siena? Giustiniani aside, why is there so paltry an amount of Venetian love poetry—and that too formulaic and imitative (Aleotti)—from the fourteenth and fifteenth centuries? Why in the world did Venice produce no surviving body of tales (*novelle*) until the sixteenth century? And why again, in matters concerning the early history of Venetian banking, are so many of the critical documents Florentine[1] rather than the fruit of Venetian sources? These are troubling questions, and no one has ever offered adequate replies.

Accordingly, when touching on Venice in my pages on sex and seduction, foiled by the lack of Venetian fifteenth-century tales, I gave more prominence to the sixteenth century. Nevertheless, the spatial perimeters for women, as extrapolated from Quattrocento Tuscan material and from northern tales of the next century, struck me as being also applicable to Venice and perfectly consistent with the known body of Venetian historical evidence.

Although the language of patronage tended to be similar up and down the peninsula, the notable differences collected around the stature of patrons. The power of princes, such as at Ferrara and Milan, was the quiddity most likely to attract the more extreme forms of figurative language. In this regard, it is instructive to watch the growing body of poetry around the Medici in Florence, as they rose to the top of the state after 1434. Siena offered something like this to the Petrucci, but Venice never saw the like.

In treating the problem of cruelty (chapter 8) and in discussion of the cruel prank (*beffa*), I was only too aware of the fact that most of the *beffa* literature comes out of Tuscany, like so much other literary activity. To what extent the voices of that material may be said to speak for upper Italy has no simple answer. Some of Bandello's tales, like those of a few others, extend the field of play for the *beffa* to more northern cities. There too, moreover, neighborhood ways and forms, as well as other social structures, paralleled Tuscan models, sufficiently so to justify claims regarding the incidence of neighborhood cruelty in a much larger ring of Italian cities. But I suspect that Florence in particular always fostered a more ruthless, less merciful, strain, owing to its keener competitive edge among tradesmen and in commercial enterprise, in a radius that ran from lowly artisan up to silk merchant and big banker. This edge was most notable in the tenacious Florentine bent for keeping close accounts of property and business affairs. No other city matched this vigilance.

Since the flood of writing that came out of Florence touches every aspect of life, the historian is often tempted to use it selectively in the search for insight into the larger world of the Italian Renaissance. Yet there can be no doubt that Florence, like Venice, was in many ways unrepresentative, atypical; so too, however, were Milan, Rome, Padua, and Ferrara. Then where *was* the typical city? Turned thus, our aggressive skepticism suddenly reminds us that historical study also imposes the need to generalize and to seek out similarities. To say, therefore, that Florence was atypical is not at all the same as to say that no Florentine document or tale may ever be used as a source of light for other Italian cities. I can only conclude that any judgments about this must belong to the discrimination of the historian.

Notes

CHAPTER I. NEIGHBORHOOD VOICES IN POETRY

1. Koenig, "Wartime Religion."

2. Some examples of the chronicles are Dino Compagni, *Cronica fiorentina;* Graziani, *Cronaca della città di Perugia; Diario ferrarese;* Infessura, *Diario della città di Roma;* and Smagliati, *Cronaca parmense.*

3. Drawing on the range of previous scholarship and altering a debated canon, Marti, *Poeti giocosi,* 111–250, publishes the reduced collection of sonnets, including those that he now enters under the name of Meo dei Tolomei. But see also Contini, *Poeti del Duecento,* 2:367–401, 883–85, for some illuminating comments on texts and manuscripts.

4. See Marti, *Poeti giocosi,* 141, 146, 148, 169, 173, 177, 194, for references both to *babbo* and to the different names, not including Becchina's.

5. Ibid., 119, 121, 124 (sonnets in the idealized mode), 122, 123 (verging on parody), 136, 138, 141 (outright parody).

6. Berni, *Rime,* 5–7.

7. Antonetti, *La vita quotidiana,* 446–57; Ruggiero, *Boundaries of Eros,* chap. 6; Labalme, "Sodomy and Venetian Justice," 217–54. Examples from statutes include *Statuta de regimine,* vol. 3, rubric 23 (death by fire); Bongi, *Bandi lucchesi,* 377–78 (threatened castration and fire); *Municipalia Cremae,* 80 (possible death by fire); and for Siena (statutes of 1545), Ascheri, *L'ultimo statuto,* 316–18 (penalties range from heavy fines to fire).

8. For the sustained campaigns against sodomy, moved by the Dominican friars San Bernardino and later Savonarola, see Rocke, *Forbidden Friendships,* 36–44, 204–12. The preachers Giovanni da Capistrano and Bernardino da Feltre were most active in the Veneto.

9. Ibid., 115. But this claim, and indeed all the book's quantitative underpinnings, have been sharply contested by S. K. Cohn's review in *Speculum* 74, no. 2 (1999): 481–83. Cohn lowers Rocke's figure to "fewer than one in every seven males," and even this he deems an inflated figure.

10. Beginning with the so-called school of homosexual poets in Perugia: Tartaro, "Forme poetiche del Trecento," 24–29; most of the texts are in Marti, *Poeti giocosi*, 559–712, 765–809, including the verse, inter alia, of Neri Moscoli, Marino Ceccoli, Cecco Nuccoli, Gilio Lelli, and others; see also verse in Saviozzo (chap. 5, this volume); Lanza, *Lirici* (some examples), 1:172–73, 323–24, 569–71; 2:240–45, 528–29, 635–36, 639–40, 646–47; and the *novellistica* (chap. 9, this volume).

11. Martines, "Amour et histoire," and chap. 4 of this volume.

12. Martines, "Séduction," and chap. 9 of this volume.

13. See Eckstein, *District of the Green Dragon;* Stella, *La révolte des Ciompi,* chaps. 1, 5; Romano, *Patricians,* chap. 6; Kent and Kent, *Neighbours and Neighbourhood;* and urban space in Crouzet-Pavan, *Venise: Une invention,* chaps. 2, 5, 6, 10.

14. Berni, *Rime,* 7, 8, 16, 21, 38, 65, 70, 201. On Berni's "lexique erotique," see the obsessional work in four volumes by Toscan, *Le carnaval du langage.* In what amounts to a remarkable *glossarium eroticum,* this French scholar takes the Florentine poet's *capitoli* as his analytical point of departure.

15. Berni, *Rime,* 92–96; Toscan, *Le carnaval du langage,* 1:39.

16. Berni, *Rime,* lines 9–10, 39–40, 62–63.

17. On the Bolognese poets, see Frati, *Rimatori bolognesi del Quattrocento.*

18. For a sounding of neighborhood attitudes, see Martines, *Renaissance Sextet,* chaps. 4, 6.

19. There was an active group of neo-Latin (humanist) poets in Ferrara. Pasquazi, *Poeti estensi.*

20. Cammelli, *I Sonetti,* 22–30.

21. Ibid., 29, lines 12, 15–17.

22. Ibid., 26, lines 3–4.

23. Ibid., 27, lines 3–4.

24. Ibid., 24, lines 1–4.

25. Berni, *Rime,* 2–4.

26. Quoted in Arnaldi and Rosa, *Poeti latini,* 1004.

27. Robin, *Filelfo,* 17–45. Reexamining the evidence and deepening the analysis, Robin argues that the assault was meant to disfigure Filelfo's face, thus "dishonoring" the man, not to assassinate him, as has traditionally been claimed.

28. See Pulci, *Opere minori,* 158–90; Pulci and Matteo, *'Libro dei sonetti.'*

29. Berni, *Rime,* 69–71.

30. Ibid., xxix–xxx; Claudio Mutini, "Berni, Francesco," in *DBI,* 9:343–57.

31. Queller, *Venetian Patriciate.* On the tentacular reach of the Medici, see Eckstein, *District of the Green Dragon,* 199–224.

32. See chaps. 2, 10, this volume.

33. On strong insult as misdemeanor, subject to prosecution, see chap. 10, notes 5 and 6.

34. See *Diario ferrarese,* 247, on anonymous "bulletini" circulated in Ferrara against the neo-Latin poet and powerful official Tito Strozzi; Smagliati, *Cronaca parmense,* 72, for a six-line ditty sung in Parma against the rich, greedy tax farmer Zan Andrea Tarascone; and Crouzet-Pavan, *Venise: Une invention,* 229, for a similar composition sung by children in the streets of Venice in 1499, against the great nobleman Antonio Grimani.

35. Meglio, *Rime,* 49–51, 54–56, 59–63.

36. Lanza, *Lirici,* 1:163–64, 178, 323, 355–56, 395; 2:144–47, 152, 264, 473–74, 481, 485, 531, 533–34, 535–36, 637.

37. Franceschi, "Il linguaggio della memoria," 220.

38. Lanza, *Lirici,* 1:211–40.

CHAPTER 2. THE VERBAL WEB OF PATRONAGE

1. "Quantunque io ti venga poco inanzi, sappi che io sono sempre teco et più che mai tuo, e quello poco so et posso e lla roba e lla vita metterò a tua posta per te . . . ma di tanto sia certo, che io non ho dimenticato tanti benefici et dal tuo padre et da te, et so che tu non hai servito a ingrato, ch'io ho tutto scolpito nel cuore. E non si credano tuo compagni che io vadi fuggendo per non pagarti, ch'io t'amo, reverisco et temo. Et è gran tempo io stimai più la gratia e ll'amicitia tua che tutte le cose del mondo; et così stimerò sempre" (Pulci, *Morgante e lettere,* 1000–1001).

2. On the carved, stamped, or sculpted heart, see Bembo, *Prose e rime,* 521 (no. 19); Galli, *Canzoniere,* 275 (no. 252); Malatesti, *Rime,* 68 (no. 34); Sforza, *Canzoniere,* 62 (no. 14). On the lover's fearing and revering, see Sforza, *Canzoniere,* 67–68.

3. Martines, "Ritual Language," 68–74; and Trexler, *Public Life,* 105–7, 157–58, on Stefano Guazzo.

4. Some recent work on patronage: Hollingsworth, *Patronage in Renaissance Italy;* Kent and Simons, *Patronage, Art, and Society;* Kent, *Rise of the Medici;* Molho, "Cosimo de' Medici," 5–33; Lowe, "Goro Gheri's Views on *amicizia,*" 91–105; and the patronage essays in Basile, *Bentivolorum magnificentia.*

5. For example, Verde, *Lo studio fiorentino;* Brown, *Isabella d'Este;* Ferrero, *Lettere del Cinquecento.*

6. See Niccolò Cieco's poem on lord-servant relations in Lanza, *Lirici,* 2:202–7.

7. Of nearly a score of Quattrocento *canzonieri,* here are four more, in addition to the four cited above (note 2): Roselli, "Canzoniere"; F. Accolti, "Le rime"; Correggio, *Opere;* Medici, *Canzoniere.*

8. The sun in Medici, *Canzoniere,* 10, 13, 15, 293; Bembo, *Prose e rime,* 519–20; stars in Poliziano, *Rime,* 286, 288, 295; and the lady as lord in Poliziano, *Rime,* 292, 323; see also Tinucci, *Rime.*

9. On the lover as beggar, see Visconti, *Rithimi,* no. 21 (unpaginated); on the lover as servant or follower, Visconti, *Rime,* 57, 61; on base/lofty, servitor/majesty, Galli, *Canzoniere,* 71, 73, 141, 163.

10. On the "vulgo obtenebrato," Visconti, *Rithimi,* n. 33; Correggio, *Opere,* 184–85; and their model, Petrarca, *Canzoniere,* e.g., 213 (no. 114), "Né del vulgo mi cal . . ./ . . . né de cose vile" (lines 9–10).

11. Trexler, *Public Life,* chaps. 1–3.

12. See Balduino, *Rimatori veneti;* and Segarizzi, "Ulisse Aleotti." There was a marked popular strain in the verse of Venice's best-known love poet, Leonardo Giustinian (see his *Poésie*). Yet, generally speaking, Petrarch was the model.

13. Malatesti was a dispenser of patronage, but Burchiello risked his life by siding with the Albizzi faction against the great patronage machine of the Medici. On Burchiello, see Lanza, *Polemiche* (1989), 347–49; Flamini, *La lirica,* 96–100, 755–56.

14. Lanza, *Lirici,* 2:55–56, lines 1–3, 57–58.

15. Poliziano, *Rime,* 282. Tinucci, *Rime,* rarely calls his lady anything but *signore.*

16. Gender relations in Klapisch-Zuber, *La maison,* strike me as more in keeping with Quattrocento realities than the rosier Venetian view in Guzzetti, "Le donne"; and Chojnacki, "Power of Love."

17. Galli, *Canzoniere,* 72 (no. 21), lines 12–14. The association of paradise with the beloved of lyric verse is of course in Petrarca, *Canzoniere,* 208 (no. 109), 226 (no. 123).

18. This convention goes back to Petrarch and beyond him to the *stilnovisti.*

19. On Giovanni di Maffeo da Barberino (c. 1376–1446), see Flamini, *La lirica,* 542. The case had gone to one of a half dozen magistracies, but I suspect the Ufficiali delle vendite or the Tribunale di mercanzia.

20. Lanza, *Lirici,* 1:691–92, lines 1–6, 19–21. The turn "povero, vecchio, infermo e peccatore" was a near-commonplace in religious verse: e.g., Malatesti, *Rime,* 201.

21. See Frati, *Rimatori bolognesi del Quattrocento;* and Pezzarossa, "Ad honorem et laudem," 35–102.

22. Niccolò Risorboli in Lanza, *Lirici,* 2:377–78, lines 27–28, 35–39. The strident biblical allusion was not out of keeping with the age's register of hyperbole.

23. In Montemagno, *Le rime,* 57, lines 1–2, 12–14.

24. Bellincioni, *Le Rime,* 1:41, 49, 50–51, 62, 65–66.

25. Bembo, *Prose e rime*, 523, line 2.

26. Pulci, *Opere minori*, 72, 86, 90, 92–93; and the letter of 22 March 1476, in Pulci, *Morgante e lettere*, 945–50, which includes the *canzone* "Da poi ch'l Lauro più, lasso, non vidi," and also in *Opere minori*, 44–50, lines 2–3.

27. I have used Quint's Italian edition of Poliziano's *Stanze*, 2–3, but for my own purposes I have slightly altered his excellent translation.

28. The word and notion "godfathers" is taken from Molho, "Cosimo de' Medici."

29. For a useful recent statement in the history-of-ideas vein, see Singer, *Nature of Love*, chaps. 1–6.

30. "Noi amamo grandemente frate Anselmo de' Conti da Padua, sì per le virtù sue, come che suo patre e parenti suoi son molto nostri, e desideramo fargli ogni piacere: e per questo, quanto ne sia possibile, lo racommandamo alla R. Paternità Vostra, che per amor nostro voglia favorirlo e averlo nel numero de li suoi più cari, e dove può farli beneficio e onore lo faccia, che tutto quello che per amor nostro gli farà avremo tanto grato quanto se in la persona nostra fusse fatto" (Ariosto, *Lettere*, 306).

31. Martines, "Ritual Language," 61–67.

32. Examples: Lanza, *Lirici*, 2:481, 485, 534; sonnets by Francesco Scambrilla and Filippo Scarlatti.

33. Poliziano, *Rime*, 359.

34. As in the violent Florentine quarrel that pitted Carlo Marsuppini and Niccolò Niccoli against Francesco Filelfo, whose face was slashed by a hired thug in 1433 and who later produced an acid, unfinished work against Cosimo de' Medici, *Commentationes florentinae de exilio*. See Rossi, *Il Quattrocento*, 37–43.

35. Lanza, *Lirici*, 1:324. Words such as *gagliofo* and *merdoso* had a strong Florentine tincture, thus tending toward my broad notion of neighborhood.

36. Calmeta, *Prose e lettere*, 88–89.

37. Bontempelli and Ghinassi, *Poliziano*, 371–72. See also Tebaldeo's more derivative Latin verse in Pasquazi, *Poeti estensi*, 19–86.

38. Cammelli (il Pistoia), *I sonetti*, 60–79, 83–89, 93, 96–100, 108–14, et seq.; Cammelli, *Rime edite e inedite*, 221–45, 249–73.

39. Bellincioni, *Le rime*. Cosmico's replies are easily inferred from evidence in Cammelli's sonnets.

40. Pulci, *Opere minori*, 151–90; and the larger collection, including many sonnets directed to others as well, in Pulci and Franco, *"Libro dei sonetti."*

41. Pulci, *Morgante e lettere*, 991–92, "mai come io fu stratiato un cane," an appropriate image for the hunter, Lorenzo. See also Jordan, *Pulci's Morgante*, 32–34.

42. Pulci, *Opere minori*, 188; and Pulci and Franco, *'Libro dei sonetti,'* 94–95.

43. Carnival was the one occasion when poets, already in the fourteenth century, could rip out vulgarities in coarse carnival songs. See Levi, *Poesia di popolo*, 5–10.

44. Edgerton, *Pictures and Punishment,* 99–100.

45. Lanza, *Lirici,* 2:94.

46. Ibid., 2:95.

47. See, for instance, the major controversy over an important murder out in eastern Florentine territory in 1421. Martines, *Lawyers and Statecraft,* 154–63.

48. Burchiello, *I sonetti,* 182.

49. Lanza, *Polemiche* (1971), 192–93, "popolaccio sozzo" and "questo popol meccancio e vile,/ch'appena può schermirsi da' pidocchi" (lines 3–4, 16). See Flamini, *La lirica,* 96–97, 755–56.

50. The accolade, on the occasion in fact of his knighting, was from Bernardo Cambini, and the derision was from Filippo Lapaccini. Lanza, *Lirici,* 1:363–64; 2:19.

51. Most of the detractors noted above, and scores of others, penned *vituperia* against anonymous men and women, many of whom would have been instantly known to neighbors and to the informed. Burchiello's sonnets swarm with sly censure. But see two candid attacks in Brunelleschi, *Sonetti,* 22–23.

52. Two contrasting examples here are the humanist Matteo Palmieri, whose contacts brought remarkable tax advantages, and Francesco d'Altobianco degli Alberti, a failed banker and poet whose ruin was completed by Florentine tax levies. See Martines, "Forced Loans," 300–311; Bracali, *Francesco Alberti;* and chap. 6, this volume.

53. Examples: G. Sacchetti, *Le rime,* 75–77; Antonio di Guido and F. Scarlatti in Lanza, *Lirici,* 1:170–72; 2:510, 526–27, 564; and Alberti's "Firenze mia" with a rich commentary in Martelli, "La canzone," 7–50. Poetry of this sort should be distinguished from verse done in the *contemptus mundi* mode. Though they seem similar, the two strains are different in tone, accent, and intention.

54. Tinucci, *Rime,* 52, lines 1–2, 5–7, 9-ll; and Flamini, *La lirica,* 292–94.

55. Muscetta and Ponchiroli, *Poesia,* 88. Brunelleschi's authorship is disputed by Tanturli and De Robertis, *Sonetti,* 17.

56. Lanza, *Lirici,* 1:127 (no. 109). BNCF, FN, II, IV, 250, fol. 34v, glosses the "quinto elemento" as "bugie."

57. Meglio, *Rime,* 77 (no. 14), 79 (no. 15).

58. Lanza, *Lirici,* 1:185, lines 23–30.

59. These themes, for other reasons, also turned up in courtly circles. Visconti, *Rime,* 93; and Malatesti, *Rime,* 201, "ingrato trovo ogni hom ch'io ho servito" (line 8).

60. Altamura, *Certame,* 20–23. This work contains all the poems for the competition.

61. On urban antagonism, see Weissman, *Ritual Brotherhood,* chap. 1, "Judas the Florentine."

62. Klapisch-Zuber, *Women, Family, and Ritual,* 13.

63. Lanza, *Lirici,* 2:526 (no. 47), lines 13–17.

64. Frati, *Rimatori bolognesi del Quattrocento,* 46, lines 1–4, 12–14.

65. Perhaps especially so in Bologna, where a tangle of papal, factional, and family interests often turned sanguinary, as in the blood feuds generated by Bentivoglio prepotence and rival claimants. See Ady, *Bentivoglio,* chaps. 1–4; also the essays on the effects of Bentivoglio patronage and cultural initiatives in Basile, *Bentivolorum magnificentia,* 13–153.

66. Frati, *Rimatori bolognesi del Quattrocento,* 339–43, lines 23–24, 39–40, 45–47, 68–69. I should add that this *canzone* has a distinct ascetic strain, for it ends, "Chi vol sieco esser giocondo/che abandoni il mondo/E che contempli quel ch'è signor vero." Once a partisan of the Bentivoglio, Bornio turned against their misrule. Ady, *Bentivoglio,* 36, 52–53.

67. The cry also went out in cities under princely rule, such as in attacks on corruption at court and in urban life. Example: Correggio, *Opere,* 142 (no. 72), 154 (no. 95), 156 (no. 99), 167 (no. 121), 171 (no. 130), 219 (no. 226).

68. Most *canzonieri* from Petrarch to Lorenzo de' Medici and Bembo show the transition to a stance against love, but a good single illustration is Roselli's "O falsa, pien d'inganni e senza fede,/femina maladetta," in Oliva, *Poesia italiana,* 15.

69. Muscetta and Ponchiroli, *Poesia,* 108, lines 1–2, 5–6, 9–17.

CHAPTER 3. PRAYER IN THE URBAN SETTING

1. Ridolfi, *Vita di Savonarola;* Pesman Cooper, "Florentine Ruling Group"; Weinstein, *Savonarola,* chaps. 1–3; Polizzotto, *Elect Nation,* chap. 1; and Pullan, *Rich and Poor,* 40–42, on fourteenth-century pessimism.

2. Corsi, *Poesie musicali,* 39; for a sampling of other ascetic statements, see Angela da Foligno, in De Luca, *Prosatori,* 856–67; Galletti, *Laude,* 3, 45, 93–94, 234, 258, 279; Staaff, *Laudario,* 150; Giustinian, *Laudario,* 294, 313, 330 (all these in Giustinian are versions of the same laud, most likely by Bianco da Siena); Tebaldeo, *Rime,* 3:ii, 603, 605, 607, 681, 685.

3. Branca, "Libertà di coscienza," 307–10.

4. Dati, in Branca, *Mercanti scrittori,* 550.

5. Dotson, *Merchant Culture,* 142, 171.

6. See, inter alia, Monti, *Le confraternite;* Meersseman, *Ordo fraternitatis;* Pullan, *Rich and Poor;* Weissman, *Ritual Brotherhood;* Banker, *Death;* Terpstra, *Lay Confraternities;* Henderson, *Piety and Charity;* Black, *Italian Confraternities;* Fortini Brown, "Scuole"; Rusconi, "Confraternite."

7. Pullan, *Rich and Poor,* 66–70; Fortini Brown, "Scuole," 308, 316–17.

8. Masi, *Ricordanze,* 80–81.

9. On the patron saints of cities, see Webb, *Patrons and Defenders.*

10. See, e.g., *Municipalia Cremae,* 72; *Statuti di Perugia,* 2:94–96; *Statuti e ordinamenti del Comune di Udine,* 47 (no. 80).

11. *Lucensis civitatis statuta,* 3:31; Waley, *Siena,* 139, 161–65; *Statuti del Comune di Ravenna,* 74–75; and *Statuta Veronae,* 1:12–14, for other obligatory processions.

12. Edgerton, *Pictures and Punishment,* 178–85; Frati, *Vita privata,* 82–85; Fanti, "La confraternità."

13. Frati, *Rimatori bolognesi del Quattrocento,* 139–44, lines 1, 7–9, 12, 22–24, 31–33, 67–69, 91–98.

14. Iacopone, *Laude,* 177–78; reproduced in Bertoni, *Laudario dei Battuti,* 33–35.

15. Ferraro, *Poesie popolari,* 57–58, lines 1–4, 15–17. Cf. Bertoni, *Laudario dei Battuti,* 29–30.

16. Guarnieri, *Laudario,* 196–202, lines 23–26. This is now the best edition of the famous Cortona lauds.

17. On Farina and "blind" Simon, see Cioni, *Poesia religiosa,* 249–50.

18. Ibid., 251–52, "Io son il gran Capitano della Morte."

19. Ferraro, *Poesie popolari,* 47–50, "Io son per nome giamata morte."

20. Ibid., 50–54.

21. Ibid., 54.

22. Saviozzo, *Rime,* 105–9, including, in the latter part of the prayer, a translation of the Magnificat (Luke 1:46–55).

23. I have called mainly on the following: Galletti, Ferraro, Staaff, Liuzzi, Iacopone, Giustinian, Bertoni, and Guarnieri. Rabboni, *Laudari e canzonieri,* should be used to correct Galletti. Note too that most poets of the period produced religious and devotional verse, occasionally on commission, e.g., Petrarch, Antonio Beccari, the two Sacchettis, Simone Serdini (Saviozzo), Leonardo Giustinian, Francesco degli Alberti, Sforza, Malatesti, Visconti, Correggio, the two Accoltis, Roselli, Cammelli, Bernardo Pulci, Lorenzo de' Medici, Boiardo, Bembo, even Poliziano, and of course an immense throng of lesser poets.

24. Malatesti, *Rime,* 176, lines 1–5, 9–11.

25. Cf. Martines, *Renaissance Sextet,* 49, Scopone's apology and plea to his lord and patron.

26. Examples: Galletti, *Laude,* 263; Iacopone, *Laude,* 42–43; Staaff, *Laudario,* 125; Liuzzi, *Lauda,* 1:356, 384 ("nostro pegno"), 402; Giustinian, *Laudario,* 1:260, 280, 287, 290, 360, 363, 368, 374, 381–82 ("pegno"); Bertoni, *Laudario dei Battuti,* 46. On the timely use of metaphor in sermons too, see Wilson, *Music,* 24–26.

27. Medici, *Opere,* 2:138–39, line 35.

28. Ibid., 137.

29. In Muscetta and Ponchiroli, *Poesia,* 53–54, lines 45–47, "Venuti siate al regno / tanto desiderato, / ch'i'comperai in sul legno."

30. Galletti, *Laude,* 169–71, octave 20, "Per cui ogni ben truovo/Per infinito mercato."

31. Staaff, *Laudario,* 244–52, stanza 33.

32. Muscetta and Ponchiroli, *Poesia,* 49–51; see also Galletti, *Laude,* 122–23; and Giustinian, *Laudario,* 1:385–86.

33. Arnaldi and Rosa, *Poeti latini,* 504, no. 19, lines 1–6.

34. Giustinian, *Laudario,* 1:270–71, lines 61–63.

35. Sapegno, *Poeti minori,* 1116–21, lines 1–4, 9–12, 53–56.

36. Corsi, *Rimatori,* 392–98, lines 23–24, 25–30; and Sacchetti, *Le rime,* 108.

37. Giustinian, *Laudario,* 1:306–8, which starts, "Madre dolce che fay?"

38. Sapegno, *Poeti minori,* 1124–26, lines 53–58.

39. Iacopone, *Laude,* 277–78, lines 1–4, 11–12.

40. Anonymous, in Galletti, *Laude,* 274–75, lines 1–4.

41. Ser Antonio Lippi is the author, in Galletti, *Laude,* 213, no. 346, lines 1, 17–20.

42. For example: D'Ancona, *Sacre rappresentazioni,* 1:224–27 (derision of "pinzocheroni"); and Alamanni, *Commedia,* 41, where Mary Magdalen's maid servant, Fulgenza, lashes out at "pinzocheroni," "sacerdotacci," and the pious Martha, who has "the shits" (la cacaiuola).

43. Rabboni, *Laudari e canzonieri,* 145–54, quatrains 1, 9, 26, 45, 52, 59, 60. Galletti, *Laude,* 88, for a nun, refers to the world as "a cage of madmen" (una gabbia di matti).

44. Giustinian, *Laudario.* My rapid count.

45. Rondeau, "Lay Piety," 216.

46. Anonymous, in Galletti, *Laude,* 9, no. 16, lines 1–2.

47. Ibid., 124, no. 172, line 20, which starts, "Vergine santa, immaculata e pia"; rather like Poliziano, *Rime,* 133, "Vergine santa, immaculata e degna."

48. Giustinian, *Laudario,* 1:344–45, no. 110, lines 19–24. Cf. ibid., 1:309–12, no. 78. On Enselmino's wider vernacular context, see Balduino, "Le esperienze," 265–367. Enselmino was actually from Montebelluna and especially known for his famous "Pianto de la Verzene Maria." See *DBI,* 42:804–6.

49. Pelikan, *Emergence of the Catholic Tradition,* 241–42, 270–77; and again Pelikan, *Growth of Medieval Theology,* 68–69, 160–75, with its summary (necessarily incomplete) of the range of things and qualities that Mary was made to equal. But see also Pelikan, *Mary,* chaps. 4, 8, 9; and Warner, *Alone of All Her Sex,* chaps. 7–8, 10.

50. A notion at the heart of a psychoanalytic interpretation of Machiavelli's view of women: Pitkin, *Fortune Is a Woman.*

51. Sforza, *Canzoniere,* 128, no. 146, lines 1–4, 12–14.

52. As set forth in part by Peyer, *Stadt und Stadtpatron;* but see also Webb, *Patrons and Defenders.*

53. By Francesco d'Albizo, in Galletti, *Laude,* 82, no. 180, lines 1–3; see lauds for Saints Agnes and Margaret in Liuzzi, *Lauda,* 2:378, 386; and for Saints Cecilia and Catherine in Staaff, *Laudario,* 241–43.

54. Anonymous, in Galletti, *Laude,* 125–26, lines 13–15, 49–51.

55. Galletti, *Laude,* 208. Poliziano, *Rime,* 243, wrote two Marian hymns in Latin, to satisfy a request from his friend Antonio Alabanti. Examples of specific devotional themes: Cappelletti, *Laude,* 191–95, 200–202 (against plague); Giustinian, *Laudario,* 1:387–88 (for Verona); Staaff, *Laudario,* 172–73 (against urban discord); Lanza, *Lirici,* 1:192–194 (by Antonio di Guido on request); Galletti, *Laude,* 31 (against calumny), 221–22, 226, 230–31, 238–39 (all against war), 254, 269–70 (for civil concord).

56. Roselli, *Canzoniere,* 188, no. 78, lines 1, 4–11. For another prayer against calumny, see B. Accolti, "Rime," 282–85.

57. Galletti, *Laude,* 138–40, no. 291, lines 93–98. The poem has forty-nine quatrains.

58. On Antonia, see Martines and Weaver, reviews of Pulci, *Florentine Drama.*

59. Pulci, *Rappresentatione di Santa Domitilla,* 2–3, or sig. Aii. Punctuation mine.

60. Newbigin, *Nuovo corpus,* xxix–xxx; Hatfield, "Compagnia de' Magi," 114.

61. D'Ancona, *Sacre rappresentazioni,* 1:248.

62. De Bartholomaeis, *Laude drammatiche,* 3:281.

63. *Dì del Giudizio,* in Banfi, *Sacre rappresentazioni,* 134–36.

64. Ibid., 130.

65. Ibid., 131.

66. Klapisch-Zuber, *La maison,* chap. 3; also Kent and Kent, *Neighbours and Neighbourhood.*

67. Banfi, *Sacre rappresentazioni,* 122–23.

68. In Ibid., 427–69.

69. Ibid., 436–37.

70. See Newbigin, *Nuovo corpus,* 31; and Castellani's *Figliuol,* in Banfi, *Sacre rappresentazioni,* 269–327.

71. Kuehn, *Emancipation;* Bellomo, "Emancipazione"; Pertile, *Storia,* 3:372–86, offers a more lenient view, for sons, of the "patria podestà." But some jurists (e.g., Baldus) ruled that such authority was "sacred."

72. *Rappresentazione del Figliuol Prodigo,* 1.

73. Ibid., 2.

74. On love's ennobling powers chez the troubadours, see Valency, *In Praise of Love,* chaps. 1–2; Boase, *Origin and Meaning of Courtly Love,* 81–83; Boase, *Troubadour Revival,* 64–66.

75. Petrarca, *Canzoniere,* 530–39, nos. 363–66.

76. Here and following I offer a summary of my own readings. See also chap. 4, "Love and History: Men against Women."

77. Ferraro, *Poesie popolari,* 76–77; and Giustinian, *Laudario,* 1:260, no. 9.

78. Fachard, "Liriche," 169–71, lines 1–4, 49–52.

79. Nappi, in Frati, *Rimatori bolognesi del Quattrocento,* 204, lines 1–5, 7–8.

80. Petrarca, *Canzoniere,* 521–27, no. 360, lines 31–32.

81. Alamanni, *Commedia.*

82. Ibid., 21–24.

83. Ibid., 46–47.

84. Ibid., 60.

85. Ibid., 10–11. The practice long continued. See a compelling use of the self-loss conceit in Buonarroti, *Rime,* 6, no. 8, "Come può esser ch'io non sia più mio?"

86. Bembo, *Prose e rime,* 605.

87. Ibid., 602. The emotive context here requires that "error" be read as something much stronger than a mere mistake.

88. B. Accolti, "Rime," 263–85.

89. Ibid., 282, and the preceding quotations, 269, 270, 278, 279, 281. He employs *giudea* as an insult (common practice in the amatory verse of the age), not to tell us that she was of Jewish descent.

90. Braccesi, *Soneti,* 29–34. He was a skillful Latin poet. See the piece on him by Perosa, "Braccesi," *DBI,* 13:602–8.

91. Fortini Brown, "Scuole," 311.

92. Pullan, *Rich and Poor,* 66–70; Fortini Brown, "Scuole," 308, 316–17.

93. Wilson, *Music,* 219.

94. Fortini Brown, "Scuole," 314; and Pullan, *"Scuole Grandi."*

95. Masi, *Ricordanze,* 80–81, 256.

96. On the careerism and corruption of the clergy, including the lax life of many female convents, suffice the quietly sulfurous lines in Hay, *Church in Italy,* 53–64.

97. Bornstein, *Bianchi.*

98. Martines, *Power and Imagination,* chaps. 6 and 10.

99. Sorelli, "La spiritualità," 1–65, revealing the mistaken tendency of most of the contributions to the special number on "spirituality" in *Studi Medievali* 28, no. 1 (1987).

100. Macey, *Bonfire Songs,* chap. 1.

101. Lesnick, *Preaching,* 146–52. Cf. the hymn to poverty in Staaff, *Laudario,* 173–75. On Quattrocento attitudes toward poverty, see Paton, *Preaching Friars,* 199–200.

102. Frati, *Rimatori bolognesi del Quattrocento,* 213, no. 8.

103. Lanza, *Lirici,* 2:634–35.

104. Spongano, *Rispetti,* 21, no. 16.

105. For the poems and Paolo Oriveto's stimulating discussion, see Pulci, *Opere minori,* 193–201, 217–29.

106. Vannozzo, *Rime,* 76–82.

107. Febvre, *Problème*, taking an early anthropological approach.

108. Machiavelli, *Libro di ricordi*.

109. As noted in chap. 7, a powerful anticlerical current runs through the large body of Italian Renaissance tales and stories—in Sercambi, Sermini, Arienti, Masuccio, Morlini, Grazzini, and others. In Ferrero and Doglio, *Novelle,* see tale 3 from Masuccio Salernitano's *Novellino,* a narrative centered on Saint Griffin's "knickers," here turned with fleering derision into a religious relic.

110. For instance: Staaff, *Laudario,* 115–20, 203; Galletti, *Laude,* 47–48.

111. Varanini, Banfi, and Burgo, *Laude cortonesi,* 3:52; Liuzzi, *Lauda,* 2:393; Staaff, *Laudario,* 137; Galletti, *Laude,* 32–33, 122, 140.

112. Staaff, *Laudario,* 15–16, 40–42, 139, 151–54; Liuzzi, *Lauda,* 2:95; Giustinian, *Laudario,* 1:290–91, 302 (Iacopone), 387; Galletti, *Laude,* 128, 130.

113. Galletti, *Laude,* 45–46, 99; Giustinian, *Laudario,* 1:363, 364, 377; Liuzzi, *Lauda,* 1:403; Staaff, *Laudario,* 113–14, 135, 136–40, 154–61.

114. Liuzzi, *Lauda,* 2:78, 342–43 (by St. Bernard); Staaff, *Laudario,* 61–62, 73–77; and F. Sacchetti, *Libro delle rime,* 294–95, his version of "Stabat mater dolorosa."

115. Wilson, *Music,* 20 n. 66.

116. Cohn, "Piety and Religious Practice," rightly emphasizes the conventional religiosity of rural and mountain folk in Tuscany but does not broach the question raised above.

CHAPTER 4. LOVE AND HISTORY: MEN AGAINST WOMEN

1. See Rougemont, *L'amour et l'occident;* Valency, *In Praise of Love;* Dronke, *Medieval Latin;* Singer, *Nature of Love.*

2. Hyde, *Society and Politics,* chaps. 4–5; Koenig, *Il "popolo" dell'Italia del Nord;* Martines, *Power and Imagination,* chaps. 3–6.

3. See Miccoli, "Storia religiosa," 609–734; D'Alatri, *Eretici e inquisitori,* vol. 1; and more recently, Merlo, *Eretici e eresie medievali.*

4. For English readers the best concise introduction is Whitfield, *Short History of Italian Literature.* See also Bertoni, *Duecento,* chaps. 7–11, 13–15; Cecchi and Sapegno, *Storia,* vols. 1–2; Muscetta, *Letteratura italiana,* vols. 1–2; Asor Rosa, *Letteratura italiana,* vols. 1, 3, 5.

5. Many basic texts are in the following anthologies: Muscetta and Rivalta, *Poesia del Duecento;* Sapegno, *Poeti minori;* Corsi, *Rimatori;* Muscetta and Ponchiroli, *Poesia;* Oliva, *Poesia italiana;* Frati, *Rimatori bolognesi del Quattrocento;* Lanza, *Lirici;* and Baldacci, *Lirici del Cinquecento.*

6. On these terms see Preminger, *Princeton Encyclopedia of Poetry and Poetics,* s.v. "Dolce stil nuovo" and "Petrarchism."

7. For a primer on the social analysis of poetry and on poetry as historical documentation, see Martines, *Society and History.*

8. Flamini, *La lirica,* 192–229; E. Levi, *I cantari leggendari,* 15–16; Lanza, *Lirici,* 1:339, 2:57; Branciforte, "Ars poetica rei publicae."

9. Examples: Saviozzo, Anselmo Calderoni, and Antonio Cornazzano. For the poets around Sigismondo Malatesta at Rimini, see Massèra, "I poeti isottei" (1911 and 1928), two articles.

10. Beccherini, "Un canta in banca fiorentino," 241–47.

11. Medin and Frati, *Lamenti storici,* 1:71–213, 2:79–113.

12. See chap. 10, this volume; also D'Ancona, *La poesia popolare italiana,* 54 ff.; and Niccoli, *Prophecy and People,* 12–19.

13. Among the numerous pertinent studies, see Pasquini, "Il codice di Filippo Scarlatti," 363–580; De Robertis, "Antonio Manetti copista," 367–409; and Tanturli, "I Benci copisti," 197–313.

14. Cornazzano, *Sonetti e canzone,* sig. A6v. Composition date: 1470s.

15. Not usually in Elizabethan verse, however, where dying in love is likely to mean the orgasm.

16. Pulci in Lanza, *Lirici,* 2:325 (no. 70); and Bembo, *Prose e rime,* 605 (no. 120).

17. See especially recent work on the ubiquity or prevalence of religious ritual: Trexler, *Public Life;* and Muir, *Civic Ritual.* In Venice, as in Florence and other cities, religious and politico-civic ritual were often fused.

18. In his *Comento;* see Medici, *Opere,* 1:10–141, at 13–17.

19. Visconti, *Canzonieri,* 6–7, "perché qual da questo [amor virtuoso] se departe intra in laberinto di sdegno, de ira, de inganno, de tradimento, de rixa, de ferite, de stroppii, et infamata morte pieno, e maxime in tanta accerba passione de animo che al parangone morte e peggio . . . felicissimo reputo."

20. Ibid., 7, "Nel quale o per transcuragine o per propria demenzia o per tenera età o per disposizion celeste . . . essendo io ne li tempi passati talmente intrato che ancora liberamente non posso affermare esserne uscito," although he confesses that his "ruina" would have been much worse, but for "questi poetici studii . . . per disfogare il core ardente."

21. For example, dirty old "crones," prostitutes, and vain or canny women.

22. Some of the basic texts are in O'Faolain and Martines, *Not in God's Image,* 118–126, 128–153; and for discussion by a team of historians, Klapisch-Zuber, *Storia delle donne,* 3–165, 330–423.

23. As in the myth of the Virgin Mary: Warner, *Alone of All Her Sex.*

24. Klapisch-Zuber, *Storia delle donne,* 88–165; on beating boys, see the poet Antonio Pucci (d. 1388) in Corsi, *Rimatori,* 808–9; and on the legal position of women in Florence, see Kuehn, *Emancipation,* 15, 116–22.

25. Brucker, *Giovanni and Lusanna,* 27.

26. Cavalcanti, in Contini, *Poeti del duecento,* 2:495, lines 1–5, in a famous sonnet with a glancing, intertextual allusion to the Virgin Mary.

27. When writing in the elevated style, all the love poets, without exception, rely on these properties.

28. Sforza, *Canzoniere,* 67–68, lines 9–13. For another terse example, see Frati, *Rime del codice isoldiano,* 1:136.

29. Poliziano, *Rime,* 106–7; Scarlatti, in Lanza, *Lirici,* 2:498–99; Nappi, in Frati, *Rimatori bolognesi del Quattrocento,* 229–39; and Meglio, *Rime,* 49–59.

30. Pelikan, *Mary,* chaps. 8–9; Warner, *Alone of All Her Sex,* 153.

31. In the fifteenth century, women very occasionally commissioned love poems, but they were composed by men in the male mode. See note 103 below.

32. In strict philosophical terms, however, the lady could be seen as agent or active intellect, inasmuch as she may actualize the lover's potential virtue. Dronke, *Medieval Latin,* 1:70–71.

33. Dante, *Vita nuova,* chap. 25; cf. Zancan, "La donna," 771.

34. Cornazzano, *Sonetti e canzone,* sig. B6 (no. 51), lines 12–14. More generally, on the metaphorical links between love and war, see Rougemont, *L'amour et l'occident,* 183–84.

35. Bembo, *Prose e rime,* 596, lines 9–11.

36. Malatesti, *Rime,* 170–71, lines 1–6.

37. At the beginning and end of our period, the two chief *canzonieri* (by Petrarch and Bembo) conclude by indicting love. See also Sarteschi, *Poesie minori del secolo XIV,* 93; Saviozzo, *Rime,* 12, 217–22; Galli, *Canzoniere,* 276 (no. 253); Poliziano, *Rime,* 84 (no. 77), 86 (no. 84); Roselli, *Canzoniere,* 138–39, 140–41, 162–63; Frati, *Rimatori bolognesi del Trecento,* 68–71; Frati, *Rimatori bolognesi del Quattrocento,* 67–73, 250–51, 345; Frati, *Rime inedite del Cinquecento,* 145, 235, 238, 244; Lanza, *Lirici,* 1:172 (no. 2), 338 (no. 3), 2:30–31, 538 (no. 64), 617–22.

38. In Lanza, *Lirici,* 1:419, lines 69–76, having just touched on Hypsipyle, Dido, Medea, and Jason.

39. Valency, *In Praise of Love,* 32; but see especially Moller, "Meaning of Courtly Love," 39–52; Koenigsberg, "Culture and Unconscious Fantasy," 36–50; and Wack, *Lovesickness in the Middle Ages,* chap. 8.

40. As in a recent interpretation of Machiavelli: Pitkin, *Fortune Is a Woman.* On wet-nursing in Florence, see Klapisch-Zuber, *Women, Family, and Ritual,* chap. 7.

41. Vossler, *Die philosophischen Grundlagen zum "süssen neuen Stil,"* 24–41; Valency, *In Praise of Love,* 205–6.

42. Of love verse written on commission, to curry favor or to favor a friend, see Saviozzo, *Rime,* 34 (no. 11); Lanza, *Lirici,* 1:295, 2:58, 60, 65, 67, 70, 72, 75, 79, 210;

Galli, *Canzoniere;* Frati, *Rimatori bolognesi del Quattrocento,* 195, 220; and Serafino, *Rime,* 40–41.

43. Correggio, *Opere,* 184, no. 156, lines 5–8. As if to deny the common assumption, Boccaccio, *Decameron,* 4.7, notes that noblemen were not alone in the capacity to feel the pangs of love.

44. Malatesti, *Rime,* 160–61; texts also in Lanza, *Lirici,* 2:457–58. Manuscripts indicate that the Florentine was either Roberto de' Rossi, the humanist, or Alberto degli Albizzi. The expressed ideals belonged to the ethical program of Renaissance humanism.

45. Lanza, *Lirici,* 2:262 (Accolti), 298–302 (Pulci).

46. Muzzarelli, *Rime,* 100 (no. 3), lines 1–4. The metaphor, revealingly, shows the predatory male (falconing) striving to see the lady as cannibal.

47. The best known of the thirteen—Bembo, Boiardo, Conti, Cornazzano, Correggio, Medici, Roselli, Visconti—may be found in *DBI,* in *DELI,* or in *DCLI.* On Galli, Malatesta, Muzzarelli, and Sforza, see Bibliography.

48. The neo-Latin poet Alessandro Braccesi (1445–1503), a jumped-up attorney (*notarius*) with excellent patronage and friends in Florentine governing circles, rather wrote his own social ticket, as is shadowed forth not only in book 1 of his *Carmina* (an *Amorum libellus*) but also in his vernacular love verse, *Soneti e canzone.* His career all but foundered after 1494, however, with the fall of the ruling Medici family. See Perosa's entry on him in *DBI,* 13:602–8.

49. Vannozzo chiefly with the Della Scala lords of Verona, Saviozzo with a variety of lesser princes and *condottieri.* See Vannozzo, *Rime,* xii–xiii; and for Saviozzo, see chap. 5, this volume.

50. Vannozzo, *Rime,* 193 (no. 137), and 97 (no. 75), for another example linking love, poverty, and *fortuna.*

51. Love-court linkage in Correggio, *Opere,* 107 (no. 1), 120 (no. 28), 139 (no. 66), 188 (no. 63), 238 (no. 264, with first quotation), 251 (no. 289, second quotation).

52. B. Pulci, in Lanza, *Lirici,* 2:281–365.

53. Not in a *canzoniere* but in the famous *stanze, rispetti* (octaves), and other poems. See Poliziano, *Rime;* and Pulci, *Stanze.*

54. See Orvieto's excellent edition of Lorenzo de' Medici's *Canzoniere;* and the shrewd, seconding observations in Kennedy, "Petrarchan Figurations of Death," 46–67.

55. Frati, *Rimatori bolognesi del Trecento;* and Frati, *Rimatori bolognesi del Quattrocento.*

56. Frati, *Rimatori bolognesi del Quattrocento,* 21, 36 ("turba bestial"), 92–93 (Refrigerio in love mode to wished-for patron), 96 and 98 (derision of provincial burgs), 115 ff. (partly in amatory language for dead patron), 203 (in praise of love code), 389–91 (love vs. the dull and lazy multitude, *vulgo inerte*).

57. Ibid., 387, 392, 394–96.

58. Frati, *Rimatori bolognesi del Trecento,* 68–71; and *Rimatori bolognesi del Quattrocento,* 345, 381 (where Aldovrandi claims that love without virtue equals vice).

59. See the essays by Pezzarossa, Fazion, and Bentivogli in Basile, *Bentivolorum magnificentia,* 35–113, 115–33, 177–214.

60. Visconti, *Rithimi,* sig. F6v ("tempi nebulosi . . ."), D7v ("Il cel nemico . . .").

61. As is evident in the many poems that are all about *fortuna.* See Medin and Frati, *Lamenti storici.*

62. On some of the preceding points, see Origo, "Domestic Enemy," 321–66; Pucci's poem on the influence of female slaves, in Corsi, *Rimatori,* 812; and Klapisch-Zuber, *Women, Family, and Ritual,* 117–31. In a commonplace of the day, much trumpeted by preachers, the widow was meant to be "dead to the world, being stripped of her carnal husband," and married to Christ: Girolamo da Siena (d. 1420), in De Luca, *Scrittori di religione,* 2:299–301. See Velluti, *Cronica domestica,* 139, exemplifying the disgust and shame of Florentine diarists when remembering a less than chaste female relative.

63. Insults drawn from cases in fourteenth-century Lucca point to incidents of adultery among married women: Marcheschi, *Ingiurie, impropri;* also Brucker, *Giovanni and Lusanna,* chap. 2; and Ruggiero, *Boundaries of Eros,* 45–69.

64. Examples: Saviozzo, *Rime,* 34–36; Lanza, *Lirici,* 1:71–72 (no. 14), 2:402 (no. 6), 405 (no. 12), 407 (no. 17), etc.; Boiardo, *Opere,* 10 (no. 14), 92 (no. 127).

65. L. B. Alberti, the great Florentine humanist, was the illegitimate son of Bianca di Carlo Fieschi, daughter of a Genoese patrician and widow of a Grimaldi. See Kuehn, "Reading between the Patrilines," 161–87. Massèra, "I poeti isotti (1)," 19–20, found that at fourteen Isotta degli Atti had a bastard son by the lord of Rimini, Sigismondo Malatesta, though he then married her. Correggio, *Opere,* 233–34 (no. 254), claims that "sex and drink" had "rotted the age" (Venere e Baco avendo il secul guasto).

66. In song, Corsi, *Poesie musicali.*

67. Herlihy and Klapisch-Zuber, *Les Toscans,* 393–419; Chojnacki, "Dowries and Kinsmen," 571–600; Romano, *Patricians,* 39–56; Kuehn, *Law,* 238–57; and Grubb, *Provincial Families,* 1–20.

68. A kind of love at first sight, well documented in verse. Examples: D'Ancona, *La poesia popolare italiana,* 508 (no. 18); Saviozzo, *Rime,* 23–30 (nos. 8, 9); Lanza, *Lirici,* 1:291.

69. Brilliantly suggestive along these lines, though apropos of the late Tudor love lyric, is Marotti, "Love Is Not Love," 396–428.

70. On Cecilia Gallerani, Bellincioni, *Rime* (1493), sig. C5, "Di che te adiri a chi invidia hai natura"; Serafino, *Rime,* 78–79.

71. See two fascinating portraits of the great beauties Cecilia Gallerani and Giulia

Farnese, drawn by the contemporary humanist Calmeta, *Prose e lettere,* 26–31. Giulia was mistress to Cardinal Rodrigo Borgia, later Pope Alexander VI.

72. Lorenzo de' Medici, *Canzoniere,* 10–12, 13–14; and Pulci, *Opere minori,* 64, where he actually names "Lucrezia" but also puns on "sun" (*sol*). On Lorenzo's sexual reputation (*tutto venereo*) and his relations with the Nasi-Benci woman, see Guicciardini, *Opere,* 194.

73. A point made absolutely clear by all court poets from Vannozzo and Saviozzo to Gasparo Visconti and Bembo, whose eulogistic verse for princes and patrons is, in effect, a kind of codification of courtly language.

74. Chojnacki, "Power of Love," 126–48; cf. Ruggiero, *Boundaries of Eros,* 23, 32 ff.

75. See Martines, "Ritual Language," and chap. 2, this volume.

76. As in the sermons of Bernardino da Siena, *La fonte della vita,* "Come il marito die amare la donna e la donna il suo marito," 237–80; and the admonitions on marital love by Girolamo da Siena, in De Luca, *Scrittori di religione,* 2:298–99.

77. Do trial records concerning sexual crime, such as adultery, throw light on "love," as seems to be done by the criminal practice of "love magic"? See Ruggiero, *Boundaries of Eros,* chap. 2; and Martin, *Witchcraft and the Inquisition,* 64, 106–10, 174–77, 205–6. Last wills and testaments, with God and death staring the testator in the face, cannot be a reliable source for checking the yearning of love, although Chojnacki, "Power of Love," relies on a scatter of last wills. In their metaphorical usage, story writers (*novellieri*) often suggested that the sexual act was a kind of people's coarse or rustic activity: see Bec, *Cultura e società,* 91.

78. Dean and Lowe, *Marriage,* 85–115, 128–51; Klapisch-Zuber, *Women, Family, and Ritual,* 178–212; Kirshner, *Pursuing Honor;* Molho, *Marriage Alliance,* 298–348; Romano, *Patricians,* chap. 3; Grubb, *Provincial Families,* 15–20; and two papers by Chojnacki, "Patrician Women" and "Dowries and Kinsmen."

79. Labalme and White, "How to (and How Not to) Get Married," 43–72; and Frati, *Vita privata,* chap. 3.

80. Brucker, *Giovanni and Lusanna,* a point at the heart of this contested marriage.

81. Exceptionally, in the 1480s, Machiavelli's sister, Primavera, seems to have married for love; but this caused enormous difficulties for the two fathers, and marriage negotiations dragged on for three years. Machiavelli, *Libro di ricordi,* 108–10, 170–86.

82. Ruggiero, *Boundaries of Eros,* 29–30. Romano, *Patricians,* 56–64, holds that broken marriages could be an economic disaster for artisans; and see the points about abandoned women and households of "*pinzochere* laborieuses" in Chabot, "La reconnaissance," 563–76. Priests in the Florentine mountains occasionally complained about the problem of runaway spouses and contested marriages, a topic

which I first met years ago, when working on my *Lawyers and Statecraft* in Florence's Archivio di Stato; but alas, it still awaits a monograph, although there is a wealth of archival material for such a study.

83. Examples: Beccari, *Rime*, 94–99; Frati, *Rime del codice isoldiano*, 155–71 (Domenico da Montichiello), 246 (Antonio da Lerro of Forlì), or 264–68 and 277–80 (Jacopo Sanguinacci).

84. In love complaint, the lover often suggests that his will has been sapped by love or that he is driven to seek his own destruction (hence the malady); and of course *fortuna* or the heavens may stand behind the illness. But for the whole intellectual and medical tradition of the *mal d'amour* as an upper-class male disease, see Wack, *Lovesickness in the Middle Ages.*

85. Adjectives in part popularized by the Neoplatonist Ficino, as in the expressions "amor vulgaris" and "amor ferinus," in a line that continued up to the mid–sixteenth century in Benedetto Varchi and others. See Jayne, *Marsilio Ficino's Commentary*, 107–14; and Varchi, on "plebeian love," cited in Martines, *Power and Imagination*, 460.

86. Giustinian, *Poesie;* Giambullari, *Rime inedite e rare;* Sassoferrato, *Madrigali;* D'Ancona, *La poesia popolare italiana;* Rubieri, *Storia della poesia popolare italiana,* 180–225, 268–88, 538–48, 559–74; and Corsi, *Poesie musicali.*

87. Sassoferrato, *Madrigali,* 36.

88. Giambullari, *Rime inedite e rare,* 177.

89. Ibid., 146 (no. 25), but see also 147 (no. 28).

90. D'Ancona, *La poesia popolare italiana,* 517 (no. 45), and another example on 504 (no. 8).

91. Sassoferrato, *Madrigali,* 72.

92. Leonardo Giustiniani was himself a Venetian patrician, although his verse is less overtly sexual than Sassoferrato's. But punning, ribald verse was much liked at Florence by Luigi Pulci, Lorenzo de' Medici, Angelo Poliziano, and others in Lorenzo's broad literary circle.

93. Prizer, "Games of Venus," 3–56.

94. Quotations from Sassoferrato, *Madrigali,* 77–78.

95. As claimed by Camporesi, in *Bread of Dreams.*

96. On the details of this procedure, with a sustained statement of theory and method, see Martines, *Society and History.*

97. De' Conti, *Il canzoniere,* 2:90, lines 1–8. Most love poets produced verse on "my lady" as a rapacious beast. Of innumerable examples, here are a few: Saviozzo, *Rime,* 145; Roselli, *Canzoniere,* 140–41, 157, 173–74; Boiardo, *Opere,* 95–96 (no. 132), 102 (no. 144); Visconti, *Rithimi,* sig. B3v, B5r, B8v, D6v, H2r; Serafino, *Die Strambotti,* 197 (no. 15), 202 (no. 33), 284 (no. 301); Tebaldeo, *Rime,* 3:737.

98. Valency, *In Praise of Love,* 32; Moller, "Meaning of Courtly Love"; Koenigs-

berg, "Culture and Unconscious Fantasy"; and Wack, *Lovesickness in the Middle Ages,* chap 8. On a more comprehensive view of the unconscious, see Siti, "L'inconscio," 717—31.

99. As in a recent interpretation of Machiavelli's political thinking: Pitkin, *Fortune Is a Woman,* where the argument pivots on the practice of wet-nursing in Florence. On this see Klapisch-Zuber, *La maison,* chap. 13.

100. Of course, *untroubled* relations of this sort are simply impossible in Freudian theory.

101. In Lanza, *Lirici,* 2:668 (no. 6), 673 (no. 17).

102. E.g., Battista da Montefeltro, in Malatesti, *Rime,* 177—78, 197; Lorenzo de' Medici's mother, Lucrezia Tornabuoni, *I poemetti sacri;* and Antonia Pulci in Banfi, *Sacre rappresentazioni;* and in D'Ancona, *Sacre rappresentazioni.*

103. Princely circles at Rimini, Camerino, and Pesaro. See Feliciangeli, "Notizie sulla vita," 1—75; and in a Tuscan-Veneto context, Rossi, "Di una rimatrice," 183—215. Visconti, *Canzonieri,* 141—42, heaps praise in three sonnets on the poetry of an unidentified lady. Lanza, *Lirici,* 2:630—33, has an amorous poem, fully in the male mode, by a certain "Caterina."

104. Cesare Nappi wrote poems on commission, such as the one for Lucrezia Bentivoglio (July 1488) on the lament of a girl whose parents are resolved to marry her to an old man, a popular theme. See Frati, *Rimatori bolognesi del Quattrocento,* 195, 220; also Lanza, *Lirici,* 1:174—78, 179—81, 279 (no. 12).

105. No "common" whore could rank as a *cortigiana,* despite the looser usage in Aretino, *Sei giornate,* 8—9, 149. Henceforth, the fussier members of Italy's aristocratic strata wanted prostitutes who had not been routinely "handled" by base commoners. Behind this precaution was the new fear of syphilis, in addition to intensified feelings about class and caste.

106. For the texts of their verse, see Salza, *Rime di Gaspara Stampa e Veronica Franco.* Notable among recent work is Zorzi, *Cortigiana veneziana;* Rosenthal, *Honest Courtesan;* and Jones, *Currency of Eros.*

107. Masson, *Courtesans of the Italian Renaissance;* Larivaille, *La vie quotidienne des courtisanes;* and the semipopular but well-illustrated book by Lawner, *Lives of the Courtesans.*

108. Colonna, *Rime.*

109. For the more somber view, see Bellomo, *La condizione giuridica,* 35—47; Klapisch-Zuber, *La maison,* chaps. 9, 10, 12; and Redon, "Aspects économiques," 441—60. For the contrasting view, see Strocchia, "Remembering the Family," 635—54; E. G. Rosenthal, "The Position of Women in Renaissance Florence," 369—81; Chojnacki, "Power of Love"; Chojnacki, "Patrician Women"; and Guzzetti, "Le donne." It is possible that upper-class women were better off in Venice than in Florence.

CHAPTER 5. THE SUICIDE OF A POET

1. The best sketch of Saviozzo's life is still Volpi, "La vita e le rime."

2. So styled by Saviozzo's great editor, Pasquini, "Saviozzo," "piccolo maestro senese."

3. Ibid.

4. Dionisotti, "Chierici e laici," 55–88

5. Bec, *Florence 1300–1600,* 47–105.

6. Murray, *Suicide,* 84–92, 238–41, 400–404; and Motta, "Suicidi," 96–100.

7. Pasquini, "Saviozzo."

8. The documents on the two assaults are in Saviozzo, *Rime,* 265–68. My conversion of lire to florins is based on computations in Caferro, *Mercenary Companies,* 51, 55.

9. This is underlined by Caferro, *Mercenary Companies,* chaps. 1–4.

10. Graziani, *Cronaca;* Chambers and Dean, *Clean Hands,* chaps. 1–2, 5, 7; Martines, *Violence and Civil Disorder.*

11. Salutati, *L'Epistolario,* 2:383, in a letter of 15 August 1392 to the lord of Imola, Ludovico Alidosi, recommending a "dear" friend, "master Simon."

12. See Gherardi, *Il paradiso.*

13. Saviozzo, *Rime,* 111, 114–15, verse done when in Imola.

14. Ibid., 20–23.

15. Colonna, *I Colonna,* 67–70; Rendina, *Capitani,* 342–45; Ammirato, *Istorie,* 4:290–91, 303.

16. Saviozzo, *Rime,* 31–33.

17. On the theme of love as virility and identity, see Martines, "Amour et histoire," 585–93, and chap. 4, this volume.

18. Saviozzo, *Rime,* 34–36.

19. Ibid., 27–30, 43–46.

20. Ibid., 265–68.

21. Ibid., 105–9.

22. Ascheri, *Siena nel Rinascimento,* 14 n. 5.

23. Siena had in fact been one of Giangaleazzo's client states since 1389.

24. Saviozzo, *Rime,* 61–65, line 108, "per parte d'ogni vero italiano."

25. Ibid., 63, lines 52–60: "Ora è venuto il tempo, ora il disio, / or la santa iustizia a vendicarsi: / ora veggio svegliarsi / Italia bella, e chiama a te vendetta! / Signor, tu vedi che ciascuno aspetta / il tuo santo vessillo e 'l tuo domino: / che 'l sangue fiorentino / purghi la sua più venenosa scabbia, / e noi siàn franchi di cotanta rabbia!"

26. Ibid., 3–5, 14–16, 82–90, 110–11, 113, 132, 162–69, 227–28. On the Malatesta, see Jones, *Malatesta of Rimini.*

27. Judging by the literary and cultural level of the foremost Sienese writer of the period, Sermini, *Novelle.*

28. The letter of 5 January 1405 (our 1406), in Saviozzo, *Rime,* 268.

29. Ibid., 82–89, 110–11, 162–69, 227–28.

30. Ibid., 113.

31. Ibid., 178–81.

32. Ibid., 99–105, a *capitolo* in 169 verses.

33. Ibid., 40–43.

34. Ricotti, *Storia,* 2:226–34, 257–75; Trease, *Condottieri,* 194–95, 206–8, 220–22.

35. Saviozzo, *Rime,* 54–58.

36. Ibid., 268–70.

37. Martines, "Ritual Language," 68–75.

38. Saviozzo, *Rime,* 162–69.

39. Ibid., 169, lines 264–67, 270–72.

40. Ibid., 54–58, lines 121–25.

41. Ibid., 100–101, 230.

42. Ibid., 126, lines 9–10 (proverb), 133–34, line 14 (upstarts).

43. Ibid., 114, lines 1–4.

44. Ibid., 58–61.

45. Ibid., 58–61, lines 1–2, 9, 20, 23, 27, 28, 33, 36, 37–38, 40, 46, 72–73, 81–83, 84–85, 92.

46. Ibid., 238–39.

47. Ibid., 238, lines 1–4.

48. Ibid., 239, lines 9–17.

49. Ibid., 159–61.

50. Ibid., 5–8, 105–9, 152–55, 155–58, 212–14, 230–31, 241–43, 245–64.

51. Ibid., 237–38, 244–45.

52. Ibid., 135–36.

53. Ibid., 236, lines 13–14.

54. Ibid., 46–50.

55. Ibid., 49, lines 86–96.

56. Ibid.; candid are 182–85, 232–33, 239–40, 241; ambiguous, 149–52, 233.

57. Chambers and Dean, *Clean Hands,* tell me that in their overall work on Mantua and Ferrara, they have never come upon a case of prosecution for sodomy at court, nor have I in research connected with other princely courts.

58. For evidence of this claim, see below.

59. Martines, "Séduction," and chap. 9, this volume.

60. Chancellors of leading mercenaries headed small teams of clerks and notaries. Caferro, *Mercenary Companies,* 39–40.

61. Saviozzo, *Rime,* 65–68, 178–81.

62. Ibid., 20–23, 23–27, 113, 178–81, 265–68.

63. Ibid., 23–27.

64. Ibid., 115–19. It seems the sequential arrangement was his.

65. Ibid., 23–27, 127–29, 144–46, 149–52, 174–77, 222–27, being some of his principal love poems.

66. Ibid., 169–74.

67. Ibid., 12–14.

68. Ibid., 217–22, lines 1–3.

69. Ibid., 185–212.

70. Ibid., 83, 133, 229. See also chap. 4, this volume.

71. Saviozzo, *Rime,* 76–82.

72. Caferro, *Mercenary Companies,* 87, notes that at its peak the greatest of the marauding companies "numbered some ten thousand men." See also Trease, *Condottieri;* and Mallett, *Mercenaries,* 25–50. In 1377, obeying the orders of a French cardinal, mercenaries in Cesena massacred five thousand civilians, including women and children. The moats of the city were piled with bodies.

73. Saviozzo, *Rime,* 72–75, lines 1–3.

74. Ibid., 215–17.

75. Ibid., 68–72.

76. Ibid., 69, lines 23–30: "O vulva adulterata, orrida e vana,/perché non ti serrasti sul dolore,/sì che con teco insieme io fusse morto?/Almen, da poi ch'uscito fui di fore,/perché non fui io dismembrato o storto,/e poi a' can dato a mangiare il core?/Maladetta la luce e lo splendore/che prima mai s'aggiunse agli occhi mei."

77. Ibid., 357, s.v. "Mongibello."

78. Ibid., 229, lines 1, 3–4, "Amor . . . /tu m' hai prestata l'eloquenza e 'l dire,/la fantasia, l'ingegno e l'intelletto."

79. Ibid., 237–38.

CHAPTER 6. ALIENATION: THE OUTSIDER AS POET

1. Flamini, *La lirica,* 259–66; Bracali, *Francesco Alberti;* and the illuminating pages in Martelli, *Letteratura fiorentina,* 285–311.

2. Passerini, *Gli Alberti;* Foster, "Ties That Bind."

3. Cited in Martines, *Social World,* 248–49.

4. Ibid., 364, no. 16, making him sixteenth in order of wealth in the Santa Croce Quarter. His 1427 tax-return inventories are in ASF, *Catasto,* 34, fols. 607r–619r.

5. ASF, *Catasto,* 354, fols. 427r–443v; 654, fols. 427r–453v. The *portata* is dated 31 Jan. 1430 (our 1431).

6. Ibid., 450, fols. 401v–402v. Dated 31 May 1433.

7. Ibid., 617, pt. 1, fols. 348r–353v, top. Dated 31 Aug. 1442.

8. Ibid., fols. 349r–352r, top. But his stricter house confinement really seems to have started in about 1437. See note 23.

9. Martines, "Forced Loans," 300–311.

10. ASF, *Balìe,* 25, fols. 4r, 36r, showing that Francesco was also accorded the privilege to bear arms.

11. Foster, "Ties That Bind," 652; Martines, *Social World,* 353, showing Altobianco as the eighth-highest taxpayer in his quarter in 1403.

12. ASF, *Catasto,* 804, fol. 270r. Looking back nearly twenty-five years in this tax return of 1458, Francesco declares, "Ho più debitori e creditori dela compagnia vechia di Roma, Brugia, Londra e Colognia vechie [*sic*], che non se ne ritrase mai uno soldo chè sono morti e faliti già è una età."

13. This court cries out for a historical survey and analysis, but see Bonolis, *La giurisidzione;* and Astorri, "Note sulla Mercanzia Fiorentina," 965–93. Evidence of the lawsuits filters through Francesco's tax returns.

14. Foster, "Ties That Bind," 202–3.

15. ASF, *Catasto,* 450, fol. 403r.

16. Ibid., 617, pt. 1 (1442), fol. 348r–v, top. On the "rag trade" and clothing prices for upper-class Florentines in this period, see Frick, "Dressing a Renaissance City," chap. 4.

17. Lanza, *Lirici,* 1:129 (no. 115), lines 1–2, 7.

18. ASF, *Catasto,* 700, fol. 561r.

19. In one case, as his returns specify, the lessees paid no rent because they were guardians to Lucrezia, daughter of Alberto degli Alberti, the cousin who had died in the joust. See Alberto's fascinating sonnet in which he all but foresees his own death: Lanza, *Lirici,* 1:51.

20. ASF, *Catasto,* 804, fols. 267r–276r.

21. Ibid., 914, fol. 336r–v (Sept. 1469).

22. Martines, *Lawyers and Statecraft,* 133–35, 216.

23. Conti, *L'imposta diretta,* 312 n. 39, citing Francesco's returns of 1447, in which the claim is made that "da 10 anni in qua non sepi che cosa Fuxe libertà."

24. Cited in Martines, *Social World,* 294.

25. ASF, *Notarile antecosimiano,* 14196, fol. 152. This document was graciously brought to my attention by Gene Brucker.

26. ASF, *Catasto,* 804, fol. 270v. All the facts concerning his illegitimate children are drawn from the candid statements in his tax returns, as cited in notes 5, 6, 7, 16, and 18 above.

27. Ibid., 914, fol. 336r–v (Sept. 1469).

28. Herlihy and Klapisch-Zuber, *Les Toscans,* 339 n. 47. See also Origo, "Domestic Enemy."

29. Trexler, "Foundlings," 266–68.

30. ASF, *Catasto*, 1005, pt. 1 (1480), fol. 53r. Here, three Alberti brothers (Antonio, Filippo, and Daniello di Francesco di Giannozzo), all in their twenties, declare, "We find ourselves without a trade (*sanza alchuno aviamento*), without earnings and without any goods."

31. Passerini, *Gli Alberti,* 1:93.

32. Knowledge of these acquaintances is gleaned from his *catasti* and poems.

33. Lanza, *Lirici,* 1:146, 149.

34. Flamini, *La lirica,* 588–89.

35. Ibid., 259–60 n. 3.

36. Lanza, *Lirici,* 1:98–99, 100–101 (no. 68), 147 (no. 148); and BNCF, FN, II, IV, 250, fol. 41r, informing us that Antonio di Guido sent his remarkable political poem "Dormi Giustiniano" to Francesco, whose "Firenze mia" (to be discussed) links perfectly with it.

37. Lanza, *Lirici,* 1:17–20.

38. Letter cited in Flamini, *La lirica,* 265. On the dedication of *Della famiglia,* bk. 3, see Gorni, "Storia del Certame," 157.

39. Lanza, *Lirici,* 1:78 (no. 27); also BNCF, FN, II, II, 39, fol. 13r; and II, IV, 250, fol. 15v.

40. Lanza, *Lirici,* 1:139–43.

41. The unpublished poems appear with the others in BNCF, *Conventi soppressi,* CI, 1746, fols., 202r–235v. The newly edited poems are in Martelli, "La canzone," 7–50; Martelli, "Il capitolo 'Di vecchiezza,' " 35–63; and Grazzini, "Un sonetto *De contemptu mundi,*" 368–77.

42. Lanza, *Lirici,* 1:76–77, 77 (no. 25), 84 (no. 33).

43. Ibid., 126–27, line 3.

44. His readiness to be distracted is more than hinted at by the frequent incidence of asides in his tax reports.

45. Lanza, *Lirici,* 1:83 (no. 31). In line 15 of the sonnet, I have elected "figlia" over Lanza's "briglia," in keeping with my source, BNCF, *Conventi Soppressi,* CI, 1746, fol. 227r. Note too that the first line in another version of this sonnet, BNCF, FN, II, II, 40, fol. 119v, begins in fact by confusing *so* and *son* in the sixth word: "Io so ch'io non son più ch'altri comprende."

46. See note 45.

47. Lanza, *Lirici,* 1:83–84, line 1.

48. Ibid., 69 (no. 7), line 1.

49. Ibid., 70 (no. 10), line 12.

50. Ibid., 83 (no. 30), lines 1–4, 12–14; also BNCF, FN, II, II, 39, fol. 16r.

51. Examples: Lanza, *Lirici,* 1:76–78, 84 (no. 33), 93 (no. 53), 94–95, 124–25, 128–29, 143 (no. 141).

52. Ibid., 84 (no. 33), lines 9–10; and BNCF, FN, II, IV, 250, fol. 23r.

53. Lanza, *Lirici*, 1:56–57.

54. Ibid., 86 (no. 38), 88–89, 90 (no. 46), 102–3, 130 (no. 117), 145 (no. 144), all on the designated imagery. Flamini, *La lirica*, 137, comments on the last of these.

55. Martelli, "La canzone," 40–42.

56. Lanza, *Lirici*, 1:96–97; Martelli, "La canzone," 29–31; Fubini, *Italia quattrocentesca*, 62–86, on the political background; and Martines, "La famiglia Martelli," for a key document on the eve of Cosimo de' Medici's return from exile.

57. Lanza, *Lirici*, 1:128 (no. 112), lines 1–6, 12–14; and BNCF, FN, II, IV, 250, fol. 4r.

58. Lanza, *Lirici*, 1:76 (no. 33); and BNCF, FN, II, IV, 250, fols. 15v–16r. This rather different version offers in line 7, for example, "a farvi servi e perder *honoranza.*"

59. Martelli, "La canzone," 7–25, is a superb edition of the poem with a rich gloss. See also Lanza, *Lirici*, 1:116–19.

60. BNCF, Magl. XXV, 650, fol. 5r. Very run-of-the-mill stuff, Giogante's poem begins and ends, "O re del cielo quant' è la tua potenza/ . . . Cantisi ancora a gran laude di Cosme."

61. Martelli, "La canzone," 13, lines 20–24.

62. Ibid., 24–25, lines 141–43.

63. On the political conflicts of the 1420s, see Pellegrini, *Sulla repubblica fiorentina;* Brucker, *Civic World,* chap. 8; Kent, *Rise of the Medici,* chap. 3; and note 56 above.

64. Martines, *Social World,* 299–300, 347–48; Martelli, "Profilo ideologico," 131–43. Jacopo was directly involved in the 1478 plot against the Medici.

65. Lanza, *Lirici*, 1:127 (no. 109), lines 1–4, 9–11. BNCF, FN, II, IV, 250, fol. 3r, glosses "quinto elemento" as "bugie." In certain poets after Francesco, the "fifth element" often refers to sodomy: see Toscan, *Le carnaval du langage,* 1:158, 655–58.

66. Lanza, *Lirici*, 1:78–82.

67. Ibid., 100 (no. 47), 124 (no. 104), 126 (no. 107), 144 (no. 143). Note that no. 104 has been edited by Martelli, "La canzone," 43–45.

68. Lanza, *Lirici*, 1:95–96, lines 12–14; and BNCF, FN, II, IV, 250, fol. 13r–v. Although condensing and allegorizing, Francesco here is looking back nearly a century to Antonio Pucci's *ternario* on the Mercato Vecchio, in Corsi, *Rimatori,* 870–80.

69. Lanza, *Lirici*, 1:76–77, 84 (no. 33), for the three sonnets; quotation, 77 (no. 25), line 12.

70. Ibid., 77 (no. 25), lines 7–8, 15–17; and BNCF, FN, II, II, 39, fol. 12v.

71. Martines, "Way of Looking at Women."

72. Lanza, *Lirici*, 1:148 (no. 150), lines 1–4. BNCF, Magl. VII, 1168, fol. 100r, glosses the theme as "dolendosi delli inganni chelli pare chessi aparecchino."

73. Lanza, *Lirici*, 1:103 (no. 74), lines 1–4; and BNCF, FN, II, II, 39, fol. 29r.

74. Lanza, *Lirici*, 1:102–3 (no. 72), lines 1, 7–9. BNCF, FN, II, IV, 250, fol. 12r, reads "puzole da ghonfiare" and "ghabbie da matti" in lines, 2, 7. Note that Italy has no skunks, but that word comes closest to rendering *puzzole*.

75. Lanza, *Lirici*, 1:101–2, 102 (no. 71), 131 (no. 118), 143–44, all these being full-fledged prayers. The following are religious poems, some really ranking as semiprayers: Ibid., 108–9, 120–22, 123 (no. 101), 124 (no. 102), 125 (no. 105), 139 (no. 138).

76. Ibid., 93 (no. 53).

77. Ibid., 143 (no. 141), line 1.

78. Examples in the Petrarchan mode: ibid., 69 (no. 8), 83 (no. 30), 120 (no. 96), 131 (no. 119), 131–32, 132 (no. 121), 133 (no. 124), 133–34, 134–35 (three sonnets), and 137 (no. 133).

79. Ibid., 148 (no. 151); and BNCF, Magl. VII, 1168, fol. 100v.

80. Lanza, *Lirici*, 1:135 (no. 128), lines 1–4; BNCF, FN, II, IV, 250, fol. 26v.

81. Lanza, *Lirici*, 1:132 (no. 122), 138 (no. 136).

82. Conti, *L'imposta diretta*, 310.

CHAPTER 7. THE TALE AS HISTORICAL TESTIMONY

1. The theoretical breakthrough came with White's *Metahistory.*

2. The best general work on the Renaissance tale is still Di Francia, *Novellistica;* but now see also Malato, *La novella.* On degrees of realism, see Martines, *Renaissance Sextet.*

3. Note meal times in Boccaccio's *Decameron* (any edition); Sermini, *Novelle;* Sercambi, *Novelliere;* and Arienti, *Porretane.*

4. Best represented perhaps by Duby, *A History of Private Life.*

5. The expanding literature on this cluster of themes is amply cited in the notes for chap. 9.

6. As demonstrated in the suggestive study by Klapisch-Zuber, "Au péril des commères."

7. Thus Hay, *Church in Italy,* 49–71; Brucker, "Ecclesiastical Courts," 229–57; and Chittolini and Miccoli, *Storia d'Italia: Annali,* 9:149–93, 221–48.

8. Examples: Boccaccio, *Decameron,* 3.1, 3.4, 3.8, 7.3, 8.2, 8.4, 9.2; Sercambi, *Novelliere,* vol. 1, tales 11, 13, 30, 33, 35–36, and passim; Sermini, *Novelle,* vol. 2, tales 2, 9, 17, 19, 23; Bandello, *Novelle,* pt. 1, tale 30; pt. 2, tales 7, 45, 48; pt. 3, tale 61; Salernitano, *Il Novellino,* tale 3, in Ferrero and Doglio, *Novelle,* 323–36.

9. M. Manetti, *Novella.*

10. The penalty once used by Bernabò Visconti, lord of Milan, as narrated by Sacchetti, *Trecentonovelle,* no. XXV, 49–50. Sacchetti's moralizing at the end of the

incident makes it clear that the priest was castrated for heterosexual misdeeds, not sodomy. On another castration tale see Firenzuola, *Opere*, 162–71.

11. Bernardino, *Prediche volgari sul campo di Siena*, nos. 22 and 23, 622–25; and Hay, *Church in Italy*, 61.

12. L. Medici, in *Scritti scelti;* also Martines, *Renaissance Sextet*, 141–52.

13. As seen, for instance, in the suicide of the poet Saviozzo of Siena. See chap. 5, this volume, and the tales in Martines, *Renaissance Sextet*.

14. Weissman, *Ritual Brotherhood*, 20.

15. As in the story of Grasso, in Manetti, *Vita di Filippo Brunelleschi*. The story is in Martines, *Renaissance Sextet*, tale 6, where the woodcarver immediately stands up for the parish priest of Santa Felicità in Florence.

16. I have treated the problem alluded to here in my *Society and History*, 1–17.

17. As attested by just about any tale of the period, showing exchanges between confessors and penitents. A detail like this, in the expectations of the period's reading audience, had to be realistic.

18. Datini, *Le lettere*.

19. I offer a sustained analysis of this story in my *Renaissance Sextet*, 213–41.

20. For an apposite reading of Boccaccio, see Weaver, "Dietro il vestito," 701–10.

21. Sercambi, *Novelliere*, 2:35–41 (tale 64).

22. Crouzet-Pavan, *Sopra le acque salse*, 1:579–606.

23. Cf. Marshall, *Local Merchants:* his averages show that the female customers of his petty tradesmen totaled no more than 10 percent of his samples. Women were seen as beginning to age by their early thirties, marriage and childbearing being decisive. Again, in Florence, women over thirty married or remarried with increasing difficulty. See Herlihy, "Viellir à Florence"; also Herlihy and Klapisch-Zuber, *Les Toscans*, 202–3, 404.

24. Bisticci, *Vite di uomini illustri*, 280.

25. Sercambi, *Novelliere*, 1:26–29.

26. Such as in the story of Grasso, in Manetti, *Vita di Filippo Brunelleschi*.

27. In Borlenghi, *Novelle;* and my *Renaissance Sextet*, tale 4.

28. As in complaints against the arranged marriage of girls who were not seldom twenty and even thirty years younger than their husbands; hence the many verse laments of the *malmaritata*, the unhappily married girl.

29. French literary scholarship has been at the forefront of work on citizen-peasant relations. See Rochon, *Ville et campagne;* and Plaisance, "Les rapports ville campagne," 61–73; and again Plaisance, "Città e campagna," 583–634.

30. Herlihy and Klapisch-Zuber, *Les Toscans*, chap. 9; Jones, *Economia e società*, 17–47, 178–89; and Cherubini, *Signori, contadini, borghesi*, 73–99.

31. My sampling is drawn from the *novellieri* listed in the appendix to chap. 9.

32. On the designated victims, see Boccaccio, *Decameron*, 8.3, 8.6, 9.3; Sercambi,

Novelliere, tale 29; Sermini, *Novelle,* vol. 2, tale 25; *Bianco Alfani,* in Ferrero and Doglio, *Novelle,* 629–52; and Lorenzo de' Medici's *Giacoppo,* in *Scritti scelti,* 603–18. The last two of these are in Martines, *Renaissance Sextet.*

33. Martines, "Politics of Love Poetry," in Smarr, *Historical Criticism,* 129–44.

34. Weissman, *Ritual Brotherhood.*

35. On Florentine confraternities, see Henderson, *Piety and Charity.*

36. A succinct study of the main one is Molho, "Cosimo de' Medici," 5–33.

37. In Manetti, *Vita di Filippo Brunelleschi;* and Martines, *Renaissance Sextet,* 171–212.

38. Sacchetti, *Trecentonovelle,* 304–8 (no. 147).

CHAPTER 8. CRUELTY IN THE COMMUNITY: A BLOODY TALE

1. In the critical edition by Le Hir, De Navarre, *Nouvelles,* 282–83. The discussion occurs in the first tale of the sixth day (tale 51 in most editions).

2. On the outlook and views of such men, Branca, *Mercanti scrittori;* Bec, *Les marchands écrivains;* Weiand, *"Libri di famiglia";* and more recently, Valori, "Con utile e con onore."

3. In Hale, *England and the Italian Renaissance,* 3; see also Hoenselaars, *Images of Englishmen and Foreigners,* 16, 44, 114, 117, 121–22, 173; and on the image of the Italian, especially Florentines, in France, see the essay by Plaisance in Dufournet, Fiorato, and Redondo, *L'Image de l'autre Européen,* 147–57.

4. *The Merry Wives of Windsor,* 3.1.101–4; and Hunter, "English Folly and Italian Vice," 103–32, for a more nuanced, literary picture.

5. See the outstanding studies in Rochon, *Formes et significations;* and Martines, *Renaissance Sextet,* 71–241. The great centers of the *beffa* were Florence, Siena, Lucca, and neighboring Perugia and Bologna.

6. Meglio, *Rime,* 55, lines 5–7, 12.

7. In Lanza, *Lirici,* 1:395.

8. B. Accolti, "Rime," 283–84, lines 3, 8–9, 12, 14, 26–27, 35–36, 46–48.

9. Cf. Martines, "Ritual Language," 59–76.

10. "Symbolic Action in a Poem by Keats," in Burke, *Grammar of Motives,* 447–63; and the diverse essays in Burke, *Language as Symbolic Action.*

11. A remarkable recent study is Evans, *Rituals of Retribution.* Peters, *Torture,* does a succinct and valuable inquiry, drawing much on Fiorelli, *La tortura giudiziaria.*

12. Dean, "Marriage and Mutilation," 3–36: note his use of statutory material and ample discussion of the secondary literature on late-medieval vendetta in Italy.

13. Corsi, *Rimatori,* 927–28, 931, and references there to other such verse; also Sapegno, *Poeti minori,* 426, 427, for another edition of the poems.

14. Graziani, *Cronaca*, 415, involving shepherds in the region of Acquapendente in 1437.

15. Grazzini, *Le cene*, 271.

16. Ibid., 3–13.

17. On the last point, see especially Donati, *L'idea di nobiltà*, chaps. 1–2.

18. Despite canon-law claims, parental consent and even parental choice were de rigueur in social practice, although such strictness was linked above all to the higher social classes and the question of dowries. See Tamassia, *La famiglia italiana*, 150–95; Kuehn, *Law*, 197–211; Klapisch-Zuber, *Le maison*, 180–83 and chaps. 7–8. Dean, "Fathers and Daughters," notes that *statuta* in Florence did not mandate parental consent; but Florentine *ricordanze* establish that the practice was all but universal in the upper classes.

19. Because this style was meant exclusively for men of the upper classes, as documented in chap. 4; see also Martines, "Amour et histoire," 575–603.

20. Fabbri, *Alleanza matrimoniale*, 213.

21. Grazzini, *Le cene*, 272, 274.

22. As first studied by Weissman, *Ritual Brotherhood*.

23. Di Blasi, "Gusto della burla," for the metaphor of the mirror.

24. Examples: the figure of Bianco Alfani (remade by a group of tricksters), Scopone (remade by his landlord), and the Fat Woodcarver (remade by friends)—all in Martines, *Renaissance Sextet*, tales 2, 4, 6. In Sercambi, *Novelliere*, 1:26–29, the tale of Ganfo, who recognizes himself only by the social signifiers of his own clothing; and in Grazzini, *Le cene*, 38–49 (supper 1, tale 3), the manner of Geri Chiaramontesi's social annihilation.

25. Henderson, *Piety and Charity*, 39.

26. As documented in chaps. 2 and 4.

27. Trexler, *Public Life*; Weissman, *Ritual Brotherhood*; Henderson, *Piety and Charity*, chaps. 2–5; and Eckstein, *The District of the Green Dragon*.

28. Grazzini, *Le cene*, 13.

29. Molho, *Marriage Alliance*, 298–348; and Litchfield, *Emergence of a Bureaucracy*, 13–41.

30. As noted in the preceding chapter.

31. Grazzini's only other story about a "pedagogue" ends, homologically, with the amputation of the man's penis: *Le cene*, 27–37 (supper 1, tale 2); but see also Plaisance, "La folie comme marquage," 29–30.

32. Plaisance, "La structure de la *beffa*," 50–57, 64, 70–73.

33. Sermini, *Novelle*, 1:437–48 (tale 25).

34. Grazzini, *Opere*, 37; Plaisance, "La structure de la *beffa*," 80 n. 113; but other scholars say that he was a quondam "spicer-pharmacist," offering no evidence for this apart from the fact that a close relative owned such a shop.

35. De Navarre, *Nouvelles*, 283; or in the handiest English edition, *The Heptameron*, 431–32.

CHAPTER 9. SEDUCTION AND FAMILY SPACE

1. Machiavelli, *La mandragola*, 7–25, for the play's early fortunes.

2. The exceptions deal mainly with Florence and the Florentine dominion: e.g., Cohn, *Laboring Classes;* Mazzi and Raveggi, *Gli uomini e le cose;* Stella, *La révolte des Ciompi;* and Franceschi, *Oltre il "Tumulto."*

3. Hence gendered and private space, as opposed to public, sacred, or ritual space.

4. Some select works on the Italian Renaissance tale: Di Francia, *Novellistica;* Porcelli, *La novella del Cinquecento;* Tartaro, "La prosa narrative antica"; Cecchi and Sapegno, *Storia: Il Trecento*, 370–569; Cecchi and Sapegno, *Il Cinquecento*, 320–51; and the best recent collection of essays, Malato, *La novella*. For two stories drawn largely from reality, see *Bianco Alfani* and *The Fat Woodcarver* in Martines, *Renaissance Sextet*, 95–116, 171–212.

5. Tanner, *Adultery in the Novel*, is a shrewd study of the background to this question.

6. Some of the canonical texts are in Lenzi, *Donne e madonne*. See also Zarri, *Le sante vive;* Barbi, "Due curiosità quattrocentesche," 217–25; and Kirshner, *Pursuing Honor.*

7. Guardacci and Ottanelli, *I servitori domestici;* Ruggiero, *Boundaries of Eros*, chap. 2; Mazzi, *Prostitute e lenoni*, 98–99, 122–23; Cohen, "No Longer Virgins," 169–91.

8. Kirshner, *Pursuing Honor;* Klapisch-Zuber, *La maison*, chaps. 1, 3, 7–8, 12; Molho, *Marriage Alliance*, chap. 6; Bellomo, *La condizione giuridica;* and Grubb, *Provincial Families*, 10, on how fathers or brothers of girls in the Veneto often spoke the *verba de praesenti.*

9. Bestor, "Kinship and Marriage," 2:344–45.

10. The figures for Florence, showing an average differential of roughly thirteen years, are the most reliable for any city in Renaissance Italy. See Herlihy, *Women, Family, and Society*, 182. Cf. also Herlihy and Klapisch-Zuber, *Les Toscans*, 394–400. In Venice, girls from the noble ranks married generally between the ages of thirteen and sixteen, as noted by Chojnacki, "Most Serious Duty," 151 n. 53. But in the Veneto generally the average age difference between spouses seems to have been closer to seven or eight years, though the gap could widen sharply among the rich and well-born. Grubb, *Provincial Families*, 4–6.

11. Cappelli, *Poesie musicali*, 44; Giambullari, *Rime inedite e rare*, 186–88; Levi, *Poesia di popolo*, 31–37. Closely related are the laments of the unhappily cloistered girl: Corsi, *Rimatori*, 993–95; Muscetta and Ponchiroli, *Poesia*, 303–4.

12. Boccaccio, *Decameron* (any modern edition), 2.10, 7.9; Bandello, *Novelle,*

732 ff., 776 ff.; Grazzini, *Le cene*, 122–34; Parabosco, *I diporti*, 30–33; Nelli, *Le amorose novelle*, the second story (unpaginated).

13. Alberti, *Dinner Pieces*, 128–33.

14. Perosa and Sparrow, *Renaissance Latin Verse*, 196–99, line 92. For the rest, on older men "rearing" their young wives, see Lenzi, *Donne e madonne*, 87; Morelli, *Ricordi*, 210; Alberti, *Della famiglia*, 164–65, 344–85; Herlihy and Klapisch-Zuber, *Tuscans and Their Families*, 228–31.

15. Strozzi, *Lettere di una gentildonna fiorentina*, letter 53, on how a young wife turned a husband into a loving dolt. Cf. Martines, "Way of Looking at Women," 22.

16. Boccaccio, *Decameron*, 2.10, 5.10, 7.9; Sacchetti, *Trecentonovelle*, 537–38; Sermini, *Novelle*, 2:401–11; Firenzuola, *Opere*, 104–14; Molza, *Novelle*, 110–17; Bandello, *Novelle*, 124–47; Grazzini, *Le cene*, 122–34; Parabosco, *I diporti*, 30–33.

17. Arienti, *Porretane*, 261–69; Alberti, *Dinner Pieces*, 198–209; Firenzuola, *Opere*, 172–77; Sercambi, *Novelliere*, 2:91–94, where the sacking of Arezzo elicits the lechery and treachery of local women with foreign soldiers.

18. Boccaccio, *Decameron*, 4.3, 4.6, 4.7; Arienti, *Porretane*, 61–70, 71–78.

19. Boccaccio, *Decameron*, 8.8; Sermini, *Novelle*, 1:215–23; 2:615–24, 601–10 (here the friend's sister is seduced); plus two late examples, Bandello, *Novelle*, 124–47; and Straparola, *Le piacevoli notti*, 2:3–9, though the last of these, by its baroque trickeries, departs too much from reality.

20. Boccaccio, *Decameron*, 3.3, 7.5, 7.8, 7.9; Sercambi, *Novelliere*, 2:255–61; 3:181–88, 203–11, 224–30; Sermini, *Novelle*, 2:423–34; Grazzini, *Le cene*, 122–34; Molza, *Novelle*, 110–17; Parabosco, *I diporti*, 39–43; Straparola, *Le piacevoli notti*, 1:35–43; Gherardi in Ferrero and Doglio, *Novelle*, 68–76, where the scheming seductress is foiled; and *Tre novelle rarissime*, 111–29, a tale by Giacomo Salvi in which pretty Angela takes a lover to avenge her "ugly" husband's serial adulteries.

21. Firenzuola, *Opere*, 104–14.

22. Burguière et al., *Histoire de la famille*, 2:189; the Venetian claim is in Newett, *Canon Pietro Casola's Pilgrimage*, 145.

23. Cf. the discussion by Kuehn, "Reading Microhistory," 11–36.

24. On the anthropological view, Pitt-Rivers, *Fate of Shechem*, 44–45, 80–83; on Macinghi-Strozzi, Martines, "Way of Looking at Women."

25. Piccolomini, *Historia de duobus amantibus*, 898.

26. To avoid the temptations of seduction and to protect her brother's honor, a young Strozzi widow, in one story, has recourse to masturbation with sausages. Sercambi, *Novelliere*, 2:58–60.

27. Examples: Boccaccio, *Decameron*, 8.7; Sermini, *Novelle*, 2:413–21; Alberti, *Dinner Pieces*, 190–97; Bandello, *Novelle*, 914–22. The lurid widow in the most misogynous work of the age is this very type: Boccaccio, *Il corbaccio*, written about 1363–65.

28. Girolamo da Siena (d. 1420), in De Luca, *Scrittori di religione*, 2:299–301; Zarri, *Le sante vive*, 36–39; and texts in Lenzi, *Donne e madonne*, 55–56, 186–87.

29. On *conversi*, Brucker, "Monasteries, Friaries and Nunneries," 45–46; on *fratesche*, Ser Giovanni, *Il Pecorone* (1974), 156; also Zarri, *Le sante vite*, 36–39; and on *ammantellate*, Weaver, review of *Florentine Drama*, 475.

30. See Masuccio's venomous attack on the religious hypocrisy of widows, in Ferrero and Doglio, *Novelle*, 460–70; also Sermini, *Novelle*, 1:259–66; and Alberti, *Dinner Pieces*, 190–97.

31. Suffice it to name Boccaccio, Sacchetti, Sercambi, Sermini, Piovano Arlotto, Arienti, Marabottino Manetti, Poggio, Masuccio Salernitano, Firenzuola, Morlini, Grazzini, Nelli, and Parabosco.

32. Grazzini, *Le cene*, 184–99; Firenzuola, *Opere*, 172–77; Sermini, *Novelle*, 2:413–21, where implicitly the heroine and her mother at first had the same confessor; and Lenzi, *Donne e madonne*, 186.

33. Bernardino da Siena, *Prediche volgari sul Campo di Siena*, 622–25; Hay, *Church in Italy*, 61; Zarri, *Le sante vive*, 39, 49–50 n. 116; Lenzi, *Donne e madonne*, 56.

34. Alberti, *Dinner Pieces*, 134–48 (note the second son's treatment of his wife); Bandello, *Novelle*, 124–47; and Doni, *Novelle*, 66–67, a tale in which a wife could never get away from her husband, save through cunning trickery on Mardi Gras.

35. On the corruption of the clergy in Italy between about 1340 and 1540, see Miccoli, "Storia religiosa," 875–96. Mazzi, *Prostitute e lenoni*, 136, notes that in 1497 the friars of Santo Spirito in Florence, having impregnated a girl named Sandra, dispatched her to a country village to give birth there.

36. Priests without Latin were not a rarity, however, owing to a variety of dodges. See Trexler, *Synodal Law*, 38–39.

37. Note the antics of a Florentine priest (c. 1470) out in a country parish, as retailed by M. Manetti, *Novella*. Sermini, *Novelle*, 1:273–88, expresses characteristic attitudes.

38. Weissman, *Ritual Brotherhood*, 20.

39. Local statutes generally barred women from appearing in courts of law and called for them to give testimony at home or in their parish churches. For example, Perugia: *Primum (-quartum) volumen*, vol. 3, rubric 46, on women not testifying in the courts, "quia non videtur licitum nec honestum," and making the church of San Lorenzo the preferred site for their testimony. Such disapproval originated in Roman law. On men strolling near city walls, see Erizzo, *Sei giornate*, 80. The public space around government buildings was much frequented and patrolled by soldiers, whereas the cosmopolitan air of large churches was inimical to the needs of prayer by women, who wanted a more restricted space. Note the opening sentence in Arlotto, *Motti e facezie*, 81 (no. 48).

40. See chap. 7.

41. Capua, *Santa Caterina da Siena,* 1.iv.76. On keeping the eyes down, see Boccaccio, *Decameron,* 8.7; Sermini, *Novelle,* 2:399; Da Dio, *Decor puellarum,* bk. 4, "De belli costumi"; and Brucker, *Giovanni and Lusanna,* 27, for a point against the widow Lusanna, who dared to look men in the face when in the streets. Even when dancing, an honorable woman was meant to "keep her eyes modestly on the ground," as called for by the contemporary dance master, Guglielmo Ebreo of Pesaro, *De pratica seu arte tripudii,* 108–9.

42. Respectively on the Florentine, Bolognese, and Pisan sites: Martines, *Renaissance Sextet,* 196–207; Arienti, *Porretane,* 43–49; Sercambi, *Novelliere,* 2:81.

43. By a law of 1440: Bongi, *Bandi lucchesi,* 378–79. In Florence too, by the late fifteenth century, they move rather freely through much of the city: Mazzi, *Prostitute e lenoni,* 249–92. And the topographic spread of prostitution in Venice is succinctly outlined by Crouzet-Pavan, *Sopra le acque salse,* 2:831–36.

44. Not, of course, all worn at the same time. On the dress and insignia of prostitutes, see Rezasco, "Segno delle meretrici," 161–220.

45. La Roncière, "Tuscan Notables," 189. On always keeping the street door locked, see the warning by a contemporary, Paolo da Certaldo, *Libro di buoni costumi,* 114, no. 138.

46. Poverty levels have been most studied in and around Florence: Herlihy and Klapisch-Zuber, *Les Toscans,* chaps. 9–10; Stella, *La révolte des Ciompi,* 111–23, 183–92. On lower-class women, Brucker, *Society of Renaissance Florence,* 190–201; Herlihy, *Women, Family, and Society,* 87–94; Ruggiero, *Boundaries of Eros,* 3–44; L. Ferrante, "L'onore ritrovato," 499–528; Rossiaud, *La prostitution médiévale,* 113, 139–42; and in the Florentine countryside, Mazzi and Raveggi, *Gli uomini e le cose,* chaps. 2, 5.

47. Masson, *Courtesans of the Italian Renaissance;* Larivaille, *La vie quotidienne des courtisanes;* in a more popular vein, Lawner, *Lives of the Courtesans;* and the major early discussion by Rezasco, "Segno delle meretrici," 192 ff.

48. Straparola, *Le piacevoli notti,* 2:13–17.

49. Arienti, *Porretane,* 270–75.

50. The language of love, examined in chaps. 2 and 4, is also delineated in Martines, "Politics of Love Poetry," 129–44.

51. Frick, "Dressing a Renaissance City," appendix 5, under "sacchi."

52. As yet an unexamined trait of the period, but perfectly evident in the literary record, as well in the *novellistica* as in the verse.

53. Guglielmo Ebreo de Pesaro, *De pratica seu arte tripudii,* 108–11, on this fifteenth-century dance master's rules for women. On dancing in Florence, Ciappelli, *Carnevale e quaresima,* 147–53. Most strict clergymen, such as Giovanni Dominici and San Bernardino, were opposed to dancing.

54. Boccaccio, *Decameron,* 9.2.

55. Petrarca, *Canzoniere*, 395 (no. 261), for the theme of the speaking eye; but see also the focus on the eyes in nos. 39, 72, 75, 231, 233, 258.

56. Parabosco, *I diporti*, 72–75, where the would-be lovers are reduced to nothing but eye contact in church.

57. Note Meina's eye signals in Lorenzo de' Medici's tale *Giacoppo*, in Martines, *Renaissance Sextet*, 145.

58. Cherubino da Siena, *Regola della vita matrimoniale*, 14; and Bindoccia's actions in Bandello, *Novelle*, 127.

59. Sermini, *Novelle*, 1:215–23.

60. Boccaccio, *Decameron*, 3.5. On the eyes as "messengers," see the anonymous fourteenth-century *rispetto* in Corsi, *Rimatori*, 1002.

61. Guicciardini, *Opere*, 194.

62. Thus at least the findings for Florence: Klapisch-Zuber, *Women, Family, and Ritual*, 172–74, where as many as 7 percent of female servants, especially if once married, might stay on in a house for five or more years. On close relations between female servants and patrician women in Venice, see D. Romano, *Patricians*, 134–38.

63. Herlihy and Klapisch-Zuber, *Tuscans and Their Families*, 291–92.

64. Boccaccio, *Decameron*, 8.3, 8.10; Bracciolini, *Facezie*, 193–94 (no. 222); Sercambi, *Novelliere*, 3:197–202; Masuccio, in Ferrero and Doglio, *Novelle*, 355–63; and Brevio, *Novelle*, 46–64, where a *compare* acts as the go-between.

65. Sermini, *Novelle*, 1:225–37, 2:401–11; Molza, *Novelle*, 110–17; and Bandello, *Novelle*, 124–47, where the husband verges on homoerotic relations with the youth.

66. Sercambi, *Novelliere*, 2:3–12, 364–66; Molza, *Novelle*, 86–94; Fortini, in Salinari, *Novelle del Cinquecento*, 417–30, where two sisters-in-law end up sharing a lover.

67. Sacchetti, *Trecentonovelle*, 27–28; Arlotto, *Motti e facezie*, 198–200; Grazzini, *Le cene*, 233–53; Bandello, *Novelle*, 354–64; Molza, *Novelle*, 124–31, where the tantalized Gabriotto rapes his mother-in-law; and Fortini, in Salinari, *Novelle del Cinquecento*, 445–51, where Lucrezia couples with her son-in-law. In Giovanni (Fiorentino), *Il Pecorone* (1804), 2:138–49, a youth tragically spurns his stepmother's "carnal" love. This tale appears in the *editio princeps* (Milan, 1558) but is suppressed by the modern editor, Esposito, because much of it is taken from Firenzuola's translation of Apuleius's *Golden Ass*.

68. Sermini, *Novelle*, 2:573–80.

69. Martines, *Renaissance Sextet*, 25–35.

70. Sercambi, *Novelliere*, 3:204–11.

71. Ibid., 225–30. The interest in counting orgasms may already be found in Antonio Pucci (c. 1350): see his use of "correr," in Corsi, *Rimatori*, 839.

72. Boccaccio, *Decameron*, 3.1; 9.2; Sermini, *Novelle*, 1:107–19; Sercambi, *Novel-*

liere, 1:190–94; Firenzuola, *Opere*, 196–201. For ample archival evidence of male entry into nunneries, see Mazzi, *Prostitute e lenoni*, 131–37; and Ruggiero, *Boundaries of Eros*, 70–88.

73. Sermini, *Novelle*, 2:561–71.

74. Ibid., 1:471–81.

75. Examples: Boccaccio, *Decameron*, 3.5; Bracciolini, *Facezie*, nos. cxxxvii and ccxxi; Sermini, *Novelle*, 2:391–400; Masuccio, in Ferrero and Doglio, *Novelle*, 356–63; Bandello, *Novelle*, 125–47; Grazzini, *Le cene*, 80–94; Fortini, in Salinari, *Novelle del Cinquecento*, 416–30. On rustic metaphors for coitus, Bec, "La figura del contadino," 91.

76. Pitt-Rivers, *Fate of Shechem*, 82. Examples: Sacchetti, *Trecentonovelle*, 171; Sercambi, *Novelliere*, 3:181–88; Sermini, *Novelle*, 2:383–89. The adulterous wife on top literally "beats" the lover underneath with her buttocks.

77. Boccaccio, *Decameron*, 9.3; Piccolomini, *Historia de duobus amantibus*, 962.

78. In Lucca, for example: Bongi, *Bandi lucchesi*, 123–24.

79. Bandello, *Novelle*, 113–24. Neri, "La contessa di Challant," 225–54, examines the historical story.

80. Venice in 1544 made extramarital intercourse with one man an act of prostitution. Martin, *Witchcraft and the Inquisition*, 235; Rezasco, "Segno delle meretrici," 212, dates this law to 1542. On the testimony of several neighbors in Perugia, see *Primum (-quartum) volumen*, vol. 3, rubric 83. In Bologna three witnesses sufficed to establish that a woman was a whore. *Statuta criminalia communis Bononiae*, 28r. On the death penalty in Milan, *Statuta criminalia mediolani*, 16; on death in Pavia, if the adultery took place in the woman's (i.e., her husband's) house, see *Statuta de regimine*, bk. 3, rubric 79; and on death in Cremona, *Statuta et ordinamenta comunis Cremonae*, 46. The item on fines at Florence was kindly communicated to me by Gene Brucker, calling on material in the state archives of Florence, in the *Atti del Podestà* and the *Atti del Esecutore*.

81. O'Faolain and Martines, *Not in God's Image*, chaps. 3, 5, 7–8, for the medieval background to misogyny. The entire range of misogynous themes is in Boccaccio, *Il corbaccio*, a dark narrative underscoring the great storyteller's altered views in old age.

82. Bracciolini, *Facezie*, nos. 139 and 279.

83. Also Martines, "Amour et histoire."

84. The near exceptions are Molza, *Novelle*, 29–68, an early fairy tale, centered on the openly incestuous feelings of a king for his beautiful daughter; and Straparola, *Le piacevoli notti*, 1:28–35.

85. Sacchetti, *Trecentonovelle*, 27–28; Ser Giovanni, *Il Pecorone* (1804), 2:138–49; Arlotto, *Motti e facezie*, 198–201; Sermini, *Novelle*, 1:383–89; Sercambi, *Novelliere*, 2:3–12; Molza, *Novelle*, 124–31. Related hereto is a widow's seduction of her son-

in-law in a tale by Fortini, in Salinari, *Novelle del Cinquecento,* 445–51; and Nelli, *Le amorose novelle* (unpaginated), the second tale, is about the married Giulia's seduction of her nephew.

86. Bandello, *Novelle,* 355–64; and Lazzari, *Parisina,* for the historical case.

87. Sacchetti, *Trecentonovelle,* 27–28, a tale echoed in Arlotto, *Motti e facezie,* 198–201.

88. Masuccio, in Ferrero and Doglio, *Novelle,* 460–70; Morlini, in Guglielminetti, *Novellieri del Cinquecento,* 8–9.

89. Brevio, *Novelle,* 33–45; the tale is reprinted in Guglielminetti, *Novellieri del Cinquecento,* 293–98.

90. Cited in Ciappelli, *Carnevale e quaresima,* 82. But *l'atto del matrimonio* is a common locution of the period: for example, Giovanni Dominici, in Lenzi, *Donne e madonne,* 48; and Arlotto, *Motti e facezie,* 186, no. 129.

91. Boccaccio, *Decameron,* 7.9.

92. Cardini, *De finibus Tuscie,* 196–214, on the falcon as phallus in a *Decameron* story (5.9). In Italian Renaissance literature, the trained hawk or falcon is often a frank metaphor for the penis. Toscan, *Le carnaval du langage,* vol. 3, chap. 42, is a sustained discussion of the whole bird-penis equivalance. See Sermini's sonnet in praise of his hawk, *Novelle,* 1:199.

93. Parabosco, *I diporti,* 39–43; Bandello, *Novelle,* 125–47; Molza, *Novelle,* 69–85; Salvi in *Tre novelle rarissime,* 111–29.

94. Bandello, *Novelle,* 134.

95. Boccaccio, *Decameron,* 7.7.

96. Grazzini, *Le cene,* 158–84.

97. Arienti, *Porretane,* 25–26. The naughty gesture was the sign of the fig, "li fece un fica"; and "blind eye" might also refer to the vagina. Toscan, *Le carnaval du langage,* 3:1204–6, misses this equivalence and relates "occhio," in matters of obscenity, to the anus.

98. Masuccio, in Ferrero and Doglio, *Novelle,* 323–36. See also Nigro, *Le bracche di San Griffone.*

99. Rusconi, *Il movimento religioso;* and *Temi e problemi;* also Papi, *In castro poenitentiae;* and Zarri, *Le sante vive.*

100. Sermini, *Novelle,* 1:257–66. Seeking obviously to protect himself and avoid scandal, Sermini hedges by saying that they were spurious friars, though they have no other life and are never challenged by ecclesiastical authority.

101. Sercambi, *Novelliere,* 1:222–25.

102. Bernardino da Siena, *Prediche volgari sul Campo di Siena,* 622–25; Hay, *Church in Italy,* 61; Zarri, *Le sante vive,* 39, 49–50 n. 116; Lenzi, *Donne e madonne,* 56.

103. Boccaccio, *Decameron,* 8.7; Sercambi, *Novelliere,* 3:225–30. Cf. Mazzi, *Prostitute e lenoni,* 88, on Letta Sassetti.

104. On arranged marriage, three recent studies, stressing social and cultural matters, correct and complement the traditional institutional approach: Molho, *Marriage Alliance,* 128–78; Grubb, *Provincial Families,* 1–33; and Bestor, "Kinship and Marriage." The legal dimensions are in Bellomo, *La condizione giuridica.* Cf. case studies in Kuehn, *Law,* chaps. 8–10; and Kirshner, "Maritus lucretur dotem," 111–55.

105. Eleven alone in Boccaccio, *Decameron,* 4.1, 4.3, 4.5, 4.6, 4.7, 4.8, 5.1–4, 5.7.

106. Bandello, *Novelle,* 117.

107. Martines, "Way of Looking at Women," 22.

108. Bestor, "Kinship and Marriage," 1:160–61.

109. Examples: Boccaccio, *Decameron,* 4.6–8; Granucci, in Salinari, *Novelle del Cinquecento,* 609–12, 612–14 (the second death being an execution); and Selva, also in Salinari, *Novelle del Cinquecento,* 619–22, where a secret, socially impossible love brings a wasting death.

110. Boccaccio, *Decameron,* 4.6.

CHAPTER 10. POETRY AS POLITICAL MEMORY

1. D'Ancona, *La poesia popolare italiana,* 53–55; Ammirato, *Istorie fiorentine,* 5:59–60.

2. The Gonfalonier of Justice, Piero Gualterotti, raised the question of "quello sia da fare circa il sonetto si è trovato facto in vergogna del Re di Francia." Fachard, *Consulte e pratiche della repubblica fiorentina, 1498–1505,* 1:426. Date: 3 August 1503.

3. ASF, Signoria. Carteggi. *Responsive originali,* 43, fol. 9r–v. I owe this reference to William J. Connell, and here render grateful thanks.

4. Molho and Sznura, *Alle bocche della piazza,* 173.

5. Evangelisti, " 'Libelli famosi,' " 181–239.

6. In the papal states, during the late fourteenth and fifteenth centuries, this offense was punishable by a fine of ten or more florins. *Aegidianae constitutiones,* 291.

7. Lazzarini, *Marino Faliero,* 135–54, rightly argues that the two verses were a fifteenth-century interpolation.

8. Cesareo, *Pasquino e pasquinate;* Dell'Arco, *Pasquino statua parlante;* and especially the two volumes, with hundreds of poems, beautifully edited by Marucci, Marzo, and Romano, *Pasquinate romane del Cinquecento.*

9. Gozzadini, *Memorie,* 214–17; Frati, "I Bentivoglio," 30.

10. See, for example, Medin, *La storia della repubblica di Venezia.*

11. Neo-Latin humanist verse was rarely read out to the populace.

12. On this and the preceding items there was much statutory prescription: e.g., *Aegidianae constitutiones,* 20–21, 216–17, 248; *Statuta populi et communis Florentiae,* 1:80–82; *Municipalia Cremae,* 113; *Statuta iurisdictionum,* 103, 105; *Statuti del Comune di Ravenna,* 50, 78, 194; Bongi, *Bandi lucchesi,* 191, 205; Frati, *Vita privata,* 78–79.

13. See Martines, "Ritual Language," 59—76.

14. Ortalli, ". . . *Pingatur in palatio* . . ."; Edgerton, *Pictures and Punishment*.

15. Lanza, *Lirici*, 2:94, words assigned to the son of the Florentine, Rinaldo degli Albizzi, leader of the anti-Medici party in 1433—34; Edgerton, *Pictures and Punishment*, 99—100; Kent, *Rise of the Medici*, chap. 5.

16. Donato di Neri, *Cronaca senese*, 743—47.

17. Novati, "Le poesie," 55—79; E. Levi, *I cantari leggendari*; and again Levi, *Poesia di popolo*, chap. 5.

18. Branciforte, "Ars poetica rei publicae"; Branciforte, "Antonio di Meglio," 9—23; Trexler, *Libro Cerimoniale*.

19. Some of them even peddled prophecies: Niccoli, *Prophecy and People*, 12—19.

20. On the last of these, see Filippo Scarlatti's sonnet cxi, in Lanza, *Lirici*, 2:575.

21. Pucci in Corsi, *Rimatori*, 883.

22. Cesareo, *Pasquino e pasquinate*, 17.

23. Frati, "I Bentivoglio," 11; Gozzadini, *Memorie*, 93—94.

24. Such as Matteo da Milano, who did recitations of his own famous lament on the travails of Bernabò Visconti. See Medin and Frati, *Lamenti storici*, 1:181—213.

25. Examples: Lanza, *Lirici*, 1:76 (no. 23), 270 (no. 7), 672—73 (no. 11); 2:87—90, 208—9; Sacchetti, *Libro delle rime*, 370—75.

26. The sonnet for Strozzi is in Montemagno, *Le rime*, 57; on Pitti, see Lanza, *Lirici*, 1:363—64.

27. Poems for the Medici: Lanza, *Lirici*, 1:146, 149, 157, 158—59, 269, 293, 344, 356, 361, 363, 372, 376, 385, 388, 429, 667, 674, 691; 2:49, 105—20, 137, 211—12, 274, 285, 286—90, 308—11, 312, 338—40, 360—65, 377—79, 469—70, 751. Not included here are poems done for the Medici by Luigi Pulci, Matteo Franco, Poliziano, Bellincioni, and neo-Latin poets such as Naldo Naldi, Ugolino Verino, and Alessandro Braccesi, on whom see Rochon, *La jeunesse*, 311—16.

28. In Corsi, *Rimatori*, 850—55.

29. Medin and Frati, *Lamenti storici*, 1:265. See Tebaldeo, *Rime*, 2:362, no. 230, for a lovely sonnet on degraded Pisa and wicked Florence, written around 1500.

30. F. Sacchetti, *Libro delle rime*, 140—42; Medin, "I Visconti," 745.

31. Antonio Beccari, *Rime*; Corsi, *Rimatori*, 319—23, 449—53; Vannozzo, *Rime*; Niccolò Cieco, in Lanza, *Lirici*, 2:167—213.

32. See the condensed treatment in Scrivano, "Bellincioni, Bernardo," 687—89.

33. Lanza, *Lirici*, 1:421.

34. Ibid., 2:16.

35. Ibid., 1:667.

36. A point best documented by the verse exchanges among poets: Lanza, *Lirici*; Frati, *Rimatori bolognesi del Quattrocento*; Lanza, *Polemiche* (2d ed.); Frati, "I Bentivoglio"; Basile, *Bentivolorum magnificentia*; and some articles on copyists of the

period, including Pasquini, "Il codice di Filippo Scarlatti," 363–580; De Robertis, "Antonio Manetti copista," 367–409; Tanturli, "I Benci copisti," 197–313.

37. See especially Bentivogli, "La poesia in volgare," 177–222, which demolishes Lodovico Frati's two-volume edition of the Codice Isoldiano (Bologna, 1913); also Messina, "Per l'edizione delle *Rime* del Burchiello," 196–296; Gorni, "Un canzoniere adespoto," 189–219.

38. Frati, *Rimatori bolognesi del Quattrocento,* on verse exchanges and the material in his summary biographies.

39. Cesareo, *Pasquino e pasquinate,* 17; but the poem itself, a *ternario* by the prominent oligarch Niccolò da Uzzano, is in Lanza, *Lirici,* 2:661–63.

40. Flamini, *La lirica,* 96–99, 292–94, on Burchiello and Tinucci; Lanza, *Polemiche* (1971 ed.), 184–85; Kent, *Rise of the Medici,* 225–33, on Tinucci; and Tinucci, *Rime.*

41. Cf. Martelli, "La canzone," 7–50.

42. Lanza, *Lirici,* 2:381–84; Volpi, *Rime di trecentisti minori,* 227–28, by Braccio Bracci; F. Accolti, "Le rime," 211–15.

43. Corsi, *Rimatori,* 415 (no. 3); Sacchetti, *Libro delle rime,* 200–204, 206–9; Sarteschi, *Poesie minori del secolo XIV,* 43, sonnet by Bracci; and Volpi, *Rime di trecentisti minori,* 245–46.

44. For example, three poems by Nicolò Malpigli, in Frati, *Rimatori bolognesi del Quattrocento,* 27–29.

45. Pulci and Franco, *"Libro dei sonetti";* and Pulci, *Opere minori,* 153–90.

46. See Martines, "Love and Hate in Renaissance Patronage," 17–18; Cammelli, *I sonetti,* 60–79 (against Bellincioni), 108–14 (against Sasso); and the excellent piece by Ricciardi, "Cosmico, Niccolò Lelio," 72–77.

47. Pallone, *Anticlericalismo,* 36. He probably attacked Savonarola, the Trotti brothers, and others. See Piromalli, *La cultura a Ferrara,* 138–46.

48. See Medin and Frati, *Lamenti storici;* Medin, *Lamenti de' secoli xiv e xv;* Ferrari, *Poesie su Ludovico il Moro;* and Russell, "Studio dei generi medievali italiani," 349–70.

49. Medin and Frati, *Lamenti storici,* 1:23–32, 55–60, 71–213, 215–75; 2:41–111, 121–229, 231–46, 321–26; 3:9–25, 55–62, 69–75, 79–113, 241–87, 347–400.

50. In Corsi, *Rimatori,* 855–63, lines 121–22.

51. Medin and Frati, *Lamenti storici,* 1:215–47.

52. Ibid., 225, 257 n. 1.

53. Ibid., 252, 256, 258–60.

54. Ibid., 273–75.

55. Ibid., 71–213.

56. Ibid., 71–139.

57. Ibid., 181–213.

58. Ibid., 209 (stanza 62).

59. Cf., for example, the anonymous Florentine sonnet (c. 1338) against Venice, in Sapegno, *Poeti minori,* 454 (no. 19), declaring that "de la carne tua far' tonnina/e del tuo proprio sangue un largo laco" (lines 13–14); and Morpurgo, *Dieci sonetti storici fiorentini,* unpaginated. Here the anonymous sonnet no. 5 (late fourteenth century) would have Florence make purses from the skins of the people of Arezzo, Siena, and Pistoia; and in Medin, *Sonetti per la lega di Cambrai,* 15 (no. 7, written about 1509), the poet would have Venice make all "Italy dark with human blood."

60. For example, Michele del Giogante to Cosimo de' Medici, in Lanza, *Lirici,* 1:670 (no. 7), "se non che vostro sono in carne e 'n ossa."

61. Medin and Frati, *Lamenti storici,* 2:233–34, 321.

62. Ibid., 79–93; for poems in favor of Venice, see Medin, *Sonetti per la lega di Cambrai;* and Novati and Pellegrini, *Poesie politiche,* 13–16.

63. Medin and Frati, *Lamenti storici,* 3:104, 106 (lines 126–27, 180–83).

64. Gozzadini, *Memorie,* 214–17; Frati, "I Bentivoglio," 29–34.

65. For example, Giovanni II Bentivoglio moans, "Son quel miser Bentivoglio/ Che già fui in tanta altura," and the personified Venice cries, "Son Venetia sconsolata/posta in pianto e gran dolore." Medin and Frati, *Lamenti storici,* 3:55, 99.

CHAPTER 11. CRISIS IN THE GENERATION OF 1494

1. See the miscellany of essays in Abulafia, *French Descent;* and Fiorato, *Italie;* also *Storia d'Italia* (Einaudi), 2:1, 346–64; and the fine piece by Denis, "Charles VIII en Italie," 57–66.

2. Villari, *Life and Times,* 1:173–211; Cordero, *Savonarola,* 276–78; Weinstein, *Savonarola,* chaps. 4–7; Polizzotto, *Elect Nation,* chaps. 1–2; and the poem in praise of the French king by an anonymous Savonarolan, Medin, *Ternario in Lodi di Carlo VIII,* written even before his descent into Italy.

3. As reflected, for instance, in verse: Marucci, Marzo, and Romano, *Pasquinate romane del Cinquecento,* 1:8–9 (no. 9). But the feeling regarding divine punishment was widespread in upper Italy: Niccoli, *Prophecy and People,* 3–23. Later, the Sack of Rome (1527) seemed to confirm this view in the eyes of all Italians.

4. Examples: Atti, *Cronaca,* 176; and Matarazzo, *Cronaca,* 1–243, at 16. Cf. Denis, "Charles VIII en Italie," 59.

5. Suffice it to comb the chroniclers: e.g., Smagliati, *Cronaca parmense;* or Masi, *Ricordanze,* 94–95, on the sacking of Prato in late August and September of 1512.

6. The evidence is scattered throughout Florence's famous political deliberations in the top tier of government, the famous *Consulte e pratiche.* The late republican ones have been edited by Fachard, *Consulte e pratiche: 1505–1512* and *Consulte e pratiche della repubblica fiorentina, 1498–1505.*

7. Burigozzo, *Cronaca di Milano,* 419–552; Atti, *Cronaca;* and the chroniclers Smagliati and Masi.

8. The best recent study is Fiorato, "Complaintes," 179–225. On love poetry as both escape from and commentary on worldly cares, see Martines, "Amour et histoire," 575–603, and chap. 4 of this volume.

9. Dionisotti, "Chierici e laici," 55–88, finds that in his large sample of one hundred writers from the early sixteenth century, about half were in holy orders, a remarkable figure, and they relied more or less fully on their ecclesiastical incomes. About twenty of them became cardinals or bishops. But see also Bec, "Le statut socioprofessionel," 47–105, which looks at 650 writers and finds that in the period 1450–1550 some 46.6 percent worked "aupres des seigneurs," hence ranked as courtiers. On the powers of secretaries as writers and servitors, see Fiorato, *Culture et professions,* 133–84.

10. As is well known, the Venetian chronicler Sanuto occasionally copied anonymous verse in its entirety into his oceanic diary: *I darii,* 1:759, 871, 1016–17, 1021; 7:63–65, 173–75 (examples). He also made a collection of Latin and vernacular poems, on which see D'Ancona and Medin, "Rime storiche," 17–35. Smagliati, *Cronaca parmense,* 71–72, cites a scorching anonymous ditty against a notorious local tax farmer; other references may be found in Cian, *La satira: Dal medioevo al Pontano,* 291–93. On "bench singers," see Niccoli, *Prophecy and People,* 12–23.

11. Marucci et al., *Pasquinate romane del Cinquecento,* 1:xviii; Previtera, *La poesia giocosa,* 310–12.

12. Marucci et al., *Pasquinate romane del Cinquecento,* 1:7.

13. Ibid., 12–13.

14. Ibid., 17, 38–40, 42–46, 49, quotations on 45, 47.

15. Ibid., 84–85, 111, 295, "Christ's cunt!" and "God's ass!"

16. Ibid., 84–85, 170–72, 197, 230, 242–44.

17. Ibid., 141–72, 232–98, 307–14.

18. Ibid., 172.

19. Ibid., 182, 214–15.

20. On particular cardinals, see Cesareo, *Pasquino e pasquinate,* 116–69; and the study by Hallman, *Italian Cardinals,* on nepotism, lucrative income, and privatizing ecclesiastical property.

21. "Where are you going, where, O Ludovico? This isn't the way to go to Milan." Text given in full by Giannessi, "Gli inizi," 482.

22. In Medin, *Lamenti dei secoli xiv e xv,* 71–84.

23. Medin and Frati, *Lamenti storici,* 3:79–93, 99–113; for two sonnets against Venice, see Medin, *Sonetti per la lega di Cambrai,* 18, 21. On Venetian foreign relations in these years, see Seneca, *Venezia e Papa Giulio II;* and Gilbert, "Venice in the Crisis," 274–92.

24. In defense of Venice, most of the sonnets in Medin, *Sonetti per la lega di Cambrai;* also Novati and Pellegrini, *Poesie politiche,* 13–16.

25. Example: Smagliati, *Cronaca parmense,* 165.

26. Guicciardini, *Opere,* 435, in *Storia d'Italia,* 1:ix.

27. Burigozzo, *Cronaca di Milano,* 431–32. The preacher hailed from Siena, a certain friar Hieronimo, who upset the upper classes and the richer Milanese clergy by assailing their immorality and corruption. In 1523 another friar worried and keenly divided the Milanese (444).

28. *DBI,* 9:343–57; Virgili, *Francesco Berni;* and especially Berni, *Poesie e prose,* v–xxxv, on Berni's life and art.

29. Berni, *Poesie e prose,* 33–34, 42–62, 69–71, 80–83, 128–38. Note the similar succinct praise of fish, oil, pans, and roast goose in the *Quaedam epigrammata* of Folengo, *Opere,* 613–15.

30. Berni, *Poesie e prose,* 62–69, 73, 76, 164–67, 103–7. The attack on love, "Mando fatto in Abruzzi: contro Amore dispettoso," begins characteristically, "Amor, io te ne incaco" (73).

31. Ibid., 114, "Sonetto contro li preti."

32. Dionisotti, "Chierici e laici," 55–88; and more generally on relations between the Church and the intelligentsia, see Prosperi, "Intelletuali e chiesa," 161–252.

33. Santoro, *Fortuna;* and Bec, "Fortune e prudence," 69–78.

34. Cremonte, *Matteo Bandello.*

35. Brevio, *Novelle.*

36. Gilbert, *Machiavelli and Guicciardini,* 193–97, 288–91; Santoro, *Fortuna;* though Machiavelli believed in striving to harness *virtù* to *fortuna,* as in the impetuosity of brilliant young generals and statesmen. Examples of key references to "fortuna" in Ariosto's *Orlando furioso:* canto 8, stanza 62; canto 19, stanza 1; canto 30, stanzas 15, 35, 53; canto 33, stanzas 35, 42, 57; canto 34, stanzas 73, 74; canto 35, stanza 5; canto 37, stanza 11; canto 40, stanza 61; canto 44, stanzas 61, 62; canto 45, stanzas 1, 2, 4, 5, 7; canto 46, stanzas 8, 71, 135.

37. Cian, *La Satira: Dall' Ariosto al Chiabrera,* 3–4.

38. Cagnola, *Storia di Milano,* 199. The Battle of Fornovo was certainly not won by the Italians. Santosuosso, "Anatomy of Defeat," 221–50.

39. See De Robertis on Cammelli and his style, "Cammelli, Antonio," 277–86; and Pallone, *Anticlericalismo.*

40. Cammelli, *I sonetti,* sonnets 273–388. Cf. Rossi, "Poesie storiche," 207–25, an informed commentary on Cammelli's political sonnets.

41. Cammelli, *I sonetti,* sonnet 383.

42. Ibid., sonnet 386.

43. Ibid., sonnet 369.

44. Machiavelli, *Discorsi*, 1:xii; Guicciardini, *Opere*, 103 (no. 28), 340–41.

45. Note two clamorous cases in the 1470s, reported by Malipiero, *Annali veneti*, 661–62, 668–70.

46. In Asor Rosa, *Letteratura italiana*, vol. 3, *Le Forme del testo*, 1, 519–30.

47. Many of the early printed editions of the war poetry have now been photographed and published in the remarkable Beer, Diamanti, and Ivaldi, *Guerre in ottava rima*, alas, utterly without notes or commentary.

48. In the famous *Prose della volgar lingua*, in Bembo, *Prose e Rime*, 71–309.

49. Asor Rosa, *Letteratura italiana*, vol. 2, *Le opere*, 3–85, esp. 26–44.

50. Folengo, *Baldus*, and xxix–xxxvi for a biographical sketch; see also Goffis, "Per la biografia dei Folengo," 193–206.

51. Ramat, "Il *Baldus*, poema dell'anarchia," in his *Sette contributi*, 73–81.

52. Folengo, *Opere*, 3–70 (*Zanitonella*), and 795–912 (for much of *Caos del tri per uno*); or the latter complete, Folengo, *Caos del tri per uno*, in Warburg Institute Library, London.

53. On Folengo's return to cloister, Goffis, "Per la biografia dei Folengo"; and Billanovich, "Per una revisione" and "Un nuovo Folengo."

54. Dionisotti, "Chierici e laici," 58–61, including his remarks on Ariosto, who was beneficed and hence a cleric but yet not a priest; also Grendler, *Critics of the Italian World*, chaps. 2, 4.

55. The best summary of this debate remains Migliorini, *Storia della lingua italiana*, 339–60. On the Quattrocento background to the linguistic crisis, see Folena, *Il linguaggio del caos*, 3–17, and (on Folengo) 147–68; also Pierre Blanc, "La crise linguistique," 27–55, which contrasts Bembo's literary *koine* with the more populist bent of the new printed book and the craze for translations from the Greek and Latin. In a rich and condensed piece, Segre, "Edonismo linguistico nel Cinquecento," 369–96, highlights experimentation, marked contrasts, and the literary validity of the language of writers such as Aretino and Folengo.

56. The key argument in Mazzacurati, *Il Rinascimento dei moderni*, chap. 1.

57. Castiglione, *Cortegiano* (Maier ed.). On the succeeding interpretation, see Martines, "Gentleman in Renaissance Italy," 77–93; cf. Carella, "Il libro del cortegiano," 1089–1126; and again Carella, "Genesi di un mito," 1, 496–516.

58. See Castiglione, *Seconda redazione;* and especially Ghinassi, "Fasi dell'elaborazione del 'Cortegiano,' " 155–96. In this second revision of the work, the question of relations between the prince and the ideal courtier is treated in bk. 3, chaps. 5–47.

59. Castiglione immediately took Francesco Maria's cause to be a lost one, however, and withdrew his support, so that when the ousted lord returned to Urbino in 1522, he stripped Castiglione of his Pesarese fief. Mutini, "Castiglione, Baldassarre," 53–68.

60. Castiglione, *Cortegiano* (Maier ed.), 161–62, 230–31; Castiglione, *Seconda redazione,* 59–60, 110–11.

61. Still bk. 4 in Castiglione, *Cortegiano* (Maier ed.), 450–510; Castiglione, *Seconda redazione,* 191–236.

62. Castiglione, *Cortegiano* (Maier ed.), 216. In Castiglione, *Seconda redazione,* 100: "Voglio adonque ch'il cortiggiano . . . se volti con tutto il pensiero e forze dell'animo suo ad amare e quasi adorare el principe, a chi serve, sopra ogni altra cosa."

63. The word *giuoco* in fact frequently recurs in the dialogue.

64. See Lawner, *I Modi.*

65. This concluding comment calls for an apposite reference: Martines, "Review Essay."

AFTERWORD: THEMES AND STRATEGIES

1. Mueller, *Venetian Money Market.*

Bibliography

ABBREVIATIONS

ASF   Archivio di stato, Florence.
ASI   *Archivio storico italiano.*
BNCF   Biblioteca Nazionale Centrale di Firenze.
DBI   *Dizionario biografico degli italiani.* Rome, 1960–.
DCLI   *Dizionario critico della letteratura italiana.* 3 vols., ed.
         Vittore Branca. Turin, 1974.
DELI   *Dizionario enciclopedico della letteratura italiana.* 6 vols.,
         ed. Giuseppe Petronio. Rome, 1966–70.
FN   Fondo Nazionale
GSLI   *Giornale Storico della Letteratura Italiana.*
Magl.   Magliabecchi
SFI   *Studi di Filologia Italiana.*

Abulafia, David, ed. 1995. *The French Descent into Renaissance Italy, 1494–95:*
   Antecedents and Effects. Aldershot, Eng.
Accolti, Benedetto. 1957. "Le rime di Benedetto Accolti d'Arezzo." Ed. Elena
   Jacoboni. *SFI* 15:241–302.
Accolti, Francesco. 1955. "Le rime di Francesco Accolti d'Arezzo: Umanista e
   giureconsulto del sec. xv." Ed. Michele Messina. *GSLI* 132:173–233.
Ady, Cecilia M. 1937. *The Bentivoglio of Bologna.* London.
Aegidianae constitutiones cum additionibus carpensibus. 1571. Venice.
Alamanni, Antonio. 1977. *Commedia della conversione di Santa Maria Maddalena.* Ed.
   Pierre Jodogne. Bologna.

Alberti, Leon Battista. 1946. *I primi tre libri della famiglia.* Ed. Francesco Carlo Pellegrini and Raffaele Spongano. Florence.

———. 1987. *Dinner Pieces.* Tr. David Marsh. Binghamton, N.Y.

Altamura, Antonio. 1974. *Il Certame Coronario.* Naples.

Ammirato, Scipione. 1853. *Istorie fiorentine.* 7 vols. Turin.

Antonetti, Pierre. 1994. *La vita quotidiana a Firenze ai tempi di Lorenzo il Magnifico.* Tr. Maria Grazia Meriggi. Milan.

Aretino, Pietro. 1969. *Sei giornate.* Ed. Giovanni Aquilecchia. Bari.

Arienti, Sabadino degli. 1981. *Le porretane.* Ed. Bruno Basile. Rome.

Ariosto, Ludovico. 1887. *Lettere.* Ed. Antonio Cappelli. Milan.

———. 1960. *Orlando furioso.* Ed. Santorre Debenedetti and Cesare Segre. Bologna.

Arlotto, Piovano. 1953. *Motti e facezie.* Ed. Gianfranco Folena. Milan.

Arnaldi, Francesco, and Lucia Gualdo Rosa, eds. 1964. *Poeti latini del Quattrocento.* Milan.

Ascheri, Mario. 1985. *Siena nel Rinascimento: Istituzioni e sistema politico.* Siena.

———, ed. 1993. *L'ultimo statuto della Repubblica di Siena (1545).* Siena. Includes the *Statutum.*

Asor Rosa, Alberto, ed. 1982–91. *Letteratura italiana.* 12 vols. Turin.

Astorri, Antonella. 1992. "Note sulla Mercanzia Fiorentina sotto Lorenzo de' Medici. Aspetti istituzionali e politici." *ASI* 150, no. 3: 965–93.

Atti, Ioan Fabrizio degli. 1979. *Cronaca.* In Mancini, *Le Cronache.*

Baldacci, Luigi, ed. 1975. *Lirici del Cinquecento.* Milan.

Balduino, Armando. 1980. "Le esperienze della poesia volgare." In Folena, *Storia,* 3, 1: 265–367.

———, ed. 1980. *Rimatori veneti del Quattrocento.* Padua.

Bandello, Matteo. 1974. *Novelle.* Ed. Giuseppe Guido Ferrero. Turin.

Banfi, Luigi, ed. 1963. *Sacre rappresentazioni del Quattrocento.* Turin.

Banker, James. 1988. *Death in the Community: Memorialization and Confraternities in an Italian Commune in the Late Middle Ages.* Athens, Ga.

Barbi, Michele. 1897. "Due curiosità quattrocentesche." In *Miscellanea nuziale Rossi-Teiss,* 217–25. Bergamo.

Basile, Bruno, ed. 1984. *Bentivolorum magnificentia: Principe e cultura a Bologna nel Rinascimento.* Rome.

Bec, Christian. 1967. *Les marchands écrivains: Affaires et humanisme à Florence, 1375–1434.* Paris.

———. 1969. "Fortune e prudence au Cinquecento." *Revue des Etudes Italiennes* 15, no. 1: 69–78.

———. 1981. *Cultura e società a Firenze nell'età della rinascenza.* Rome.

———. 1981. "La figura del contadino nella novellistica toscana del secondo Trecento e del primo Quattrocento." In Bec, *Cultura e società.*

———. 1986. *Florence 1300–1600: Histoire et culture.* Nancy.

———. 1986. "Le statut socio-professionel des écrivains italiens (XIIIe–XVIe siècles)." In Bec, *Florence 1300–1600.*

———, ed. 1976. *Italie 1500–1550: Une situation de crise?* Annales de l'Université Jean Moulin Series. Lyon.

Beccari, Antonio da Ferrara. 1967. *Rime.* Ed. Laura Bellucci. Bologna.

Beccherini, Bianca. 1948. "Un canta in banca fiorentino: Antonio di Guido." *Rivista Musicale Italiana* 50:241–47.

Beer, Marina, Donatella Diamanti, and Cristina Ivaldi, eds. 1988–89. *Guerre in ottava rima.* 4 vols. Modena.

Bellincioni, Bernardo. 1493. *Rime.* Milan.

———. 1876–78. *Le Rime.* Ed. Pietro Fanfani. 2 vols. Bologna.

Bellomo, Manlio. 1965. "Emancipazione (diritto intermedio)." In *Enciclopedia del diritto,* 14:809–19. Milan.

———. 1970. *La condizione giuridica della donna in Italia: Vicende antiche e moderne.* Turin.

Bembo, Pietro. 1966. *Prose e rime.* Ed. Carlo Dionisotti. Turin.

Bentivogli, Bruno. 1984. "La poesia in volgare: Appunti sulla tradizione manoscritta." In Basile, *Bentivolorum magnificentia,* 177–222.

Bernardino da Siena, San. 1964. *La fonte della vita: Prediche volgari scelte e annotate.* Ed. Giacomo V. Sabatelli. Florence.

———. 1989. *Prediche volgari sul Campo di Siena 1427.* Ed. Carlo Delcorno. Milan.

Berni, Francesco. 1934. *Poesie e prose.* Ed. E. Chiorboli. Geneva.

———. 1969. *Rime.* Ed. Giorgio Bàrberi Squarotti. Turin.

Bertoni, Giulio, ed. 1909. *Il laudario dei Battuti di Modena.* In *Beihefte zür Zeitschrift für Romanische Philologie,* no. 20.

———. 1930. *Il Duecento.* Milan.

Bestor, Jane Fair. 1992. "Kinship and Marriage in the Politics of an Italian Ruling House: The Este of Ferrara in the Reign of Ercole I (1471–1505)." 2 vols. Ph.D. diss., University of Chicago.

Billanovich, Giuseppe. 1936–37. "Per una revisione della biografia di Teofilo Folengo," *Atti del Reale Istituto Veneto di Scienze Lettere e Arti* 96, no. 2: 775–96.

———. 1937–38. "Un nuovo Folengo: Conclusione del mito di Merlino," *Atti del Reale Istituto Veneto di Scienze Lettere e Arti* 97, no. 2: 365–481.

Bisticci, Vespasiano da. 1938. *Vite di uomini illustri del secolo XV.* Florence.

Black, Christopher F. 1989. *Italian Confraternities in the Sixteenth Century.* Cambridge, Eng.

Blanc, Pierre. 1976. "La crise linguistique dans la premiere moitié du Cinquecento: Symptomes et modalités." In Bec, *Italie 1500–1550,* 27–55.

Boase, Roger. 1977. *The Origin and Meaning of Courtly Love: A Critical Study of European Scholarship*. Manchester.

———. 1978. *The Troubadour Revival: A Study of Social Change and Traditionalism in Late Medieval Spain*. London.

Boccaccio, Giovanni. 1960. *Decameron*. Ed. Vittore Branca. 2 vols.

———. 1992. *Il corbaccio*. Ed. Giulia Natali. Milan.

Boiardo, Matteo Maria. 1962. *Opere volgari*. Ed. Pier Vincenzo Mengaldo. Bari.

Bongi, Salvatore, ed. 1863. *Bandi lucchesi del secolo decimoquarto*. Bologna.

Bonolis, Guido. 1901. *La giurisdizione della Mercanzia in Firenze nel secolo xiv.* Florence.

Bontempelli, Massimo, and Ghino Ghinassi, eds. 1969. *Il Poliziano, il Magnifico: Lirici del Quattrocento*. Florence.

Borlenghi, Aldo, ed. 1962. *Novelle del Quattrocento*. Milan.

Bornstein, Daniel E. 1993. *The Bianchi of 1399: Popular Devotion in Late Medieval Italy*. Ithaca, N.Y.

Bracali, Gherardo. 1910. *Francesco Alberti: Poeta fiorentino del Quattrocento*. Pistoia.

Braccesi, Alessandro. 1985. *Soneti e canzone*. Ed. Franca Magnani. Verona.

Bracciolini, Poggio. 1950. *Facezie*. Milan.

Branca, Vittore, ed. 1986. *Mercanti scrittori: Ricordi nella Firenze tra Medioevo e Rinascimento*. Milan.

———. 1995. "Libertà di coscienza e dignità dell'uomo: Il messagio di Poliziano e Pico della Mirandola." *Atti della Accademia Nazionale dei Lincei* 9, no. 6: 303–11.

Branciforte, Suzanne. 1990. "Ars poetica rei publicae: The Herald of the Florentine Signoria." Ph.D. diss., University of California, Los Angeles.

———. 1995. "Antonio di Meglio, Dante, and Cosimo de' Medici." *Italian Studies* 50:9–23.

Brevio, Giovanni. 1799. *Novelle*. Rome.

Brown, Alison, ed. 1995. *Language and Images of Renaissance Italy*. Oxford.

Brown, Clifford M. 1982. *Isabella d'Este and Lorenzo da Pavia: Documents for the History of Art and Culture in Renaissance Mantua*. Geneva.

Brucker, Gene. 1971. *The Society of Renaissance Florence: A Documentary Study*. New York.

———. 1977. *The Civic World of Early Renaissance Florence*. Princeton, N.J.

———. 1986. *Giovanni and Lusanna: Love and Marriage in Renaissance Florence*. Berkeley, Calif.

———. 1990. "Monasteries, Friaries, and Nunneries in Quattrocento Florence." In Verdon and Henderson, *Christianity and the Renaissance*, 41–62.

———. 1991. "Ecclesiastical Courts in Fifteenth-Century Florence and Fiesole." *Medieval Studies* 53:229–57.

Brunelleschi, Filippo. 1977. *Sonetti di Filippo Brunelleschi*. Ed. Giuliano Tanturli and Domenico de Robertis. Florence.

Buonarroti, Michelangelo. 1960. *Rime*. Ed. Enzo N. Girardi. Bari.

Burchiello. 1940. *I sonetti*. Ed. A. Viviani. Milan.

Burguière, André, Christiane Klapisch-Zuber, Martine Segalen, and Françoise Zonabend, eds. 1986. *Histoire de la famille*. 3 vols. Paris.

Burigozzo, Giovanni Marco. 1842. *Cronaca di Milano (1500–1544)*. *ASI* 3:419–552.

Burke, Kenneth. 1945. *A Grammar of Motives*. New York.

———. 1968. *Language as Symbolic Action*. Berkeley, Calif.

Caferro, William. 1998. *Mercenary Companies and the Decline of Siena*. Baltimore.

Cagnola, Giovan Pietro. 1842. *Storia di Milano*. *ASI* 3:1–215.

Calmeta, Vincenzo. 1959. *Prose e lettere edite e inedite*. Ed. Cecil Grayson. Bologna.

Cammelli, Antonio. 1884. *Rime edite e inedite di Antonio Cammelli detto il Pistoia*. Ed. Antonio Cappelli and Severino Ferrari. Livorno.

———. 1888. *I sonetti del Pistoia*. Ed. Rodolfo Renier. Turin.

Camporesi, Piero. 1989. *Bread of Dreams: Food and Fantasy in Early Modern Europe*. Tr. David Gentilcore. Chicago.

Cappelletti, Ermanno, ed. 1986. *Laude di Borgo San Sepolcro*. Florence.

Cappelli, Antonio, ed. 1868. *Poesie musicali dei secoli xiv, xv e xvi*. Bologna.

Capua, Raimundo da. 1934. *Santa Caterina da Siena: Vita*. Tr. P. G. Tinagli. Siena.

Cardini, Francesco. 1989. *De finibus Tuscie: Il Medioeveo in Toscana*. Florence.

Carella, Angela. 1988. "Genesi di un mito: Il libro del cortegiano." In Asor Rosa, *Letteratura italiana*, vol. 2, *Storia*, pt. 1, 496–516.

———. 1992. "Il libro del cortegiano di Baldassare Castiglione." In Asor Rosa, *Letteratura italiana*, vol. 1, *Opere*, 1089–1126.

Castiglione, Baldassare. 1964. *Il libro del cortegiano, con una scelta delle opere minori*. Ed. Bruno Maier. Turin.

———. 1968. *La seconda redazione del "Cortegiano."* Ed. Ghino Ghinassi. Florence.

Cavaciocchi, Simonetta, ed. 1990. *La donna nell'economia: Secc. xiii–xviii*. Prato.

Cecchi, Emilio, and Natalino Sapegno, eds. 1965–69. *Storia della letteratura italiana*. 9 vols. Milan.

———. 1965. *Storia: Il Trecento*. Vol. 2 of *Storia della letteratura italiana*, 370–569. Milan.

———. 1966. *Il Cinquecento*. Vol. 4 of *Storia della letteratura italiana*, 320–51. Milan.

Cesareo, Giovanni A. 1938. *Pasquino e pasquinate nella Roma di Leone X*. Rome.

Chabot, Isabelle. 1990. "La reconnaissance du travail des femmes dans la Florence du Bas Moyen Age." In Cavaciocchi, *La donna nell'economia*, 563–76.

Chambers, David S., and Trevor Dean. 1997. *Clean Hands and Rough Justice: An Investigating Magistrate in Renaissance Italy*. Ann Arbor, Mich.

Cherubini, Giovanni. 1974. *Signori, contadini, borghesi: Ricerche sulla società italiana del basso medioevo.* Florence.

Cherubino da Siena. 1888. *Regola della vita matrimoniale.* Ed. Francesco Zambrini and Carlo Negroni. Bologna.

Chiffoleau, Jacques, Lauro Martines, and Agostino Paravicini Bagliani, eds. 1994. *Riti e rituali nelle società medievali.* Spoleto.

Chittolini, Giorgio, and Giovanni Miccoli, eds. 1986. *Storia d'Italia: Annali* (Einaudi). Turin. 9:149–93, 221–48.

Chojnacki, Stanley. 1974. "Patrician Women in Early Renaissance Venice." *Studies in the Renaissance* 21:176–203.

———. 1975. "Dowries and Kinsmen in Early Renaissance Venice." *Journal of Interdisciplinary History* 4:571–600.

———. 1988. "The Power of Love: Wives and Husbands in Late Medieval Venice." In Erler and Kowaleski, *Women and Power,* 126–48.

———. 1991. " 'The Most Serious Duty': Motherhood, Gender, and Patrician Culture in Renaissance Venice." In Migiel and Schiesari, *Refiguring Women,* 133–54.

Cian, Vittorio. 1938–39. *La satira: Dall'Ariosto al Chiabrera.* Milan.

———. 1945. *La satira: Dal medioevo al Pontano.* Milan.

Ciappelli, Giovanni. 1997. *Carnevale e quaresima. Comportamenti sociali e cultura a Firenze nel Rinascimento.* Rome.

Cioni, Alfredo, ed. 1963. *La poesia religiosa: I cantari agiografici e le rime di argomento sacro.* Florence.

Cohen, Elizabeth S. 1991. "No Longer Virgins: Self-Presentation by Young Women in Late Renaissance Rome." in Migiel and Schiesari, *Refiguring Women,* 169–91.

Cohn, Samuel Kline, Jr. 1980. *The Laboring Classes in Renaissance Florence.* New York.

———. 1999. "Piety and Religious Practice in the Rural Dependencies of Renaissance Florence." *English Historical Review* 114:1121–42.

———. 1999. Review of *Forbidden Friendships,* by Rocke. *Speculum* 74, no. 2: 481–83.

Colonna, Prospero. 1927. *I Colonna.* Rome.

Colonna, Vittoria. 1982. *Rime.* Ed. Alan Bullock. Rome.

Conti, Elio. 1984. *L'imposta diretta a Firenze nel quattrocento (1427–1494).* Rome.

Contini, Gianfranco, ed. 1960. *Poeti del Duecento.* 2 vols. Milan.

Cordero, Francesco. 1986. *Savonarola: I. Voce calamitosa 1452–1494.* Rome.

Cornazzano, Antonio. 1503. *Sonetti e canzone.* Venice.

Correggio, Niccolò da. 1969. *Opere.* Ed. Antonia Tissoni Benvenuti. Bari.

Corsi, Giuseppe, ed. 1969. *Rimatori del Trecento.* Turin.

———, ed. 1970. *Poesie musicali del Trecento.* Bologna.

Cremonte, L. 1966. *Matteo Bandello e i casi vari e mirabili delle sue novelle.* Alessandria.

Crouzet-Pavan, Elisabeth. 1992. *Sopra le acque salse: Espaces, pouvoir et société à Venise à la fin du Moyen Age.* 2 vols. Rome.

———. 1997. *Venise: Une invention de la ville, XIIIe–XVe siècle.* Seyssel.

Culture et société en Italie du Moyen Age à la Renaissance: Hommage a André Rochon. 1985. Paris.

Da Dio, Giovanni. 1471. *Decor puellarum.* Venice.

D'Alatri, Mariano. 1986. *Eretici e inquisitori in Italia.* 2 vols. Rome.

D'Ancona, Alessandro. 1906. *La poesia popolare italiana.* 2d ed. Livorno.

———, ed. 1872. *Sacre rappresentazioni dei secoli xiv, xv e xvi.* 3 vols. Florence.

D'Ancona, Alessandro, and Antonio Medin. 1888. "Rime storiche del sec. xv." *Bullettino dell'Istituto Storico Italiano* 5:17–35.

Dante Alighieri. 1932. *La vita nuova.* Ed. Michele Barbi. Florence.

Datini, Margherita. 1977. *Le lettere di Margherita Datini a Francesco di Marco.* Ed. Valeria Rosati. Prato.

Dean, Trevor. 1997. "Marriage and Mutilation: Vendetta in Late Medieval Italy." *Past and Present* 157:3–36.

———. 1998. "Fathers and Daughters: Marriage Laws and Marriage Disputes in Bologna and Italy, 1200–1500." In Dean and Lowe, *Marriage,* 85–106,

Dean, Trevor, and K. J. P. Lowe, eds. 1998. *Marriage in Italy, 1300–1650.* Cambridge, Eng.

De Bartholomaeis, Vincenzo, ed. 1943. *Laude drammatiche e rappresentazioni sacre.* 3 vols. Florence.

De' Conti, Giusto. 1918. *Il canzoniere.* 2 vols., ed. Leonardo Vitetti. Lanciano.

Dell'Arco, Mario. 1967. *Pasquino statua parlante.* Rome.

De Luca, Giuseppe. 1954. *Prosatori minori del Trecento: Scrittori di religione.* Milan.

———. 1977. *Scrittori di religione del Trecento: Testi originali.* 2 vols. Turin.

De Navarre, Marguerite. 1967. *Nouvelles.* Ed. Yves Le Hir. Paris.

———. 1984. *The Heptameron.* Tr. Paul A. Chilton. London.

Denis, Anne. 1976. "Charles VIII en Italie: Catalyseur et/ou symbole de la crise." in Bec, *Italie 1500–1550,* 57–66.

Denley, Peter, and Caroline Elam, eds. 1988. *Florence and Italy: Renaissance Studies in Honour of Nicolai Rubinstein.* London.

De Robertis, Domenico. 1974. "Antonio Manetti copista." In *Tra Latino,* 2:367–409.

———. 1974. "Cammelli, Antonio." in *DBI,* 17:277–86.

Diario ferrarese dall'anno 1409 sino al 1502. 1928–33. Ed. Giuseppe Pardi. In *Rerum italicarum scriptores,* vol. 24, pt. 7, sec. 1. Bologna.

Di Blasi, Patrizia. 1985. "Gusto della burla e mito dell' onore: Oralità e scrittura nella novella del Grasso Legnaiuolo." In Squarotti, *Metamorfosi.*

Di Francia, Letterio. 1924. *Novellistica: Dalle origini al Bandello.* Milan.

Dionisotti, Carlo. 1967. *Geografia e storia della letteratura italiana.* Turin.

———. 1967. "Chierici e laici." In Dionisotti, *Geografia,* 55–88.

Donati, Claudio. 1988. *L'idea di nobiltà in Italia, secoli xiv–xviii.* Rome.

Donato di Neri. 1937–38. *Cronaca senese,* in *Rerum italicarum scriptores,* vol. 15, pt. 6, fasc. 8–10. Bologna.

Doni, Antonfrancesco. 1852. *Novelle.* Ed. Salvatore Bongi. Lucca.

Dotson, John E., ed., tr. 1994. *Merchant Culture in Fourteenth-Century Venice: The Zibaldone da Canal.* Binghamton. *See also* Strussi.

Dronke, Peter. 1968. *Medieval Latin and the Rise of the European Love Lyric.* 2 vols. 2d ed. Oxford.

Duby, Georges, ed. 1988. *A History of Private Life.* Vol. 2, *Revelations of the Medieval World.* Tr. Arthur Goldhammer. Cambridge, Mass.

Dufournet, Jean, Adelin C. Fiorato, and Augustin Redondo, eds. 1992. *L'image de l'autre Européen, XVe–XVIIe siècles.* Nancy.

Eckstein, Nicholas A. 1995. *The District of the Green Dragon: Neighbourhood Life and Social Change in Renaissance Florence.* Florence.

Edgerton, Samuel Y., Jr. 1985. *Pictures and Punishment: Art and Criminal Prosecution during the Florentine Renaissance.* Ithaca, N.Y.

Erizzo, Sebastiano. 1977. *Le sei giornate.* Ed. Renzo Bragantini. Rome.

Erler, Mary, and Maryanne Kowaleski, eds. 1988. *Women and Power in the Middle Ages.* Athens, Ga.

Evangelisti, Claudia. 1992. " 'Libelli famosi': Processi per scritte infamanti nella Bologna di fine '500." *Annali della Fondazione Luigi Einaudi* 26:181–239.

Evans, Richard J. 1996. *Rituals of Retribution: Capital Punishment in Germany, 1600–1987.* Oxford.

Fabbri, Lorenzo. 1991. *Alleanza matrimoniale e patriziato nella Firenze del '400: Studio sulla famiglia Strozzi.* Florence.

Fachard, Denis, ed. 1973. "Liriche edite e inedite di Biagio Buonaccorsi." *SFI* 31:157–206.

———, ed. 1988. *Consulte e pratiche: 1505–1512.* Geneva.

———, ed. 1993. *Consulte e pratiche della repubblica fiorentina, 1498–1505.* 2 vols. Geneva.

Fanti, Mario. 1978. "La confraternità di Santa Maria della Morte e la conforteria dei condannati in Bologna nei secoli XIV e XV." *Quaderni del Centro di Ricerca di Studio sul Movimento dei Disciplinati* 20:3–101.

Febvre, Lucien. 1942. *Le problème de l'incroyance au XVIe siècle: La religion de Rabelais.* Paris.

Feliciangeli, Bernardo. 1894. "Notizie sulla vita e sugli scritti di Costanza Varano-Sforza (1426–1447)." *GSLI* 23:1–75.

Ferrante, Lucia. 1983. "L'onore ritrovato: Donne nella Casa del Soccorso di San Paolo a Bologna (sec. xvi–xvii)." *Quaderni Storici* 53:499–528.

Ferrari, Severino, ed. 1887. *Poesie su Ludovico il Moro.* Bologna.

Ferraro, Giuseppe, ed. 1877. *Poesie popolari religiose del secolo xiv.* Bologna.

Ferrero, Giuseppe G., ed. 1948. *Lettere del Cinquecento.* Turin.

Ferrero, Giuseppe G., and Maria Luisa Doglio, eds. 1975. *Novelle del Quattrocento.* Turin.

Fiorato, Adelin Charles. 1994. "Complaintes, *cantari,* et poésies satiriques inspirées par la campagne de 1494–1495." In Fiorato, *Italie,* 179–225.

———, ed. 1989. *Culture et professions en Italie (fin XVe–début XVIIe siècle).* Paris.

———, ed. 1994. *Italie 1494.* Paris.

Fiorelli, Piero. 1953–54. *La tortura giudiziaria del diritto romano.* 2 vols. Milan.

Firenzuola, Agnolo. 1991. *Opere.* Ed. Adriano Seroni. Florence.

Flamini, Francesco. 1977. *La lirica toscana del Rinascimento anteriore ai tempi del Magnifico.* Reprint, Bologna.

Folena, Gianfranco. 1991. *Il linguaggio del caos: Studi sul plurilinguismo rinascimentale.* Turin.

———, ed. 1976–86. *Storia della cultura veneta.* 6 vols. in 9 tomes. Vicenza.

Folengo, Teofilo. 1527. *Caos del tri per uno.* Venice.

———. 1977. *Opere.* Ed. Carlo Cordié. Milan.

———. 1989. *Baldus.* Ed. Emilio Faccioli. Turin.

Fortini Brown, Patricia. 1996. "Le 'Scuole.'" In Tenenti and Tucci, *Storia di Venezia,* 5:307–54.

Foster, Susannah Kerr. 1985. "The Ties That Bind: Kinship Association and Marriage in the Alberti Family 1378–1428." Ph.D. diss., Cornell University.

Franceschi, Franco. 1991. "Il linguaggio della memoria: Le deposizioni dei testimoni in un tribunale corporativo fiorentino fra XIV e XV secolo." In Maire Vigueur and Paravicini Bagliani, *La parola,* 213–32.

———. 1993. *Oltre il "Tumulto": I lavoratori fiorentini dell'Arte della Lana fra Tre e Quattrocento.* Florence.

Frati, Lodovico. 1900. *La vita privata di Bologna dal secolo xiii al xvii.* Bologna.

———. 1905. "I Bentivoglio nella poesia contemporanea." *GSLI* 45:1–34.

———, ed. 1908. *Rimatori bolognesi del Quattrocento.* Bologna.

———, ed. 1913. *Le rime del codice isoldiano.* 2 vols. Bologna.

———, ed. 1915. *Rimatori bolognesi del Trecento.* Bologna.

———, ed. 1918. *Rime inedite del Cinquecento.* Bologna.

Frick, Carole Collier. 1995. "Dressing a Renaissance City: Society, Economics, and Gender in the Clothing of Fifteenth-Century Florence." Ph.D. diss., University of California, Los Angeles.

Fubini, Riccardo. 1994. *Italia quattrocentesca: Politica e diplomazia nell'età di Lorenzo il Magnifico.* Milan.

Galletti, G., ed. 1864. *Laude spirituali di Feo Belcari, di Lorenzo de' Medici, di Francesco d'Albizzo, di Castellano Castellani, e di altri.* Florence.

Galli, Angelo. 1987. *Canzoniere.* Ed. Giorgio Nonni. Urbino.

Gherardi (da Prato), Giovanni. 1975. *Il paradiso degli Alberti.* Ed. Antonio Lanza. Rome.

Ghinassi, Ghino. 1967. "Fasi dell'elaborazione del 'Cortigiano.'" *SFI* 25:155–96.

Giambullari, Bernardo. 1955. *Rime inedite e rare.* Ed. Italiano Marchetti. Florence.

Giannessi, Ferdinando. 1957. "Gli inizi della tradizione poetica milanese." In *Storia di Milano,* 8:457–84.

Gilbert, Felix. 1965. *Machiavelli and Guicciardini: Politics and History in Sixteenth-Century Florence.* Princeton, N.J.

———. 1973. "Venice in the Crisis of the League of Cambrai." In Hale, *Renaissance Venice,* 274–92.

Giovanni (Fiorentino), Ser. 1804. *Il Pecorone.* 2 vols. Milan.

———. 1974. *Il Pecorone.* Ed. Enzo Esposito. Ravenna.

Giustinian, Leonardo. 1883. *Poésie edite ed inedite,* ed. Bertold Wiese. Bologna.

———. 1983. *Laudario giustinianeo.* 2 vols. Ed. Francesco Luisi. Venice.

Goffis, Cesare F. 1960. "Per la biografia dei Folengo." *Rinascimento* 11:193–206.

Gorni, Guglielmo. 1972. "Storia del Certame Coronario." *Rinascimento* 12:135–81.

———. 1975. "Un canzoniere adespoto di Mariotto Davanzati." *SFI* 33:189–219.

Gozzadini, Giovanni. 1839. *Memorie per la vita di Giovanni II Bentivoglio.* Bologna.

Graziani. 1850. *Cronaca della città di Perugia dal 1309 al 1491: Nota col nome di DIARIO del Graziani.* Ed. Ariodante Fabretti. *ASI* 16, no. 1.

Grazzini, Anton Francesco. 1974. *Opere.* Ed. Guido Davico Bonino. Turin.

———. 1976. *Le cene.* Ed. Roberto Bruscagli. Rome.

Grazzini, Stefano. 1996. "Un sonetto *De contemptu mundi* di Francesco d'Altobianco degli Alberti." *Interpres* 15:368–77.

Grendler, Paul F. 1969. *Critics of the Italian World (1530–1560): Anton Francesco Doni, Nicolo Franco & Ortensio Lando.* Madison, Wis.

Grubb, James S. 1996. *Provincial Families of the Renaissance: Public and Private Life in the Veneto.* Baltimore.

Guarducci, Piero, and Valeria Ottanelli. 1982. *I servitori domestici della casa borghese toscana nel basso medioevo.* Florence.

Guarnieri, Anna Maria, ed. 1991. *Laudario di Cortona.* Spoleto.

Guglielminetti, Marziano, ed. 1972. *Novellieri del Cinquecento.* Milan.

Guglielmo Ebreo de Pesaro. 1993. *De pratica seu arte tripudii: On the Practice or Art of Dancing.* Ed. and Tr. Barbara Sparti. Oxford.

Guicciardini, Francesco. 1953. *Opere.* Ed. Vittorio de Caprariis. Milan.

Guzzetti, Linda. 1998. "Le donne a Venezia nel XIV secolo." *Studi Veneziani* 35:15–88.

Hale, John Rigby. 1996. *England and the Italian Renaissance.* London.

———, ed. 1973. *Renaissance Venice.* Totowa.

Hallman, Barbara McClung. 1985. *Italian Cardinals: Reform and the Church as Property, 1492–1563.* Berkeley, Calif.

Hatfield, Rab. 1970. "The Compagnia de' Magi." *Journal of the Warburg and Courtauld Institutes* 33:107–61.

Hay, Denys. 1977. *The Church in Italy in the Fifteenth Century.* Cambridge, Eng.

Henderson, John. 1994. *Piety and Charity in Late Medieval Florence.* Oxford.

Herlihy, David. 1969. "Vieillir à Florence au Quattrocento." *Annales ESC* 24:1338–52.

———. 1995. *Women, Family, and Society in Medieval Europe: Historical Essays (1978–1991).* Ed. Anthony Molho. Providence, R.I.

Herlihy, David, and Christiane Klapisch-Zuber. 1978. *Les Toscans et leurs familles: Une étude du catasto florentin de 1427.* Paris.

———. 1985. *Tuscans and Their Families: A Study of the Florentine Catasto of 1427.* New Haven, Conn.

Hoenselaars, A. J. 1992. *Images of Englishmen and Foreigners in the Drama of Shakespeare and His Contemporaries.* London.

Hollingsworth, Mary. 1994. *Patronage in Renaissance Italy: From 1400 to the Early Sixteenth Century.* London.

Hunter, G. K. 1978. "English Folly and Italian Vice." In G. K. Hunter, ed. *Dramatic Identities and Cultural Tradition,* 103–32. Liverpool.

Hyde, J. K. 1973. *Society and Politics in Medieval Italy.* London.

Iacopone da Todi. 1974. *Laude.* Ed. Franco Mancini. Rome.

Infessura, Stefano. 1890. *Diario della città di Roma.* Ed. Oreste Tommasini. Rome.

Jayne, Sears R., ed. 1940. *Marsilio Ficino's Commentary on Plato's Symposium.* Columbia, Mo.

Jones, Ann Rosalind. 1990. *The Currency of Eros: Women's Love Lyric in Europe, 1540–1620.* Bloomington, Ind.

Jones, Philip J. 1974. *The Malatesta of Rimini and the Papal State: A Political History.* Cambridge, Eng.

———. 1980. *Economia e società nell'Italia medievale.* Tr. C. S. Jones and A. Serafini. Turin.

Jordan, Constance. 1986. *Pulci's Morgante: Poetry and History in Fifteenth-Century Florence.* Washington, D.C.

Kennedy, William J. 1989. "Petrarchan Figurations of Death in Lorenzo de' Medici's Sonnets and *Comento*." In Tetel et al., *Life and Death,* 46–67.

Kent, Dale. 1978. *The Rise of the Medici: Faction in Florence, 1426–1434.* Oxford.

Kent, Dale, and F. W. Kent. 1982. *Neighbours and Neighbourhood in Renaissance Florence: The District of the Red Lion in the Fifteenth Century.* Locust Valley, N.Y.

Kent, F. W., and Patricia Simons, eds. 1987. *Patronage, Art, and Society in Renaissance Italy.* New York.

Kinsman, Robert S., ed. 1974. *The Darker Vision of the Renaissance.* Berkeley, Calif.

Kirshner, Julius. 1977. *Pursuing Honor While Avoiding Sin: The Monte delle Doti of Florence.* Milan.

———. 1991. "Maritus Lucretur Dotem Uxoris Sue Premortue in Late Medieval Florence." *Zeitschrift der Savigny-Stiftung für Rechtsgeschichte* 77:111–55.

Klapisch-Zuber, Christiane. 1985. *Women, Family, and Ritual in Renaissance Italy.* Tr. Lydia Cochrane. Chicago.

———. 1990. *La maison et le nom: Stratégies et rituels dans l'Italie de la Renaissance.* Paris.

———. 1992. "Au péril des commères. L'alliance spirituelle par les femmes à Florence." In André Joris and Pierre Toubert, eds., *Femmes, mariages-lignages: XIIe-XIVe siècles. Mélanges offerts à Georges Duby.* De Boeck Université.

———, ed. 1990. *Storia dell donne: Il Medioevo.* Rome.

Koenig, John. 1986. *Il "popolo" dell'Italia del Nord nel XIII secolo.* Bologna.

———. 1999. "Wartime Religion: The Pre-Montaperti Sienese Supplication and Ritual Submission." *Bullettino Senese* 105:7–62.

Koenigsberg, Richard. 1967. "Culture and Unconscious Fantasy: Observations on Courtly Love." *Psychoanalytic Review* 54:36–50.

Kuehn, Thomas. 1982. *Emancipation in Late Medieval Florence.* New Brunswick, N.J.

———. 1985. "Reading between the Patrilines: Leon Battista Alberti's *Della Famiglia* in Light of His Illegitimacy." *I Tatti Studies* 1:161–87.

———. 1989. "Reading Microhistory: The Example of Giovanni and Lusanna." *Journal of Modern History* 61:11–36.

———. 1991. *Law, Family & Women: Toward a Legal Anthropology of Renaissance Italy.* Chicago.

Labalme, Patricia H. 1984. "Sodomy and Venetian Justice in the Renaissance." *Legal History Review* 52:217–54.

Labalme, Patricia H., and Laura Sanguinetti White. 1999. "How to (and How Not to) Get Married in Sixteenth-Century Venice." *Renaissance Quarterly* 52, no. 1: 43–72.

Lanza, Antonio. 1971. *Polemiche e berte letterarie nella Firenze del primo quattrocento: Storia e testi.* Rome. First ed. of Lanza, *Polemiche* (1989).

———. 1989. *Polemiche e berte letterarie nella Firenze del primo Rinascimento (1375–1449).* 2d ed. Rome.

———, ed. 1973–75. *Lirici toscani del Quattrocento.* 2 vols. Rome.

Larivaille, Paul. 1975. *La vie quotidienne des courtisanes en Italie au temps de la Renaissance: Rome et Venise, 15e et 16e siècles.* Paris.

La Roncière, Charles de. 1988. "Tuscan Notables on the Eve of the Renaissance." In Duby, *History of Private Life,* 2:157–310.

Lawner, Lynne. 1987. *Lives of the Courtesans: Portraits of the Renaissance.* New York.

———, ed. and tr. 1988. *I Modi: The Sixteen Pleasures: An Erotic Album of the Italian Renaissance.* Evanston.

Lazzari, Alfonso. 1949. *Parisina.* Florence.

Lazzarini, Vittorio. 1963. *Marino Faliero.* Florence.

Lenzi, Maria Ludovica. 1982. *Donne e madonne: L'educazione femminile nel primo Rinascimento italiano.* Turin.

Lesnick, Daniel R. 1989. *Preaching in Medieval Florence: The Social World of Franciscan and Dominican Spirituality.* Athens, Ga.

Levi, Ezio. 1914. *I cantari leggendari del popolo italiano nei secoli xiv e xv. GSLI,* supplement 16.

———. 1915. *Poesia di popolo e poesia di corte nel Trecento.* Livorno.

Litchfield, R. Burr. 1986. *Emergence of a Bureaucracy: The Florentine Patricians, 1530–1790.* Princeton, N.J.

Liuzzi, Fernando. 1935. *La Lauda e i primordi della melodia italiana.* 2 vols. Rome.

Lowe, K. J. P. 1988. "Towards an Understanding of Goro Gheri's Views on *amicizia* in Early Sixteenth-Century Medicean Florence." In Denley and Elam, *Florence and Italy,* 91–105.

Lucensis civitatis statuta nuperrime castigata. 1539. Lucca.

Macey, Patrick. 1998. *Bonfire Songs: Savonarola's Musical Legacy.* Oxford.

Machiavelli, Bernardo. 1954. *Libro di ricordi.* Ed. Cesare Olschki. Florence.

Machiavelli, Niccolò. 1965. *La mandragola.* Ed. Roberto Ridolfi. Florence.

———. 1984. *Discorsi sopra la prima deca di Tito Livio.* Ed. Gennaro Sasso and Giorgio Inglese. Milan.

Maire Vigueur, Jean-Claude, and Agostino Paravicini Bagliani, eds. 1991. *La parola all'accusato.* Palermo.

Malatesti, Malatesta. 1982. *Rime.* Ed. Domizia Trolli. Parma.

Malato, Enrico, ed. 1989. *La novella italiana: Atti del Convegno di Caprarola, 19–24 settembre 1988.* 2 vols. Rome.

Malipiero, Domenico. 1843. *Annali veneti dall' anno 1457 al 1500. ASI 7,* no. 2.

Mallett, Michael. 1974. *Mercenaries and Their Masters: Warfare in Renaissance Italy.* London.

Mancini, Franco, ed. 1979. *Le Cronache di Todi, secoli xiii–xvi.* Florence.

Manetti, Antonio. 1976. *Vita di Filippo Brunelleschi preceduta da La Novella del Grasso.* Ed. Domenico de Robertis and Giuliano Tanturli. Milan.

Manetti, Marabottino. 1858. *Novella*. Lucca.

Marcheschi, Daniela, ed. 1983. *Ingiurie, impropri, ecc.: Saggio di lingua parlata del Trecento cavati dai libri criminali di Lucca per opera di Salvatore Bongi*. Lucca.

Marotti, Arthur F. 1982. " 'Love Is Not Love': Elizabethan Sonnet Sequences and the Social Order." *Journal of English Literary History* 49:396–428.

Marshall, Richard K. 1999. *The Local Merchants of Prato: Small Entrepreneurs in the Late Medieval Economy*. Baltimore.

Martelli, Mario. 1985. "Profilo ideologico di Alamanno Rinuccini." In *Culture et société en Italie*, 1:131–43. Paris.

———. 1986. "La canzone a Firenze di Francesco d'Altobianco degli Alberti: Testo e commento." *Interpres* 6:7–50.

———. 1989. "Il capitolo 'Di vecchiezza' di Francesco d'Altobianco degli Alberti." *Interpres* 9:35–63.

———. 1996. *Letteratura fiorentina del Quattrocento: Il filtro degli anni Sessanta*. Florence.

Marti, Mario. 1956. *Poeti giocosi del tempo di Dante*. Milan.

Martin, Ruth. 1989. *Witchcraft and the Inquisition in Venice, 1550–1650*. Oxford.

Martines, Lauro. 1959. "La famiglia Martelli e un documento sulla vigilia del ritorno dall' esilio di Cosimo de' Medici." *ASI* 117:29–43.

———. 1963. *The Social World of the Florentine Humanists: 1390–1460*. Princeton, N.J.

———. 1968. *Lawyers and Statecraft in Renaissance Florence*. Princeton, N.J.

———. 1974. "A Way of Looking at Women in Renaissance Florence." *Journal of Medieval and Renaissance Studies* 4, no. 1: 15–28.

———. 1974. "The Gentleman in Renaissance Italy: Strains of Isolation in the Body Politic." In Kinsman, *Darker Vision*, 77–93.

———. [1979] 1988. *Power and Imagination: City-States in Renaissance Italy*. New York.

———. 1985. *Society and History in English Renaissance Verse*. Oxford.

———. 1988. "Forced Loans: Political and Social Strain in Quattrocento Florence." *Journal of Modern History* 60:300–311.

———. 1993. "The Politics of Love Poetry in Renaissance Italy." In Smarr, *Historical Criticism*, 129–44.

———. 1994. *An Italian Renaissance Sextet: Six Tales in Historical Context*. Tr. Murtha Baca. New York.

———. 1994. "Love and Hate in Renaissance Patronage: Italy." *italianist* 14:5–31.

———. 1994. "Ritual Language in Renaissance Italy." In *Riti e rituali* (see Chiffoleau, Martines, and Paravicini Bagliani).

———. 1995. "The Italian Renaissance Tale as History." In Brown, *Language and Images*, 313–30.

———. 1996. "Amour et histoire dans la poésie de la Renaissance italienne." *Annales HSS* 3:575–603.

———. 1998. "Séduction, espace familial et autorité dans la Renaissance italienne." *Annales HSS* 2:255–90.

———. 1998. "Review Essay: The Renaissance and the Birth of Consumer Society." *Renaissance Quarterly* 51, no. 1: 193–203.

———. 1998. Review of *Florentine Drama,* by Antonia Pulci. *Renaissance Studies* 12:298–301.

———, ed. 1972. *Violence and Civil Disorder in Italian Cities: 1200–1500.* Berkeley, Calif.

Marucci, Valerio, Antonio Marzo, and Angelo Romano, eds. 1983. *Pasquinate romane del Cinquecento.* 2 vols. Rome.

Masi, Bartolomeo. 1906. *Ricordanze di B. Masi, calderaio fiorentino, dal 1478 al 1526.* Ed. Giuseppe Odoardo Corazzini. Florence.

Massèra, Aldo F. 1911. "I poeti isottei (1)." *GSLI* 57:1–32.

———. 1928. "I poeti isottei (2)." *GSLI* 92:1–55.

Masson, Giorgina. 1975. *Courtesans of the Italian Renaissance.* London.

Matarazzo, Francesco. 1851. *Cronaca della città di Perugia dal 1492 al 1503.* Ed. Ariodante Fabretti. *ASI* 16, no. 2: 1–243.

Mazzacurati, Giancarlo. 1985. *Il Rinascimento dei moderni: La crisi culturale del XVI secolo e la negazione delle origini.* Bologna.

Mazzi, Maria Serena. 1991. *Prostitute e lenoni nella Firenze del Quattrocento.* Florence.

Mazzi, Maria Serena, and Sergio Raveggi. 1983. *Gli uomini e le cose nelle campagne fiorentine del Quattrocento.* Florence.

Medici, Lorenzo de'. 1939. *Opere.* Ed. Attilio Simioni. 2 vols. Bari.

———. 1955. *Scritti scelti di Lorenzo de' Medici.* Ed. Emilio Bigi. Turin.

———. 1984. *Canzoniere.* Ed. Paolo Orvieto. Milan.

Medin, Antonio. 1891. "I Visconti nella poesia contemporanea." *Archivio storico lombardo,* 2d ser., 8:733–95.

———. 1904. *La storia della repubblica di Venezia nella poesia.* Milan.

———, ed. 1883. *Lamenti de' secoli xiv e xv.* Florence.

———, ed. 1896. *Ternario in Lodi di Carlo VIII.* Padua.

———, ed. 1900. *Sonetti per la lega di Cambrai.* Padua.

Medin, Antonio, and Lodovico Frati, eds. 1887–94. *Lamenti storici dei secoli xiv, xv, e xvi.* 4 vols. Bologna and Padua.

Meersseman, Giles G., with Gian Piero Pacini. 1977. *Ordo fraternitatis.* 3 vols. Rome.

Meglio, Giovan Matteo di. 1977. *Rime.* Ed. Giuseppe Brincat. Florence.

Merlo, Grado Giovanni. 1989. *Eretici e eresie medievali.* Bologna.

Messina, Michele. 1978. "Per l'edizione delle *Rime* del Burchiello. I. Censimento dei manoscritti e delle stampe." *Filologia e Critica* 3:196–296.

Miccoli, Giovanni. 1974. "La storia religiosa." In *Storia d'Italia* (Einaudi), 2:1:609–734, 875–96.

Migiel, Marilyn, and Juliana Schiesari, eds. 1991. *Refiguring Women: Perspectives on Gender and the Italian Renaissance.* Cornell.

Migliorini, Bruno. 1960. *Storia della lingua italiana.* Florence.

Molho, Anthony. 1979. "Cosimo de' Medici: Pater Patriae or Padrino." *Stanford Italian Review* 1:5–33.

———. 1994. *Marriage Alliance in Late Medieval Florence.* Cambridge, Mass.

Molho, Anthony, and Franek Sznura, eds. 1986. *Alle bocche della piazza: Diario di anonimo fiorentino 1382–1401.* Florence.

Moller, Herbert. 1960. "The Meaning of Courtly Love." *Journal of American Folklore* 73:39–52.

Molza, Francesco Maria. 1992. *Novelle.* Ed. Stefano Bianchi. Rome.

Montemagno, Buonaccorso da. 1970. *Le rime dei due Buonaccorso.* Ed. Raffaele Spongano. Bologna.

Monti, Gunnaro Maria. 1927. *Le confraternite medievali dell'alta e media Italia.* 2 vols. Venice.

Morelli, Giovanni. 1956. *Ricordi.* Ed. Vittore Branca. Florence.

Morlini, Girolamo. 1983. *Novelle e favole.* Ed. Giovanni Villani. Rome.

Morpurgo, Salomone, ed. 1893. *Dieci sonetti storici fiorentini.* Florence.

Motta, Emilio. 1888. "Suicidi nel Quattrocento e nel Cinquecento." *Archivio Storico Lombardo* 15:96–100.

Mueller, Reinhold C. 1997. *The Venetian Money Market: Banks, Panics, and the Public Debt, 1200–1500.* Baltimore.

Muir, Edward. 1981. *Civic Ritual in Renaissance Venice.* Princeton, N.J.

Municipalia Cremae. 1723. Crema.

Murray, Alexander. 1998. *Suicide in the Middle Ages.* Vol. 1, *The Violent against Themselves.* Oxford.

Muscetta, Carlo, ed. 1970–76. *Letteratura italiana Laterza.* Vols. 1–4. Rome.

Muscetta, Carlo, and Daniele Ponchiroli, eds. 1968. *Poesia del Quattrocento e del Cinquecento.* Turin.

Muscetta, Carlo, and Paolo Rivalta, eds. 1956. *Poesia del Duecento e del Trecento.* Turin.

Mutini, Claudio. 1979. "Castiglione, Baldassare." *DBI,* 22:53–68.

Muzzarelli, Giovanni. 1983. *Rime.* Ed. Giuseppina H. Palazzini. Mantua.

Nelli, Giustiniano. 1550. *Le amorose novelle.* Siena?

Neri, Ferdinando. 1931. "La contessa di Challant." *GSLI* 98:225–54.

Newbigin, Nerida, ed. 1983. *Nuovo corpus di sacre rappresentazioni fiorentine del Quattrocento,* vol. 139 of "Collezione di opere inedite e rare." Bologna.

Newett, M. Margaret, ed. 1907. *Canon Pietro Casola's Pilgrimage to Jerusalem: In the Year 1494.* Manchester.

Niccoli, Ottavia. 1990. *Prophecy and People in Renaissance Italy.* Tr. Lydia G. Cochrane. Princeton.

Nigro, Salvatore S. 1983. *Le brache di San Griffone: Novellistica e predicazione tra '400 e '500.* Bari.

Novati, Francesco. 1892. "Le poesie sulla natura delle frutte e i canterini del comune di Firenze nel Trecento." *GSLI* 19:55–79.

Novati, Francesco, and Francesco Carlo Pellegrini, eds. 1885. *Poesie politiche popolari dei secoli xv e xvi.* Ancona.

O'Faolain, Julia, and Lauro Martines. 1973. *Not in God's Image: Women in History from the Greeks to the Victorians.* New York.

Oliva, Carlo, ed. 1978. *Poesia italiana del Quattrocento.* Milan.

Origo, Iris. 1955. "The Domestic Enemy: Eastern Slaves in Tuscany in the Fourteenth and Fifteenth Centuries." *Speculum* 30:321–66.

Ortalli, Gherardo. 1979. *". . . Pingatur in palatio . . .": La pittura infamante nei secoli xiii–xvi.* Rome.

Pallone, Rocco. 1975. *Anticlericalismo e giustizia sociale nell' Italia del '400: L'opera poetica e satirica di Antonio Cammelli detto "il Pistoia."* Rome.

Paolo da Certaldo. 1945. *Libro di buoni costumi.* Ed. Alfredo Schiaffini. Florence.

Papi, Anna Benvenuti. 1990. *In castro poenitentiae: Santità e società femminile nell'Italia medievale.* Rome.

Parabosco, Girolamo. 1558. *I diporti.* Venice.

Pasquazi, Silvio. 1966. *Poeti estensi del Rinascimento: Con due appendici.* Florence.

Pasquini, Emilio. 1964. "Il Codice di Filippo Scarlatti." *SFI* 22:363–580.

———. 1974. "Saviozzo." *DCLI*, 3:317–23.

Passerini, Luigi. 1869. *Gli Alberti di Firenze.* 2 vols. Florence.

Paton, Bernadette. 1992. *Preaching Friars and the Civic Ethos: Siena, 1380–1480.* London.

Pelikan, Jaroslav. 1971. *The Emergence of the Catholic Tradition (100–600).* Vol. 1 of *The Christian Tradition: A History of the Development of Doctrine,* 5 vols. Chicago.

———. 1978. *The Growth of Medieval Theology (600–1300).* Vol. 3 of *The Christian Tradition: A History of the Development of Doctrine,* 5 vols. Chicago.

———. 1996. *Mary through the Centuries: Her Place in the History of Culture.* New Haven, Conn.

Pellegrini, Francesco Carlo. 1889. *Sulla repubblica fiorentina a tempo di Cosimo il Vecchio: Saggio di studii.* Pisa.

Perosa, Alessandro. 1971. "Braccesi, Alessandro." *DBI,* 13:602–8.

Perosa, Alessandro, and John Sparrow, eds. 1979. *Renaissance Latin Verse: An Anthology.* London.

Pertile, Antonio. 1894. *Storia del diritto italiano.* 2d ed. 6 vols. Turin.

Pesman Cooper, Roslyn. 1984–85. "The Florentine Ruling Group under the *governo popolare* 1494–1512." *Studies in Medieval and Renaissance History* 7:71–181.

Peters, Edward. 1983. *Torture.* Oxford.

Petrarca, Francesco. 1985. *Canzoniere.* Ed. Alberto Chiari. Rome.

Peyer, Hans C. 1955. *Stadt und Stadtpatron im Mittelalterlichen Italien.* Zurich.

Pezzarossa, Fulvio. 1984. "Ad honorem et laudem del nome Bentivoglio. La letteratura della festa nel secondo quattrocento." In Basile, *Bentivolorum magnificentia,* 35–113.

Piccolomini, Enea Silvio. 1975. *Historia de duobus amantibus.* In Ferrero and Doglio, *Novelle,* 858–957.

Piromalli, Antonio. 1975. *La cultura a Ferrara al tempo di Ludovico Ariosto.* Rome.

Pistoia, il. *See* Antonio Cammelli.

Pitkin, Hanna Fenichel. 1984. *Fortune Is a Woman: Gender and Politics in the Thought of Niccolò Machiavelli.* Berkeley, Calif.

Pitt-Rivers, Julian. 1977. *The Fate of Shechem, or the Politics of Sex: Essays in the Anthropology of the Mediterranean.* Cambridge, Eng.

Plaisance, Michel. 1972. "La structure de la *beffa* dans les *Cene* d'Antonfrancesco Grazzini." In Rochon, *Formes et significations,* 1:45–97.

———. 1981. "La folie comme marquage et moyen d'exclusion dans la nouvelle florentine du XVIe siècle." In Redondo and Rochon, *Visages,* 23–32.

———. 1985. "Les rapports ville campagne dans les nouvelles de Sacchetti, Sercambi et Sermini." In *Culture et société en Italie, du Moyen-Age à la Renaissance: Hommage à André Rochon,* 61–73. Paris.

———. 1986. "Città e campagna." In Asor Rosa, *Letteratura italiana,* 5:583–634.

Poliziano, Angelo. 1979. *The Stanze of Angelo Poliziano.* Tr. David Quint. Amherst, Mass.

———. 1990. *Rime.* Ed. Daniela Delcorno Branca. Venice.

Polizzotto, Lorenzo. 1994. *The Elect Nation: The Savonarolan Movement in Florence 1494–1545.* Oxford.

Porcelli, Bruno. 1973. *La novella del Cinquecento.* Rome. Also in Muscetta, *Letteratura italiana,* vol. 4.

Preminger, Alex, ed. 1974. *Princeton Encyclopedia of Poetry and Poetics.* London.

Previtera, Carmelo. 1939. *La poesia giocosa e l'umorismo: Dalle origini al Rinascimento.* Milan.

Primum (-quartum) volumen statutorum Auguste Perusie magistratuum ordines. 1526–28. 4 vols. Perugia.

Prizer, William F. 1991. "Games of Venus: Secular Vocal Music in the Late Quattrocento and Early Cinquecento." *Journal of Musicology* 9, no. 1: 3–56.

Prosperi, Adriano. 1981. "Intellettuali e chiesa all' inizio dell'età moderna." In *Storia d'Italia: Annali* (Einaudi), ed. Romano and Vivanti, 4:159–252. Turin.

Pulci, Antonia. 1554. *La Rappresentatione di Santa Domitilla*. Florence.

———. 1996. *Florentine Drama for Convent and Festival: Seven Sacred Plays*. Ed. and tr. James W. Cook and Barbara C. Cook. Chicago.

Pulci, Luigi. 1962. *Morgante e lettere*. Ed. Domenico de Robertis. Florence.

———. 1986. *Opere minori*. Ed. Paolo Orvieto. Milan.

Pulci, Luigi, and Matteo Franco. 1933. *Il 'Libro dei sonetti.'* Ed. G. Dolci. Milan.

Pullan, Brian. 1971. *Rich and Poor in Renaissance Venice: The Social Institutions of a Catholic State, to 1620*. Oxford.

———. 1990. "The *Scuole Grandi* of Venice." In Verdon and Henderson, *Christianity and the Renaissance*, 272–301.

Queller, Donald E. 1986. *The Venetian Patriciate: Reality versus Myth*. Urbana, Ill.

Rabboni, Renzo. 1991. *Laudari e canzonieri nella Firenze del '400: Scrittura privata e modelli nel 'Vat, Barb. lat. 3679'*. Bologna.

Ramat, Raffaello. 1958. *Sette contributi agli studi di storia della letteratura italiana*. Palermo.

La rappresentazione del Figliuol Prodigo. 1584. Florence.

Redon, Odile. 1990. "Aspects économiques de la discrimination et de la 'marginalisation' des femmes." In Cavaciocchi, *La donna nell'economia*, 441–60.

Redondo, Augustin, and André Rochon, eds. 1981. *Visages de la folie (1500–1650)*. Paris.

Rendina, Claudio. 1985. *I capitani di ventura: Storia e segreti*. Rome.

Rezasco, Giulio. 1889. "Segno delle meretrici." *Giornale Ligustico di Archeologia, Storia e Letteratura* 16:161–220.

Ricciardi, Roberto. 1984. "Cosmico, Niccolò Lelio." *DBI*, 30:72–77.

Ricotti, Ercole. 1844–45. *Storia delle compagnie di ventura in Italia*. 4 vols. Turin.

Ridolfi, Roberto. 1974. *Vita di Girolamo Savonarola*. 4th ed. 2 vols. Florence.

Robin, Diana. 1991. *Filelfo in Milan: Writings 1451–1477*. Princeton, N.J.

Rochon, André. 1963. *La jeunesse de Laurent de Médicis (1449–1478)*. Paris.

———, ed. 1972–75. *Formes et significations de la "Beffa" dans la littérature italienne de la Renaissance*. 2 vols. Paris.

———, ed. 1976. *Ville et campagne dans la littérature italienne de la Renaissance*. 2 vols. Paris.

Rocke, Michael. 1996. *Forbidden Friendships: Homosexuality and Male Culture in Renaissance Florence*. New York.

Romano, Dennis. 1987. *Patricians and Popolani: The Social Foundations of the Venetian Renaissance State*. Baltimore.

Rondeau, Jennifer Fisk. 1988. "Lay Piety and Spirituality in the Late Middle Ages: The Confraternities of North-Central Italy, ca. 1250 to 1348." Ph.D. diss., Cornell University.

Roselli, Rosello. 1925. "Il Canzoniere di Rosello Roselli." Ed. Ezio Bruti. *Atti della Accademia Rovertana degli Agiati*, ser. 4, 7:81–199.

Rosenthal, Elaine G. 1988. "The Position of Women in Renaissance Florence: Neither Autonomy nor Subjection." In Denley and Elam, *Florence and Italy*, 369–81.

Rosenthal, Margaret F. 1992. *The Honest Courtesan: Veronica Franco, Citizen and Writer in Sixteenth-Century Venice*. Chicago.

Rossi, Vittorio. 1888. "Poesie storiche del sec. xv." *Archivio Veneto* 35, no. 1: 207–25.

———. 1890. "Di una rimatrice e di un rimatore del sec. xv: Girolama Corsi Ramos e Jacopo Corsi." *GSLI* 15:183–215.

———. 1956. *Il Quattrocento*. Milan.

Rossiaud, Jacques. 1988. *La prostitution médiévale*. Paris.

Rougement, Denis de. 1972. *L'amour et l'occident*. Paris.

Rubieri, Ermolao. 1877. *Storia della poesia popolare italiana*. Florence.

Ruggiero, Guido. 1985. *The Boundaries of Eros: Sex Crime and Sexuality in Renaissance Venice*. New York.

Rusconi, Roberto. 1986. "Confraternite." In Chittolini and Miccoli, *Storia d'Italia: Annali*, 9:469–506.

———, ed. 1984. *Il movimento religioso femminile in Umbria nei secoli xiii–xiv*. Florence.

Russell, Rinaldina. 1977. "Studio dei generi medievali italiani: Il compianto per un personaggio illustre." *Forum Italicum* 4, no. 4: 349–70.

Sacchetti, Franco. 1936. *Il libro delle rime*. Ed. Alberto Chiari. Bari.

———. 1984. *Il Trecentonovelle*. Ed. Antonio Lanza. Florence.

Sacchetti, Giannozzo. 1948. *Giannozzo Sacchetti: Le rime edite e inedite*. Ed. Oretta Sacchetti. Rome.

Salinari, Giambattista, ed. 1976. *Novelle del Cinquecento*. Turin.

Salutati, Coluccio. 1891–1911. *L'Epistolario*. Ed. Francesco Novati. Rome.

Salza, Abdelkedar, ed. 1913. *Rime di Gaspara Stampa e Veronica Franco*. Bari.

Santoro, Mario. 1966. *Fortuna, ragione e prudenza nella civiltà letteraria del Cinquecento*. Naples.

Santosuosso, Antonio. 1994. "Anatomy of Defeat in Renaissance Italy: The Battle of Fornovo in 1495." *International History Review* 16, no. 2: 221–50.

Sanuto, Marin. 1879–1903. *I darii*. 58 vols. Ed. Rinaldo Fulin et al. Venice.

Sapegno, Natalino, ed. 1952. *Poeti minori del Trecento*. Milan.

Sarteschi, E., ed. 1867. *Poesie minori del secolo XIV*. Bologna.

Sassoferrato, Olimpo da. 1974. *Madrigali e altre poesie d'amore*. Ed. Franco Scataglini. Ancona.

Saviozzo, Simone Serdini da Siena, il. 1965. *Rime*. Ed. Emilio Pasquini. Bologna.

Scrivano, Riccardo. 1965. "Bellincioni, Bernardo." *DBI,* 7:687–89.

Segarizzi, Arnaldo. 1906. "Ulisse Aleotti: Rimatore veneziano del sec. xv." *GSLI* 47:41–66.

Segre, Cesare. 1974. *Lingua, stile, e società.* New ed. Milan.

———. 1974. "Edonismo linguistico nel Cinquecento." In Segre, *Lingua, stile,* 369– 96.

Seneca, Federico. 1962. *Venezia e Papa Giulio II.* Padua.

Serafino de' Ciminelli. 1894. *Le Rime.* Ed. Mario Menghini. Bologna.

———. 1967. *Die Strambotti des Serafino dall'Aquila: Studien und Texte zur Italienischen Spiel- und Scherzdichtung des ausgehenden 15. Jahrhunderts.* Ed. Barbara Bauer-Formiconi. Munich.

Sercambi, Giovanni. 1974. *Il novelliere.* Ed. Luciano Rossi. Roma.

Sermini, Gentile. 1968. *Novelle.* 2 vols. Ed. Giuseppe Vettori. Rome.

Sforza, Alessandro. 1973. *Canzoniere.* Ed. Luciana Cocito. Milan.

Singer, Irving. 1984. *The Nature of Love.* Vol. 2, *Courtly and Romantic.* Chicago.

Siti, Walter. 1986. "L'inconscio." In Asor Rosa, *Letteratura italiana,* 5:717–31.

Smagliati, Leone. 1970. *Cronaca parmense (1494–1518).* Ed. Sergio di Noto. Parma.

Smarr, Janet Laverie, ed. 1993. *Historical Criticism and the Challenge of Theory.* Urbana, Ill.

Sorelli, Fernanda. 1987. "La spiritualità medievale." *Studi Medievali* 28, no. 1: 1–65.

Spongano, Raffaele, ed. 1971. *Rispetti e strambotti del Quattrocento.* Bologna.

Squarotti, Giorgio Bàrberi, ed. 1985. *Metamorfosi della novella.* Foggia.

Staaff, Erik, ed. 1931–32. *Le laudario de Pise: Du ms. 8521 de la Bibliothèque de l'Arsenal de Paris.* Uppsala.

Statuta criminalia communis Bononiae. 1524. Bologna.

Statuta criminalia mediolani. 1619. Milan.

Statuta de regimine praetoris civilia et criminalia civitatis et comitatus papie. 1505. Pavia.

Statuta et ordinamenta comunis Cremonae facta et compilata currente anno domini mcccxxxix. 1952. Ed. Ugo Gualazzini. Milan.

Statuta iurisdictionum mediolani saeculo xiv. 1869. Ed. Antonio Ceruti. Milan.

Statuta magnificae civitatis Veronae libri quinque una cum privilegiis. 1747. 2 vols. Venice.

Statuta populi et communis Florentiae publica auctoritate collecta castigata et praeposita anno salutis mccccxv. 1778–83. 3 vols. Freiburg.

Statuta Veronae. 1588. Verona.

Statuti del Comune di Ravenna. Ed. Antonio Tarlazzi. Ravenna, 1886.

Statuti di Perugia dell'anno Mcccxlii. 1913. 2 vols. Ed. Giustiniano degli Azzi. Rome.

Statuti e ordinamenti del Comune di Udine. 1898. Udine.

Statutum reipublicae senensis anno domini mdxlv. 1993. In Ascheri, *L'ultimo statuto.*

Stella, Alessandro. 1993. *La révolte des Ciompi: Les hommes, les lieux, le travail.* Paris.

Storia di Milano. 1953–60. 14 vols. Fondazione Treccani degli Alfieri. Milan.

Storia d'Italia (Einaudi). 1972–76. Ed. Ruggiero Romano and Corrado Vivanti. 4 vols. Turin.

Straparola, Giovan Francesco. 1550–55. *Le piacevoli notti.* 2 vols. Venice.

Strocchia, Sharon T. 1989. "Remembering the Family: Women, Kin, and Commemorative Masses in Renaissance Florence." *Renaissance Quarterly* 42, no. 4: 635–54.

Strozzi, Alessandra Macinghi. 1877. *Lettere di una gentildonna fiorentina del secolo xv ai figliuoli esuli.* Ed. Cesare Guasti. Florence.

Strussi, Alfredo, ed. 1967. *Zibaldone da Canal.* Venice. *See also* Dotson, *Merchant Culture.*

Tamassia, Nino. 1971. *La famiglia italiana nei secoli decimoquinto e decimosesto.* Rome.

Tanner, Tony. 1979. *Adultery in the Novel: Contract and Transgression.* Baltimore.

Tanturli, Giuliano. 1978. "I Benci copisti: Vicende della cultura fiorentina volgare fra Antonio Pucci e il Ficino." *SFI* 36:197–313.

Tartaro, Achile. 1980. *Forme poetiche del Trecento.* Rome.

———. 1984. "La prosa narrativa antica." In Asor Rosa, *Letteratura italiana,* 3:2:652–713.

Tebaldeo, Antonio. 1992. *Rime.* 3 vols. Ed. Tania Basile and Jean-Jacques Marchand. Modena.

Temi e problemi della mistica femminile trecentesca. 1983. Todi.

Tenenti, Alberto, and Ugo Tucci, eds. 1996. *Storia di Venezia.* Vol. 5. Rome.

Terpstra, Nicholas. 1995. *Lay Confraternities and Civic Religion in Renaissance Bologna.* Cambridge, Eng.

Tetel, Marcel, Ronald G. Witt, and Rona Goffen, eds. 1989. *Life and Death in Fifteenth-Century Florence.* Durham, N.C.

Tinucci, Niccolò. 1974. *Rime.* Ed. Clemente Mazzotta. Bologna.

Tornabuoni, Lucrezia. 1978. *I poemetti sacri.* Ed. Fulvio Pezzarossa. Florence.

Toscan, Jean. 1981. *Le carnaval du langage: Le lexique érotique des poètes de l'équivoque, de Burchiello à Marino (XVe–XVIIe siècle).* 4 vols. Lille.

Tra Latino e volgare per Carlo Dionisotti. 1974. 2 vols. Padua.

Trease, Geoffrey. 1970. *The Condottieri: Soldiers of Fortune.* London.

Tre novelle rarissime del secolo XVI. 1867. Bologna.

Trexler, Richard C. 1971. *Synodal Law in Florence and Fiesole, 1306–1518.* Vatican City.

———. 1973. "The Foundlings of Florence." *History of Childhood Quarterly* 1:259–84.

———. 1980. *Public Life in Renaissance Florence.* New York.

———, ed. 1978. *The Libro Cerimoniale of the Florentine Republic by Francesco Filarete and Angelo Manfidi: Introduction and Text.* Geneva.

Valency, Maurice. 1958. *In Praise of Love: An Introduction to the Love Poetry of the Renaissance*. New York.

Valori, Alessandro. 1996. " 'Con utile e con onore per l'anima e per il corpo': Il concetto di onore in alcune lettere e libri di ricordi tardo-medievali." Ph.D. diss., Brown University.

Vannozzo, Francesco di. 1928. *Rime*. Ed. Antonio Medin. Bologna.

Varanini, Giorgio, Luigi Banfi, and Anna Ceruti Burgo, eds. 1981. *Laude cortonesi dal secolo xiii al xv*. 4 vols. Florence.

Velluti, Donato. 1914. *La cronica domestica di Messer Donato Velluti*. Ed. I. del Lungo and G. Volpi. Florence.

Verde, Armando, F. 1973–85. *Lo studio fiorentino, 1473–1503: Ricerche e documenti*. 4 vols. Florence.

Verdon, Timothy, and John Henderson, eds. 1990. *Christianity and the Renaissance: Image and Religious Imagination in the Quattrocento*. Syracuse, N.Y.

Villari, Pasquale. 1888. *Life and Times of Girolamo Savonarola*. 2 vols. Tr. Linda Villari. London.

Virgili, Antonio. 1881. *Francesco Berni con documenti inediti*. Florence.

Visconti, Gasparo. 1494. *Rithimi*. Milan.

———. 1952. *Rime*. Ed. Alessandro Cutolo. Bologna.

———. 1979. *I canzonieri per Beatrice d'Este e per Bianca Maria Sforza*. Ed. Paolo Bongrani. Milan.

Volpi, Guglielmo. 1890. "La vita e le rime di Simone Serdini detto il Saviozzo." *GSLI* 15:1–78.

———, ed. 1907. *Rime di trecentisti minori*. Florence.

Vossler, Karl. 1904. *Die philosophischen Grundlagen zum "süssen neuen Stil."* Heidelberg.

Wack, Mary Frances. 1990. *Lovesickness in the Middle Ages: The Viaticum and Its Commentaries*. Philadelphia.

Waley, Daniel. 1991. *Siena and the Sienese in the Thirteenth Century*. Cambridge, Eng.

Warner, Marina. 1990. *Alone of All Her Sex: The Myth and Cult of the Virgin Mary*. New ed. London.

Weaver, Elissa. 1989. "Dietro il vestito: La semiotica del vestire nel *Decameron*." In Malato, *La novella*, 2:701–10.

———. 1999. Review of *Florentine Drama*, by Antonia Pulci. *Speculum* 74, no. 2: 474–76.

Webb, Diana. 1996. *Patrons and Defenders: The Saints in the Italian City-States*. London.

Weiand, Christof. 1993. *"Libri di famiglia" und Autobiographie in Italien zwischen Treund Cinquecento: Studien zur Entwicklung des Schreibens über sich selbst*. Tübingen.

Weinstein, Donald. 1970. *Savonarola and Florence: Prophecy and Patriotism in the Renaissance.* Princeton, N.J.

Weissman, Ronald, F. E. 1982. *Ritual Brotherhood in Renaissance Florence.* New York.

White, Hayden V. 1974. *Metahistory: The Historical Imagination in Nineteenth-Century Europe.* Baltimore.

Whitfield, John Humphreys. 1960. *A Short History of Italian Literature.* Harmondsworth, Eng.

Wilson, Blake. 1992. *Music and Merchants: The Laudesi Companies of Republican Florence.* Oxford.

Zancan, Marina. 1986. "La donna." In Asor Rosa, *Letteratura italiana,* 5:765–811.

Zarri, Gabriella. 1990. *Le sante vive: Profezie di corti e devozione femminile tra '400 e '500.* Turin.

Zorzi, Alvise. 1986. *Cortigiana veneziana: Veronica Franco e i suoi poeti, 1546–1591.* Milan.

Index

About the Author

Lauro Martines is a former professor of history at the University of California, Los Angeles. A noted expert on the Italian Renaissance, his books include *The Social World of the Florentine Humanists, Lawyers and Statecraft in Renaissance Florence, Society and History in English Renaissance Verse, Power and Imagination: City-States in Renaissance Italy,* and *An Italian Renaissance Sextet: Six Tales in Historical Context.* He resides in London.